TEXT TO TRADITION

SOUTH ASIA ACROSS THE DISCIPLINES

SOUTH ASIA ACROSS THE DISCIPLINES

Funded by a grant from the Andrew W. Mellon Foundation and jointly published by the University of California Press, the University of Chicago Press, and Columbia University Press.

South Asia Across the Disciplines is a series devoted to publishing first books across a wide range of South Asian studies, including art, history, philology or textual studies, philosophy, religion, and the interpretive social sciences. Series authors all share the goal of opening up new archives and suggesting new methods and approaches, while demonstrating that South Asian scholarship can be at once deep in expertise and broad in appeal.

For a list of books in this series, see page 279.

TEXT TO TRADITION

THE *NAIṢADHĪYACARITA* AND LITERARY COMMUNITY IN SOUTH ASIA

Deven M. Patel

COLUMBIA UNIVERSITY PRESS   NEW YORK

Columbia University Press
Publishers Since 1893
New York Chichester, West Sussex
cup.columbia.edu

Library of Congress Cataloging-in-Publication Data
Patel, Deven M.
Text to tradition : the Naisadhiyacarita and literary community in South Asia / Deven M. Patel.
pages cm. — (South Asia Across the Disciplines)
Includes bibliographical references and index.
ISBN 978-0-231-16680-5 (cloth) — ISBN 978-0-231-53653-0 (electronic)
1. Sriharsa, active 12th century. Naisadhiyacarita. 2. Sanskrit poetry—History and criticism.
I. Title.

PK3798.S77N364 2014
891′.21—dc23

2013010312

Cover design: Jordan Wannemacher
Cover image: Enthroned Couple Entertained by Musicians, Indian Pahari, early 19th century.
Object Place: Kangra style, Punjab Hills, Northern India. © 2014 Museum of Fine Arts, Boston

In memory of Aditya Behl,

friend and mentor

CONTENTS

ACKNOWLEDGMENTS

THIS BOOK has my name attached to it, and all the shortcomings in it are indeed mine alone. However, from the beginning, I am proud that this project has been a collaboration of learned people from all over the world, from Berkeley to Ujjain to Philadelphia and many places in between. I first acknowledge the formative role in my education and life played by Robert Goldman, with whom I earnestly began my study of Sanskrit *kāvya* and commentaries. His erudition regarding these subjects left such a deep impression on me that I could not have written anything but a dissertation that fused the two. I also thank Profs. Theodore Riccardi, Nadine Berardi, and especially Gary Tubb and Sally Goldman for teaching me to read and enjoy the Sanskrit language as an undergraduate and graduate student. I owe a profound debt to Prof. Ram Karan Sharma, with whom I've had the privilege and pleasure of studentship and friendship for more than fifteen years. His encouragement and seemingly limitless expertise on all matters related to Sanskrit shaped this book at every turn. As well, I express my deep gratitude to Shrimati Annapurna Sharma and to all members of Sharmaji's household in Vigyan Vihar for their hospitality over the years.

I learned much from many Sanskrit scholars in India during my various stays. Among them, special recognition goes to Srinivas Rath. I had initially planned to visit with him for one or two days in spring 2003. Instead, he became my host and mentor for almost a full year. Sitting in his room on Kalidas Marg in Ujjain, India, I spent magical days listening to one of the finest contemporary Sanskrit poets sing poetry and explain the subtle arts of the Sanskrit *kavi*. Among other works, we read the entire *Naiṣadhīyacarita* together during this time, and I am eternally grateful for this experience, as I am to the entire Rath family for making Ujjain a second home in India. I also benefited greatly from conversations with many fine scholars of Sanskrit poetry in India, including Kamaleshdatta Tripathi, V. Kutumba Sastry, Ramaranjan Mukherji, Gautam Patel, Harinarayana Bhat, Ramji Upadhyaya, Narayan Mishra, and Rewa Prasad Dvivedi. I would also like to extend my gratefulness to the various institutions (and people) in India that supported me during the past decade. Included among them are the Ecole Francaise D'Extreme Orient in Pondicherry, the Kuppuswami Sastri Institute in Chennai, and the Kalidas Akademi and Scindia Oriental Institute in Ujjain. Among the various people at these places, I express my gratitude especially to Francois Grimal, Dominic Goodall, SAS Sharma, Shankar Sharma, Prerna Patel, Balkrishna Sharma, and Sitanshu Rath.

Special thanks go to Yigal Bronner, David Shulman, and all of the members of the 2008 Summer Academy devoted to the *Naiṣadhīyacarita* ("Sanskrit Poetry at the Zenith") at the Institute for Advanced Studies in Jerusalem, Israel: V. Narayana Rao, Maya Tevet-Dayan, Lawrence McCrea, H.V. Nagaraja Rao, Charles Malamoud, Luther Obrock, Whitney Cox, Ilanit Levi-Shacham, Maayan Nidbach, Tammy Klein, Joseph Vayalil, Bhavani and Anasuya Pendyala, and Alex Cherniak. Additionally, I wish to thank several colleagues (and friends) who have offered me their friendship and specific advice for making this book better: Eun Sun Jang (Kyungseo), Jesse Knutson, David Mellins, Travis Smith, Adheesh Sathaye, Andrew Nicholson, John Nemec, Gil Ben-Herut, and Frank Hoffman. Among friends who closely followed my trail as I finished this book, I especially thank Michael Ero, Gene Terry, Deana Heath, Dev Rana, Michael Granros, Birjoo Patel, Chris Strnad, Kevin Jackson, Alfredo Rossi, Lois Darlington, Kevin Lin, Ronnie Lin, Sanjay Kansupada, Cheng-dar Yang, Jamie Bennett, Chris Morray-Jones, Jane Downey, and Ron denBroeder.

The final product could not have been possible without the astonishing generosity of my colleagues at the University of Pennsylvania. I thank especially the South Asia Studies Faculty Writing Group at the University of Pennsylvania: Daud Ali, Ramya Sreenivasan, and Lisa Mitchell. For weeks, they spent their precious time sharpening my rhetoric and challenging me to rethink portions of my arguments. I feel very fortunate to have received their learned support when I did. Consistently for the past five years, other colleagues, students, and friends at the University of Pennsylvania lent a helping hand whenever I asked for or needed it. Among them, I thank George Cardona, Michael Meister, Jamal Elias, Babubhai

Suthar, Allyn Miner, Jody Chavez, Kathleen Hall, Zoe Beckerman, Sanjukta Banerjee, Haimanti Banerjee, Raili Roy, Rita Copeland, Victor Mair, Phil Miraglia, David Nelson, Surendra Gambhir, Vijay Gambhir, Pushkar Sohoni, Nachiket Chanchani, Justin McDaniel, Rupa Viswanath, Ramnarayan Rawat, Walt Hakala, David Buchta, Steven Vose, Sarah Pierce-Taylor, Jonathan Dickstein, Simone Barretta-McCarter, Theodore Benke, and Rosane and Ludo Rocher.

I thank the institutional support I received from the Muktabodha Indological Research Institute, the Fulbright-Hays Doctoral Dissertation Research Abroad Program, the Mellon Penn Humanities Forum, and the University of California, Berkeley. I also cannot thank enough the two learned reviewers of my manuscript for Columbia University Press. Perhaps only they and I know the extent to which the original draft of my manuscript was transformed in light of their generous comments. I also thank Kathryn Schell of Columbia University Press and Marc Johnston of Cenveo Publisher Services for their patient help with all my questions during this process.

I reserve the last words of thanks for my mother and father (for their sacrifice and support), my older brother Amrish (for his unconditional support and tough love), and to Iza, who provided the acumen, support, and love I needed to make this a better book.

TEXT TO TRADITION

INTRODUCTION

COMPARED TO what we know about classic works with long reception histories from other parts of the world, we have a surprisingly shadowy understanding of what great literary works composed in South Asia meant to generations of audiences. In earlier "histories of literature," individual works were often presented as static texts with an intrinsic set of features and values that could be uncritically implicated in a narrow or generalized history of a period, a region, or a genre. Accordingly, the emphasis in these works was almost always on the *text* itself (or, more commonly, groups of texts) and rarely ventured to address how an indigenous literary tradition received and *experienced* one of its key texts. As such, after more than a century of scholarship, even now we can only gather a vague idea of what kinds of reading communities—and reading practices—clustered around works of literature that continued to remain relevant for a culture over centuries. The case of Sanskrit poetry (*kāvya*) and specifically a genre known as *mahākāvya* (literally, a "long" or "great" poem) is emblematic of this poverty in our historical comprehension. Several Sanskrit *mahākāvya* are widely understood as classics of South Asian literature, and while sophisticated studies of individual *mahākāvya* have become available recently, no existing work has yet treated a single poem's literary history from the point of view of its audiences.[1] Considerable advances and important contributions to the understanding of the intellectual history of Sanskrit culture have been made in the past few decades—especially concerning rich traditions of poetics (*alaṅkāraśāstra*) from the sixth through seventeenth centuries. However, outside of understanding literary culture through the universalizing rubrics of formalized poetics, more investigation into other aspects of the lives of texts is needed to fully explain a literary tradition's view of itself.

Missing, for instance, are serious discussions about an individual Sanskrit poem's reading communities and their reading *practices*, a sense of what tied a particular work's readership together over centuries, and what the dynamics of difference between these audiences, separated by time and space, were. There is a complex relationship, as philosophers like Paul Ricoeur have argued, between "the world of the text" and "the world of the reader," but the two have been conflated to such an extent in much of the early scholarship on Sanskrit literature that, even today, it is virtually impossible to think of individual works as having a complicated history mediated by various approaches to explain and interpret a text over time.[2] Missing also is an acknowledgment of the complex, conflicted, and even contradictory *effect* that knowledge of a text's long history has on readers at varying points in history, including the present. Admittedly, linking individual texts, or even genres, with real communities of readers from premodern South Asia is a difficult task. This is especially the case for texts with long reception histories for which we have centuries-long gaps in tangible evidence to explain how individuals and certain social groups approached them or how they might have functioned within institutions dedicated to learning and teaching literature. Nevertheless, based on the evidence we do have, certain questions can and remain to be addressed. For example, outside of the *alaṅkāraśāstra*, what are the different types of readership a Sanskrit poem attracted across centuries? What were some of the diverse explanatory or interpretive practices readers brought to the text? What tied all of them together?

Some of these questions first came up for me while encountering references to a twelfth-century Sanskrit poem entitled the *Naiṣadhīyacarita*. Histories of Sanskrit literature consistently noted that the *Naiṣadhīyacarita* (literally, the *Deeds* or *Adventures of Nala, King of Niṣadha*), or simply the *Naiṣadhīya*,[3] was considered to be the "last" of the great poems of the classical Sanskrit tradition and that "to the purely native taste," it had been preferable to all other long Sanskrit poems, studied and praised more frequently than even Kālidāsa's works.[4] But I also read contrary statements in other histories of Sanskrit literature:

> The *Naiṣadhīyacarita* is the last masterpiece of industry and ingenuity but to class it with the masterpieces of Kālidāsa, Bhāravi, and even Māgha is to betray an ignorance of the difference between poetry and its counterfeit. Śrīharṣa not only shares but emphasizes to an extreme degree the worst kind of artificialities of his tribe; and no sound-hearted, sound-minded

> reader will ever include him in the small class of great poets. . . . Even if a modern critic has the inclination to share the enthusiasm of Śrīharṣa's admirers, the poet's impossible and incessant affectations rise up in witness against such an attitude. [The] modern reader often perhaps lacks [the] equipment and aptitude [to appreciate the poem] and therefore finds little interest in a work that, for its cult of style, has always been so popular with scholars of a traditional type.[5]

I was confused by the stark gulf that these authors suggested: that the *Naiṣadhīya* could once be considered, by some, as the finest poem in Sanskrit while others now would barely recommend, if not dismiss altogether, the idea of picking it up. Some years of actually reading Sanskrit poetry, and not just secondary reviews of it, disabused me of trusting the opinions of literary scholars trained to write about it under the spell of nineteenth-century and early-twentieth-century aesthetic expectations.[6] I gathered that while centuries of premodern reading must have embraced feelings of identification with the poet, most colonial-era scholarship on the *Naiṣadhīya*—and on much of Sanskrit literature—sought to separate itself from the premodern practices of *Naiṣadhīya* commentary. Premodern audiences addressed the *Naiṣadhīya* as part of a *tradition* of classic *mahākāvya*, and, therefore, to write a commentary on the poem meant to try to become an *ideal* reader for a poem one clearly respected. Modern critics from the colonial period, by and large, ignored or underplayed the tradition in which the text was understood, received, and taught. At the same time, however, much of this literary-historical scholarship desired some form of connection with scholastic engagements from the past and, thus, to maintain a relationship with a continuous discourse of the *Naiṣadhīya*.

Recognition of this shift in scholarly attitude notwithstanding, the modern critiques of the *Naiṣadhīya* also inspired a strong curiosity: What could the "native taste" have actually meant across time, and what did a "traditional type" of reader like about the *Naiṣadhīya* that these later critics clearly despised? Could we recover forms of literary awareness and criticism about the poem that might have existed in the past, and might still—or no longer—exist in the present? Ultimately, this curiosity led me to investigate documents, agents, and social contexts that would otherwise have remained invisible to a project solely focused on the text itself. What began, therefore, as a modest exploration of one of the greatest works of South Asian poetry has now also become a book about dozens of arguably less-important works, composed by dozens of men over hundreds of years. Rather than speak of a single literary work, therefore, I claim to write here about a singular *tradition* of a literary work: the *Naiṣadhīya* tradition.

A *TRADITION* OF A TEXT

The word *tradition*, even when applied to literary texts, can be a protean designation, open to being shaped (or disfigured) to suit hosts of possible pasts, presents, and futures. Most simply, a literary tradition may refer to sets of textual and scholarly practices that grow up around a root or source text (*mūla-grantha* in Sanskrit). *Tradition*, thus, explains an ongoing set of self-aware text-critical and aesthetic engagements with a powerful literary object that span centuries. These engagements include, but are not limited to, formal commentaries, narrative texts, encomia, pseudepigrapha,[7] translations, visual representations,[8] anonymous snatches of literary-critical discourse available from oral tradition, and modern forms of literary criticism.

A well-known maxim in Sanskrit explains: "a commentator knows but not the poet" (*vyākhyātā jānāti na tu kaviḥ*). Accordingly, the most important documents for my study are commentaries on the *Naiṣadhīya* written in Sanskrit from the thirteenth to twentieth centuries. In addition to being different hermeneutic orientations to the poem, commentaries serve as storehouses for encomia (*praśasti*) to the *Naiṣadhīya* and biographical information about the text, the author, and the reception history of the poem. Commentaries help us, among other things, to trace the poem's legibility through history. They present sites for competing aesthetics and draw out important contrasts between the creative and critical enterprises intrinsic to Sanskrit literary culture—the work of the poet (*kavi*) and the scholar (*paṇḍita*). *Tradition* also frames sets of shared tastes and values that, over time, undergo subtle changes and even reversals. Recognizing that certain literary texts can, in many situations, be encountered autonomous to any mediating influences, it seems that very many other works, by dint of their age and reputation, can never be approached through such a naïve lens. *Tradition*, therefore, rather than fortifying the idea that literary works are received unmediated, trans-historically, and are available to all people at all times in all contexts, actually helps us to move away from this fiction.

Finally, *tradition* serves as a label for the effect produced in readers when encountering and sustaining an older and influential work that brings with it centuries of readings, reading practices, and dramatic shifts in context of reading. In applying a concept like *tradition* to frame a diverse reception history for an 800-year-old poem like the *Naiṣadhīya*, this book pays special attention to the critical concepts associated with reader-reception theories developed in the latter half of the twentieth century. In particular, my understanding of a *Naiṣadhīya* tradition encompasses seeing commentators, at different turns, as different types of readers and part of different types of reading communities. Thus, following one stream of reader-response theory, *Text to Tradition* delineates the reading practices of empirical readers and reading communities in specific historical situations in order to reconstruct the contributions of human agents in forming the *Naiṣadhīya* tradition as it exists for us today.[9] I see the literary-historical agenda of my study as less guided by an urge to understand the *Naiṣadhīya* as such and more focused on the critical engagements that explore its changing intelligibility from the point of view of different audiences at different periods. I plot, therefore, a selective trajectory that focuses on those moments when the *Naiṣadhīya* tradition turns to analyze its own history, as my primary concern is with the way readers of the poem throughout history imagine and write about their relationship with each other and with their predecessors. I have sought to articulate those changes, tracing the history of the tradition through some of its most important transitional moments.

I am also sympathetic to other understandings of an "audience" as largely a critical fiction—an *implied* reader—and wish fruitfully to see the *Naiṣadhīya* tradition as largely an *effect* the poem has had on readers throughout history. Here I interpret reader identifications with Śrīharṣa and the *Naiṣadhīya* as largely an affinity to effects rather than objective entities. Thus, we may posit readers' response to a *Śrīharṣa* effect or to a *Naiṣadhīya* effect rather than to an actual poet and poem. Each discursive engagement with the poem sees it as something different. There are multiple *Naiṣadhīyas*, in other words, conceived in different ways by commentators-as-editors, commentators-as-interpreters, biographers and hagiographers, or by literary critics. The poem's discursive genres also develop independently of the poetic traditions of encomia, imitation, and oral verses speaking of rivalry between poems and generally produce a different kind of *Naiṣadhīya* as the object of scholarship, evaluation, and commentary. The shifting and unpredictable nature I identify with the

Naiṣadhīya tradition at various historical moments also speaks to a notion that neither the text nor its empirical readers have an independent status but are rather mutually constituted/absorbed into an "interpretive community" that determines, at any given point, what the text is.[10]

THE TEXT OF THE *TRADITION*

The text at the heart of the tradition is an extraordinary one. The following chapters, where I explore and discuss the *Naiṣadhīya*'s unique aesthetic as a poem and what I am calling the *Naiṣadhīya* tradition, will make clear what makes it so extraordinary. First, however, I briefly address the choice of this particular work over and above hundreds of other candidates, especially when the reception histories of equally neglected works of more well-known poets like Kālidāsa remain to be written.

The *Naiṣadhīya* emerged at an important moment in South Asian literary and intellectual history. It was produced at the eve of a new political dispensation in northern India that would gradually but definitively realign the patronage networks of Sanskrit literary and intellectual production. At a time when vernacular languages were boldly moving into the literary realm, the *Naiṣadhīya* had an unprecedented role in catalyzing change in various literary cultures of South Asia. The *Naiṣadhīya*'s awareness of regional languages is manifested, for example, in a twelfth-century Sanskrit enriched by neologisms, a distinctive style and syntax, a turn toward the use of popular subgenres well represented in the literary cultures of the newly emergent languages, and the use of vernacular meters. New works on poetics dealing with topics of trope and rhetoric crop up during the time of Śrīharṣa to keep pace with the transforming aesthetics of *kāvya* in Sanskrit and the regional languages. It is the first, and in some cases the only, *mahākāvya* translated into the early literary cultures of South Asia's regional languages. In addition to being a source text for Pahāri painters during the eighteenth century and Kathakali dramatists since the seventeenth century, it has also been read as religious allegory by audiences since the sixteenth century.

The poem is an emblem of a literary age in transition. The *Naiṣadhīya* was both a distillation of past *mahākāvya* practices and a model for future poets working in multiple South Asian languages. Less than a century after its composition, the legacy of the poem began to take shape through the emergence of Sanskrit commentaries and biographies of both the poem and poet. By the fourteenth century, literary communities across the subcontinent came to see the *Naiṣadhīya* as the fifth and final text in a canonical formulation known as the *pañcamahākāvya*, or "the five [classic] *mahākāvya*," which include the works of Kālidāsa (fourth century CE?), Bhāravi (sixth century), and Māgha (seventh century). The *Naiṣadhīya* both affirms inherited norms of the *mahākāvya* tradition (from earlier poets like Kālidāsa, Bhāravi, and Māgha) and also galvanizes new trends in Sanskrit and regional South Asian literatures. As we shall see, however, the energy it infused in the genre was not unanimously lauded among the critics historically. Its unstable position as a "great work," therefore, in the divergent evaluative matrices of Sanskrit literary communities has rendered the poem both a confirmation and a disruption of familiar patterns in works that precede it. Finally, its relative lateness (the twelfth century), in relation to other established classics, makes the poem coeval with the unprecedented increase of secondary *kāvya*-related documents in South Asia (formal commentaries, narrative accounts, translations, and adaptations), supplying its historical record with a richly detailed and textured archive—clearly the most extensive of any *mahākāvya* we have. The diverse history of this important Sanskrit literary work's reception from the twelfth to twentieth centuries, therefore, effectively indexes the wider changes that characterize the literary landscape of South Asia in the second millennium.

ŚRĪHARṢA: THE POET AT THE HEAD OF THE TRADITION

Playfully broken are the tusks of that mad elephant,
that group of Cārvākas who hold that
only perception leads to true knowledge.
The attack is executed by the hands of a lion,
whose human form is Śrīharṣa.
These actions of his are well known in the world.[11]

Varadarāja Paṇḍita, commentator on the *Khaṇḍanakhaṇḍakhādya*

Śrīharṣa, in addition to being the single most remarkable poet of his age, is also among the most important philosophers working during this period. His philosophical masterpiece *Khaṇḍanakhaṇḍakhādya* (Edible Pieces of Hostile Argument), what he calls a companion piece to the *Naiṣadhīya*, revolutionizes Indian philosophy and will be considered by later audiences as a foundational text of a mature phase of Advaita Vedānta, an influential school propounding the nonduality (*advaita*) of Being.[12] One of the epilogue verses of the *Naiṣadhīya* mentions that the king of Kānyakubja (Kanauj) honored Śrīharṣa. Throughout the first millennium CE, the kings of Kanauj supported the development of Sanskrit poetry and poetics, giving patronage to authors like Bāṇabhaṭṭa, Bhavabhūti, Trivikramabhaṭṭa, and Rājaśekhara.[13] Fixing Śrīharṣa's date and patronage in Kanauj, however, has vexed modern scholars as it had the earlier Sanskrit commentators of the *Naiṣadhīya*. The only certainty is that the poet-philosopher worked in the courts of one or more of the Gāhaḍavāla kings of the twelfth century (Govindacandra, Vijayacandra, and Jayacandra)—somewhere between 1125 and 1180 CE.[14] Govindacandra (1114–1155 CE) was followed by his son Vijayacandra (1155–1170 CE), who, according to a standard historical narrative, presided over the beginning of Gāhaḍavāla decline: the loss of the Delhi region to Turuṣkas (Turks) and encroachment from the east by then-prince and soon-to-be Sena king Lakṣmaṇasena.[15] The Gāhaḍavāla dynasty effectively ended with the death of Vijayacandra's son Jayacandra (1170–1193 CE) at the battle of Candwar, where he was reportedly killed by Mu'izz ud-Dīn Ghūri's general Quṭb ud-Dīn Aibak.[16]

Historical records do not provide a definite indication of which Kānyakubja king patronized Śrīharṣa. The traditional Sanskrit commentators of *Naiṣadhīya* variously place Śrīharṣa at the courts of three of the Gāhaḍavāla kings. The fifteenth-century *Naiṣadhīya* commentator Gadādhara comments on a stray detail from the epilogue verse that mentions Śrīharṣa as honored by a king of Kānyakubja (*kānyakubjeśvara*). Gadādhara thus places Śrīharṣa in the court of Govindacandra, but without any justification. In the final verse of the fifth canto of the *Naiṣadhīya* (v. 138), Śrīharṣa mentions that he composed a praise poem honoring a certain king "Vijaya" in his *Śrīvijayapraśasti*; on this basis, several scholars have speculated that Govindacandra's son Vijayacandra was his patron. The *Naiṣadhīya*'s seventh canto (v. 110) mentions a lost work by Śrīharṣa in honor of an unnamed Bengali king (the *Gauḍorvīśakulapraśasti*); on this basis, seventeenth-century commentator Gopinātha writes in his *Harṣahṛdaya* that Śrīharṣa was in the court of the Sena king Vijayasena (1097–1160 CE). References from later texts outside the commentarial tradition, such as Rājaśekharasūri's *Prabhandhakośa*, place Śrīharṣa in Jayacandra's court. In light of the well-established notion that Jayacandra emphasized the "ideals of dharma symbolized by Viṣṇu and Rāma," some also highlight as noteworthy to the argument of Jayacandra as Śrīharṣa's patron the hymn to the twelve forms of Viṣṇu found in the twenty-first canto of the *Naiṣadhīya*.[17] G.R. Watve, in his history of Sanskrit literature in Marathi, suggests that Śrīharṣa wrote the *Naiṣadhīya* to commemorate the groom-choosing ceremony (*svayaṃvara*) of Jayacandra's daughter Saṃyogitā (Saṃyuktā).[18] I find it probable that the poet worked under the patronage of all, or at least two, of the Gāhaḍavāla kings but composed the *Naiṣadhīya* at the court of Jayacandra, the last of the Gāhaḍavālas.

THE NALA–DAMAYANTĪ STORY

Karkoṭaka the snake,
the king Ṛtuparṇa, and
Nala and Damayantī:
Singing their praise
destroys Kali's effect.[19]

The *Mahābhārata*, The Forest Book

The *Naiṣadhīya* focuses on the famous romance of Nala and Damayantī, a crucial episode in a larger story about the famous couple's union, exile, separation, and ultimate reunion. Śrīharṣa chooses only to focus on the couple's falling in love, marriage, and honeymoon. The entire story, known to generations of South Asian audiences, is narrated in the *Mahābhārata* and Somadeva's eleventh-century *Kathāsaritsāgara* (Ocean of Rivers of Stories). The narrative begins with Nala, king of Niṣadha, who, upon hearing of Damayantī's beauty and virtue, longs to be with her. As he pines for her in the palace garden, a golden *haṃsa* (the Indian goose) alights nearby. Nala captures the bird but sets it free when it promises to fly to Damayantī's country (Vidarbha) in order to unite him with the princess. The *haṃsa* reaches Damayantī and describes Nala to her in the most favorable terms. Instantly, she falls in love and feels the weight of being separated from him. Seeing her lovesick, Damayantī's father organizes a *svayaṃvara*, a royal ceremony where Damayantī would choose her husband among eligible princes.

Nala eagerly sets out to attend the ceremony. On his way, he encounters four Vedic divinities who preside over one of the four regions of the universe: Indra, king of the gods, presides over the East; Agni, god of fire, the North; Varuṇa, god of waters, the West; and Yama, god of death, the South. To his surprise, each of these gods expresses a desire to marry

Damayantī, and, in a cruel twist of fate, they pressure Nala to be their go-between to convince her to marry one of them. Stunned at first, but careful to respect the gods' wishes, he smartly points out that it will be impossible for him to enter her secret quarters without arousing suspicion from the guards. Indra cleverly counters this argument by offering to grant Nala the power to become temporarily invisible when entering the palace. Dejected by the mission, but resolved to carry it out, Nala enters the palace invisibly and, as he stands in front of the princess as an anonymous messenger, diligently persuades her to marry one of the four gods. She adamantly refuses to entertain his multiple pleas and insists that she will either marry her beloved Nala or take her own life. Satisfied that he tried his best to do what was asked of him, Nala proceeds to the *svayaṃvara*. The gods, recognizing Damayantī's stubborn refusal to marry any of them, now decide to come as Nala and assume his form as they take their place among the other suitors. Five Nalas now appear to Damayantī. Confused at first, she notices after a while that four of the five do not blink their eyes, nor do their flower garlands wilt. Also, their feet do not touch the ground. She realizes all of these to be signs that they are gods and chooses the real Nala to be her husband.

As the gods return unsatisfied, they encounter Dvāpara and Kali, personifications of the previous and current degraded age (*yuga*). Both were late to Damayantī's ceremony and, angered that they could not win her, vow to bring the happy couple to misery. As Nala and Damayantī settle into their newly married life, Kali seizes an opportunity to take control of Nala's body, when the young king forgets to wash himself before performing a ritual. Kali also enters into the mind of Nala's brother Puṣkara and drives him to challenge Nala to a gambling contest. With the dice loaded against him and unable to resist the next roll, Nala loses his entire kingdom. Exiled and each wearing only a single piece of clothing, Nala and Damayantī wander in the wilderness. Adding to his woe, a bird flies off with Nala's clothes when he tries to trap it. After this point, the couple shares Damayantī's single piece of clothing. Nala pleads with Damayantī to go back to her father's home but she refuses. Desperate and possessed by Kali, Nala abandons her one night while she is sleeping, ripping off half of her dress to cover himself. As he enters deeper into the forest, he sees a snake trapped in a forest fire. He rescues the snake (named Karkoṭaka) and is, at once, bitten by it. The poisonous bite, Karkoṭaka tells him, will disfigure him and transform him into a dwarf so that he can remain hidden and enter the service of King Ṛtuparṇa of Ayodhyā. The benevolent snake also gives Nala a special garment that will, at the right moment, return him to his original form. When he arrives to Ayodhyā, Nala finds employment in King Ṛtuparṇa's stables and in the kitchen as a cook. Taking on the name Bāhuka, he also eventually becomes the king's most trusted advisor. Damayantī, meanwhile, after undergoing some harrowing trials while searching for Nala, reaches the palace of the king of the Cedi country. Here she becomes a servant for the queen until an emissary from her father's kingdom recognizes her and arranges for her return to Vidarbha.

Damayantī at once sends a search party to find Nala, realizing that her husband may be in disguise. When one of the messengers infers Bāhuka might be Nala—based on his skills as a charioteer and cook—he poses a question to him that Damayantī had suggested might confirm his identity: "What kind of man abandons his wife in the middle of the night and takes half of her clothes?" Nala/Bāhuka responds to the messenger: "The kind of man who tried to make his stubborn wife return to her father's house." Calling for a public announcement that Nala can be presumed dead, but secretly suspecting that this Bāhuka might be Nala, Damayantī proposes that a second *svayaṃvara* be announced. As it would be hastily put together, only those kings who could arrive the quickest would be able to attend. Ṛtuparṇa desires to attend and asks his skilled charioteer Bāhuka to take him to Vidarbha as quickly as he can. During the journey, Ṛtuparṇa teaches Bāhuka the art of "counting" in the context of gambling (*akṣa-hṛdaya*). In return, Bāhuka teaches Ṛtuparṇa how to control horses. Once they arrive at Vidarbha, Damayantī asks Bāhuka why a man would want to send his wife back to her father's house. He responds: "Because he has gambled away his kingdom and cannot fittingly support her." Damayantī immediately recognizes Bāhuka to be none other than Nala. Thus recognized by his wife, Nala puts on the magic garment given to him by Karkoṭaka the snake and reverts to his human form. Thus reunited, the couple spends some time in Ṛtuparṇa's kingdom before returning to the capital of Niṣadha to confront Puṣkara. Confident in his newly acquired skill as a gambler (staking even Damayantī in exchange for the entire kingdom), Nala wins the contest this time and regains his kingdom. Magnanimously, however, instead of exiling his brother, he grants Puṣkara half of the kingdom. Nala and Damayantī resume their married life together.

Explanations for the popularity of the Nala-Damayantī story have been numerous. A frequent reason cited is that Damayantī's choice of a mortal husband, when divine ones were available, offers a powerful statement about love intensely shared between humans. Linking the story's "humanness" with its underlying erotic intensity, Narayana Rao and Shulman note that the numerous tellings of the Nala–Damayantī story speak to the "inventiveness of human modes of loving" and that "being human also presupposes anxiety about identity and integrity of the self in relation to others and to the field of metaphysical forces within which the human being must act."[20] Another reason rests in the poem's appeal to audiences as a talisman of sorts to ward off the deleterious effects of the present world-age (*kaliyuga*), regarded as hopelessly debased. This tradition perhaps owes its source to the second book of the *Mahābhārata* where we are told of the inherent power that lies in recounting Nala and Damayantī's story for eradicating the ill effects of the *kaliyuga* and for providing solace in times of hardship.[21] This, in fact, was the putative purpose of telling the story in the *Mahābhārata* in the first place: to console the exiled king Yudhiṣṭhira, who, like Nala, loses everything in an ill-fated gambling match. Śrīharṣa himself alerts the reader to this tradition in the third verse of the poem, which rhetorically asks that as telling the Nala story purifies the *kaliyuga*, why wouldn't it also purify his own poetry, which is fully devoted to telling this story (*Naiṣadhīya* 1.3)?

THE *NAIṢADHĪYA*'S PLOT

> *Glory to Nala, the jewel in the crown of all kings!*
> *To praise him makes everything auspicious.*
> *A collection of the pearls of Nala's fame,*
> *Śrīharṣa's elegant poem confers a special delight.*[22]
>
> Gopinātha Ratha, seventeenth-century commentator

The number of texts directly inspired by Śrīharṣa's *Naiṣadhīyacarita* makes his telling of the first part of the Nala story arguably the most influential of them all. It conforms to the custom of the Sanskrit *mahākāvya* genre (discussed in the next chapter) to explore the mood and details of a portion of a story over and above the impulse to bring it to a hasty completion. The *Naiṣadhīya* dwells only on a fragment of the Nala story—the happy scene that ends with the couple's marriage and honeymoon. The poet nevertheless makes references to the darker aspects of the larger story throughout his poem, lest the stakes involved in the narrative be forgotten. What the

Mahābhārata presents in two hundred couplets, Śrīharṣa expands to some 2,760 verses, spanning twenty-two cantos (*sarga*). The story in Śrīharṣa's poem begins with the premise that Prince Nala and Princess Damayantī have fallen in love without ever having met or without having seen each other face to face (except in paintings and in their dreams). Each experiences a deeply felt longing for the other. Nala, elaborately described by the poet as the archetypal noble and learned king, wanders depressed in his palace garden while the lovelorn Damayantī curses the moon and all things that inspire desire in her. While in the palace garden, Nala captures a magical talking bird (*haṃsa*). Thinking he will be killed, the *haṃsa* cries out to his own absent beloved in desperation, wondering how she and their children will survive without him. The bird's pity-inducing laments and its promise to act as special envoy to Nala's beloved Damayantī lead the king to set it free. Thus liberated, the *haṃsa* flies to Kuṇḍinapura (Damayantī's home) to bear Nala's message of love.

What follows are exquisite scenes of a courtly game of love, revealing in full display the poet's verbal skills (cantos two through four). Neither Nala nor Damayantī want to reveal their love for each other *completely*, and so the *haṃsa* makes sure to play an even-handed go-between, extracting coded confessions of love from both. Damayantī's father, meanwhile, senses his daughter's misery and sets up a groom-choosing ceremony (*svayaṃvara*) in order for her to find an appropriate husband. The major narrative complication follows (canto five): four Vedic gods (Indra, Agni, Varuṇa, and Yama) hear about Damayantī from sage Nārada, who explains that all the regents of the earth have neglected their wars in their obsession for Damayantī's hand in marriage. So overtaken are they with her description that the heavenly beings decide that they also want to marry this mortal princess. In a cruel irony, they hire Nala to be their messenger and go-between to convince the princess to choose one of them as a husband. A devastated Nala accepts this disheartening mission out of pious obligation to the gods. Because he cannot enter the women's living quarters, the gods grant him the power of invisibility so that he can enter incognito.

An entire canto (six) is dedicated to Nala's crossing seven different chambers of Damayantī's palace before finally reaching her; his presence is felt by the other women and ultimately by Damayantī herself even though no real contact has yet been made. He observes from a distance as the princess rejects a marriage proposal from Indra, who, distrustful of Nala, had already sent another envoy on his behalf prior to

Nala's arrival. Another canto (seven) is devoted to Nala's mental picture of Damayantī's body—from head to toe—allowing the poet to create an erotic intensity hidden in submerged metaphors connecting the princess's body with various other physical images and inventive abstractions. Finally, at the end of this canto and the beginning of the succeeding one, Nala reveals himself to Damayantī and her friends—simultaneously preserving his anonymity (he does not give his name to them) and fulfilling his own obligations as messenger by arguing persuasively on behalf of the gods (cantos eight and nine). Despite Nala's lawyer-like argumentation, Damayantī adamantly refuses any other suitor. When she is ready to break down completely in the desperate thought that she will never be united with Nala, the *haṃsa* reappears and guides Nala to reveal himself to her (canto nine). Upon processing the revelation, Damayantī falls silent and only secretly hints that Nala should come to her *svayaṃvara.* The next three cantos (ten, eleven, and twelve) are devoted to describing the various kings that attended the *svayaṃvara* in the ultimately vain hope of marrying Damayantī. These cantos describe why other human and divine suitors could not make it, how the ones that could attend were each received and communicated with each other, and how the goddess Sarasvatī—Speech herself—comes to describe each of the gathered kings and lends Damayantī some aid in choosing the right man. Unfortunately, when she gets to Nala, the four Vedic gods have already transformed themselves to look like Nala, realizing that he is the only suitor Damayantī is interested in. As Sarasvatī describes the "five Nalas" (*pañcanalīya*) in a tour de force of double meaning (where each description of the multiple Nalas also reveals their underlying identity), Damayantī is literally at a loss for words, suffocated by language, when confronted by this conundrum—where Sarasvatī's coded introductions serve only to highlight the guile and irony of the situation (canto thirteen).

In a brilliant turn, Damayantī prays to the gods themselves for advice and grace. The four Vedic gods relent, bless her, and Damayantī places the garland around the real Nala's neck, sealing their betrothal (canto fourteen). The next two cantos (fifteen and sixteen) describe the extended plan of the traditional Hindu wedding: the preparations of the bride and groom on the night before the ceremony, the groom's procession to the bride's home, the bride's entourage singing songs of love and marriage, the wedding day itself, the reception feast, and finally the return of the now-married couple to the husband's home. In an innovation from the *Mahābhārata*, the next canto (seventeen) is an interlude to the romance narrative, with Kali (the representative of the "dark age" we currently live in) making an appearance. Apparently, Kali had intended to attend the *svayaṃvara* himself but arrived late. Being told by the Vedic gods (who are returning to heaven) that he has missed his chance, Kali vengefully vows to separate the couple. Śrīharṣa uses this opportunity in the narrative to stage a fascinating debate between Kali (a spokesman for atheism and materialism) and the gods (defenders of traditional religion) on the finer points of ethics, morality, and the ultimate aims of human life. Eventually, Kali (and his friend Dvāpara, symbolic of the second-to-worst age where social life is imbued with deceit at every level) leave the scene and proceed to the outskirts of Nala's capital, where they will plot their scheme for years to separate the couple. Śrīharṣa leaves them here and proceeds in the next canto (canto eighteen) to describe "the first night" spent together by Nala and Damayantī after the wedding. The next and final four cantos describe the following morning, day, and evening. Poets come to awaken Nala, not realizing that he has already left to do his morning prayers (canto nineteen); when Nala returns, he shares some light moments of fun with his bride and her friend (canto twenty). Upon completing his political and military tasks as king by midday, he takes a bath and delivers a long hymn of praise to Lord Viṣṇu. After lunch, he spends the afternoon with Damayantī and her friends, who play games and sing songs in their honor. As evening approaches, Nala goes to the river for his twilight prayers (canto twenty-one). The poem ends with Nala and Damayantī together describing the moonrise (canto twenty-two).

OUTLINE OF THE *NAIṢADHĪYA* TRADITION

In pinpointing the critical moments in the poem's history, *Text to Tradition* follows the logic of the *Naiṣadhīya* tradition's primary sources. The chapters of this book are loosely structured along both a chronology (of changing patterns of reception from the thirteenth to twentieth centuries) and along source types with their varying and often overlapping functions. As far as we can tell, the *Naiṣadhīya* tradition begins in the late twelfth century, and the first documents related to the poem are early commentaries from the mid-thirteenth century. These works essentially respond to the text as an object of awe in need of explication and analysis. Sometime in the late fourteenth century, the tradition turns to the *Naiṣadhīya* as a technology for the examination and promotion of advanced literary practice. Eventually, by the fifteenth and sixteenth centuries, the work is recognized as a classic worthy of imitation, translation, and veneration.

Chapter 1 commences the study of the *Naiṣadhīya* tradition by framing the *Naiṣadhīya* within the broader fold of the *mahākāvya* genre and exploring the poem's aesthetic, to give the reader an idea of why this particular poem deserved so much varied attention by so many generations of readers. The remaining chapters draw out the distinctive aspects of this attention. Chapters 2 to 5 discuss the wide-ranging nature of Sanskrit commentaries on the *Naiṣadhīya* and form the core of this book. Chapter 2 provides a historical account of commentarial production on the poem, dividing up eight centuries of engagement into three distinct phases: an early phase (thirteenth to fourteenth centuries), middle phase (fifteenth century), and late phase (post–sixteenth century) that roughly correspond to the critical turning points in commentarial attitudes toward the *Naiṣadhīya*. Chapter 3 takes up the *act* of commentary—writing itself and the ways in which commentators variously interpret the verses of the *Naiṣadhīya*—and chapter 4 describes the editorial practices of commentators and the impact of these practices in shaping the reception of the poem. Chapter 5 explores the commentarial influence on what I call "secondary waves" of reading, emphases on the poem's semantic polyvalence, and its openness to allegorical interpretation.

Chapter 6 treats the fascinating legends available in commentaries and specialized narrative texts. These largely reflect on the poem's transmission history and the literary-critical reception it received at the hands of imagined audiences. The narratives also provide us a glimpse into premodern forms of biography in South Asia, the ways in which authors and texts were imagined in narrative to address curiosities insufficiently satisfied by facts gleaned from other types of sources. Chapter 7 positions the *Naiṣadhīya* and its commentarial cultures within the changing literary landscape of South Asia during the second millennium by exploring the regional-language translations of the poem. I conclude with a general discussion of how the *Naiṣadhīya* was represented, in centuries of commentary, through various carefully crafted encomia and pseudepigrapha that followed and bolstered its rise as a classic text. I also observe the ways in which the poem has continued to function in the canons of Sanskrit literature in the twentieth century.

1 ◈ THE *NAIṢADHĪYA'S* AESTHETIC

After adopting a superb path,
a path untrodden by other poets,
and initiated by his own pioneering steps,
the poet Śrīharṣa—the glorious Harṣa—
strides about gloriously.[1]

Gadādhara, fifteenth-century commentator

THE *MAHĀKĀVYA* GENRE

IF THERE is a canonical genre in Sanskrit from the early centuries of the first millennium CE to the early centuries of the second millennium CE, it is the *mahākāvya*. Important to critics and commentators from the seventh century CE onward, it became especially important after 1000 CE with the rise of the *kāvya* commentary, now the mechanism through which to preserve, control, and teach elegant language and to carry forward the values of Sanskrit culture. The *mahākāvya* is, literally, a "long poem." Although sometimes termed a "court epic," it is misleading to conflate the *mahākāvya* with the massive mytho-historical epics *Mahābhārata* and *Rāmāyaṇa*, from which the Sanskrit *mahākāvya* usually draws its subject matter.[2] Though the early history of the genre may be "lost in the mists of time,"[3] the earliest extant examples of the genre date to the early centuries of the first millennium CE, when the great epics were perhaps still taking their final form as redacted texts. The first and only known poets from this period are Aśvaghoṣa and Kālidāsa. Aśvaghoṣa is well known for two *mahākāvya* compositions: the *Buddhacarita* (Life of the Buddha) and the *Saundarānanda* (Handsome Nanda). Similarly, Kālidāsa is known for two *mahākāvya* works: the *Kumārasambhava* (The Birth of Kumāra) and the *Raghuvaṃśa* (The Lineage of Raghu), an archetypal specimen of the genre for later theorists. The *mahākāvya* is still not a very well understood genre of Indian literature. Differing markedly from explicitly religious or didactic poetry in early India, *mahākāvya* from the time of Kālidāsa until the thirteenth century was the genre most closely tied to the culture of the royal court, both in its emphasis on political and ethical themes and in its absorption with crafting a sophisticated language to correspond to the poet's refined aesthetic intentions. However, over the centuries, the *mahākāvya* has served as a literary form for poets composing in Sanskrit, Prakrit, and South Asia's regional languages. In fact, its range of themes and linguistic forms often exceeds what is usually thought of as "courtly."

From between the early centuries of the first millennium CE and the middle of the twentieth century, at least 350 specimens of Sanskrit *mahākāvya* survive, only a handful of which have been carefully studied. The history of the first thousand years of the genre, from Kālidāsa to Śrīharṣa in the twelfth century, demonstrates two distinct phases. Scholars often consider the poems of Aśvaghoṣa and Kālidāsa as part of a "golden age" of *mahākāvya*. After Aśvaghoṣa and Kālidāsa, there is an apparent gap in the historical record of *mahākāvya* that has not yet been fully understood. Then, from the sixth century, three poems emerged that reveal significant transformations within the genre in terms of form, content, and aesthetic: the sixth-century *Kirātārjunīya* (Arjuna and the Kirāta) of Bhāravi; Bhaṭṭi's sixth- or seventh-century *Rāvaṇavadha* (The Slaying of Rāvaṇa), usually referred to as simply *Bhaṭṭikāvya* (Bhaṭṭi's Poem); and the seventh-century work by Māgha known as *Śiśupālavadha* (The Slaying of Śiśupāla). Sanskrit audiences considered all three as classic works. From the eighth century until the time of Śrīharṣa, notable Sanskrit *mahākāvya* poems include Meṇṭha's now-lost *Hayagrīvavadha* (Slaying of Hayagrīva), Kumāradāsa's *Jānakīharaṇa* (The Abduction of Sītā), Ratnākara's *Haravijaya* (The Victory of Hara),[4] Śivasvāmin's *Kapphiṇābhyudaya* (The Exaltation of King Kapphiṇa),[5] Padmagupta's *Navasāhasāṅkacarita* (The Adventures of King Navasāhasāṅka), Bilhaṇa's *Vikramāṅkadevacarita* (The Career of His Majesty Vikramāṅka), and Maṅkha's *Śrīkaṇṭhacarita* (The Feats of Śrīkaṇṭha).

Although the defining of *mahākāvya* is part of the general discourse of literature, individual *mahākāvya* actively participate in extending the possibilities of the genre, which, in turn, leads to a revision and refinement of poetics on the *mahākāvya* throughout the centuries. Each *mahākāvya*, therefore, represents a poetic practice that consistently outpaces the theory, continually stimulating new literary-theoretical understandings. Thus, in the seventh century, Daṇḍin formulated a preliminary description of the *mahākāvya*, very probably with either Kālidāsa's *Raghuvaṃśa* or perhaps Bhāravi's sixth-century *Kirātārjunīya* as his model poem. In the course of his wide discussion on poetry, he succinctly identified certain elements of the genre.[6] For example, *mahākāvya* begins with a verse that acts as either a benediction (*āśīḥ*), a tribute to a divinity (*namas-kriyā*), or a reference to the subject of the poem (*vastu-nirdeśa*); it delineates one or more of the Vedic aims of human life (*puruṣārtha*)—religious duty (*dharma*), sensual pleasure (*kāma*), social and economic success (*artha*), and ultimate freedom from human suffering (*mokṣa*)—and details the victorious ascent (*abhyudaya*) of a noble hero; it contains descriptions of cities and of nature, the variety of leisurely life at court, relationships, war, and so forth; it is subdivided into cantos (*sarga*) that are proportional, slowly descriptive in sonorous meter, and fluid in their transitions from one to the other, keeping the continuity of the larger narrative in sight; finally, and most importantly, it is filled with and evokes in the audience different kinds of *rasa*, the essential emotional content that gives a work a distinctive aesthetic flavor.[7]

Foremost is the *mahākavi*'s sensitivity to literary craft: attention to metrics and sound patterns (assonance, consonance, and alliteration) as well as the targeted use of trope to transform mundane details and experiences into meaningful and charming images. Almost equally significant for the Sanskrit poet is the integration, within the narrative, of ethical reflections, didactic prescriptions, and references to learned and everyday bodies of knowledge. Coming at a mature point (some scholars regard it as the culminating moment) in the *mahākāvya* genre's development, the *Naiṣadhīya* is a composite album of a classical Sanskrit poet's praxis. In this regard, Śrīharṣa displays a mastery that has been instantly recognizable to the cognoscenti (*sahṛdaya*) of Sanskrit poetry. For this, he is praised as a fit successor to the earlier giants of the *mahākāvya* genre. For example, the late-nineteenth- and early-twentieth-century editor of *Bibliotheca Indica*, Dr. E. Röer, echoes sentiments of acclaim for the *Naiṣadhīya* that must have been common among the Sanskrit scholars of his day:

> With the structure or frame of the poem our delight is nearly unqualified. The language is highly elaborate, bearing the mirror's polish. It never becomes commonplace, and bears throughout a sustained tone of sprightliness and elevation. Although we find a continual play upon words for many verses together, yet not only is the sense not lost in a mere jingle of syllables, but the general effect is often much enhanced by the harmonious contrast of open and concealed meanings. The variety of meters are handled by the poet with admirable art and propriety; the subject sparkles under his tread, as gleams the ocean-track in a ship's wake, rich in imagery showered unceasingly from the poet's mind.[8]

Röer softens the praise at the end of this passage, however: "To sum up, in structure, force and elegance of diction, in propriety and graceful ease of meter, in powerful description, and felicitous use of imagery the *Naiṣadhīya* ranks high and may enter the lists with any work of Sanskrit literature, but to fit it for a place among the poems of the first order, it wants incident, action, and dignity."

As readily as critical readers of *mahākāvya* accept the canonical status of Śrīharṣa's poem, they also routinely highlight features that run counter to their conditioned expectations. Thus their analysis, refracted through the lens of an inherited poetics, implicitly identifies the *Naiṣadhīya*'s specific intervention in the history of Sanskrit literature and also foreshadows trends that will follow in many of South Asia's literary cultures after the twelfth century. First, there is the matter of literary craft. Substantial portions of the *Naiṣadhīya* present play with sounds, words, and images that deliberately violate or twist established norms, a radical form of catachresis that has struck many past and present readers as inordinately flippant or utterly outlandish. Thus, for example, G.C. Jhala calls the *Naiṣadhīya* "the high-water mark of decadence which gives primacy to artifice over inspiration in creative literature."[9] Indeed there is a lightheartedness that the *Naiṣadhīya* lends to an otherwise serious literary genre that elicits a shock of wonder in some cases and of discomfort in others. Furthermore, by the twelfth century, while *mahākāvya* audiences came to expect their poet to exhibit learning and multiple bodies of knowledge, the sheer weight of erudition in the *Naiṣadhīya* has also led to divergent responses: consternation in some readers, absolute delight in others. Usually, modern audiences find the poem's erudition burdensome and distracting from the poetry, while premodern audiences view it more favorably. Another important feature of the *Naiṣadhīya* that has aroused attention throughout the centuries is Śrīharṣa's claim of possessing what we could describe as a polymath subjectivity that is ultimately governed by a special spiritual insight. Like other Sanskrit *mahākavis*, he is equally at home with articulating the intellectual, emotional, and material worlds of both a rarified court society and of various non-elite societies in South Asia. What is novel with Śrīharṣa, however, is his claim that his powers as a poet are rooted in a special spiritual realization; accordingly, not only do many verses of the *Naiṣadhīya* have incorporated within them principles of yogic practice, but also the poet sees his entire oeuvre as the product of a particular spiritual mastery. This, again, is a rare feature of *mahākāvya* prior to the twelfth century but more common afterward.

I begin the discussion of the *Naiṣadhīya*'s aesthetic, therefore, with a summary of ten distinct arguments for the *Naiṣadhīya*'s significance made by K.K. Handiqui, perhaps the most serious scholar of the poem from the early twentieth century and its first English-language translator (in the 1930s). Handiqui explains, first, that there is something particularly modern about Śrīharṣa's treatment of the character of Nala, who faces "a conflict of emotions, a clash of love and duty, rare in Sanskrit poetry, but which is not without its appeal to the imagination of the modern reader"; Handiqui is especially taken with Śrīharṣa's power to "handle tense moments of emotion and pathos." The learned translator is also taken with Śrīharṣa's ethical reflections that "glorify the individual conscience as the criterion of right and wrong." He notes that Śrīharṣa does not dwell much on describing nature, a preoccupation of other Sanskrit poets, but "limits himself to a few elaborate pictures of sunrise and the rising moon." Instead, Śrīharṣa's emphasis is clearly on the urban and urbane life of his characters, with their "animated dialogues, enlivened by wit and repartee." Reflecting on the poem's relationship to earlier *mahākāvya*, Handiqui indulges in the critical rhetoric of his early-twentieth-century colleagues in speaking of the *Naiṣadhīya* as "peculiar to the age of decline in which it was written." In other words, on one level, Śrīharṣa's poem holds the reader's interest precisely because it falls into a class of "decadent" poetry, a degenerative successor to the golden age of Kālidāsa. Nevertheless, "in spite of the abundance of artificial fancies and conceits, and the fondness for word-play and obscure learning," Handiqui urges for the rehabilitation of the *Naiṣadhīya*'s status in light of its "high level of style," which "has been for ages a rare intellectual treat to students in India." He concludes, however, that the primary reason for the poem's interest lies in its role as a "repository of traditional learning" that is vital to the "study of the cultural history of medieval India."[10]

To Handiqui's assessment of the *Naiṣadhīya*, I would add that what remains consistent in the *Naiṣadhīya* is a virtuosity of language use and a masterful expression of thoughts and feelings partly inherited from earlier poets, but digested and reformed in unprecedented ways. Noteworthy also is his ability to move between distinct registers: between eroticism and subdued conjugal domesticity; between bouts of snappy dialogue and extended meditations on the emotional lives of his characters; between reconfigurations of the usages of past *mahākāvya* masters and subtle jibes at those very conventions. Śrīharṣa displays great versatility in mingling multiple, sometimes mutually contradictory, approaches to comprehend the world he represents. Many verses are replete with obscure references to mythology or to technical, linguistic, or scientific knowledge. Most verses display a richly textured surface: alliterative rhythms, disjointed syntax, unconventional imagery, obscure diction, and equally obscure references to diverse realms of cultural knowledge.

There are also apparent contradictions in the poem's execution that remarkably sit quite comfortably with each other. Sitting cheek by jowl with a profound learnedness in Śrīharṣa's verse, for example, is a magnificent nonseriousness. The poetry stacks trope upon trope that, in light of earlier *mahākāvya* practices, may occasionally seem excessive, bombastic, or over-the-top. A jarring break in the ordered, linear telling of the Nala story, however, never looms; Śrīharṣa always stays on point and makes sure not to leave the reader behind even when he decides to develop an idea over several verses. He simultaneously culls from a rich classicism that precedes him, and his elevation of a peculiar style and tone for treating *mahākāvya* themes in myriad ways sways a direction that will be taken up by future generations of poets for centuries to come. The *Naiṣadhīya*, therefore, functions as both a distillation of the past and a model for the future. While the poem as a whole deserves close textual analysis and careful attention to every feature of its aesthetic, the next few paragraphs offer only a glimpse into the *Naiṣadhīya* in order to locate Śrīharṣa's accomplishment in the context of his past predecessors and to give the reader an idea of why this particular poem garnered such a rich and multilayered reception.

POETRY AND PHILOSOPHY CONJOINTLY CONCEIVED

In technical matters of philosophy, Sarasvatī
became the Khaṇḍanakhaṇḍakhādya.
In the world of poetry, she became the Naiṣadhīya.
These two works represent the sun and the moon
and are sung about everywhere.
Scholars—competitive soldiers—
bent on defeating their rivals, and pushing their own ideas
on the battlefield of scholarship, adore Śrīharṣa
for his pungent and sweet qualities.
With the Khaṇḍanakhaṇḍakhādya, *he is pungent.*
Sweet he is in the Naiṣadhīya.[11]

Gadādhara, fifteenth-century commentator

The *Naiṣadhīya* resembles a conventional *mahākāvya* in its general conformity to the customs of the genre but not enough wholly to identify it with any of its predecessors or contemporaries. Arguably, like many works that become canonical, nothing that follows it really captures the *Naiṣadhīya*'s unique aesthetic either. Śrīharṣa is an unusual example of a poet, of a philosopher, and of a poet who is also a scholar (*kavi-paṇḍita*). In verse after verse, the learning of a *paṇḍita* resonates alongside the rhetoric of a *kavi*. Thus, Śrīharṣa considers his *Khaṇḍanakhaṇḍakhādya*, also known as *Anirvacanīyatāsarvasvam* (The Essence of the Doctrine of Unspeakability), a "sibling piece to his *mahākāvya*"; he boasts, in fact, that the *Naiṣadhīya* is better "able to hold up to crushing scrutiny" than even the *Khaṇḍanakhaṇḍakhādya*.[12] The general purpose of this technical work is to undermine the epistemological premises of logicians who cling to a pragmatic linguistic regime that holds that words truly describe objects and lead to coherent meanings. Thus the poet declares in the opening of this book (verse 1.3):

Intelligent ones! Repeat what I've said, like parrots,
and you may go forth to conquer the whole world!—
By demolishing explanations that fix meanings to words,
in every case, you will render speechless your immensely arrogant opponents.

śabdārtha-nirvacana-khaṇḍa**nayā naya**ntaḥ
sarvatra nirvacana-bhāvam a**kharva-garvā**n /

dhīrā yathoktam api kīra**vad etad** uktvā
lokeṣu dig-vijaya-kautu**kam** ātanu**dhvam** //

To drive home his philosophical point, Śrīharṣa plays on the word *nirvacana* by using it twice in two different meanings: once in the technical sense of "explanations that fix meanings to words" (i.e., etymologies) and a second time to more conventionally mean "speechless." He alerts his audience—and in the verse, his logician opponents—that the very technical term used to indicate the practice of fixing an apparently satisfactory meaning onto a verbal expression (*nirvacana*) also has itself a more conventional etymology that indicates speechlessness (*nirvacanatva*). Suggestive here is the ultimate goal Śrīharṣa argues for throughout the *Khaṇḍanakhaṇḍakhādya*: the eventual realization of that which is beyond speech or is unspeakable (*anirvacanīya*), a consciousness of nondual oneness (*advaita*) that lies beyond verbal designations that intrinsically rely on the duality of word and meaning. According to Śrīharṣa, this insight is only gained by the relentless deconstruction of conventional binaries of word and meaning and the striving to expose their underlying contradictions.

While *the philosopher* Śrīharṣa's skills are clearly on display here, the poet's sensitivity to craft is no less on display. In addition to his clever play with the word *nirvacana*, Śrīharṣa carefully attends to the sound effects in this stanza to create a desired effect. Composed in a meter called *vasantatilaka* ("Mark of Spring"), which has fourteen syllables with a caesura after the eighth syllable and is often set to melodious tunes in recitation, Śrīharṣa here mingles double consonants (especially rhotic clusters using the sound "r") with a chiming internal rhyme scheme in the second half of each foot (in boldface italic in the extract). The effect for readers and listeners of Sanskrit strikes a vigorous tone (a technical description of a certain quality, or *guṇa*, of poetry, called *ojas* in Sanskrit) that matches the subject matter, pitch-perfect notes of fusion between form and content, sound and feeling. This feature of blending a complex philosophical reference alongside a meticulous consideration of rhetorical effects (involving syllables, consonant clusters, word choice, etc.) constitutes one consistent element in the *Naiṣadhīya*.

Take, for example, the following verse (2.32) from the second canto, which builds on a common trope of comparing a woman's breasts to pots, or in Śrīharṣa's odd twist on a familiar image in the verse immediately preceding (2.31), to pots used as flotation devices while swimming (*plava-kumbha*):

> Is it possible that the turning of a potter's wheel is an attribute of a pot?
> Is the potter's stick, then, also a material cause of the pot?
> For her two upraised breasts produce a spinning effect,
> with cascades of beautiful sparks.[13]

Philosophers in early India perennially used the metaphor of the pot to discuss causality. The philosophical problem Śrīharṣa raises in the first two quarters is basic to formal logic. He implies rhetorical questions in asking if the pot can have the attributes (*guṇa*) of the potter's instruments, the wheel and stick: Can the object inherit the attributes of its instrumental cause (*nimitta-kāraṇa*)? Can the object have as its material cause (*samavāyi-kāraṇa*) the attributes of the instruments that bring it about? The response from the logicians, of course, is resoundingly negative because an object only inherits the attributes of its material constituents: The pot can only have the attributes of the material it is made of (e.g., clay) and not the attributes of the wheel and the stick that serve as instruments in the making of the pot. How is it, then, Śrīharṣa asks, that Damayantī's breasts, compared to pots, have acquired the attributes of making viewers eyes spin (*cakra-bhrama*), as it were, in the cascades of her beauty (*prabhā-jhara*) just like a potter's wheel spins (*cakra-bhrama*) and gives off cascades of lustrous sparks (*prabhā-jhara*) when turned by the potter's stick? In the first half of the verse, Śrīharṣa is a philosopher. In the second half, he is a poet. The shift is smooth and seamless in that the latter half of the verse (the poetry) reads like a natural extension of the former part (the philosophy). First he challenges the epistemological premises of formal logic and then playfully exemplifies his doubts about its efficacy to understand reality. His choice of metaphor (the pot, the potter, the potter's wheel and stick) is in keeping with an essential proposition of his philosophical position: that the singular ground of being (*brahman*) is both the nondifferentiated instrumental cause and the material cause of the world.[14]

Śrīharṣa consistently reveals this kind of learnedness in the *Naiṣadhīya*. About his prowess as a philosopher, Śrīharṣa tells the reader that he has "no equal in composing works in the field of philosophical logic" (10.138c) and that his "logical formulations can silence any opponent" (22.153c). The concluding verses of the fourth and eighteenth cantos (4.123; 18.154) respectively reveal that Śrīharṣa authored (now-lost) philosophical texts challenging the Buddhist view of "momentariness" (*Sthairyavicāraṇaprakaraṇa*) and a work on Śaiva tantra known as *Śivaśaktisiddhi.* I count some 250 references to technical philosophical doctrines in the *Naiṣadhīya*, almost all of which are seamlessly woven into the narrative or descriptive context of the poetry.

Clearly, Śrīharṣa's philosophical orientation deeply informs many of his literary choices in the *Naiṣadhīya.* The same philosophical orientation also structures the Nala narrative's core problem, which, like Advaita Vedānta, involves singling out what *seems* from what *is*, a problem that gives Śrīharṣa ample opportunities to create a symbolic world of ambiguous linguistic configurations alongside multiple levels of meaning. Take, for example, the next set of verses (6.49–.56) describing the unusual circumstance of the heroine Damayantī encountering her beloved as an invisible man that she can feel but cannot see. Here, Śrīharṣa shows a great sensitivity for his characters' psychological states during a moment of extreme emotional intensity. He describes first how Damayantī perceives Nala standing near her and spontaneously throws a flower garland in his direction. Though he was an optical illusion for the princess, the poet explains, because Nala was *actually* standing right there, the garland actually reached him. Here is how both characters respond to the startling event:

> This garland was real!
> The lord of the earth was astonished.
> The garland she threw became invisible!
> The young lady was astonished.
> The garland was truly a token of grace from someone
> who was repeatedly seen and deeply felt.

Bewildered, both Nala and Damayantī are now described as standing face to face, thinking they are somewhere else. Śrīharṣa then stunningly reveals that their illusions of each other embraced and, in doing so, the two human lovers actually embraced each other:

> Bhīma's daughter felt Nala's touch but could not see him.
> It must have been a hallucination, she thought.
> The king saw her but, suddenly frozen
> in passion's bewilderment, could not hold her.

With each touch, they experienced immense joy
and so, they were convinced their feelings were real.
Then their touches diminished and they thought
the initial awareness must have been false.
Both were in contact with what was true,
but their confusion led them to not trust it.

So beautiful in every respect, each so inviting to the other,
they could not resist making love.
Seeing how mutually satisfying were their actions,
they could not believe that they were somehow not real.

The separation they felt in their hearts
was momentary at first but then doubled in intensity,
because of the rush of happiness they got from touching each other.
It was like adding too much oil to a lamp's flame,
dulling it for a moment and then doubling its brightness.

Alternating between being steadfast and sad, the poet tells us, Damayantī made it home, going back and forth between awareness and delusion. Nala, however, wandered around the place seeing Damayantī in front of him, again and again. Śrīharṣa demonstrates a striking ability in these verses to capture the real and the virtually real in a language that both rings natural to the feelings of both lovers and remains curiously surreal, owing to the situation of each character being both visible and invisible to the other on multiple levels. Nothing like it, as far as I am aware, exists elsewhere in Sanskrit literature, and the Pahāri painters of the seventeenth century were especially drawn to representing this scene in sketch and color.[15]

A POEM BORN OF SPECIAL INSIGHT

It has the syllable Om as its ornament.
Admired by all the critics,
its elegant expressions sparkle.
It is simply beautiful, to the extent that
its superb sequence of words
gives pleasure to the goddess of Beauty.

The delight it gives to the heart lingers long.
Truly, it serves as a means to accomplish the aims of life.
Śrīharṣa's poem is a scripture par excellence.
Ah, so dear to connoisseurs of poetry,
how intense is its brilliance![16]

Śrīdhara, sixteenth-century commentator

Śrīharṣa's intensive skepticism about the reality of empirical experiences leads inevitably to his positing an "unspeakable" Truth that can only be ultimately apprehended through yogic practice.[17] Unsurprisingly, then, Śrīharṣa's fascination with yogic practice and its use as a stock metaphor is apparent throughout the *Naiṣadhīya*. For example, the third canto begins with a description of the *haṃsa* alighting to meet with Damayantī, to deliver to her a message of love from Nala. After describing the bird's descent—its wings, the sound it makes, and the effect it has on the princess—the poet launches into two verses that take the reader into the imaginative world of ascetics and their spiritual experiences, as Damayantī and her friends fix their attention on the bird:

The way that vow-observant yogis lead their minds
away from the world,
toward the singularly indescribable Truth—
that is how Damayantī's friends were:
their eyes were led away
from other distractions
to that one indescribably beautiful *haṃsa*.

The way the mind's fluctuations become still
in the yogi's own body
so that the mind can approach the Soul within,
that's how Damayantī plunged into stillness:
the desire to catch with her hand
the bird stirring nearby
was a cautious effort, out of both fear and respect.

It is clear that the *Naiṣadhīya* imaginatively revels in a language of logical paradoxes and esotericism. Evident in the two verses above, as in the earlier part of this discussion, is Śrīharṣa's characteristic ability to move seamlessly through metaphor from one realm of experience to another. Just as abruptly as the poet transports the readers in one direction—toward the abstractions underlying yogic practice—he returns them swiftly to the scene at hand: the bird and Damayantī staring at each other and ready for a conversation.

When Nala enters Damayantī's inner apartments (as an invisible man), the poet marvels at the situation with a characteristic metaphor (6.46):

> Being invisible, spreading across
> a bejeweled surface that reflects a series of bodies,
> the separated lover (*viyogi*), entering another's city (*parasya puram*),
> was like a spiritual adept (*yogi*), since
> he could enter another's body (*parasya puram*).
> Astonishing indeed was that king!

Later, during a pivotal scene when Damayantī first has the inkling that the messenger of the gods is Nala himself, the poet describes her feelings as follows (8.15):

> She was Delight itself.
> She was under an inexpressible delusion.
> In that single instant,
> she tasted the transient happiness of the world
> and the eternal bliss of ultimate liberation.

In this verse, Śrīharṣa again uses the word *anirvacanīya* ("inexpressible"), a marked term throughout the poet's corpus. Culminating this scene, Nala irrationally discloses his true identity to Damayantī. Recognizing his dramatic mistake, he quickly responds to her as a messenger should. Śrīharṣa explains the situation through the metaphor of a yogi's response after he has achieved his liberating gnosis (9.121):

> In spite of his being inwardly
> awakened to his own soul,
> a liberated sage still responds
> to the world around him
> because of the force of his karma from previous births.
> In the same way, in spite of awakening
> to what he had just revealed,
> seeing Damayantī regaining her composure,
> Nala spoke to her
> because of his commitment to being a messenger.

The *Naiṣadhīya* is one among several texts from this period that claim to be both a product of spiritual realization and an inspiration and code for those who would strive for such realization. Śrīharṣa says as much at the end of the first canto (1.145c), describing his poem as "the fruit of meditation on the *cintāmaṇi mantra*." He is referring here to a gem akin to the philosopher's stone (*cintāmaṇi*); the meditation on this particular mantra (*hrīṃ*) is held by various religious groups in South Asia to yield special creative powers for poets, scholars, and orators.[18] The mantra associated with this jewel is thought to be particularly sacred to Sarasvatī, Goddess of Speech herself. In the *Naiṣadhīya*'s fourteenth canto, while blessing Nala and Damayantī as a married couple, Sarasvatī explicitly spells out the mantra and elaborates on its benefits to the one who chants it with devotion (14.88–14.90):

Remember and repeatedly chant, King,
that hidden mantra of mine.
It has no form and represents
the form of the Lord called Śiva,
who is pure and moon-endowed,
and who is Whole but twofold,
on account of being joined by two aspects.
Let this mantra grant you success!

The good man who fixes in his heart my mantra
masters speech moistened with the nectar of *rasa*.
Acting as the God of Love,
he commands heaven's doe-eyed ladies.
The *cintāmaṇi mantra* brings a man whatever he desires.
What more is there to say about its power?

If somebody worships me by offering sweet-smelling flowers
and perfumes and, chanting the *mantra*, devotes himself
to that image of me moving about on the *haṃsa*,
at the end of one year he would attain its fruits.
Whoever's head he were to place his hands on,
that person also could—all of a sudden—
compose beautiful verses.
A wonder to behold such a powerful mantra!

Sarasvatī's most significant appearance in the *Naiṣadhīya* occurs at a pivotal moment in the plot: She introduces Damayantī to her suitors and assists her in distinguishing the real Nala from the four divine imposters who have taken his form.[19] This episode consists of thirty-two verses in the thirteenth canto and is sometimes read separately from the rest of the poem, as the "The Five Nalas" (*pañcanalīya*). "The Five Nalas" consists wholly of double-meaning stanzas delivered by Sarasvatī herself. A full discussion of this section, in light of how Sanskrit commentators elucidate its ambiguity, is offered in chapter 5 of this book.

STRETCHING THE LIMITS OF LANGUAGE AND CONVENTION

Even outside the *Pañcanalīya*, Speech as a trope (embodied in the figure of Sarasvatī) is used persistently by Śrīharṣa to draw the reader's attention to his larger aesthetic and philosophical agenda in the poem. In the third canto, for instance, Śrīharṣa imagines the husband of Speech—the Creator Brahma—as maintaining silence during his prayers because he wants to imprison his wife, as it were. Instead, however, Speech jilts the Creator in favor of Nala (3.30):

> Under the pretext of silent prayers,
> the Creator tried to stifle Speech.
> Dulled by his focus on the Veda,
> he didn't notice that She,
> the "crooked one," had wrapped
> her arms around Nala's neck,
> finding happiness in *rasa*.

Śrīharṣa at one point describes Sarasvatī's body (10.74–10.88), each part with its various adornments metaphorically connected with some area of learning: her throat, music; her belly fold, the three Vedas; her glances, poetry; her two hands, the Purāṇas; her two arms, poetic meters; her teeth, logic; her thighs, the two types of Mīmāṃsā philosophy; the girdle on her belly, grammar; her necklace, astronomy; and so on. In another place (9.4), Śrīharṣa plays with the dual significance of Sarasvatī—as Speech and as a mysterious river—to underscore the slippery nature of language; sometimes speech is straightforward, sometimes it is unfathomable just like a river, now visible and now only a trickle. The sheer pleasure Śrīharṣa takes in the virtuosity of his linguistic inventions is constantly underscored by his explicit frustration with language's limited abilities to adequately express his imagination's desire. For example, though he eventually goes on to describe Damayantī's body (from head to toe) using all manner of complex trope, he prefaces his catalog with the following disclaimer (7.14):

> In spite of a resemblance,
> can the quality of her limbs
> be compared to anything else?
> To compare the beauty of her body with anything else
> is an insult to the act of comparison itself.

Having said this, however, his similes and hyperboles run wild: dazzled by her beauty, poets honored beautiful things by comparing them to Damayantī's features and not the other way around (7.16); her locks of hair trumped the peacock's tail to such an extent that the Creator painted half-moons on the feathers to indicate their inferiority, as the "half-moon" resembles a semicircle one makes with a hand to grab an intruder by the scruff of the neck to throw him out forcefully (7.22); the ridged lines on her lower lip are really notches to mark how many arts and sciences she has mastered (7.41); the dimple on her chin was the thumbprint the Creator made when he lifted her face to see what he had artfully shaped; and so on.

In these and in many other verses, Śrīharṣa's style verges on the kind of lighthearted silliness—rare among high *mahākāvya* before his time—that compels an involuntary smile. Take, for example, his charming description of Damayantī's ear, which plays upon the resemblance of the *nāgarī* script's sign denoting the number nine (9) to the shape the curve of the inner ear takes (7.63):

> Is it the familiar numeral 9 firmly drawn inside her ear?
> Or is it something new altogether,
> with each ear sustaining half of the
> eighteen existing branches of knowledge?

Śrīharṣa's ability to combine unlikely images into an analogy that evokes two scenes at once is one of the hallmark traits of his poetry, such as in the following comparison of a beautiful woman with the feast at a wedding reception (16.107):

> The beautiful setting of the feast was a lovely woman,
> inviting with enjoyments worth enjoying:
> The milk was her smile,
> the savory snacks her jeweled blouse.
> The fritters were like her moon face,
> the plump sweet balls were her breasts, and
> the glistening rice her yellow jasmine necklace.

Or, again, in the context of the after-wedding party, Śrīharṣa flashes his intrepidness to paint farcical scenes, such as this one that describes the pranks that Damayantī's brother plays (16.52):

> One of Dama's maidservants secretly put a lizard
> near the foot of a young girl who was fanning Nala.
> As the creature crawled up the length of her leg,
> she squirmed out of her dress—terrified.
> The crowd had a good laugh.

There are quite a few other instances in the *Naiṣadhīya* where Śrīharṣa brazenly inserts explicitly sexual images or bathroom humor that Handiqui awkwardly labels "indelicate," "vulgar," or "obscene" in his translation. Modern critics have frequently perceived the *Naiṣadhīya* as distastefully obscene. Winternitz speaks of it as "vulgar" in parts and often "disgusting to persons of refined taste or religious sentiments," explaining that "the poet does not hesitate to introduce vulgar innuendos in what is supposed to be witty repartee of a more or less cultured society." "It is not a wonder, therefore," Winternitz continues, "that, judging by modern standards, an impatient Western critic should stigmatize the work as a perfect masterpiece of bad taste and bad style!"[20] Clearly, Śrīharṣa's *mahākāvya* stands apart in this regard from most of the other classic works of the genre, and readers throughout history have either been attracted to this feature of the poem or, as we glean from Winternitz's comments, repelled by it.

More common to the *Naiṣadhīya*'s aesthetic than snatches of audacious content, however, are the multiplying intricate figures of speech that are scattered throughout the poem. In particular, Śrīharṣa clearly favors the complex integration of one figure with several others in a single verse.

Take for example the following verse that compares Damayantī to the god of Love's bow. Here Śrīharṣa plays on the somewhat overused trope of comparing the body of a beautiful woman to a bow for the god of Love to shoot arrows at some male suitor. However, Śrīharṣa offers a few less-than-common flourishes to the well-worn conceit (3.127):

> Understand yourself, Damayantī, as the charming, blossom-clustered bow
> of the mind-born god of Love:
> pearls on your necklace are the circular clusters of "flower missiles";
> Nala, the best of kings, like a hunted bird, is the target;
> the silky line of hair on your belly is the supple bow-string, well-used,
> as it lies constant in the bow, your lap, and tied into a loop in the middle,
> your shimmery navel.

Another verse describes the valor of a king Damayantī passes over while choosing her groom (11.105):

> The scar from the bowstring is a line of smoke, which signifies
> that your arms—like kindling sticks—have produced a martial fire.
> The fire is meant for rival hosts—like mosquitoes—and its smoke
> brings tears to the lotus eyes of your enemies' wives.

Here the reader can observe the poet's ability imaginatively to fuse tropes and conventions found in other *mahākāvya* (bringing tears to the wives of enemies, in this case) into a complex description of the king's valor, using the strikingly down-to-earth, even discordant, image of getting smoke in one's eyes while lighting a fire to get rid of mosquitoes. Again and again, we see a poet unafraid to attempt a complex analogy that risks interfering with the alliterative effect he seeks to reproduce in every verse. A statistical analysis would probably confirm the impression that the poet is partial to tropes that produce complex conceptualizations that help him to refashion the rhetoric familiar from easily identifiable archetypes in Sanskrit *kāvya*. Such strategies also allow Śrīharṣa to substitute customary patterns of description with original, totally unexpected formulations. For instance, he can replace a familiar expression for a common motif, such as describing a young woman as "thin in the waist" (*kṛṣodarī*), by rendering it in unpredictable variants like "she, the existence or nonexistence of whose waist comes under the scope of doubt" (2.40) or "one whose middle is an alternate manifestation of Śiva's supernatural ability to become minuscule" (3.64).

Clearly concerned with the artistry that goes into composing verse and the analytical gaze applied to it, Śrīharṣa's verses demonstrate an intimacy with and ebullient use of language, as he plucks metaphors from here and there to represent further fields of experience. He calls the *Naiṣadhīya* "a traveler on a road unseen by the family of poets" (8.109), as a poem that "describes things to be emotionally experienced and known," a pioneer on a path, as it were, "not trod on by others" (20.162c); he also tells us that he "does not let a single opportunity to innovate escape him" (19.67). Śrīharṣa's style is consciously excessive, conspicuous in its quest for the next synonym or in its demonstration of how even the most circumscribed vocabularies and sets of *kāvya* conventions can take in fresh signifiers without fundamentally altering the comprehensibility of established conventions. The poet repetitively reminds the reader—in his typically periphrastic style of expression—that the *Naiṣadhīya* is "not lean on delicious poetic feeling" (15.93c). Śrīharṣa sees himself as avant-garde, venturing into uncharted landscapes of poetry, but, at the same time, does not totally rebel against the normalizing tendencies of *mahākāvya* practice.

In addition to the proliferation of complex tropes in Śrīharṣa's verses, the *Naiṣadhīya* does not lack verses that are plainer in style, content, and emotional register. At the same time, the *Naiṣadhīya* elaborates on *śṛṅgāra rasa*, an emotional aesthetic of love and eroticism. Śrīharṣa, in his inimitable style, elaborates this *śṛṅgāra rasa* by depicting lovers united and lovers-in-separation. He also skillfully represents a distinctive type of courtly flirtation that the two lovers enact verbally. This scene in the poem mediates between their initial pining for each other and their ultimate marriage. Here are a few selected verses from their extended dialogue. First, Nala speaks (9.8–9.10):

Ah, my tongue has remained indifferent to your two questions
(about my family and my name). Neither matters much really.
Both flowery and fluffy statements are poisons.
Eloquence in speech rests in brevity and substance.

What is my name?
In what order is the sequence of letters in my name?
These questions are futile.
Face to face, we can carry on our discussion
by using "you" and "I."
That should be enough.

If my family is not dignified by nature,
what is the propriety of its disclosure?
And if it is, then it is ridiculous for me
to have presented myself as a messenger or as a servant.

[To which Damayantī replies (9.15–9.16):]

I hear you adorn the lunar dynasty.
Still, my desire for details is not satisfied.
You stay quiet in certain matters, you go on and on about others.
Ah! Stupendous is your mastery of deception.

Well, you haven't made your name nectar for my ears
and, therefore, it is not proper for me to give a response.
Custom does not tolerate decent women
to sit and converse with strange men.

The contrivance of the plot here allows for a gripping dialogue between Nala and Damayantī where both sense that they are speaking to the other but where, on account of lacking certainty, neither wants to make the first move toward revealing themselves. As expected, the poet seizes on the narrative situation to play his characteristic word games where Nala's slippery response to Damayantī's request for identification is swiftly followed with Damayantī's equally clever counterresponses.

Before they arrive face to face, however, they both suffer through the symptoms of unrequited love so graphically depicted by South Asian poets, painters, and sculptors before and after Śrīharṣa. Perhaps weary of the scores of such descriptions already available to him, when the *Naiṣadhīya*'s poet focuses on the passionate moods of lovers ill-fatedly separated from each other, he often oscillates—sometimes in one and the same verse—between playing it straight and poking fun at conventional tropes that describe tormented lovers. While the more conventional imagery is fruitfully explored by Śrīharṣa as well, here are a few examples of verses from the fourth canto that guide the trope toward another, more outlandish aesthetic (4.11; 4.44; 4.49):

Just imagine the pain produced by a small splinter
entering the sole of the foot?
What to say of a mountain—the lord of the earth, Nala—
entering the soft-bodied Damayantī's heart and staying lodged in there?

Time for humans, for gods, and for the Creator
is reckoned differently for each.
Why do mathematicians not calculate time for lovers?
A moment for those separated is surely different
than a moment for those who are united.

For the sin of killing women separated from their lovers
the criminal moon is exiled, flung from the heavens,
and smashed on the rocks of the moonless black night.
The bright sparks add to the stars of the sky.

Another verse speaks to Damayantī's true feelings hidden beneath a misconstruing of her friend's intent in a polyvalent description of Damayantī's physical/emotional condition (4.109):

(Damayantī's friend says:) Love's heat dislodges the jewel in your necklace.
Your chest (*hṛdaya*) today, therefore, is unornamented (*analaṃkṛta*).
[Your heart (*hṛdaya*) today, therefore, is without Nala (*analaṃkṛta*)].
(Damayantī says:) Ah, friend, then I am lost indeed if the one I love most
is distanced from my heart (*hṛdaya*).

Eventually the two lovers do unite, and Śrīharṣa's vivid descriptions of Nala and Damayantī's first night after the wedding represent a stunningly poetic interpretation of details from texts like the *Kāmasūtra*. Here are two particularly fine verses that the poet provides after he has described their love-making (152–153):

The couple slept,
seeing each other in dream,
moving, lips locked, thighs rubbing,
entwined in deep embrace.

When they'd made love, the couple slept in bliss.
Leaves seemed to sprout from the girl's breasts,
stamping designs on her lord's chest,
elephants and dolphins.
Their hearts united, the sudden merging of breath
in and out, in and out,
indicating that their lives are now one.

It should be emphasized that, as often as Śrīharṣa chooses to be funny or impolite, he can be as frequently soft and moving. The end of the first canto, for instance, demonstrates Śrīharṣa's delicate skill as a poet to produce the *rasa* of compassion (*karuṇa-rasa*). While in his palace garden, Nala catches hold of the golden *haṃsa* who will ultimately bear his message of love to Damayantī. The bird, thinking itself near death, paints a shockingly dismal picture of his future (1.134–1.139):

I am the only son of an old mother.
My poor beloved has just given birth.
I am the only shelter for both.
Persecuting me, O fate, does compassion not restrain you?

Friends will show compassion and gather with tears a-flowing.
They will complain how unfair the world is.
Then, they will go.
But, mother, the ocean of grief facing you—
how will you cross it?

"Where is he?"
"Why is he late to send a message and
bring stalks for our dinner?"
"How far off is he from coming home?"
When you ask these questions to those birds,
they will give you a reply—weeping.
What will that moment be like for you, my wife?

Oh God! How can a lotuslike hand
that paints the coolness and softness of a beloved
write these letters that burn the forehead, cruel like
  the sun's rays:
"You will be separated from the one you love"?

For sure, lady of darting glances,
you will look around and see emptiness in all ten directions.
As soon as you hear from my friends
the news of my death,
it will be like being struck by lightning.

This episode in the poem, aptly called the "Lament of the Haṃsa" (*haṃsa-vilāpa*) by later audiences, demonstrates Śrīharṣa's range as a poet and also his insistence on making inherited tropes somehow novel. Here, on one level, the bird's pathos is surely coding the imminent suffering of the human protagonists, and the audience thus immediately enters the mood developed by the poet. However, on another level, the displacement of the lamentation onto the avian realm softens, to some extent, the emotional impact. Śrīharṣa's poem likes to stay light on the surface and lets the turbulent stirrings underneath develop and manifest for the audience in quiet, unexpected ways. Take, for example, these two crucial verses at the end of the ninth canto, where Nala throws off his mask and reveals himself to his beloved Damayantī, who has dissolved into tears at the thought of never uniting with him (9.103–9.104):

Ah love! Who are you crying for?
You are smearing your face with these tears.
With those eyes, darting and dancing,
don't you see Nala bowing here before you?

Under the pretext of dropping so many tears,
from the sapphirelike pupils of your eyes,
you show expertise in the wordplay
where a nasal letter is dropped from words.
Doubtless, that's how you make
life (*saṃsāra*) so meaningful (*sasāra*).

Even when a verse of intense emotional content appears (the first one here), the poet quickly muffles the moment with a second verse in a ludic pitch. That second verse, however, which puns on the compound word *bindu-cyutaka*, which can mean both "dropping of tears" (an involuntary natural response) and "dropping of a nasal consonant" (a word game), is nevertheless psychologically consonant with how a lover might console a beloved that has burst into tears—by making him or her smile with some totally absurd observation. Nala's citing Damayantī's expertise in a special kind of wordplay is, on a superficial level, an utterly incongruous statement given the situation. But, it is not an emotionally implausible response. Once again, Śrīharṣa draws our attention to the limited understanding one can have using logic bereft of an emotional intelligence.

ŚRĪHARṢA'S VOICE

To whose heart does Śrīharṣa not give pleasure?
Entertaining through his poetry,
he is a hill that playfully sways in the waves
of the nectar of rasa.
Attractive with his philosophizing,
he is a craggy mountain churning the sea
with deeply penetrating arguments,
a boatman skilled enough to cross the ocean
of both schools of Mīmāṃsā![21]

Rāmacandra Śeṣa, sixteenth-century commentator

This, then, is what Śrīharṣa's voice is like. For him, there is a consistent effort to rescue language that slides into convention or fades into abstraction. The poem's texture is symphonic, with the poet's voice dashing from the elevated to the colloquial or disappearing into lyrical bursts. The fluid movement of verses refuses to settle into any steady pattern. Strange articulations and images are frequently juxtaposed with familiar ones in consecutive verses, extrinsic to the reader's expectations but well within the reach of her imagination. He often cuts with a single bold stroke of language not only the knots of his oeuvre's recurring philosophical thesis (that speech is ultimately futile to describe reality) but also the pride of rival philosophers—and poets—who would dare to challenge him. A steady preoccupation with language and of his power as a poet leads Śrīharṣa to regularly import the meta-language of poetics into his verses. He thus highlights the technical language of formalized poetics by playfully interspersing in his verses the technical terms for various figures of speech in addition to specialized concepts from the history of Sanskrit poetics. For example, exploiting the homonym *vaidarbhī*, which signifies one of Damayantī's epithets, Lady from Vidarbha, and the name of a particular poetic style of composition (*vaidarbhī-rīti*) that favors lucid, melodious, and generally charming types of sonic and semantic expressivity, Śrīharṣa offers the following verse (3.116):

You are fortunate indeed, Lady of Vidarbha [Vaidarbhī style]!
Your high character [poetic virtue] attracts Nala.
What more praise could we give to the light of the moon,
for it attracts and stirs up even the deep ocean?[22]

Throughout the poem, Śrīharṣa explicitly invokes technical terms of poetics. In verse 9.50, for example, he cites the terms *dhvani* (literally, "sound" or "resonance"), the concept of a special suggestive power of poetic language beyond the denoted and intended meaning, and *vakrokti* ("crooked speech"), the oblique use and expressivity of ordinary language that makes it distinctively poetic.

Naiṣadhīya commentators throughout the centuries seem to agree that their poet relies heavily on figures such as imaginative ascription (*utprekṣā*), expressions that offer double meanings (*śleṣa*), and new approaches to the ubiquitous simile (*upamā*). Arguably, Śrīharṣa is the Sanskrit literary tradition's greatest master of *utprekṣā* and certainly one of its most celebrated *śleṣa* poets. A.N. Jani, for example, cites Pt. K.L.V. Shastri's comment in the Sanskrit preface to the 1924 Palghat edition of the *Naiṣadhīya*: "In the imaginative construction of striking expressions, Śrīharṣa is king (*ittham vācyārtha-vaicitrya-kalpanāyāṃ śrīharṣaḥ siṃhāsanam arhati*)."[23] The poet draws attention to his own literary powers in 22.144, where Nala directs Damayantī to notice the way in which poets who use the figure *utprekṣā* can effortlessly conjure up an image of the moon as a sunstone jar (white and made of nectar) and the black space in the moon as a rabbit carrying a bowl of sapphires out of which nectar is scooped up and drunk by the attendant stars.[24] In this verse, Śrīharṣa suggests the powers of the *utprekṣā-kavi* but leaves it to his sixteenth-century commentator Nārāyaṇa to make the reference to Śrīharṣa himself explicit—"*utprekṣā-kavi* means here great poets like Śrīharṣa" (*śrīharṣādibhir mahākavibhir*).

By the time Śrīharṣa was writing in the twelfth century, poetics on the *mahākāvya* had reached a mature point, as had the *mahākāvya* genre itself. The *Naiṣadhīya*'s complex reception, therefore, has as much to do with how the work of past *mahākāvya* masters is distilled in it as much as what the poem contributes as a model to future literary work in South Asia. Intertextuality with the entire history of pre-twelfth-century poetry in India reaches new heights with Śrīharṣa. Consistently, the well-known trope is fully assimilated and then thoroughly reformed. Śrīharṣa primarily demonstrates his awareness of Kālidāsa's influence. Notice, however, how inheritance transforms into something altogether new in the two verses below, the first from Kālidāsa's *Kumārasambhava* (1.43) and the second from the first canto of the *Naiṣadhīya* (1.24):

> Beauty goes to the moon but does not share in the softness of the lotus.
> Beauty in the lotus makes no claim on the soothing radiance of the moon.

Beauty, however, that has waywardly reached Umā's face—
there it can rest happily and enjoy both!

His eyes defeated the lotus.
His smile conquered the moon's beauty.
Beauty-wise, what else is there greater than the lotus and the moon?
Ah the poverty of things to compare to his face!

Kālidāsa's sublime verse uses well-worn tropes for comparing two beautiful things. Śrīharṣa, however, invokes them as tropes themselves (*upamitau*) merely to indicate how useless they are to serve as analogies. Śrīharṣa takes stock of the entire range of *mahākāvya* that precedes him but is probably closest in spirit to poets such as Bhāravi and Māgha, with whom he is usually compared. Both of these poets produced stanzas that took great pleasure in complexity, stacking trope upon trope to produce feats with language generally unavailable in Kālidāsa's poetry. What separates Śrīharṣa from these two poets is twofold. First is his noticeable self-consciousness that often lends a droll sensibility to an otherwise astounding rhetorical mastery. Second, and related to the first point, is Śrīharṣa's unfettered impulse to add poetic dazzle (*camatkāra*) to his verses, so that the reader does not feel in any way that they have already encountered a given trope in another poet's composition.

Thus, for instance, to describe the morning, Māgha sets up a series of marvelous contrasts, each suggestive of common poetic conventions, and then ends with a lofty revelation (11.64):

The night-lotus loses its beauty. The day-lotus becomes beautiful.
The owl loses its delight. The *cakravāka* duck is overjoyed.
The magnificent-rayed sun rises as the cool-beamed moon sets.
Astonishing indeed are the bitter consequences emanating from
the whimsy of cruel Fate!

Māgha's verse ends on a general statement about ruthless Nature and uses heavily condensed language that is unobtrusively evocative and clever—different types of lotuses are said to bloom at different times, the owl cannot see during the day, and the *cakravāka* ducks separate in the night and reunite during the day. Here is how Śrīharṣa describes the advance of morning in one of several verses sung by Nala's bards to awaken the king after the first night with his new bride (19.12):

> The sun is on the hunt:
> sunbeams—hawks hovering in the sky—
> kill the darkness, the black crows.
> The moon shrinks to the west, afraid
> his rabbit will be killed by the rabbit-eating hawks.
> The stars—pigeons—scatter too on hearing the news.

While also calling upon common poetic tropes (the rabbit in the moon, for example), Śrīharṣa's juxtaposition of the setting of the sun and the rising of the moon to a scene of hunters and hunted winks rather than nods to conventional treatments of this theme. The clincher, rather than a general statement that seals the thought, is an even more startling image (comparing stars to scattering pigeons) that protracts the scene rather than closing it down.

Like many poets after Kālidāsa, Māgha and Śrīharṣa incorporate a high degree of scholasticism into their poetry. Unlike other poets, however, Śrīharṣa's treatment of early India's philosophical thought and poetic conventions is virtually encyclopedic. The *Naiṣadhīya* makes reference to topics from virtually all of the technical texts on the arts and sciences. It provides exhaustive geographical and political data and alludes to a range of occupations and livelihoods that shed light on the social and economic realities of the twelfth century, including all manner of popular belief and cultural practice of the time. The *Naiṣadhīya* brings the entire textbook culture of the Sanskrit world into focus, including the twelve well-known sources (*kāvyārthānāṃ dvādaśa-yonayaḥ*) from which Sanskrit poetry generally draws: Vedic literature, *smṛti* texts, traditional histories (*itihāsa*), ancient lore (*purāṇa*), logic (*pramāṇa-vidyā*), astrology (*samaya-vidyā*), three different kinds of political texts (*rāja-siddhānta-trayī*), knowledge of common practices (*loka*), other literary compositions (*viracanā*), and miscellany of different kinds (*prakīrṇaka*). In addition, Śrīharṣa demonstrates his astonishing familiarity with virtually all of the primary scientific disciplines (*śāstra*) and ancillary Vedic sciences (*vedāṅga*): medicine (*āyurveda*), military science (*dhanurveda*), law (*dharma*), political science (*artha* and *nīti*), erotics (*kāma*), mystico-ritual science (*tantra*), musicology (*saṅgīta*), mathematics (*gaṇita*), science of horses (*aśva*), science of jewels (*ratna*), lexicons (*kośa*), poetics and rhetoric (*alaṅkāra*), dramaturgy (*nāṭya*), astrology (*mauhūrtika-vidyā*), the science of bodily signs (*sāmudrika-śāstra*), domestic rituals (*kalpa*), phonetics (*śikṣā*), etymology (*nirukta*), prosody (*chandas*), grammar (*vyākaraṇa*), and astronomy (*jyotiṣa*).

Encountering something new and strange in Śrīharṣa's poetry, therefore, surely left many contemporaries and later readers uneasy with the poem. Hostile criticism and passionate defense of the poem coexist in the *Naiṣadhīya*'s receptive history right down through to the twentieth century. Thus, the final four verses of the *Naiṣadhīya* (and to the *Khaṇḍanakhaṇḍakhādya* as well) partially lay out the future of the poem's reception, as a work that will be honored by some, rejected by others, and misunderstood by most (22.150–22.153)[25]:

Beautiful women take hold of a young man's imagination.
They cannot be appreciated by prepubescent boys.
My sweet verses delight learned connoisseurs.
Why should I care for disparagement from insipid critics?

In every direction, loud sounds leak out of falling mountain rivulets.
Let people compare these noises to see which is better (if they wish).
But the milky ocean, once churned for its nectar, relieves all exhaustions
and gives delight to delight itself. That's what makes it altogether distinctive.

I have made an effort to lodge some tough knots—here and there—
in this text.
Louts who think themselves educated, but are really only superficial readers,
should not play around with this book.
Only an appreciative reader, who has had the knots loosened for him
by a competent teacher, faithfully served,
can feel the delight of taking a dip into the waves of this poem's *rasa*.

I received two betel leaves and a high position from the lord of Kānyakubja.
I realized the supreme Brahman, an ocean of bliss, during meditation.
My poetry showers rains of honey
and my philosophical arguments best all rivals.
This work of Śrīharṣa the poet—
may it spread and may it bring about delight to generous connoisseurs.

The *Naiṣadhīya* suggests that Śrīharṣa's interest at least partially lies in authenticating his work for a specialized audience of readers who will be able to notice his wide-ranging references and then retrace his logic for using them. The poet puts his audience, like his characters, in a position of having to apprehend reality from illusion. As Śrīharṣa himself predicts, the poem will become an ideal locus of study for the formalist scholars of medieval India, those who saw within its twenty-two cantos a kind of literariness meant to destabilize the very notions of what the *mahākāvya* genre (and *kāvya* itself) was and could become.

Śrīharṣa's truculent "voice," heard in the verses above and previously unheard of altogether, is taken up by many poets thereafter, including the seventeenth-century Paṇḍitarāja Jagannātha, who many claim may have been the most recent of the great Sanskrit intellectuals. Here are two verses from his oeuvre that may remind one of *kavi-paṇḍita* Śrīharṣa. The first of these is a proud declaration from the *Rasagaṅgādhara* (1.6), a classic of Sanskrit poetics, and the second is a coded warning to unreceptive critics (blind elephants) from one of Jagannātha's collection of poems known as *Bhāminīvilāsa*:

When I needed to illustrate something apropos to the context,
I composed the verses myself. Nothing of another poet
can be found here.
Does a deer, which has the power to produce musk scent,
even consider chasing the fragrance of flowers?

Friend, you may be commander of a herd of elephants,
but your eyes are blind with intoxication.
Don't halt even for a moment here,
on this forest ground of twists and turns!
The lord of lions just tore through the boulders
of a big mountain mistaking it for an elephant.
He sleeps now here in this cave.

One can clearly hear echoes of Śrīharṣa in Jagannātha's boasts. Anthologists went a step further and directly attributed stanzas to Śrīharṣa in their collections, even though there is little likelihood that they were actually his verses. Take, for example, this verse from a thirteenth-century anthology known as the *Saduktikarṇāmṛta* (Ear-Nectar of Good Verse):

When the Creator was sculpting her body,
up to her moonlike face, with radiance itself,
he ran out of the stuff.
Even when he was creating the world, this never happened.
So with what he had left over—the darkness—
he used up to make her hair.[26]

While the verse above resembles something Śrīharṣa might have written, it is almost certainly not by him; similarly this verse, also from the *Saduktikarṇāmṛta*:

Sometimes the nose is slightly bent,
or a smirk appears on the face,
their mouths emitting a donkeylike voice.
This is how they gesture
their displeasure and derision.
Or with an uncharitable critique,
a critical silence,
or the recitation of fine verses by *other* poets.
Ah, poetry! How many prejudiced critics
can you possibly tolerate?[27]

Well-known anthologies of Sanskrit verse from the early- to mid-thirteenth century included multiple verses from the *Naiṣadhīya* and many more like the ones above that are attributed to Śrīharṣa but not found anywhere else.[28] As we shall see, the long history of the *Naiṣadhīya*'s reception is not merely an important archive. These pseudepigraphal verses demonstrate that *Śrīharṣa* and the *Naiṣadhīya*—released from their social, historical, and cultural contexts—became an imaginative style, a tonal nuance, an attitude, a particular way of treating a set of themes. The ability to appreciate these fictional representations depended not so much on Śrīharṣa's poem as it did on the codes that the *Naiṣadhīya* conjured for a model readership that could comprehend them. These verses are *oblique* forms of *praśasti*, as their ventriloquism comes across as a form of inspired flattery. Take, for example, this verse from the seventeenth-century Hindi poet Bihārīlal, one of Śrīharṣa's literary descendants:

My eyes travelled upwards
after negotiating the mountain heights of your breasts;
they wished to climb to the wondrous beauty
of your face; but alas, having fallen
in the pit of the dimples of your chin,
they got stuck up there forever.[29]

While the *praśasti* verses reflect the cumulative momentum built up around critical engagements with the *Naiṣadhīya*, verses attributed to

Śrīharṣa speak to the existence of an *effect* that the *Naiṣadhīya* tradition comes to possess, whereby audiences feel they can gain access to Śrīharṣa's voice, style, and personality and creatively redeploy his imaginative consciousness in contexts that transcend the *Naiṣadhīya* and its poet.[30]

The desire on the part of premodern literary communities in South Asia to emulate Śrīharṣa's style rests on a sympathetic identification that we generally find absent in colonial-era scholarship that has introduced the poem to many students both within and outside of India. Colonial-era critical approaches often connected the *Naiṣadhīya* to new ideologies of aesthetic order that sometimes valorized though often punitively judged the "decadence" of the *Naiṣadhīya* in light of the earlier classical models fashioned by the foundational poet Kālidāsa. Very often, critics from this era uncompromisingly privileged a type of Romantic poetry that held favor among the European writers on aesthetics at the time. As Bronner has suggested with regard to the reception of Sanskrit *śleṣa* poetry during this period, the standard-bearer for "good" poetry was Kālidāsa, whose work was "natural, simple, humane, and expressive."[31] Guided by these principles, critics of Sanskrit literature, while acknowledging Śrīharṣa's achievements, could not restrain themselves from comparing his work to Kālidāsa's.[32] Thus, for example, we have a train of reflections on what Śrīharṣa's work *lacks*:

> We have grace of expression and melody of verse in abundance in Śrīharṣa, but we miss the charming simplicity of Kālidāsa. In spite of neatness of versification and beauty of diction, richness of imagery and parade of learning, it fails to touch the heart of the reader like Kālidāsa's poems, where the words flow spontaneously from the pen of the poet even as the tiny *śefālikā* flowers drop down, of themselves, in the early autumn morn. Where we have *svabhāvokti* in Kālidāsa, we find *vakrokti* and *atiśayokti* in Śrīharṣa; where we have *upamā* in Kālidāsa, we find *utprekṣā* in Śrīharṣa; where we have suggestiveness in Kālidāsa, we find double entendre in Śrīharṣa.[33]

Baldev Upadhyaya, in his encyclopedic Hindi work on the Sanskrit pandits of Benaras, calls the *Naiṣadhīya* "unique" (*anūṭhī*), a poem that is more rational (*mastiṣk kā poṣ*) than emotional (*man kā toṣ*). W. Yates, who also recognized the importance of the poem for scholars in Benaras, favorably compares Śrīharṣa with the Latin poets, but still within a rubric of "good poetry" that is not necessarily reflective of attitudes held by premodern Indian audiences:

> In glowing descriptions of the passions and particularly the passion of Love, he resembles Ovid; in the easy flow of his language he is Virgil's equal or perhaps superior; in the variety of meters and moral reflections, he competes with Horace; while in pomp of expression, diversity of imagery and minuteness of delineation he far exceeds them all.[34]

Many of these modern perspectives, as I will now demonstrate in the next chapters, bear only a faint trace of earlier attitudes taken toward the *Naiṣadhīya* in commentaries and other premodern genres of literary criticism.

2 ◈ EIGHT CENTURIES OF COMMENTARY

In terms of inaugurating a tradition of the poem, the first significant complement to Śrīharṣa's own autobiographical gestures is a set of Sanskrit commentaries on the *Naiṣadhīya*. Over eight centuries, the poem has been an object that commentators have enthusiastically gravitated toward and, in distinctive ways, have invested with a gravitas befitting a classic work. From the thirteenth to twentieth centuries, the *Naiṣadhīya* attracted more commentaries than any other Sanskrit *mahākāvya*, and, because the first one appears only fifty years after the poem does, Śrīharṣa's masterwork offers an ideal site to study a relatively uninterrupted commentarial tradition of a major premodern South Asian literary work. Our study of the *Naiṣadhīya*'s influential role in the history of South Asia's literary traditions, therefore, begins with these commentaries and their authors. Individually and collectively, as far as we can tell, commentators constitute both an early community of creators *and* the long-standing subjects of what I have been calling a *Naiṣadhīya* tradition. Accordingly, this chapter sets out first to locate the major commentaries on the poem in time and space and to identify, where possible, lineages and relationships among them and the turning points in the poem's reception they ultimately come to represent.

Sheldon Pollock, in writing about the difficulties implicit in historicizing various aspects of Sanskrit's literary culture, notes the following:

> The generations of Sanskrit poets could be thought of as simultaneous because in one important sense they were. They continued to be read and copied, discussed and debated, and to provide important models of artistic fashioning for uninterrupted centuries. However scholars might wish to

> periodize Sanskrit literary culture, it is crucial to bear in mind such local procedures, by which, as part of its fundamental self-understanding, the culture sought to resist all periodization.[1]

In important ways, which I will discuss shortly, I think the works of commentators also "resist all periodization." Nevertheless, I argue now, we find several distinct phases of commentary writing that can be historically graphed into blocks of, more or less, two or three centuries. Thus, I identify commentaries from the thirteenth and fourteenth centuries as *early encounters* with the *Naiṣadhīya*; commentaries from this period seek to find an appropriate lens with which to interpret this relatively new poem. Only two generations removed from Śrīharṣa, these works generally hold the poem's virtuosity in awe and, following the poet's implicit and explicit indications, respond to it either as an extraordinary aesthetic creation or as a challenging work of profound scholarship in need of thoughtful explication. By the second phase, in contrast, which begins sometime early in the fifteenth century, the *Naiṣadhīya* is already well established in the institutions of *scholastic culture*. Unlike the earlier commentaries before the fourteenth century, which arguably operated under a precanonical consciousness that largely identified with the author, commentaries from this later period show that the *Naiṣadhīya* had become an object of tense debate around which an audience of readers and scholars competed for hermeneutic control. Whereas a spate of encomia (*praśasti*) dedicated to Śrīharṣa and the *Naiṣadhīya* can be found in earlier commentaries, the works from this second period of scholarship hardly mention *this* particular poet and poem as entities distinct from other poets and poems.

I argue that they focused, rather, on the *Naiṣadhīya* as one among several works marked for use in institutions of Sanskrit learning. Discussed during this period as much for its virtuosity as for the properties it held in tension, the *Naiṣadhīya* became a locus for arguments about the very *norms* of good poetry. Taken up in greater detail in chapter 4 of this book, arguments that are implied in commentaries over the interpretations of single verses appear to be emblematic of larger conflicts in motion. Most prominently, during this period, the *Naiṣadhīya* seems to have become as notorious for its literary transgressions (*doṣa*) as it became renowned for its literary virtues (*guṇa*). Commentators reveal at various turns in their analysis ambivalent feelings about the *Naiṣadhīya*'s radically imaginative use of language and trope, what one might call in Sanskrit its *kalpanā-jaṭilā* ("twisted forms of imaginative expression"); or, using a Greek term from Western classical rhetoric that the rubric of *doṣa* implies, they identify the poem's *catachresis* (literally "[deliberate] misuse"), which, as a literary term, connotes daring overextensions of language use that challenge, or perhaps fly in the face of, linguistic norms and conventions. Thus, within commentarial culture, an ironic situation arose during the fifteenth century whereby the very quality of the *Naiṣadhīya* upon which much of its reputation was built also became a site for critical disapproval.

Closely related to this developing discourse about the poem's suitability as a model of elegant, if not stylistically normative, usage is the *Naiṣadhīya*'s being classed with other classics of the *mahākāvya* genre. Commentators from the fifteenth century were also the first to write commentaries on a fixed set of five Sanskrit poems to which they gave the name *pañcamahākāvya* ("the five [classic] *mahākāvya*"), a category I discuss in this chapter. I suggest that the *Naiṣadhīya* had a prominent role in galvanizing the *pañcamahākāvya* formulation and fortifying its appeal as a useful canonical category. And *Naiṣadhīya* commentators of the fifteenth century (Mallinātha and Cāritravardhana), owing to the popularity of their gloss on all five of these poems, had an influential role in establishing and facilitating the propagation of the *Naiṣadhīya* as a canonical work. From the sixteenth to eighteenth centuries, commentary writing on the *Naiṣadhīya* reveals that the debates and tensions manifested in the works of a previous generation of scholars reached some measure of equilibrium and ultimately consolidated the *Naiṣadhīya*'s status as a classic of Sanskrit literature. Commentaries from this era are far more demanding works, as they now confidently treat the *Naiṣadhīya* as a classic work that deserves an interpretive energy that transcends the merely referential function of earlier works to include finding polyvalent meanings and scholastic references at every turn in Śrīharṣa's verses. As we shall see later, only two commentaries are available from the nineteenth century and a single one from the twentieth century, all of which largely follow earlier trends in *Naiṣadhīya* scholarship.

Surveying the development of *Naiṣadhīya* commentaries from the thirteenth to twentieth centuries, we learn that the very *genre* of commentary, as it develops around the *Naiṣadhīya*, evolves and shifts in unpredictable trajectories and that, despite the rhetoric and appearance of commentaries as uniform documents moving in fixed patterns across time and space, they are situated in specific historical contexts. Commentaries on the poem first appear in thirteenth-century western India and seem to reach their zenith in the seventeenth century as a pan-Indian phenomenon. Relatively few are composed in the nineteenth and twentieth centuries, and the ones available are generally derivative of earlier works. A detailed chronology of all known commentaries poses an insurmountable challenge, as quite a few of the works we know about prove difficult to date with any certainty. We can reconstruct, however, a fairly clear understanding of the major commentaries whose manuscripts were copied down over centuries and safeguarded in libraries and private collections. While the names of approximately fifty such commentaries on the poem have come down to us, many more were probably composed than have survived. Of these fifty, only about ten complete commentaries before the twentieth century are available in manuscript form, five of which have now been partially or fully edited and published as books or dissertations. These five include the three printed editions of the *Naiṣadhīya* with commentaries by Mallinātha (fifteenth century), Nārāyaṇa (sixteenth century), and Cāṇḍupaṇḍita (thirteenth century), as well as partial editions with the commentaries of Narahari and Gadādhara (both dissertations recently completed in India).[2]

WHAT COMMENTARIES DO

On the one hand, Sanskrit commentaries, in general, appear to have a format that is uniform and formulaic.[3] Each resembles the other and, using Sheldon Pollock's phrase, its style "memorializes, even mimics, an oral pedagogy."[4] They are structured to maximize efficiency and perform standard functions that include: reordering the syntax of the original text to make it easier to read; explaining difficult Sanskrit words or phrases with simpler ones (a sort of intralinear gloss); supplying references to texts on grammar and poetics to identify distinctive linguistic usages and tropes; and occasionally providing remarkable interpretations to either clarify or stretch the text's intended semantic structures. Along with the foundational science of grammar (*vyākaraṇa*)—all commentators, it seems, are required to be first-rate grammarians—the hermeneutic impulses of a Sanskrit commentator on *kāvya* invariably presuppose a critical investment in the fundamentals of literary science (*sāhitya-śāstra*) as well, which, among other things, includes: identifying the poem's literariness (*kāvya-lakṣaṇa*) in terms of its chief emotional sentiments (*rasa*), figures of speech and sense (*alaṅkāra*), diction (*vṛtti*), style (*rīti*), and poetic conventions (*kavi-samaya*); discovering the dynamics of its language (*śabda-vyāpāra*) in connection with its denotative (*abhidhā*), connotative (*lakṣaṇā*), and suggestive (*vyañjanā*) power; delineating the hero (*nāyaka*) and heroine's (*nāyikā*) various psychological states; and deliberating on felicitous and infelicitous poetic usages (*guṇa* and *doṣa*, respectively) from the point of view of an acculturated sense of taste customarily prescribed, or at least described, within several centuries of texts on poetics.

Technical information in these commentaries is often conveyed in technical language and generally deals with the grammaticality of an utterance, its meter, and the important figures of speech and sense. Finally, the semantic dimension of each verse is generally accounted for through the provision of synonyms, complex rewordings, or allusions to dictionaries (*kośa*). Though they occasionally open up the text's semantic and pragmatic potential for the reader, rarely do these commentaries move away from their literalist mentality. In assimilating the literary text into a discursive order that reflects organic unity and coherence with an absence of the strange or deviant, the Sanskrit commentator usually employs conventional formulas rationally to explain, justify, or elaborate through the prism of well-defined and acceptable methods of analysis. Taking an unassuming approach to interpretation, these formal commentaries follow a conservative structuring. Either they conform to a subject-centered word-by-word method (*daṇḍānvaya*) or take a verb-centered approach that tackles syntactic units (*khaṇḍānvaya*). Both of these formats (and their permutations) will be discussed in chapter 3, especially as they relate to the interpretive and pedagogical logic of *Naiṣadhīya* commentarial practice.

It is very likely that historically the Sanskrit commentary, and its utilization in institutional contexts, established works like the *Naiṣadhīya* as instruments necessary for the preservation and creative continuity of Sanskrit learning. Through the writing of a commentary, the Sanskrit intellectual's dual functions of research scholar and teacher were tested. The *Naiṣadhīya*'s reception history demonstrates the extent to which its commentators were conscious of the investments demanded of them to undertake the task of commenting on the poem. The challenge posed by a work like *Naiṣadhīya* subsumed for them an exciting glimpse into genuine literary progress and, I argue, deeper access into an elite culture of pedagogy.

EARLY ENCOUNTERS WITH THE *NAIṢADHĪYA*

I begin with the first two commentators of the poem, both of whom worked in the second half of the thirteenth century in the Vāghela courts of western India, whose capital city Dhavalakkaka (Dholakā) was near modern-day Ahmedabad. The first commentary is by Vidyādhara and is eponymously entitled the *Sāhityavidyādharī* (Commentary of Vidyādhara, Expert on Literature); the second is by Cāṇḍupaṇḍita and is called *Naiṣadhadīpikā* (A Bright Lamp on the *Naiṣadhīya*). The Vāghela kings succeeded the Solaṅkīs (Cālukyas) in the region of Gujarat in the late thirteenth century and apparently continued Solaṅkī traditions of patronage for scholars and artists. According to a later legend found in Rājaśekharasūri's sixteenth-century *Prabandhakośa*, a collection of quasi-historical narratives (*prabandha*), the *Naiṣadhīya* was introduced to the Solaṅkī courts in the latter part of the twelfth century or during the early years of the thirteenth century (only a short time after it was originally composed) under the stewardship of Vastupāla, the chief minister of King Bhīma II (1179–1239 CE).[5] The earliest known commentator, Vidyādhara, belonged to the court of Viśāladeva (c. 1250 CE), the son of Vīradhavala (founder of the Vāghela lineage).[6] The *Sāhityavidyādharī* commentary stresses the value of the *Naiṣadhīya*'s literary craft and the necessity of understanding literature (*sāhitya-śāstra*) systematically to grasp the text's elusive meanings. Aptly named, therefore, this inaugural work of the *Naiṣadhīya* tradition concentrates almost solely on the poem's rhetorical excellence by identifying, and then supplying, the technical names of various figures of speech used by Śrīharṣa. In a verse found in one manuscript of this commentary, an unnamed scribe summarizes Vidyādhara's contribution as follows:

> Long live that commentary called *Sāhityavidyādharī*,
> always beautiful and respectably established alongside
> the *Naiṣadhīya*, a poem of incomparable delight for the heart and mind.
> This commentary shines a light on the poem's fresh *rasas*.
> Meant for connoisseurs, it illuminates with ease the poem's
> deep sentiments, hidden meanings, and elegant figures of speech.[7]

As the comments of the scribe above suggest, Vidyādhara's work is clear, focused, and precise in its efficient explanations of the *Naiṣadhīya*'s language and tropes. Vidyādhara seems to have been the first of a long string of commentators and critics drawn to the rhetorical dimension of the poem. Commentators that follow him, in fact, mention his commentary by name when they reflect on Śrīharṣa's eminence as a wordsmith.

A second commentator, Cāṇḍupaṇḍita (c. 1290 CE), was a near contemporary of Vidyādhara and received patronage from the Vāghela king Śārańgadeva during the last decade of the thirteenth century. Cāṇḍupaṇḍita provides us information about his scholastic family and the distinctions he earned as scholar (*paṇḍita*) and as Vedic priest (*samrāṭ, sthapati, dīkṣita*). He tells us that his Bright Lamp commentary was on the "new poem called *Naiṣadha*" (*kāvyaṃ navam naiṣadham*), which he studied with his poetry teacher Munideva.[8] From the earliest available manuscript of the commentary (1386 CE), we also learn that Cāṇḍupaṇḍita's younger brother Talhaṇa (also a scholar) filled in some of the lacunae left after most manuscripts of the *Naiṣadhadīpikā* were burned by "barbarians" (*mleccha*).[9] Cāṇḍupaṇḍita is fully aware of Vidyādhara's commentary, and it is likely, according to J. Jani (the recent editor of Cāṇḍupaṇḍita's commentary), that his commentary's manuscript record is conflated in places with Vidyādhara's; it appears that scribes of Vidyādhara's commentary frequently supplied Cāṇḍupaṇḍita's gloss when they seem to have found that Vidyādhara's comment was no longer extant.[10]

Cāṇḍupaṇḍita writes in his preface that his predecessor Vidyādhara, while "helpful," neglected to pay sufficient attention to the more learned aspects of Śrīharṣa's poem:

> Vidyādhara has composed a helpful commentary
> but its eloquence doesn't quite release Śrīharṣa's profundity.
> Moving clouds frequently carry water
> from one shore of the ocean to the other and in all directions.
> Can that water be knee-deep anywhere?[11]

Here, Cāṇḍupaṇḍita suggests that Vidyādhara's commentary is adequate insofar as the elucidation of Śrīharṣa's rhetoric—the poet's mastery over literary figuration (*alaṅkāra*)—goes. However, for Cāṇḍupaṇḍita, the *Naiṣadhīya*'s explicit and embedded references to other learned disciplines (*śāstra*) also need explanation to do full justice to Śrīharṣa's "profundity" (*gambhīratā*). Therefore, through citations and discussions of varying lengths on the entire range of Sanskrit *śāstra* (grammar, logic, ritual, metaphysics, law, science, etc.) available in the *Naiṣadhīya*, Cāṇḍupaṇḍita takes us through the vast intellectual worlds Śrīharṣa lived in as he wrote the poem.[12] He also provides us with the first set of details about Śrīharṣa's biography, a topic I take up separately in a later chapter.

While three other commentaries from the thirteenth century are attested to in manuscript catalogs, they are either too fragmentary to be of any use or no longer survive.[13] In the fourteenth century, however, several fascinating commentaries on the *Naiṣadhīya* were composed. Two especially notable ones seem to have emerged in monastic contexts in northern and southern India. One was by a Śaiva ascetic from Vārāṇasī named Īśānadeva, and the other was by Vijayanagara's Narahari, a scholar-ascetic of the Daśanāmī order (exponents of Advaita Vedānta). Īśānadeva notes in the beginning of his commentary, entitled *Naiṣadhaṭippaṇam* (A Brief Gloss on the *Naiṣadhīya*), that he is aware of and indebted to both Vidyādhara's and Cāṇḍupaṇḍita's commentaries on the *Naiṣadhīya*. He offers warm praise to Vidyādhara's contribution in a series of verses at the beginning of his commentary and provides a short explanation of his methodology:

> Let those scholars who are curious
> about the delineation of poetic figures in Śrīharṣa's poem
> either employ their own aptitude toward discovering it
> or let them consult Vidyādhara's commentary,
> a thorough exploration of the subject from all perspectives.
> Whatever I might say on the matter
> is generally in deference to him alone
> and is not the result of my own diligence.
> I have composed this commentary on *Naiṣadhīya*
> from a Śaiva point of view to please the good.
> I've produced this work adopting the method of bees
> gathering small gobbets of honey (*mādhukari*).
> Therefore, scholars of poetry should not ridicule it.
> Every commentator's work tries its best to explain its source.
> And so, I admit that my own work follows
> my teacher's commentary on the source poem.[14]

Īśānadeva describes his commentary here as taking the form of *mādhukari*, which can refer to: the way bees gather honey, the custom by which ascetics accept food from selected households, or, as is probably meant in this context, an eclectic method of commenting whereby portions from other commentaries are cobbled together to produce a synthetic work.[15]

Some fifty years after Īśānadeva in Vārāṇasī (c. 1320 CE), Narahari composed the first commentary available from South India. The colophons at the end of each canto of his commentary inform us that Narahari worked under the king of Triliṅga (Telangana), a Vijayanagara prince ruling during the mid-fourteenth century, and that he was a pupil of the great Advaita teacher Mādhava Vidyāraṇya.[16] This would make Narahari's commentary the earliest from a philosophical lineage closely affiliated with Śrīharṣa's own Advaita orientation. His commentary, however, does not reflect a particularly sectarian mode of interpretation. In fact, bearing the same name as Cāṇḍupaṇḍita's commentary, *Naiṣadhadīpikā* (Bright Lamp on the *Naiṣadhīya*), Narahari's commentary also mirrors his colleague's strategy of reading the *Naiṣadhīya* as a repository of learned references.[17] A noteworthy fact about Narahari's commentary is that among the early commentaries on this poem, it had the widest circulation geographically. It was popular in Kashmir for centuries, and manuscripts of it in Śāradā script can be found in several manuscript libraries in India today.[18] The dispersion of commentaries across vast geographical spaces and the development of regional recensions are phenomena not very well understood, but, as Pollock explains, the "provenance of commentators is likely to be a key factor in textual regionalization":

> Commentators were editors as much as exegetes, and the editions they established often became dominant in a given region (these, too, however, circulated widely outside their script area, so much so that commentaries of the tenth-century Kashmiri scholar Vallabhadeva were studied assiduously in fifteenth-century Āndhra). Just how such editions were established also largely escapes us, as do the text-critical principles they were based on. We do know that commentators typically collected and compared manuscripts in order to constitute their text. In some instances efforts were made to secure copies from all over the subcontinent.[19]

Admittedly working with limited source material, Pollock suggests that the wide distribution of commentaries, such as Vallabhadeva's work on Kālidāsa and, in the case of the *Naiṣadhīya*, Narahari's Bright Lamp, may imply forms of text-editing practices of which we have little knowledge now. One thing that is certain is that geography did not restrict the transmission of commentaries between and among commentators working distantly from each other. As I mentioned earlier, Īśānadeva (in Vārāṇasī) acknowledges his debt to both Vidyādhara and Cāṇḍupaṇḍita, commentators from Gujarat, whose commentaries he had before him while he composed his own gloss of the *Naiṣadhīya*.

Another notable commentary from the fourteenth century (1335 CE) was by a scholar named Bhavadatta (or Bhavadeva). His commentary has two names, *Naiṣadhasārasarasvatī* (The Learned Essence of the *Naiṣadhīya*) and *Naiṣadhagūḍhapadavivṛti* (Explanations of the *Naiṣadhīya*'s Esoteric Words). Bhavadatta was from Vārāṇasī and evidently belonged to the same clan as the tenth-century polymath Vācaspati Miśra. He makes an intriguing point that there were "many" (*anekā*) commentaries available when he was writing his, which would indicate that already, by his time, the *Naiṣadhīya* had become an immensely popular poem. After making this point, in a spirit characteristic of his contemporaries (Īśānadeva and Narahari), Bhavadatta deferentially writes the following:

> Mine cannot stand in comparison to these other commentaries. Having not studied with several teachers, even a learned scholar is unable to say anything about the *Naiṣadhīya*. My own sophomoric effort to comment on the poem will certainly be ridiculous to the learned literary specialists. Still, helpless as I am, I carry on here to compose a commentary on the poem on account of my youthful rashness. How does one judge an act of a child?[20]

He concludes that his work, therefore, in light of other commentaries, gives off light like a glowworm (*khadyota*) in the presence of the moon's luster (*indu-kānti*). Bhavadatta also apparently wrote a commentary on another difficult poem, Māgha's *Śiśupālavadha*, and it seems that his work continued to be popular for centuries, as the seventeenth-century commentator Bharatasena (Bharatamallikā) from Bengal seems to have been familiar with Bhavadatta's *Naiṣadhīya* commentary when he wrote his own.

Many of these early encounters with the *Naiṣadhīya* (from the thirteenth and fourteenth centuries) suggest attempts to structure, through the writing of a commentary, an experience of reading a new and strange poem, to harness, as it were, what a tenth-century Sanskrit literary theorist (Rājaśekhara) speaks of as a form of connoisseurship that entails the ability to "imaginatively re-create" (*bhāvayitrī pratibhā*) for oneself what the poet has the power genuinely to create (*kārayitrī pratibhā*).[21] Borrowing language from post-structuralist literary theory, we might say that commentaries from this period are *open*, to the extent that, before the poem becomes ensconced in normative (and thus passive) patterns of reception in the fifteenth century, they are still *writing* the *Naiṣadhīya*'s significance under the influence of the poem's own overt indications or implicit suggestions.[22]

THE *NAIṢADHĪYA* IN SCHOLASTIC CULTURE

The late-fourteenth and early-fifteenth centuries represent a turning point in scholarship on the *Naiṣadhīya*. By this time, the poem had become a fixture in scholarly discussions and debates about *mahākāvya*. We can infer this partly, I submit, because, for the first time, eschewing a singular focus on issues of interpretation, commentaries from this era begin explicitly to argue with each other about text-critical issues concerning correct readings and the identification of interpolations in the manuscript record. As such, they also find it challenging to fix a final version of the text that, presumably, can be claimed as authentic to Śrīharṣa's original vision and then used as an exemplar in pedagogical contexts. I discuss these hypotheses and other topics related to editorial practices of *Naiṣadhīya* commentators in chapter 4 but, from a historical point of view, it is important to note that commentaries explicitly emphasizing these concerns do not seem to emerge until the second half of the fourteenth century.

The first Jain commentaries on the *Naiṣadhīya* also emerged during this period as did the first translations of the poem into South Asia's regional languages. The two most well-known names from this new era of *Naiṣadhīya* scholarship are Mallinātha and Cāritravardhana. Both Mallinātha and Cāritravardhana have written works on all five of what prove to be enduring classics of the *mahākāvya* genre, the so-called *pañcamahākāvya* ("the five [classic] *mahākāvya*"). The five works included two by Kālidāsa, who probably wrote some time in the fourth or fifth centuries CE: the *Raghuvaṃśa* (The Lineage of Raghu) and the *Kumārasambhava* (The Birth of Kumāra). The other three works were distinguished from Kālidāsa's work both temporally and stylistically; they were the seventh-century poet Bhāravi's *Kirātārjunīya* (Arjuna and the Kirāta); eighth-century Māgha's *Śiśupālavadha* (The Slaying of Śiśupāla); and, of course, Śrīharṣa's *Naiṣadhīya*. One of the earliest sources we have that places all four of these authors together is in a Jain Sanskrit work by Munibhadrasūri entitled *Śāntināthacarita*, which was composed, according to A.N. Jani, in 1354 CE.[23]

From what I can tell, the category of *pañcamahākāvya* is the earliest—and most important—articulation of a Sanskrit literary canon in South Asia, emblematic to the *mahākāvya* genre and central to *mahākāvya* education, of which Śrīharṣa and the *Naiṣadhīya* are the final members. This list, in turn, engenders several other sublists that rearrange the works and poets along other numerical vectors. Ultimately, the *pañcamahākāvya* formulation, which began, I surmise, as a nascent formation of a Sanskrit literary canon in the fourteenth century, became a dominant paradigm in

South Asia to frame canonical works, and similar lists emerge in regional-language literary cultures.[24] My postulation is that the *Naiṣadhīya* had an equally significant role in catalyzing the second most common subdivision of the *pañcamahākāvya* formation, which follows a modeling perhaps first seen in the context of Āyurveda classics. As the eponymous *Carakasaṃhitā* and *Śuśrutasaṃhitā* along with Vāgbhaṭa's *Aṣṭāṅgahṛdaya* compose the "big three" (*bṛhattrayī*) of Āyurveda's textual corpus, so too do the *Kirātārjunīya*, the *Śiśupālavadha*, and the *Naiṣadhīya* form the *bṛhattrayī* of *mahākāvya*. As a complement to the *bṛhattrayī* formulation, the two *mahākāvya* of Kālidāsa, the *Raghuvaṃśa* and the *Kumārasambhava*, are combined with the shorter poem *Meghadūta* (The Cloud Messenger) to form the "light three" (*laghutrayī*). In some contexts, Bhaṭṭi's *Rāvaṇavadha* (The Killing of Rāvaṇa)—usually referred to as the *Bhaṭṭikāvya*—is sometimes added for symmetry to the *laghutrayī* instead of *Meghadūta*. By displacing canonicity to the works and not to the individual personas, the idea of "five great works" or to the *laghutrayī*/*bṛhattrayī* distinction leaves room for changes as, for example, the *Bhaṭṭikāvya*'s inclusion into the canon.

The significance of the *laghutrayī*/*bṛhattrayī* formulation in *kāvya* contexts historically invites different interpretations but becomes rather crudely transformed in much of twentieth-century criticism as a critical code of so-called natural versus decadent poetry—the *laghutrayī* of Kālidāsa being chaste, lucid, natural but the *bṛhattrayī* artificial, overwrought, decadent. Initially, however, my hypothesis is that the distinction between the two sets of texts probably emerged out of a need in Sanskrit pedagogical culture to distinguish the "easier" texts of Kālidāsa from the more intellectually demanding works of Bhāravi, Māgha, and Śrīharṣa. These three latter poets from the sixth, seventh, and twelfth centuries, respectively, came also to be called the "trio of poets" (*kavitrayī*), a collective epithet that echoes an earlier representation of the "three sages" of the grammatical tradition (*munitrayī*).[25]

Mallinātha is the commentator most famously associated with commentaries on the *pañcamahākāvya*. In fact, the commentator, whose long career probably crosses over from the late-fourteenth century to the early decades of the fifteenth century, is probably the most widely read and written about Sanskrit commentator of *kāvya* in general.[26] Born in western Andhra Pradesh, he worked in the courts of Siṅgabhūpāla at Rāchakonda (c. 1370) and Devarāya I of Vijayanagara (1400–1410 CE). He explains in the preface to his commentary on *Naiṣadhīya* why he entitled it the *Jīvātu* (The Enlivener) and follows it with another verse about his commentary's methodology, one that he repeats in all of his *mahākāvya* commentaries:

> For the sake of bringing back to life poet Śrīharṣa's true words,
> deadened by the poison of inferior commentaries,
> I have composed this commentary on *Naiṣadhīya*
> called the "The Enlivener" (*Jīvātu*).
>
> Nothing irrelevant and extrinsic to the root text is written here.
> I have commented on everything,
> using a method that properly construes
> words and their syntax (*anvaya-mukha*).[27]

Cluing us in to his critical temperament and disdain for much of the scholarship on *kāvya* that preceded him, Mallinātha strikes a tone that is more professional and polemical—a stark contrast to the largely saccharine statements of deference we witnessed in commentaries from earlier centuries. Mallinātha's frustration with *kāvya* commentaries resonates with tenth-century *Yogasūtra* commentator Bhoja's well-known remark about bad commentaries:

> Whatever is rather difficult to understand,
> that they avoid by saying "It is clear."
> With respect to the clear meanings,
> they over-elaborate with useless analysis of compounds, etc.
> Commentaries seem to confuse issues for readers
> by aimlessly prattling on unhelpfully at the wrong places.[28]

Bhoja suggests that commentaries should do something similar to what Mallinātha claims his commentaries do: stay relevant and prove useful.

The nature of the statements that Mallinātha makes also raises questions about to whom the commentaries are addressed. Implied in his words—and the very title of his commentary—is that he is writing both for what we may assume to be his students (if we presume that his commentary was intended for general students of *kāvya*, which it does seem to be, and is certainly now) *and* for his community of rival commentators, whom he ironically depends upon to be an audience. We may cautiously speculate here that since the *Naiṣadhīya*, at this time, has begun to attract a great deal of attention from scholars from all over South Asia, with statements like these, commentators like Mallinātha are resisting identification with what they deem to be the work of lesser scholars. In defending the superiority of his work against rival works, Mallinātha explicitly acknowledges the existence of other readers but implicitly shows himself to be a better, if not the best, reader of the *Naiṣadhīya*.[29] His approach to the *Naiṣadhīya* suggests a stark contrast with other commentaries that precede and follow his work. For example, his *Jīvātu* lacks any kind of *praśasti* directed toward the poet or the poem, a departure from earlier (and later) commentarial practice. Furthermore, his preface is virtually uniform to all of the other outstanding *mahākāvya* he comments on, and it appears that he has no special affection for the *Naiṣadhīya*—that for him it is just another "great text" that necessitated a commentary.

These features about his commentary, coupled with the fact that other commentators from this period mirror his approach to write formulaic commentaries on the same set of poems (Cāritravardhana, for example, discussed later), leads one to think that a commentary on *Naiṣadhīya* during this period served a function over and above the need for a gloss to a difficult poem. One hypothesis is that writing a commentary on the *Naiṣadhīya* conferred upon a scholar the title of *mahāmahopadhyāya*, Sanskrit pedagogical culture's equivalent of a modern university professorship.[30] Indeed, many commentators on the *Naiṣadhīya*, as we gather from the prefaces to their work, emphasize their own youth when beginning to write their commentary. It is quite possible, therefore, that a commentary on the *Naiṣadhīya* inaugurated the career of trained scholars rather than coming at the end of it. If an anonymous saying is to be believed—"My vigor was spent on Māgha's poem and the *Meghadūta*" (*māghe meghe gataṃ vayaḥ*)—Mallinātha apparently spent most of his years commenting on Kālidāsa's *Meghadūta* (Cloud Messenger) and Māgha's *Śiśupālavadha* (The Slaying of Śiśupāla). I contend that as he refers in all of his works to commentaries he wrote on all the other *mahākāvya*—except for the *Jīvātu*, which makes no mention of any commentary—it is very likely that he composed his commentary on the *Naiṣadhīya* first, an intriguing postulation in light of the notion just cited that *Naiṣadhīya* was *the* poetic text one commented upon to receive credibility in courtly intellectual circles, in the form of the title *mahāmahopadhyāya*.

All of Mallinātha's commentaries convey the practice of a dedicated teacher explaining the technical points of grammar, meter, and lexicography. In contemporary times, Mallinātha has become the butt of jokes that poke fun at gratuitous, self-righteous clinging to one's own perspective—thus, in present-day Maharashtra, there is an expression of "doing a Mallināthi" (*mallināthī-karaṇam*) if one goes on and on about something.[31] While Mallinātha's is the most well known among commentaries that begin with strong polemical statements, it appears that many commentators by the early sixteenth century might have embraced the *Naiṣadhīya* as a site of contestation to emphasize the distinctive merits of their work as superior to that of their predecessors in terms of its usefulness as a critical and pedagogical work. Although we do not see this tone in important commentaries in the latter half of the sixteenth and seventeenth centuries, twentieth-century commentaries, as we shall see later, return to this pugnacious style perhaps, in no small measure, on account of Mallinātha's influence. For lack of any corroborating evidence, it is difficult to understand how exactly the *Naiṣadhīya* might have functioned in the fifteenth century in pedagogical contexts. However, we may postulate its function during that period from the function it currently plays and has played for the past century: as an advanced-level text that culminates *kāvya* education.

Edwin Gerow notes in his article on primary Sanskrit education in contemporary India that Kālidāsa's texts are used as part of the "intermediate" training of the Sanskrit student (the *kāvya* level), roughly corresponding to the fourth and fifth years of study, while more complex texts like the *Śiśupālavadha* and the *Naiṣadhīya* are undertaken for the more advanced *sāhitya* level.[32] In assessing the graded nature of the Sanskrit curriculum in his essay, Gerow finds that the study of the "best literature" reverses course from the way students are generally trained in the earlier phases of their instruction, where "mechanistic and repetitive techniques of study" dominate. He concludes, therefore, that the reading of more difficult *kāvya*, such as the *Śiśupālavadha* and the *Naiṣadhacarita*, "represent, in the literary history of Sanskrit, a kind of obscuring of the quality of limpidness and directness thought to be characteristic of 'classical' Sanskrit—and its most distinguished representative, Kālidāsa."[33] Corroborating Gerow's observations, modern university textbooks and exam-review manuals confirm that students are commonly assigned the *Raghuvaṃśa* at the beginning of their course of study and at least the first canto of the *Śiśupālavadha* and/or *Naiṣadhīya* at the end of their requisite curriculum.[34] It seems that works of certain poets like Kālidāsa—through works like *Ṛtusaṃhāra* (the first printed Sanskrit work) and *Raghuvaṃśa*—were used to establish a standard language for Sanskrit students at the lower level of the school system, and others were used to regulate a graded relaxation of norms and a more sophisticated usage of an ever-increasing complexity of linguistic and stylistic forms. It seems that collectively, the *pañcamahākāvya* represent a vital mechanism for reproducing cultural value from a moral and aesthetic point of view. The *bṛhattrayī* especially makes requisite close readings of linguistically and conceptually difficult poems, something highly desirable for the pedagogical aim of teaching elegant uses of Sanskrit.

During the twentieth century, the *Naiṣadhīya* has been a staple text of Sanskrit *pāṭhaśālā* and university culture. The steady formation of the *Naiṣadhīya*'s literary identity today as an advanced textbook *par excellence* in the Sanskrit curriculum was probably a result conditioned by centuries of critical engagements, chief among them being the numerous commentaries on the poem. Jaydev Jani informed me, for instance, that up until the mid-twentieth century, the entire the *Naiṣadhīya* was required during the examination period (*śrāvana-māsa-dakṣinā-parīkṣā*) to attain the Sanskrit degree of *ācārya* in the Gaekwad-established Sanskrit curriculum at the MS University of Baroda.[35] A.N. Jani, citing S. Bhattacharya, mentions that up until the twentieth century, the *Naiṣadhīya* was a required text in the Bengal university system as well.[36] In fact, A.N. Jani cites a passage from the sixteenth-century Bengali poem *Kavikaṅkana Caṇḍi* that charts the course of *kāvya* study for the hero of the poem (Śrīmanta Saudāgar) and includes Kālidāsa's *Meghadūta* and *Kumārasambhava* in addition to *Naiṣadhīya* (*jaimini-bhārata-pūta tave paḍe meghadūta naiṣadha kumārasambhava*).

Contemporary scholars of *mahākāvya* in India invariably connect the *Naiṣadhīya* with its role in school culture. For example, in the introduction to his important monograph on *Naiṣadhīya* (in Hindi), Candika Prasad Shukla explains that the study of the poem and the love of learning Sanskrit arose together for him during his student days, confessing that he and his peers in Sanskrit class eagerly anticipated the day that they would know enough of the language to be able to enjoy Śrīharṣa's great *mahākāvya*.[37] The most important reason Shukla gives for the anticipation rests on the idea (by Shukla's time widely impressed into Sanskrit school culture) that the *Naiṣadhīya* was a "challenging" work and, as such, offered something different from the poems of Kālidāsa. Recalling a personal memory, Sanskrit scholar Rewa Prasad Dvivedi recounted to me how his own teacher (the legendary Mahadev Shastri of Benares) used to participate in all-night bouts of *antyākṣari* where solely the verses of the *Naiṣadhīya* were allowed.[38] He also remembered that his teacher would finish sessions of philosophy or *śāstra* study with verses from the *Naiṣadhīya*, apparently to add levity to their otherwise serious studies. Anecdotes like this give some insight into the informal sites where *mahākāvya* like the *Naiṣadhīya* might have been enjoyed in the recent past. They also reinforce the *Naiṣadhīya*'s unsurprising popularity in Benares through seven centuries.[39]

The other prominent commentator from the fifteenth century is the renowned Jain scholar Cāritravardhana from Gujarat, who belonged to the Kharatara-gaccha in the lineage of the fourteenth-century polymath Jinaprabhasūri and was a pupil of Kalyāṇarāja. Entitling it the *Naiṣadhatilaka* (An Ornament to the *Naiṣadhīya*), Cāritravardhana probably composed his commentary during the middle of the century (c. 1455 CE). From the few passages available to me, it seems that Cāritravardhana, like Vidyādhara, focuses on Śrīharṣa's use of trope. He provides, for example, a quasi-statistical breakdown of the poet's most frequent usages [alliteration (*anuprāsa*) followed by double meaning (*śleṣa*) and repeated phoneme "twinning" (*yamaka*)] and also emphasizes, as Vidyādhara had, that Śrīharṣa primarily uses trope to enhance the narrative and not simply to craft clever, pictorial verse (*citrabandha*).[40] He also aims to clarify textual readings in various places, and glosses from his commentary are frequently found as marginalia in the manuscripts of other, even earlier, commentaries.[41]

Alongside Cāritravardhana and Mallinātha, the third major *Naiṣadhīya* commentator from the latter half of this century, named Gadādhara, has only recently become more widely known.[42] Gadādhara's commentary, simply referred to as "Gadādhara's Commentary" (*Gādādharī*), was composed in a city called Kroḍā in an area known as the Antarvedi, the country lying between the two sacred rivers Gaṅgā and Yamunā (Doab). Like Cāṇḍupaṇḍita, Gadādhara also provides biographical details about Śrīharṣa, locating him under Govindacandra's patronage and not in the court of Govindacandra's grandson Jayacandra. The role commentaries play in filling out the details of Śrīharṣa's life is discussed at length in chapter 6. There are names of several other commentaries from the fifteenth century in older lists, some that seem to have been very long and involved works, such as the commentary of a certain Jain scholar named Municandra Sūri.[43] Nevertheless, the three that have come down to us, especially Mallinātha's and Gadādhara's, prove indispensable to understanding some of the major trends in *Naiṣadhīya* text-critical scholarship among pre–sixteenth century exegetes.

A POSTCANONICAL CULTURE OF COMMENTARY

The early sixteenth century marks yet another turning point in the history of the *Naiṣadhīya*'s reception among commentators. It was at this point that the most widely used commentary of the *Naiṣadhīya*, and, indeed, one of the most unique commentaries in all of Sanskrit literary culture, emerged from western India (Maharashtra), written by a scholar named Nārāyaṇa Beḍarakara. Nārāyaṇa's *Naiṣadhīyaprakāśa* (A Light on the *Naiṣadhīya*), in the words of nineteenth-century Indologist E. Röer, "has a thorough appreciation of the beauties of Śrīharṣa, and is fully able to follow him into the labyrinthine windings whether of fancy or expression. He explains with accuracy and nicety all those passages which, from the double meanings of words or their rare use, from the elaborate structure of the sentence or from the obscurity of allusion or circumstance, would, otherwise remain unintelligible."[44] The *Naiṣadhīyaprakāśa* (or *Prakāśa*), following the trend in *Naiṣadhīya* scholarship begun in the fifteenth century, participated in fixing correct readings but adds to this project an interpretive exuberance, beyond Cāṇḍupaṇḍita's obsession with finding philosophical references, to locate as many esoteric meanings as possible from Śrīharṣa's poetry. This he does, as we shall see in the next chapter, largely through creatively reconfiguring word divisions and using a series of conventional strategies (like dropping or adding a syllable) to yield alternate or double meanings (*śleṣa*). Nārāyaṇa is not consistent in this approach throughout the poem but picks choice opportunities to demonstrate the elasticity of Śrīharṣa's language.

Unlike earlier commentators, Nārāyaṇa seems to treat the *text* of the *Naiṣadhīya* as an object that can be both interpreted and performed. In his commentary, he dutifully explains standard, generally accepted, meanings of Śrīharṣa's verses first; however, at the next moment, he converts, replaces, or supplements them with new ones. His commentary is deeply sensitive to the overt and covert intertextuality of the poem—a consistent feature we identified in Śrīharṣa's propensity to shuttle back and forth between narrative tasks and adventurous forays into linguistic play or scholastic reference. Nārāyaṇa, I argue, adapts a reading process that mirrors Śrīharṣa's own resistance to habitual linguistic categories that deliver illusory forms of clarity and semantic closure and reflects what may be termed a "complexity effect" produced in Śrīharṣa's poetry. As we will see in the next chapter, Nārāyaṇa frequently reconfigures the linguistic signs of Śrīharṣa's verse, often privileging a playful search for polyvalent significance in it over and above any kind of stable interpretive context.[45]

The other two major commentaries from the sixteenth century seem to be anthological in scope. The first is by a scholar named Śrīdharasūri, who may have been a court scholar and poet of the Jain Tuḷuva king Sālvamalla, who ruled around 1550.[46] His commentary is eponymously entitled *Śrīdharīya* and contains in the preface a note that the *Naiṣadhīya* is a very popular text that is capable of yielding many meanings.[47] Like many earlier commentators, Śrīdhara also describes the learning necessary to write a commentary on the *Naiṣadhīya* at the end of his commentary on the seventeenth canto. He gives us a snapshot of the intellectual training he needed to acquire before tackling the *Naiṣadhīya*:

> Śrīdhara is victorious—an ocean of learning
> in poetry, Vedānta, logic, *smṛti*, metrics,
> poetics, drama, *purāṇa*, Veda, and Śaiva doctrine.
> He has knowledge of medicine, yoga, economics,
> political science, mystical doctrines, ritual literature, and astrology.[48]

The other important commentary comes from the last quarter of the sixteenth century and is by Lakṣmaṇabhaṭṭa. Lakṣmaṇabhaṭṭa was from a well-known family of scholars who had come from southern India (the colophon uses the term *dākṣinātya*) but were settled in Vārāṇasī. His nephew Viśveśvara (better known as Gāgābhaṭṭa) also composed a commentary on *Naiṣadhīya* in the late seventeenth century. Lakṣmaṇabhaṭṭa's commentary is entitled *Guḍhārthaprakāśika* (A Light on Hidden Meanings), and like Śrīdhara's work, his commentary also appears to be a sort of an anthology of previous scholarship on the *Naiṣadhīya*. He cites, for example, Narahari, Mallinātha, and Bhavadatta in his commentary and claims to have gone through hundreds of others before writing his own work, even though his work, he claims, is better:

> I have commented on the *Naiṣadha* by following
> a path not seen by the others.
> Although there may be a hundred decent commentaries
> on the *Naiṣadhīya* by good scholars,
> still at least a handful among them will be able to discern
> how special this one is.[49]

We see in Lakṣmaṇabhaṭṭa's commentary yet another change in attitude toward commentary writing. In channeling the language of Śrīharṣa's boasts about the *Naiṣadhīya*, who, as we saw earlier, had famously written that his poem clears a path never trod upon by other poets, Lakṣmaṇabhaṭṭa seems to elevate the status of the commentary genre by suggesting its worthiness to be spoken of with a rhetoric one usually associates with the creative text. Drawing attention to his work's distinction in the same language Śrīharṣa uses to distinguish the *Naiṣadhīya* from other works, Lakṣmaṇabhaṭṭa appears rhetorically to erase the assumed alterity between poems and commentaries. In other words, his bold assertion suggests that by the sixteenth century, the *kāvya* commentary had become an acknowledged subgenre in its own right.

Lakṣmaṇabhaṭṭa also quotes the commentary of a near-contemporary scholar named Rāmacandra Śeṣa, the only other significant commentator we have evidence for from this century. Rāmacandra belongs to the famous Śeṣa family of Vārāṇasī, which produced notable scholars like the *dharmaśāstra* author Kṛṣṇaśeṣa. Rāmacandra's commentary is entitled *Bhāvadyotanikā* (The Illuminator of Meanings), and, like Cāritravardhana, defends Śrīharṣa's unorthodox *mahākāvya* style. He writes, for example, that even though Śrīharṣa resists stock descriptions prescribed by various texts on poetics (introduction of the seasons, mountains, flower plucking, water sports, wine drinking, amorous games, etc.) if they clash with his narrative design, "it is not appropriate to say that the *Naiṣadhīya* is not a *mahākāvya*." He goes on to cite Daṇḍin's *Kāvyādarśa* (1.20) to bolster his argument that leaving out some conventional aspect or other does not ruin a poem.[50]

THE CONSOLIDATION OF A *NAIṢADHĪYA* TRADITION

Śrīharṣa, king of poets, has produced an extraordinary composition:
The stage for her play is the peak of the palace of the learned heart.
The activity backstage is the fashioning of novel sentiments.
Her friends are the expressive manifestations of rasa.
Her skillful acting is the careful use of words.
Naiṣadha—Nala—is the husband she has chosen for herself.[51]

Viśveśvara (aka Gāgābhaṭṭa), seventeenth-century commentator

All three commentaries—of Śrīdhara, Lakṣmaṇabhaṭṭa, and Rāmacandra—suggest that by the end of the sixteenth century, the *Naiṣadhīya* had attracted a significant following among scholars and that a *tradition* of writing commentaries upon it had become well established. The seventeenth century was then a time for consolidation of the tradition. Numerous commentaries seem to have sprung up during this period, and many of them seem to be derivative works that bring together earlier readings rather than produce novel interpretations. One such example is the commentary of Bhagīratha. Bhagīratha wrote his commentary in the northern courts of Uddyotacandra and Rudracandra, who ruled in Kūrmācala (Kumaon) in what is now the Himalayan state of Uttarakhand. His eponymous *Bhāgīrathī* commentary attempts to distill in a succinct way all of the various interpretations that have proliferated in the eras preceding his. Bhagīratha quotes in his anthological work the *Naiṣadhīya* commentaries of Narahari, Lakṣmaṇabhaṭṭa, Nārāyaṇa, Viśveśvara, Jagaddhara, Tāṇḍava, Mukuṭa, and Mallinātha, among others.[52]

Two especially notable commentaries from this period are Jinarāja's *Naiṣadhasukhāvabodha* (Guide to Easy Comprehension of the *Naiṣadhīya*) and the *Naiṣadhīyapadavākyārthapañjikā* (Short Commentary on the Interpretation of the *Naiṣadhīya*'s Expressions) by Viśveśvara (Gāgābhaṭṭa). Both were immensely learned scholars and leaders of their respective religious communities. Jinarāja was born in Gujarat in 1591 CE, received initiation at Bikaner into a Jain order in 1600, and served as a Jain guru of great repute until his death in 1643. His work reflects a culmination of centuries of importance Jain scholarship had given to the *Naiṣadhīya*.[53] Jinarāja alludes to this fact at the end of his gloss on the seventeenth canto:

> My work has been prepared with the assistance of many researchers who are aware of the numerous recent philosophical texts referenced in the *Naiṣadhīya*. These researchers, who are expounders of the Jain point of view, are learned men in all the various *śāstras*, including literature, the dictionaries, poetics, metrics, grammar, logic, etc.[54]

Like Jinarāja, Gāgābhaṭṭa was a prolific writer and is famous for officiating at the coronation of the Maratha emperor Chatrapati Shivāji in 1674 CE. As mentioned earlier, he was a nephew to *Naiṣadhīya* commentator Lakṣmaṇabhaṭṭa and his two brothers Dinakarabhaṭṭa and Kamalākarabhaṭṭa, both important late-sixteenth-century commentators of *kāvya*, Vedic, and *dharmaśāstra* texts. Other notable commentaries from this century include Kashmiri commentator Ānanda Rājānaka (*Naiṣadhīyatattvavivṛti* [Gloss on the Essence of the *Naiṣadhīya*]), who also wrote a commentary on Mammaṭa's mid-eleventh-century poetics work *Kāvyaprakāśa* in 1665 CE; the *Naiṣadhīyasubodha* (Guide to Easy Comprehension of the *Naiṣadhīya*) by Bengali commentator Bharatasena (or Bharatamallika), who lived in the village of Kāñcrāpāra in Hooghly District[55]; a work called *Harṣahṛdayam* (The Heart of Joy [or, alternatively, Śrīharṣa Secret]) by Gopinātha, a scholar probably from South India or perhaps Orissa[56]; a brief unnamed commentary by Bengali commentator Mahādeva Vidyāvāgīśa; and *Naiṣadhīyavivṛti* (A Brief Gloss on the *Naiṣadhīya*) by the well-known Gujarati Jain commentator Ratnacandra, who says in his commentary on *Raghuvaṃśa* that he composed his *Naiṣadhīya* commentary (now unavailable) early in his career (1612 CE).

The poem's verses also serve as a source of inspiration for a seventeenth-century series of Pahāri paintings on the Nala–Damayantī story; many of the frames of this series are accompanied by a Sanskrit commentarial gloss that exhibits an interesting nexus of textual commentary with visual representation. About the paintings themselves, the art historian B.N. Goswamy writes: "The present set of paintings . . . present a largely secular setting. Nala and Damayantī in these paintings emerge as archetypal lovers in a story full of romance and intrigue, mystery and magic. In the hands of these anonymous artists of two centuries ago, the personages and events of the Nala-Damayantī story take on a new significance."[57] He explains some of the approaches the artists take with the *Naiṣadhīya*'s contents. For example, with respect to condensing the content of Śrīharṣa's lush poetry into a painting's manageable frames, Goswamy writes: "This happens especially in paintings in which a long conversation occurs, like that between Nala and Damayantī when Nala comes as messenger of the gods. The poet, in the original text, lingers lovingly and long over this, but the artist condenses the sequence into four paintings and the *paṇḍita* has to confine himself to describing the gist of the conversation on the fly-leaves of these four paintings."[58] The *paṇḍita* that Goswamy refers to above is the commentator of the *Citrārthadīpikā* (Lamp on the Meanings in the Painting), an anonymous Sanskrit commentary appended to the paintings, whereby the relationship between each individual painting and Śrīharṣa's verses is elucidated for the viewer.[59]

Unlike the proliferation of commentaries in the seventeenth century, the eighteenth century presents an inexplicable lacuna in the record. Although there is a likelihood that several commentaries listed in manuscript catalogs were composed in the eighteenth century, none of them can be fixed to this century with any certainty. The only known commentator likely from the early part of this century is another Viśveśvara (son of Lakṣmīdhara), who seems to have resided in a place called Anūpasāgara on the Ganges. He composed a number of works of poetry, drama, poetics, and logic as well as several scholarly commentaries, including one on Bhānudatta's work on poetics (*Rasamañjarī*) and the *Naiṣadhīya*, which is entitled *Bhāvapradīpa* (Bright Light on *Naiṣadhīya*'s Meanings).[60] From the nineteenth century, again only two commentators can be identified with any certainty: an eminent scholar and poet of Vishakhapatnam named Veṅkaṭa Raṅganātha, who lived between 1822 and 1900, and a professor of rhetoric named Premacandra Tarkavāgīśa at the Sanskrit College in Calcutta. Jani offers a few colorful details about Raṅganātha's oeuvre, which includes an unnamed commentary on *Naiṣadhīya*: that he held the customary title of "Eminent Preceptor" (*mahāmahopadhyāya*), indicating his having many pupils, that he was "an exponent of the rational basis of the tales in Indian mythology," and that he composed a "gigantic Encyclopedia" of Sanskrit language and literature that still needs an editor.[61] Premacandra composed a commentary entitled *Naiṣadhānvayabodhikā* (Elucidation on How to Construe the *Naiṣadhīya*), which was edited by E. Röer for the *Bibliotheca Indica Series* in 1856.[62] He justifies his commentary in formulaic terms by insisting that it does not intend to supplant the numerous other commentaries that precede it but rather to help himself "better understand the subtle ideas of the *Naiṣadhīya*."[63]

One important scholar from the Bengal region wrote a commentary in the twentieth century: a *mahāmahopadhyāya* from Bangladesh (from the village Unaśiyā in the former East Bengal) named Śrī Haridāsa Siddhāntavāgīśa. Haridāsa, born into a family of scholars and working under the patronage of a certain Zamindar of Nakipūra for much of his life, wrote numerous original works in Sanskrit and Bengali. He also penned commentaries on virtually all of the major works of Sanskrit literature and edited the text of the *Mahābhārata* in Bengali script.[64] His *Naiṣadhīya* commentary is entitled *Jayantī* (The Victorious One), and, similar to commentaries like Mallinātha's *Jīvātu*, it claims superiority over other lackluster commentaries in its preface: "Cast aside the string of older commentaries: they lack poetic finery; they are dry of poetic sentiment and stripped of any excellence; they are difficult to understand and incomprehensible, wanting in any distinctive value and generally unexceptional. Use this commentary on *Naiṣadhīya* instead: it is new, clear, and composed with elegance."[65]

We have names (and occasional details) for twenty other commentators in the manuscript catalogs, potentially including works by the grandsons of commentator Mallinātha (Peḍḍabhaṭṭa) and of the poet Śrīharṣa himself, a man named Kamalākara Gupta, who apparently composed a commentary of sixty thousand stanzas (in the eight-syllabic *śloka* meter).[66] It is likely that the claim about Peḍḍabhaṭṭa is merely due to confusion, but the Kamalākara reference seems worthy to be entertained, if not entirely plausible.[67] A.N. Jani writes wistfully about this lost commentary:

> This commentary is not mentioned in any catalogue including that of Aufrecht. The only source of information is a list of old works. The authenticity of this list need not be questioned as the commentary of Gadādhara, mentioned therein, and not referred to in other catalogues, has come down to us. [Kamalākara's] *Bhāṣya* [commentary] has unfortunately not come down to us. If the extent mentioned in the list is correct, it must certainly be the most important [commentarial] work and when it will come to light it will solve many problems such as the biography of the poet, his native place, the extent of the poem, etc. for which at present we have to fall back upon conjectures. It is also important, because it comes from the grandson of the poet. Hence an authoritative commentary like this will throw, whenever found, much light on the external problems mentioned above, as well as the internal ones such as the correct text etc. But at present we can say only this much that we have to lament for the loss of such an important work like this and pray to the Almighty to bring it to light from some corner of India.[68]

In addition to recovering a commentary from the poet's grandson, two other amazing discoveries would be if commentaries supposedly written by famous poets associated with the *Naiṣadhīya* tradition were to be rediscovered or discovered. Śrīnātha, the fifteenth-century Telugu poet of the famous (and first) translation of the *Naiṣadhīya*, is believed by several scholars to have been a commentator on the poem. Almost certainly, however, the *Naiṣadhīya* commentator Śrīnātha cannot be the same Śrīnātha who composed the *Śṛṅgāranaiṣadham* (or *Naiṣadhamu*), as the fragment of the commentary (entitled *Naiṣadhīyaprakāśana* [Light on the *Naiṣadhīya*]) indicates that the author was the son of a certain Śrīkarācārya and was patronized by a Racherla-Velama king (of Andhra Pradesh) named Śiṅgama Nāyaḍu (Sarvajña) in the early fourteenth century, at least a few decades before the birth of the Telugu poet.[69] The fourteenth-century commentary, nevertheless, would be an important one to have, as it would mark one of the earliest from South India and, judging from the fragmentary verses available from it, would provide valuable information about the poem's reception during this early period:

> Bowing my head to those who are virtuous and praiseworthy and who know tradition, I write this commentary abandoning what should be abandoned as wrong and replace it with something that's right, even if it is brief. Damn those so-called scholars who, themselves being ignorant of correct meaning, spoil the poet's poem with their worthlessly wordy expositions. If a crow goes up to the sky and hovers above the ocean cawing, then what does it know of the depth and the jewels therein?[70]

Another intriguing possibility, built wholly on fragmentary evidence and conjecture, is that Kṛṣṇānanda, a Sanskrit *mahākavi* from thirteenth-century Orissa celebrated for his *Naiṣadhīya*-inspired poem *Sahṛdayānanda* (Pleasure for the Connoisseur), wrote a Sanskrit commentary on the *Naiṣadhīya* as well. If this commentary did actually exist, it could be considered one of the earliest on the poem, contemporaneous with Cāṇḍupaṇḍita's.[71]

CONCLUDING OBSERVATIONS

> *The existing monuments form an ideal order among themselves, which is modified by the introduction of the new (the really new) work of art among them. The existing order is complete before the new work arrives; for order to persist after the supervention of novelty, the whole existing order must be, if ever so slightly, altered; and so the relations, proportions, values of each work of art the whole are readjusted; and this is conformity between the old and the new.*[72]
>
> T.S. Eliot

When the *Naiṣadhīya* became a classic for premodern audiences cannot be exactly traced to a particular moment. Being the most recent and the "last" of the great classic *mahākāvyas*, the poem's historicity is more intensively scrutinized by the Sanskrit commentators than perhaps that of any other of the canonical *mahākāvyas*. This may be largely because the *Naiṣadhīya* seems actively to embed itself in a socio-historical moment. Its tradition has definite markers of who wrote the poem, where it was written, who it might have been written for, and how it came to be read in multiple spaces and within multiple temporalities. And yet, there are few fixed, historical certainties. From the few hints we can gather from commentaries and premodern oral traditions, the *Naiṣadhīya* appears to have been squeezed into preexisting canonical formulations during the fifteenth century. Thus, for example, there is a famous couplet that groups the four *mahākavis* associated with the *pañcamahākāvya*, a designation that became prominent during the fourteenth and fifteenth centuries:

> Kālidāsa's analogies,
> Bhāravi's profound meanings,
> and the graceful elegance of the *Naiṣadhīya*'s verse—
> in Māgha all three virtues are there.[73]

An earlier version of this verse reads:

> Kālidāsa's analogies,
> Bhāravi's profound articulations,
> and the graceful elegance of Daṇḍin's verse—
> in Māgha, all three virtues are there.[74]

The move of replacing a new poet (Śrīharṣa) for an older one (Daṇḍin) while retaining the structure of a traditional verse here occurs in a eulogistic stanza devoted to Māgha's superiority, where each canonical author is distinguished for a particular virtue. In the reformulated verse, the sixth-/seventh-century prose master Daṇḍin's poetry is replaced with the *Naiṣadhīya*, signaling perhaps a curricular move that foregrounds Śrīharṣa's melodious verse to the diminishment of an earlier usage of Daṇḍin's. The replacement may suggest a particular strategy to account for newer works that emerge alongside earlier classics. The persistence of this aphorism's popularity is seen in local adaptations of the formula as well. For example, a Sanskrit verse from twentieth-century scholar of Oriya literature Pt. Mrutyuñjaya Rath reads:

> The heroic Bhañja's analogies
> and profound meanings
> and the graceful elegance of the *Kallola*'s verse—
> in the *Cintāmaṇi*, all three exist.[75]

Rath's reproduction of the verse connects up the greats of the Oriya canon: seventeenth-century Upendra Bhañja, Dinakṛṣṇa Dāsa (seventeenth-century author of the *Rasa'kallola*), and the eighteenth-century author of *Bidaddha Cintāmaṇi*, Abhimanyu Sāmanta Sinhāra. It seems that during the second phase of the *Naiṣadhīya* tradition's development (after the fifteenth century), evaluative criticism in the form of an influential store of anonymous verses about the *Naiṣadhīya* and its relationship to other canonical poems suddenly springs up and mushrooms around the reception of the text. For at least the past few hundred years, it appears that no study of the *Naiṣadhīya* in India is complete without accounting for these verses, which have become integral parts of the tradition of the text itself.

Instead of substituting the *Naiṣadhīya*, another formulation adds it to a preexisting formula of great authors and works. The original verses cleverly dramatize (through *śleṣa*) a competitive rapport between Bhāravi (seventh century) and Māgha (eighth century), two of Śrīharṣa's famous predecessors:

The Sun's light (*bhāravi*) brightly shines
as long as the wintry month (*māgha*) has not emerged.
Just so was the case that when the poet Māgha appeared,
the splendor of Bhāravi dimmed, just like the sunlight in winter.

Bhāravi's speech is like the sun:
it wakes everybody up.
And, like winter's approach,
who doesn't shiver on account of Māgha?

Just like monkeys (*kapaya*)
who think back on the sunlight (*bhāravi*)
that has been diminished by a winter (*māgha*)
that discourages their movement (*pada-krama*),
so too are the poets (*kavaya*)
unable to compose verse (*pada-krama*),
thinking back on Bhāravi
and how he was overshadowed by Māgha.[76]

To these verses is added the following one:

Bhāravi's (the sun's) light shone
so long as Māgha (the wintry month) had not emerged.
But when the *Naiṣadhīya* came onto the scene,
where indeed was Bhāravi? Where was Māgha?[77]

The original verses summarize the widely understood relationship between Bhāravi and Māgha among Sanskrit audiences—that both poets, in their own distinctive ways, set the standard for post-Kālidāsa *mahākāvya*, that the later poet Māgha was locked in direct competition with his predecessor Bhāravi, and that arguably Māgha's work not only successfully outdid Bhāravi's but also became *the* standard work of *mahākāvya*. Until, of course, as the progress narrative of canon would have it, Śrīharṣa's *Naiṣadhīya* came along four centuries later to trump both of them. The modular displacement of the final two quarters in this more recent verse not only neatly expresses the dynamic and transformative emergence of the new poet (Śrīharṣa) and his poem *Naiṣadhīyacarita* but also suggests a novel reckoning of the final phase in the consolidation of the most widely understood canon of *mahākāvya* works.

To conclude this chapter, I offer a few general observations about the commentarial tradition on *Naiṣadhīya* taken as a whole. These observations are largely based on information gleaned from prefatory statements made by commentators and, where available, from a broader survey of their exegetical practices in commenting on the *Naiṣadhīya*. Essentially, from the perspective of formal commentary, the reception of *Naiṣadhīya* went through three identifiable phases. First were the early readers from the thirteenth and fourteenth centuries, for whom the poem was an exciting encounter with Śrīharṣa's unique gifts as a poet and scholar. Thus, the commentaries of Vidyādhara and Cāṇḍupaṇḍita in the thirteenth century—the first formalized readings of *Naiṣadhīya*, as far as we are concerned—encountered a relatively new work. As was cited earlier, Cāṇḍupaṇḍita, in fact, referred to it as "a new poem" (*navam kāvyam*). While he acknowledges the existence of commentaries other than Vidyādhara's, it seems that both he and Vidyādhara had very few secondary sources upon which to model their own scholarly interpretations. They both, therefore, attempt to provide coherent and univocal criteria by which to access and evaluate this new and strange poem. Vidyādhara's commentary primarily helps the reader to identify the *Naiṣadhīya*'s literary excellence and its complex figures of speech and thought, while Cāṇḍupaṇḍita assists the reader through what he believes is the *Naiṣadhīya*'s culture of opaque philosophical reference.

Both of these early commentaries suggest a precanonization phase, where the *Naiṣadhīya* is presented as something new but not overtly canonical. From a critical standpoint, they set the tone for the kind of perceptions and analysis this poem came to engender in later centuries.

Thus, for example, Jaydev Jani, the editor of Cāṇḍupaṇḍita's commentary, writes: "Cāṇḍupaṇḍita is the first scholar who has made the *Naiṣadha* an arena to exhibit one's scholarship. It is perhaps after his commentary that the *Naiṣadha* might have been extolled as *naiṣadhaṃ vidvad-auṣadham* [a medicine for scholars]" (J. Jani 2003: xxxxix). The famous characterization (anonymous) of the *Naiṣadhīya* as a "medicine for scholars" (*vidvad-auṣadha*) not only seems to find its earliest advocate in Cāṇḍupaṇḍita, but the aphorism also hearkens back to the title of Śrīharṣa's philosophical masterpiece *Khaṇḍanakhaṇḍakhādya*, the term *khaṇḍa-khādya* being often associated with a disease-curing tonic mentioned in the Āyurvedic literature.[78] Later *praśasti* in the works of commentators constantly recall this image of this poem:

A union of sound and sense,
elegantly bound up within choice meters,
is its powerful roots.
The range of logical arguments
makes for a beautiful roof of rough *śiphā* branches.
Śrīharṣa's expressive words are the flowers,
and its sole fruit is *śṛṅgāra*, ripe and glistening with lots of *rasa*.
What can excel this great medicinal plant?[79]

Going through inferior poems of other poets
has led many to mental strain.
These works aggravate the mind's *doṣas*
and cause an unhealthy imbalance.
May the poetry of Śrīharṣa,
the lord of the family poets,
be a rejuvenating medicine!
Drink it up with your ears![80]

These two verses, the first by sixteenth-century commentator Śrīdhara and the second by the seventeenth-century Gāgābhaṭṭa, play on the poem's corrective potency to remedy ignorance and rejuvenate lifeless verse.

Just as Cāṇḍupaṇḍita directs our lens to the *Naiṣadhīya*'s scholasticism, similarly, Vidyādhara, given the telling moniker of Sāhityavidyādhara ("Vidyādhara, expert in literature") by scribes, draws his audience's attention to the *Naiṣadhīya*'s special contribution to poetic language. In addition to inaugurating interpretive frameworks and rhetorical structures within which many later readers will derive meaning, both of these commentaries integrate information that a self-aware poet gives about his own (and his poem's) identity with their own imagined, supplementary narrative. The fourteenth-century commentators that follow Vidyādhara and Cāṇḍupaṇḍita also reinforce the trends set by these two early readers; in fact, the interpretive pathways they inaugurate will endure as valid approaches to enter the poem throughout the succeeding centuries. These two readers also establish the earliest textual history of the *Naiṣadhīya*, even though some later editor-commentators question the authoritativeness of many of their readings.[81]

The commentators of the early- to mid-fourteenth century—Īśānadeva, Narahari, and Bhavadatta—demonstrate an awareness of their predecessors' insights and approach their task to comment on the poem with humility. Īśānadeva's statements convey a sense that he looked upon his work as an exercise to enhance his own intellectual development. Narahari, in addition to seeing the poem as an intellectual challenge, expresses awe over the poem's aesthetic power and sees his own work as a sort of tribute to it. Bhavadatta explains that he is composing his commentary to initiate others into it, as he himself had numerous teachers to help him understand the poem; even so, he admits, his work may come up short in the eyes of the truly learned. All three of these commentaries represent a bridge between a nascent tradition of *Naiṣadhīya* scholarship and a full-fledged scholastic culture around the poem that forms in the late-fourteenth/early-fifteenth and sixteenth centuries. With the commentaries of Mallinātha, Cāritravardhana, and Gadādhara, we see the rise of a distinctive professionalism that distinguishes them from earlier commentaries. Especially notable among these "professional" readers—teachers in institutional contexts of court or schools of Sanskrit learning (*pāṭhaśālā*)—are Mallinātha and perhaps Cāritravardhana, the earliest two commentators to have commented on most of the *mahākāvya* we now understand as canonical, including the *pañcamahākāvya* of Kālidāsa, Bhāravi, Māgha, and Śrīharṣa.

During this phase, commentators turn toward the *Naiṣadhīya* as a now-established object of value in need of accurate textual preservation and correct (appropriate) interpretation. Their work, as I argue at length in chapter 4, had a major role in shaping the narrative of Sanskrit literary history, as it is currently understood. In text-critical and literary-critical terms, the late-fourteenth and early-fifteenth century marks a decisive shift in the commentarial tradition of the *Naiṣadhīya*. As the poem grows more popular, and commentaries on it begin to proliferate (apparently), commentators like Mallinātha set the tone for this new era of scholarship with strident rejections of the value of earlier attempts to comment on *Naiṣadhīya*. As we shall see in the next chapter, his work also uses a particular style of commentary writing aimed at providing an exacting coherence to *Naiṣadhīya* scholarship. I argue that his mode of interpretation fit the needs of his contemporary audiences, who wanted an interpretation that was both accessible and authoritative in its tone. Mallinātha's commentaries have had the single greatest influence on *kāvya* studies throughout the past five centuries, and, even today, most students of canonical *mahākāvya* read the poem with his commentary underneath the source text. We will also see in a following chapter the extent to which commentators like Gadādhara, whose work from this century is relatively unknown, contributed to a growing academic discourse designed to provide "correct" readings and interpretations for an audience of students, scholar-colleagues, and critics.

As the *Naiṣadhīya* became part of a broader academic culture of Sanskrit learning, another type of commentary emerged in the sixteenth century that focused solely on seeking polyvalent meanings in the poem. Whereas earlier commentaries interpreted *Naiṣadhīya* through the prism of its literary effects or philosophical references, as the poem acquired a canonical status in the fifteenth century, commentaries like Nārāyaṇa's sixteenth-century *Prakāśa*—one of the truly unique commentaries of Sanskrit literary culture—looked to *overinterpret* the *Naiṣadhīya* and read it as an inexhaustible resource for nonliteral and allegorical sense in Śrīharṣa's poetry.[82] By Nārāyaṇa's time, the *Naiṣadhīya*, I surmise, was fundamentally understood as an exercise in extraordinary creative practice, a work that consistently exhibited a propensity to question the logic of linguistic norms. Consequently, several commentaries from this period (Nārāyaṇa's being most paradigmatic) appear to be premised on the logic that their engagement with the poem should seek to bring out the fundamental inexhaustibility and transcendent nature of an imagination that resists being circumscribed by conventional exegetical practice. Nārāyaṇa does not obsessively identify figures of speech, he does not provide many references to philosophical texts while analyzing Śrīharṣa's verses, nor does he position himself as bent on displacing inferior commentaries. His primary impulse is to explore all possible meanings and alternative interpretations the poem (and Sanskrit grammar) can yield. It is a hermeneutic desire rooted in a belief that the *Naiṣadhīya* is an esoteric work that conceals all sorts of meanings from plain view. His adopted task, therefore, is to follow the logic of the poem itself and uncover what, to him, is hidden.

Although we do not have complete works available from the two other surviving commentators from this century, Śrīdhara and Lakṣmaṇabhaṭṭa, both of them note that their commentaries bring out the *Naiṣadhīya*'s hidden meanings and esoteric significance. While nothing like Nārāyaṇa's commentary is replicated in any of the succeeding centuries, perhaps on account of the overwhelming popularity of the *Prakāśa*, the seventeenth to twentieth centuries produce two distinct kinds of commentaries. First is the anthological work that attempted to systematize earlier readings and interpretations, such as Jinarāja's and Bhagīratha's, for example. The archival impulse of these commentaries, to rein in the proliferation of exegeses on the poem and to distill the essence of its hermeneutic traditions for readers, appears consonant with the movement to make the *Naiṣadhīya* a permanent part of the *mahākāvya* canon. The other type of commentary, evident from the two works available from the twentieth century, was the derivative work of exegesis that largely recapitulated earlier explanations and interpretations. While Śrī Haridāsa occasionally offers an emended textual reading, his and Premacandra's commentaries reflect practices seen in earlier commentaries. Both also reflect in their prefatory remarks a tonal stance encountered earlier: Haridāsa exudes a polemical spirit bent on minimizing the value of others' contributions, while Premacandra humbly submits that his commentary is merely an exercise to better his own understanding of the poem.

The notion that modes of exegesis evolve historically from commentator to commentator also applies to other similar *mahākāvya* traditions, such as those associated with the works of Kālidāsa and Māgha, for example. The types of continuities and disjunctions that form the intertextual cultures of commentary on the *Naiṣadhīya*, however, seem unique to the extent that *Naiṣadhīya* commentators overtly present their commentary as an argument for how the poem *should* be read. So whereas Cāṇḍupaṇḍita finds the *Naiṣadhīya* to be primarily a learned work, Nārāyaṇa sees in the *Naiṣadhīya* both an allegory and an unfolding of a mantra that presents the reader with a treasure of potential interpretations. Although in many cases one can only speculate on the awareness of commentators of other commentaries that preceded them—and of "families" of commentaries that build upon each other—specific examples will guide us toward understanding the diverse ways in which a later commentator elaborates, clarifies, corrects, or redirects in a wholly new direction the analysis of his predecessors. This constitutes the subject of the next two chapters.

3 ◈ THE *NAIṢADHĪYA* INTERPRETED AND OVERINTERPRETED

> *But there has never been a creative age that has not been critical also. For it is the critical faculty that invents fresh forms. The tendency of creation is to repeat itself. It is to the critical instinct that we owe each new school that springs up, each new mould that art finds ready to its hand. . . . The critic as an interpreter will be always showing us the work of art in some new relation to our age. He will always be reminding us that great works of art are living things—are, in fact, the only things that live.*[1]
>
> Oscar Wilde, from "The Critic as Artist"

I REPEAT A Sanskrit maxim cited in the introduction: *vyākhyātā jānāti na tu kaviḥ* ("the commentator knows but not the poet"), a recognition that, indeed, once the poem is out of the poet's hand, the critical reader, for better or worse, holds the reins to govern which direction its interpretation takes. The case of the *Naiṣadhīya* offers a striking example of this phenomenon, as lineages of ardent readers have put the poem to uses the poet may never have approved of or even envisioned. Or, then again, perhaps Śrīharṣa anticipated and authorized their readings in the very form he gave to his poem. While the latter question is an imponderable one, this chapter historicizes the relationship between the *Naiṣadhīya* and its commentator-critics. I propose here three special relationships that link commentary writing with the interpretation of the *Naiṣadhīya*. The first of these relationships is between the structure and form of the commentary and its putative function. The second proposition relates the function of a particular commentary with the context of reception within which it operated and that it shaped. Finally, I seek to explain correspondence between a particular series of commentaries with the broader historiography outlined in the previous chapter, as earlier commentaries play specific roles in their own historical contexts but also exist as coeval and equally available sources for later commentators. In elaborating these three relationships, I show how the types of commentaries that emerged in successive periods formed shifting paradigms of social and aesthetic practices of reading, teaching, and learning in Sanskrit literary culture.

THE AUTHOR AND PREMODERN LINEAGES OF COMMENTARY

Before exploring the changing relationships between the commentary's formal features, its multiple functions, and the reception contexts within which it functions, it is necessary to assess the *continuity* that these documents share with their founding source. On the one hand, it could be argued that the connection between the commentary and the source text is somewhat tenuous and arbitrary, whereby a particular reader's strategy of interpretation, arbitrarily chosen, inevitably produces findings that link up with the adopted strategy. On the other hand, another approach to understanding the relationship between texts and readers is to argue that, fundamentally, commentaries are largely shaped according to the triangulated bonds of affiliation that commentators share with the author, the text, and with each other. As such, Eco argues, texts and interpretations essentially validate each other, "[s]ince the intention of the text is basically to produce a model reader able to make conjectures about it, [and] the initiative of the model reader consists in figuring out a model author that is not the empirical one and that, in the end, coincides with the intention of the text."[2] Occupying a middle ground between seeing the hermeneutic circle as a vicious circle—where readers see in the text what they want to see—and perceiving interpretation as if primarily guided by an author's direct communiqué to a competent reader, Pierre Bourdieu has the following statement about the author's relation to his commentators:

> A virtuoso of the art of playing with all the possibilities offered by the game, [the author] gives the appearance of coming back to simple common sense in order to denounce the convoluted interpretations which the most zealous

> commentators have given his works; or else he leaves hanging in doubt, by irony or humor, the meaning of a work which is *deliberately polysemic*. By thus reinforcing the ambiguity which makes the work transcendent over all interpretations, including those of the author himself, he methodically draws on the possibilities of a willed polysemy which, with the appearance of a corps of professional interpreters—meaning professionally determined to find meaning and necessity, however much work of interpretation or overinterpretation is involved—is found inscribed in the field itself, and therefore in the creative intention of producers.[3]

Bourdieu suggests the art of interpretation to be prefigured in the artist's intentions and, therefore, not something to be understood outside the *field* that binds poets and commentators—perhaps "model" readers—together.

Among many modern readers of Sanskrit literature, the value of commentaries as interpretations has hardly been understood along the lines of any of the perspectives given above. The value of commentaries has often been reduced to their being mere entry points to understanding the lexical and syntactical structures of texts or, in the case of virtuosic acts of exegesis, as idiosyncratic musings of an eccentric mind. Seeing the diversity of these documents across time, however, at least as they pertain to the *Naiṣadhīya* tradition, should lead us to extend the possible scope of commentary writing and see them collectively as noteworthy artifacts of a poem's various reading lineages in history. The commentaries on the *Naisadhīya* implicitly inform us of the ways in which the poem was preserved, read, re-formed, and performed. At the head of this lineage is the poet himself, who, as we saw earlier, had explained in verse 22.152 (one of the epilogue stanzas) that his poem will not be fully enjoyable—and, in all likelihood, will be largely inaccessible—to those who are too proud to resort to the mediation of a competent teacher (or a good commentator). Judging by some of the verses commentators from all eras insert at some point in their commentaries, it would seem that the scholar-commentators of *Naiṣadhīya* took the poet's challenge seriously and dutifully slotted themselves into the roles of teachers (and students), assigned first with the task of training themselves and, afterward, training others to read the poem.

Take, for example, the following passages from the respective commentaries of Vidyādhara (thirteenth century), Narahari (fourteenth century),

Gadādhara (late fifteenth century), Rāmacandra Śeṣa (sixteenth century), and Gāgābhaṭṭa (seventeenth century):

The commentator has to have knowledge
of the eight grammars and of the various sub-branches of logic;
of the essence of literature and of political science;
knowledge of the meanings of the Vedas
and a familiarity with the ancient lore.
He has to know all of the other sciences as well.
With this lamp of knowledge eternally burning
to dispel the darkness of ignorance,
that learned commentator might be able to
interpret this unique aesthetic creation.[4] [Vidyādhara]

I have neither the imagination born of learning from previous births,
nor can I bear the heavy load of books on various subjects.
Praised by the entire world, it is only the *Naiṣadhīyacarita*
that makes my heart and the hearts of other poets quiver.
Even a fool strives to dive into this poem,
holding as it does the essence of deep meanings and emotions.
Just as a young child who, even though toothless,
eagerly grabs at candy.

On account of mistaken judgment, inability, or other such cause,
sometimes even clearly existent meanings
in this impenetrable forest of great profundity
that is the *Naiṣadhīya* cannot be fixed with any certainty.
Therefore, please do not fault me for my failure
to completely extract correct meanings from Śrīharṣa's poem.
Who can totally scoop out the heaps of jewels
found at the bottom of the ocean?[5] [Narahari]

The source of things itself takes shelter, again and again,
among the shadows of authority cast by this poet,
whose mind is sharper than that of Bṛhaspati,
the teacher of the lords of heaven.
In general, however, I lack the competence
correctly to interpret this poem. And so,
if there is something here I fail to appreciate,
literary minds ought not to show me contempt.[6] [Gadādhara]

Brahma is four-faced,
Lord Śiva has five faces and
his son Skanda, six.
Śeśanāga, lord of hooded cobras,
is thousand-faced!
If even these divinities
cannot describe the subtleties
of Śrīharṣa's verse,
where are we in this enterprise?
Still, whatever little we do say
can be chalked up to our insolence.[7] [Rāmacandra Śeṣa]

There have been books written about it.
Commentaries on it by learned scholars are superb.
They have supplied the technical terms for figures of speech
and a gloss for difficult vocabulary.
They have told us everything about this poem,
written by one who adorns the family of poets.
Whatever I now say in my own commentary
is a collection of all their findings, so
think of it as a synthesis and not as a redundancy.[8] [Gāgābhaṭṭa]

Setting aside the formulaic nature of the self-effacing humility found in each of these verses,[9] we notice the extent to which commentators simultaneously position themselves in a mode of deference and pride as they proceed to recover Śrīharṣa's original voice through the medium of the scholarly commentary.

It seems clear that all of them approach the poem with trepidation precisely because the poet warns them to do so. Likewise, as will become evident throughout the chapters of this book, all commentarial glosses and many of their paraphrases and interpretations are guided by the strategies the poet lays out for them and expects them to use. As most, if not all, of the premodern commentators will share in this empathetic feeling for their poet, we can begin to think of the commentators collectively as part of a literary community that shares similar readings, interpretations, and panegyric dispositions largely because they also use similar modes of text-critical and interpretive strategies that, to their sensibility, the poet *expects* them to use.[10] Thus, as the above passages reflect, in defining their own deference to the commentarial task at hand and while praising those who have preceded them, commentators speak to the very features of the *Naiṣadhīya* that Śrīharṣa indicates are the hallmarks of his work: that his poem is a pioneering piece of literature (literally, "a path newly blazed," as he says); that it is purposefully knotted and weighed down with arcane forms of scholasticism; and that it is a composition divinely inspired and awe-inspiring even for the learned.

INTERPRETATION AND FORM

The *Naiṣadhīya*, like all verse *mahākāvya*, presents a semiotic density that invites multiple forms of commentarial analysis. All the commentators share an approach of sustained and intricate contemplation of the poem, but each of them brings to it a particularized appreciation and pedagogical strategy. A translation of each verse of the poem based on the specificity of each commentary would demonstrate, therefore, a range of difference between and among them. To illustrate some of the variations of form and interpretive focus among *Naiṣadhīya* commentators, below I provide a translation and analysis of several commentaries on the very first verse of the poem.

The following translation of *Naiṣadhīya* 1.1 is informed by a conventional paraphrase of the verse shared and supplied by all of the Sanskrit commentators. As one will notice, however, it is certainly not the only legitimate, or even most likely, reading upon which one can settle:

> That Nala was a treasure-house of resplendence,
> a great and dazzling festival,
> the orbit of whose fame is represented by
> the white royal umbrella.
> Drinking in the stories of this earth protector,
> even the gods do not care as much for the divine nectar.

Both Vidyādhara and Cāṇḍupaṇḍita provide a similar type of gloss on this verse, although they have a different emphasis on what should be deemed important about it. Because his is a more complete and well-preserved text, I give here Cāṇḍupaṇḍita's complete commentary on this verse, followed with Vidyādhara's distinctive analysis. I have indicated the source text in **boldface** and used the equal sign (=) to mark the gloss (either a synonym or an alternative meaning) that follows. Cāṇḍupaṇḍita's commentary on *Naiṣadhīya* 1.1 reads as follows:

> The beginning of a text gives homage to a preferred deity in order to honor custom, to bless the audience, and to bring about the successful completion of the work without complications. That is not the case here. How could the utterance of the name of Nala—himself auspiciousness embodied, whose glory destroys sin—not bring about the removal of any complications? Indeed, remembering great men like Pṛthu, Sahasrārjuna, Bharata, and Nala is the highest kind of benediction. Thus the tradition says that the very mentioning of Nala and Damayantī's name obliterates this debased age (*kaliyuga*). The poet, therefore, mentions Nala first and, in doing so, composes his benediction.
>
> There was a king named **Nala.** What was special about him? He was a treasure **of greatness** = of glorious valor. And he was a **dazzling festival** because of his beauty; or rather, he was dazzling on account of festivals [as a patron or a participant]. This alone marks his auspiciousness. How to describe him? He was accompanied by a **white royal umbrella** that represented the **orbit of his fame**, which means that he was a repository of such virtues as fame, charm, and bravery. **Drinking in** (the verbal root 'pi' here used in the sense of 'drinking') **whose stories** = narrative episodes, **the gods** = learned ones **do not care much** = in such a manner **for divine nectar** = well-crafted speech.
>
> What were these stories about? They were about a protector of the earth. And so, upon hearing these stories, the gods do not care much for nectar. This marks Nala's universal lordship among the cadre of kings. Or, it was that, like the glorious sun, Nala was a **treasure-house of resplendence.** Or, that he was dazzling on account of [patronizing or participating in many] festivals. Nala is also glorious, foremost among the handsome, and a representative of the stoic and charming type of hero known as the *dhīralalita*. Or else, **drinking in whose stories, the earth protectors** = kings **do not care much for nectar** = earth.[11]

There are two important features to identify here. The first is Cāṇḍupaṇḍita's apologia for Śrīharṣa's apparent breach of *mahākāvya* convention. Justifying Śrīharṣa's benedictory verse (or lack thereof), Cāṇḍupaṇḍita sets the pattern that many commentators of *Naiṣadhīya* will feel compelled to follow: to harmonize the conventionalized prescriptions of poetics manuals, such as the influential *Kāvyaprakāśa* (Light on Poetry) of Mammaṭa (c. 1100 CE), with the unconventional practices of this poet.

The second feature, more germane to drawing connections between commentarial form and function, is the style of Cāṇḍupaṇḍita's gloss. Cāṇḍupaṇḍita adopts the analytical verb-centered method of Sanskrit commentary that deals with syntactic units (*khaṇḍānvaya*), sometimes referred to as the *kathambhūtinī* style, so named for its preference for syntactical analysis around a series of questions like *kiṃ bhūta* ("of what nature"/"being how"/"what kind of . . ."?).[12] This style of commentary contrasts with the so-called *anvayamukhī* commentary, which "arranges the words 'by means of the normal construction' (*anvaya-mukhena*)"; Tubb and Boose explain this second approach as going "straight through all the words of the [root text] in one long string, merely rearranging them so as to place them in the most easily understandable prose order."[13] Rather than asking questions and answers that gradually open up the syntax of the verses, this method follows the constituents of each line (*daṇḍānvaya*). Some have argued that the *kathambhūtinī* style was particularly prominent in Kashmir and northwestern India, largely on the grounds that the early *kāvya* commentator Vallabhadeva (tenth century; from Kashmir) used this method.[14] Others have argued that it was an older technique that became less popular than the *anvayamukhī* as time went on.

Commentators like Cāṇḍupaṇḍita, who use the *kathambhūtinī* method, take the verb as the main core of the sentence and pose a series of leading questions around it to elucidate a certain kind of answer. Tubb and Boose explain this approach as the provision of a basic "skeleton sentence" of the original text and then a gradual filling in of each of the remaining parts of the source text, "by asking questions that bring out the ways in which those parts fit into the construction of the original text."[15] Next they analyze the verse around these questions and sometimes supply a prose order to the verse at the end; they then take the nominative element first (in the case above, Nala), followed by *bahuvrīhi* compounds (exocentric nominal compounds) that denote the referent in terms of a specific quality (e.g., Nala was dazzling on account of festivals), and then deal with other qualifiers that may be present. Kishorenath Jha thus speaks of this method as "natural" and empowering for the student "to discover truths about the language himself [as] the pupil is led step-by-step in a logical manner to arrive at the complete syntactic unit."[16] Finally, they provide an explanation.

Regarding the example above (Cāṇḍupaṇḍita's commentary on *Naiṣadhīya* 1.1), Cāṇḍupaṇḍita's special emphasis is placed on identifying the type of hero Nala represents in dramaturgical discourse; he identifies him as a *dhīralalita* hero, one whose charm lies in his steadfast character.

Vidyādhara's gloss is virtually identical with Cāṇḍupaṇḍita's, but his explanation of the verse is more involved than his successor's:

> In this verse, there is alliteration (*anuprāsa*), the poetic figure of sound. There is also an inverted simile (*vyatireka*) here: by first drawing an analogy between divine nectar and stories of Nala, the poet then expresses the superiority of the stories about Nala over and above the divinity-conferring nectar. There is also the trope of "double meaning" (*śleṣa*) as the poet simultaneously describes both Nala and the Sun, depending on how one breaks the words up. Taking the words to mean "Nala" fits the narrative context (*prākaraṇika*) while reading "sun" points to an extra-narrative context (*aprākaraṇika*). There is a metaphor (*rūpaka*) here also as Nala is posited as no different from the sun. Thus, overall, there is a mixture of tropes here (*saṅkara*) along the lines of the maxim of the mixture of sesame seeds and husked rise, indicating an intimate commingling of elements.[17]

We see here that, in his comment on the verse as a whole, Vidyādhara prepares his reader to expect from his commentary a thoroughgoing analysis of figures of speech and thought, a favored mode of interpretation for him. Cāṇḍupaṇḍita, as we shall see later, only provides such detailed explanations on technical matters when they relate to philosophical references embedded in Śrīharṣa's verse. Both commentators, however, in using this question-answer-explanation style of commentary, open up the text to the reader gradually, allowing them to follow the logic of the poet and to construct their own significance around it. This method, I suggested, is premised on a *weak* pedagogy, in the sense that its form privileges description through a staged curiosity (in the form of leading questions) rather than a stronger regime of gloss encouraged by asserting the order of the syntax. By doing so, the reader can slowly follow for himself how the syntactic units fit together rather than be given the order of the syntax by the commentator as the only one possible.[18] It also encourages the search for polyvalence in the text (and potentially arguments over the propriety of certain interpretations) as well as multiple rearrangements of syntax are possible. Although a milder version of this phenomenon of polyvalence is available in Cāṇḍupaṇḍita's commentary cited earlier, it is more vigorously manifested in later commentaries that use a hybrid form of the *kathambhūtinī* method.

The form, and likewise the function, of the next phase of *Naiṣadhīya* commentaries is markedly different from Cāṇḍupaṇḍita's and Vidyādhara's in style while generally following them in terms of content. The major difference is that the commentaries of the late-fourteenth and early-fifteenth centuries did not rhetorically or practically approach the *Naiṣadhīya* through a singular interpretive prism. Nor did they see the need to emphasize the idea that meaning in Śrīharṣa's verses could proliferate in multiple, and even contradictory, ways. On the contrary, I argue, in their form these commentaries actually sought to *control* the interpretation of the poem. This development speaks to what I deem to have been the function of the *Naiṣadhīya* and its commentaries during this period: The *Naiṣadhīya* emerged as a key component in the literature curriculum as a text for advanced students, and commentaries on it were treated as credentials-conferring exercises. As such, the method commentators like Mallinātha prefer is the subject-centered word-by-word method that takes each word in the order it appears in the verse, the *daṇḍānvaya* or *anvayamukhī* type of commentary discussed earlier.

In the case of Mallinātha's analysis of 1.1, for example, he begins much in the way Cāṇḍupaṇḍita begins his, with the exception that he frames his gloss to Śrīharṣa's opening verse assertively rather than apologetically:

> Authoritative opinion of literary scholars holds that a poem is a vehicle "to achieve fame, to gain wealth, to acquire knowledge of life in the world, to dispel the nonbeneficial, and to become instantly enlightened. It is like advice given by a lover" [*Kāvyaprakāśa* 1.1]. Poetry, therefore, is a means toward many good ends. And because the venerable Śrīharṣa is aware of the warning against serious literary discussion of inferior poems, he wanted to compose a poem called the *Naiṣadhīya*. A poem begins with an auspicious benediction, meant to wipe away obstacles toward a desired end. It is said, therefore, "the beginning of a poem should either be a blessing, homage to a deity, or an indication of the subject matter." Therefore, here with this verse beginning with "Drinking in," Śrīharṣa indicates the auspicious subject of the poem as taking the form of king Nala, the hero of the story.[19]

Mallinātha then provides his gloss of the verse's syntax, which strictly follows the *anvayamukhī* method:

> **Drinking in** = having fully relished; **the stories** = episodes; **of this earth protector** = Nala; **the gods** = deities or learned people (according to the lexicographer Kśirasvāmin, the word *budhā* relates to a deity, to the moon, and to

> learned ones); **do not care much for the divine nectar** = nectar is just like this story; referring to nectar amounts to saying that they regard the story very highly; **represented by a white royal umbrella** = it was made into a white umbrella, or rather, made into a royal umbrella; the **orbit of his fame** was made into a white umbrella; **treasure-house of resplendence** = the sense is that Nala is comparable to the sun; **a great and dazzling festival** = he was resplendent because of constantly participating in festivities [the lexicographer Amara says that the word *ujjvala* is synonymous with other words for "festival" (*maha*, *uddhava*, and *utsava* are synonyms)]. He was Nala.[20]

Mallinātha straightens out the syntax by reordering the sequence of words (in **boldface**) that appear in the verse to provide the reader with an easy comprehension of what he seems to imagine to be the conventional and intended sense. In the process of doing so, he explains the case inflections of all nouns, compounds, and grammatical formations:

> Drinking in the stories of this earth protector, the gods do not care much for the divine nectar. Represented by a white royal umbrella, the orbit of his fame, a treasure-house of resplendence, a great and dazzling festival, he was Nala.

Then, like Vidyādhara, he gives the audience an exposition on what he believes is important for them to take away from the verse:

> Here, referring to Nala as a "treasure-house of resplendence" and superimposing the form of a white umbrella onto an "orbit of his fame" there is a metaphor (*rūpaka*). And because of the superiority of Nala's stories as compared to nectar, there is the figure of contrast (*vyatireka*). And regarding the combination of the two, there is the figure of commingling (*saṃśṛṣti*). These are spoken of in the poetics manual *Sāhityadarpaṇa* in the following way: a metaphor is when a form is superimposed onto an object, which is then not thereby denied; a figurative contrast (*vyatireka*) is when the vehicle is inferior to a superior tenor; and the figure of commingling is spoken of as a condition where these figures are understood as mutually connected. In this canto, the meter is *vaṃśastha*, a twelve-syllabic meter whose sequence of syllables runs as follows: light-heavy-light, heavy-heavy-light, light-heavy-light, heavy-light-heavy.[21]

Here Mallinātha follows Vidyādhara in supplying the technical names to Śrīharṣa's various figurative usages in the verse. Unlike Vidyādhara, however, he adds references to well-known poetics texts, like the fourteenth-century *Sāhityadarpaṇa* (A Mirror on Literature), and the technical definition of the meter of the verse.

Such referential and technical accretions to a basic explanation are, to my mind, reminders that Mallinātha's commentary was, in all likelihood, intended to function as a comprehensive lesson to students of literature. On the whole, one also sees in Mallinātha's commentary an economy of expression that resists bringing in anything unconnected to the literal meaning or, where applicable, probable double-meanings. As he famously boasts in his preface (discussed in the previous chapter), he does not wish to go the way of other commentaries that "kill" the *Naiṣadhīya* by bringing in extrinsic significance to the verses of the poem. Here and elsewhere, he takes Śrīharṣa's text as a basically self-illuminating entity that must be interpreted according to what it itself provides the commentator, not on the basis of what he would arguably perceive as extraneous, supplementary material that the commentator might desire to superimpose onto it. Thus, Mallinātha appears narrowly to conceive of interpretation as a determination of the text's meaning and is less interested in the hermeneutic understandings of readers that might extend the potentialities of the poem beyond the surface layer of meaning. For him, then, the structure he gives to his commentary would probably reflect a natural reading process that sufficiently deals with the immediate contexts of word and syntax, on the one hand, and with the total contexts of interpretation and information about grammar, trope, and narrative, on the other. It bears repeating that Mallinātha hardly even speaks of the *Naiṣadhīya* specifically. In fact, all of his *kāvya* commentaries have virtually the same prefatory verses and a seemingly identical approach procedurally. Even the titles to his early commentaries—on the *Naiṣadhīya* and on Kālidāsa's *mahākāvyas*—refer to some version of "bringing back to life" works presumably deadened by poor literary-critical attention.[22]

All in all, therefore, it seems Mallinātha's pedagogical impulse is guided by the need to draw out the structural similarities among all the *mahākāvyas* he comments on rather than to identify each work's individuated character, which was an earlier generation's impetus for commentary writing. Whereas the technique of the thirteenth-century commentators represents an oral teaching style that invites the audience logically to discover the basic meaning of the verse around the action of the verb, the fifteenth-century works of Mallinātha most likely reflect the professional teacher's attempt to provide a clear and largely unambiguous gloss to his audience. Once the intricate syntax of a Sanskrit verse has been put into a linear prose order, the tropes and meter identified, relevant grammar lessons reinforced, and the appropriate reference texts cited, commentators like Mallinātha see their hermeneutic challenges—and, by extension, those of their audience—as resolved.[23] Nevertheless, the nature of all of the customary, text-oriented paradigms seems both epistemologically and pedagogically premised on a semiotic approach to the material, where a persevering reader is rewarded for following the text's "rules" of selection, arrangement, and emphasis. Literary discourse itself is seen as essentially mimetic and referential, and the ultimate goal is to develop a normative respect for an "authoritative" reading that focuses solely on determining the text's significance according to what the commentator believes the poet originally intended. As the reception contexts changed for commentary writing—one from limited and selective interpretive prisms for a more sophisticated audience (Cāṇḍupaṇḍita and Vidyādhara) to a more targeted, pedagogically motivated work for general institutional purposes (Mallinātha)—so too did the method of commentary change to fit the function.

READING MULTIPLE MEANINGS INTO THE *NAIṢADHĪYA*

Below I exemplify the ways in which Cāṇḍupaṇḍita especially shaped his commentary to suit an audience that would appreciate his ferreting out Śrīharṣa's numerous philosophical references in *Naiṣadhīya*, much as Vidyādhara's audiences presumably valued his attention to the poem's extravagant use of trope. However, remaining for a moment with the thesis that the choice of commentarial style is bound up with temporally conditioned shifts in the context and function where and how commentaries are respectively read and used, Nārāyaṇa's commentary on *Naiṣadhīya* 1.1 also merits consideration.[24] In the sixteenth century, Nārāyaṇa uses a hybrid style that neither wholly takes the form of the *kathambhūtinī* type of commentary nor of the *anvayamukhī* but rather shifts back and forth between them.[25] Thus, for example, Nārāyaṇa first arranges his commentary of 1.1 in the standard prose order favored by the *anvayamukhī* approach, beginning with the subject Nala and stating clearly the core sentence of the verse: "That Nala was . . ." (*sa nala āsīt* . . .). Then he proceeds to segment his analysis through the *kathambhūtinī* commentary's method of asking strategic questions: "What was special about Nala?" (*kim viśiṣṭo nalaḥ*?). In between recapitulating the prose order and supplying questions to organize the flow of his gloss, Nārāyaṇa associatively provides all sorts of technical analysis and information (grammatical, lexicographical, intertextual, names of tropes, etc.) alongside multiple layers of potential interpretations, each one commonly separated by a transitional phrase like "Or else . . ." (*yadvā*). The entire discussion of just this first verse runs several pages, demonstrating the full repertoire of techniques available to the Sanskrit commentator to identify, even create, polyvalence. All of the reworked elements of the verse graphed collectively yield at least nine translations of this verse, the most conventional one being:

> That Nala was a treasure-house of resplendence,
> a great and dazzling festival,
> the orbit of whose fame is represented by
> the white royal umbrella.
> Drinking in the stories of this earth protector,
> even gods do not care as much for the divine nectar.

The other eight versions bear the same meaning for the first two quarters of the verse (that Nala was a "treasure-house of resplendence," "a great and dazzling festival," and that his fame is "represented by the white royal umbrella"). The succeeding half of the verse, however, is open to a remarkable assortment of possibilities:

> Drinking in the stories of this earth protector,
> even the learned ones do not care as much for the
> immortal state of liberation from worldly unhappiness.

> Drinking in the stories of this earth protector,
> the gods used to, but no longer, care as much
> for the exquisitely beautiful moon.

> Drinking in the stories of this earth protector,
> the gods do not desire nectar,
> what is normally their daily meal.

> Drinking in the stories of this earth protector,
> the divine serpents that bear the earth on their hoods,
> like Takṣaka and Śeśanāga,
> do not take the nectar offered to them by Indra.

Drinking in the stories of this earth protector,
other enlightened kings do not care as much
for the immortality that comes from performing Vedic sacrifices.

Drinking in the stories of this earth protector,
the evil effects of Kali—the sinister spirit in the gambling dice—
and his debased age is destroyed.

Drinking in the stories of the sun, the earth's protector,
the learned ones do not care as much for the moon,
who is the keeper of the immortal nectar.

In spite of the fact that Nala was a gambler, he was the king.
Drinking in his stories, even the gods do not care as much
for the divine nectar.

Thus, from this verse words used for "gods" (*budha*), "nectar" (*sudhā*), and the compound "earth protector" (*kṣiti-rakṣin*) are redistributed, in accordance with what Sanskrit grammar and lexicons allow, to startling effect. And so, the word whose most likely meaning in this context would be "gods" (*budha*), the ones who receive Nala's stories, comes also to mean "learned people," "kings," "mountains," "elephants who hold the earth up," and "divine serpents." All of these can, in turn, be modified with the epithet of being "earth protectors" according to various scenarios consonant with lexical meanings and Purāṇic mythology. As such, these stories respectively confer to each a unique reward that matches a cherished desire: to ordinary people, the cessation of worldly suffering (*mokṣa*); to kings, sovereignty over the earth (*bhūpālana*); to gods, immortality-sustaining nectar (*amṛta*); and to mountains, elephants, and snakes, a lofty seat of power (*mahatsthāna*), as each is thought to bear the weight of the earth in different contexts.

Nārāyaṇa treats other modifiers the same way. Thus, the "earth protector" can be broken up differently to render two separate words: *kṣiti*, which can mean "earth" and "destruction"; and *akṣin*, which can mean a "dice-playing gambler" or "Kali," the representative of the rotten, debased age we currently live in. And so, Nala would not only be the "earth protector" but also the "destroyer of Kali." Nārāyaṇa reconfigures the word used for "nectar" (*sudhā*) to mean "the moon" and "immortality itself that comes from performing Vedic sacrifices."

In a similar reading by Nārāyaṇa's contemporary Śrīdhara, Nala and his "stories" (*kathā*) are reimagined variously. Nala is not only a great king but also the destroyer of Kali, the Absolute (*paramātman*), Viṣṇu, Śiva, the sun, and the moon. Nala is also Rāma (replacing the word *nala* with *nara*)[26] where, as Śrīdhara explains, the killing of Rāvaṇa qualifies him as an "earth protector." Śrīdhara continues: Nala's stories (*kathā*) are respectively compared to the end of worldly suffering, as valuable as the earth, equivalent to immortality-granting nectar, synonymous with the stories of Viṣṇu's avatars (*avatāra-kathā*), and superior to lofty positions of power (in the case of mountains, elephants, and snakes). In addition to Nārāyaṇa's nine interpretations, Śrīdhara adds a tenth one, using a clever lipogram known as *varṇa-cyuti-nyāya*, where "dropped letters" (*varṇa-cyuti*) are restored to bring forth a desirable significance:

> That Nala was a treasure-house of resplendence,
> a great and dazzling festival,
> the orbit of whose fame is represented by
> the white royal umbrella.
> Drinking in the stories of this earth protector,
> kings do not care as much
> for the earth itself.

Here, to get the meaning of "earth" (*vasudhā*) from the word "nectar" (*sudhā*) to convey the esoteric meaning that intelligent kings (*budhā*) dismiss even lordship of the earth in favor of Nala's stories, Śrīdhara invokes the *varṇa-cyuti-nyāya* and adds the phoneme *va* to the root word *sudhā*, thus justifying *vasudhā*.[27] For commentators such as Nārāyaṇa and Śrīdhara, these kinds of reading strategies are in evidence at virtually every opportunity afforded by Śrīharṣa's language. With each new reading, these commentators cite a range of texts to justify each interpretation: from Vedic texts (*Bṛhadāraṇyaka Upaniṣad*) and philosophical works (*Vivekacūḍāmaṇi*), to *dharmaśāstra* (*Manusmṛti*) and *tantra* (*Durgātantra*), to different dictionaries (*Abhidhānaratna* and *Amarakośa*) and poetics works (*Sarasvatīkaṇṭhābharaṇa* and *Sāhityadarpaṇa*), to the various Purāṇa texts and the compositions of other poets like Kālidāsa.

I also attribute Nārāyaṇa and Śrīdhara's choice of an eclectic and synthetic mode of exegesis largely to the sixteenth-century milieu of readers and critics for whom they wrote. They were not introducing a new text, as the thirteenth-century commentators were, nor were they embroiled in pedagogical debates aimed at controlling the interpretation of *Naiṣadhīya*, as Mallinātha seems to have been. Instead, internal evidence suggests that both Nārāyaṇa and Śrīdhara probably wrote for an audience that was far more diverse: advanced students of *kāvya*, other *Naiṣadhīya* scholars, and perhaps even a new kind of "religious" reader interested in *Naiṣadhīya*'s reputation as an esoteric text. The latter group, I will argue later, include those who transform *Naiṣadhīya* into allegory—a seed for future interpretation that Nārāyaṇa merely plants in the preface of his commentary on *Naiṣadhīya* 1.1 without bringing it up much again later:

> To complete a desired composition without obstacles and to fulfill the mandates of tradition, it is said that one ought to perform a benediction. It is said, therefore, that "the beginning of a poem should either be a blessing, homage to a deity, or an indication of the subject matter." The poet named Śrīharṣa, the composer of the *Naiṣadhīya*, mysteriously seeds his benediction by paying homage to his preferred deity Rāma, lord of the Raghus. Others, however, say that the benediction simply takes the conventional form of citing the subject matter of the poem.[28]

Like his predecessors, Nārāyaṇa here addresses the technical problem other scholars of *Naiṣadhīya* also take up; that is, whether the verse conforms to the common practice of performing a benediction at the beginning of a poem. In fact, after giving his own idiosyncratic opinion—that the benediction is really directed to Rāma—he cites the more common view of his predecessors that the verse introduces the subject matter of the *Naiṣadhīya*. Noteworthy here, however, is that unlike an earlier generation of commentators, who occasionally mentioned alternative opinions (usually on textual matters) and generally only emphasized a singular interpretation, Nārāyaṇa often foregrounds multiple nonconventional readings before supplying more established and standardized positions. No wonder, therefore, his text is dramatically longer than those of other commentators who provide little more than a simple gloss.

Neither Nārāyaṇa nor Śrīdhara appear interested in arguing for a singular (and constraining) way of reading a given verse. Furthermore, neither commentary gives the impression that interpretation is a naïve search for a *correct* meaning, nor as simply a recounting of alternative meanings in order to highlight a correct meaning, but rather as a peculiar kind of exercise in intellectual pleasure—what in Sanskrit might be called *manovinoda*—that the *Naiṣadhīya* itself seems to relish. In other words, their exegetical practice self-admittedly does not provide what is necessary for thoroughly *understanding* the text but rather what their learned, resourceful, and witty intelligence finds *interesting*.[29] Interpretation, thus, seems to be more about guiding the reader to reflect on the text's underlying potencies and how the text functions. The three centuries of scholarship that intervene between Cāṇḍupaṇḍita in the thirteenth century and Nārāyaṇa in the sixteenth century represent a period of gradual progression that leads ultimately to a veritable field of *Naiṣadhīya* studies. By the sixteenth century, commentators feel confident to suggest that the *Naiṣadhīya* is a profoundly coded poem with an intrinsic polysemy that requires skillful decoding.

PHILOSOPHICAL READINGS OF THE *NAIṢADHĪYA*

Cāṇḍupaṇḍita is the first of a long line of decoder-critics. After Cāṇḍupaṇḍita, the notion that the *Naiṣadhīya* is a "difficult" text becomes proverbial among the poem's professional readers. His perspective on the text, however, is not one of radical polysemy (like later commentators) but rather targeted and singularly obsessed with Śrīharṣa's philosophical agenda. What follows is an example of his commentary on a verse from the sixth canto (6.51) where Nala, wandering as an invisible man in search of Damayantī, finally comes face-to-face with her. The verse reads:

> They were two.
> Even though in the same place, facing each other,
> they thought they were somewhere else.
> Their illusory selves embraced each other.
> In doing so, they actually embraced each other.

Occurring during a pivotal turn in the fortunes of the hero and heroine, the context of this verse is that Nala (playing messenger for the gods) accidentally brushes up against a flustered Damayantī in the corridors of the women's quarters. The two lovers cannot *truly* meet in a normative setting because one is invisible (the hero Nala) and the other (the heroine Damayantī) is certain that no one can infiltrate the security of the women's quarters. Furthermore, the physical embrace of two strangers of good breeding (they have never met) and the ethics of a messenger overstepping his boundaries can never strike audiences of this kind of poetry as, in any way, culturally consistent with what is conventionally appropriate (and, therefore, aesthetically acceptable or plausible). Śrīharṣa here dramatically captures the ways in which a Sanskrit poet can project onto an imaginative plane what he cannot express in putatively real situations. Their "embrace" *must be* illusory, or must it? In reality, they must experience each other as different—this is the only way they can—but their "illusory" selves embrace each other, the poet tells us. What is not normative, and therefore appropriate, in reality becomes available and potentially fulfilling in an imaginary plane. It is important that they are enclosed by four walls, in close proximity, unable to flee, and magnetically drawn to each other. The scene works because the audience knows that the couple (observant of court manners and moral norms) could not possibly have any actual physical contact with each other. And so they wonder, like the audience, if a particular cognition implies the absence of another, if something simultaneous can be revealed that is not the immediate object of awareness.

The verse is indeed bursting with philosophical possibilities. But, other than Cāṇḍupaṇḍita, no other commentators take it up. Nārāyaṇa and Mallinātha, for example, do not seem entranced at all by this verse's potential for philosophical insight. They both convey that Nala and Damayantī were in the same room and, while they had an illusory embrace, the two probably had some real touches also. Nārāyaṇa remarks that the intended meaning of the verse is that in the midst of their seeing illusions of each other, they (or their hearts) grasped each other's true form also. Cāṇḍupaṇḍita, however, spots in the verse a reference to a specific philosophical school's theory of error (*akhyātivāda*) and proceeds comprehensively to provide a justification for his find. Before engaging in a rather technical philosophical discussion, he initially sets up the situation using his standard question-and-answer (*kathambhūtinī*) approach toward defining the words and explaining their syntactical relationship with each other:

> The two, Nala and Damayantī, embraced each other in actuality. Where? In the middle of her inner chambers, the two embraced the illusion of each other. In the midst of an illusion of making contact, a true connection occurred. Or else, one may take the modifier "actually" (*tathyam*) as an adverb whereby during the embrace, their minds illusorily embraced each other. The true Damayantī was embraced by Nala, whose mind grasped a false Damayantī. And a true Nala was embraced by Damayantī, whose mind had become engrossed in a false Nala. Here the distinction rests in the origin of the reason. What were they doing? They are seeing each other as if they were in different places. Where? Both inhabit the same space, in a single location.

Having provided the narrative context, Cāṇḍupaṇḍita then frames the situation with a preliminary discussion of its philosophical implications, analogizing the subject of the verse with standard images from philosophical texts.

> Just as a delusion always accounts for experiencing an illusory embrace, in such a way these two on account of delusion thought they had embraced their many selves—as at the time of a delusion, another delusion also arises, and another, etc. Just as a dream that is true at the time of dreaming afterwards finds its reality logically objectionable, just so an illusory embrace also is true at that time of the illusion and is only afterwards logically objectionable. And, just so, the shell (mother-of-pearl) is truly apprehended as silver at the time of apprehension and afterwards is found to be logically objectionable. But here is the distinction. On account of the delusion of perceiving such things as a shell as silver, an anxiety arises that if this spontaneous perception of silver will be logically objectionable, then perhaps I will not be able to apprehend real silver in the future. But here (in the context of this verse), even when there is an actual embrace, an experience akin to an illusory embrace arises.

Setting up the philosophical problem, Cāṇḍupaṇḍita proceeds strategically to delineate the positions that might be put forth by several important philosophical traditions of early India.[30]

According to the learned commentator, because the Sāṅkhya philosophers hold that the object of an erroneous cognition is real (*satkhyātivāda*), for them, when there is an error (as when a shell is apprehended as silver) that apprehension is, in some form or other, understood as actually real. Contrary to the Sāṅkhya view, Cāṇḍupaṇḍita elucidates that some Buddhist philosophers argue that the object of an erroneous cognition is not real (*asatkhyātivāda*). Other Buddhists like the "Middle-Path" philosophers (*mādhyāmika*) radically propound the doctrine of an erroneous cognition's nonexistence or emptiness (*śūnyavāda*); for them, silver is apprehended but that apprehension is delusional (i.e., empty). Likewise, Cāṇḍupaṇḍita gives protracted explanations of the views of the Nyāya and Vedānta schools of philosophy on the subject of erroneous cognition. Thus, Nyāya philosophers speak of the object of error as something altogether "other" (*anyathākhyāti*); seeing a shell as silver (a delusion) is an altogether distinct apprehension from the shell that is actually being seen; therefore, one may conclude that it is possible that something that is actually unreal takes on a reality all its own.[31] Similarly, Cāṇḍupaṇḍita analyzes the position of Vedānta philosophers who essentially hold that the object of erroneous cognition is indefinable. Because a shell cannot be silver, the perception of silver cannot be real; however, because silver is apprehended, it is also not unreal. Because the existence and nonexistence of the perceived silver mutually contradict each other, the commentator explains, Vedānta philosophy holds that it is neither real nor unreal and nor is it something other than the real and the unreal; rather, it is inexpressible and, therefore, indefinable.

Having established the ground for discussing the philosophical subject of error, Cāṇḍupaṇḍita now comes to his thesis: that Śrīharṣa's verse actually reflects the perspective of the Prābhākara-mīmāṃsā school, which holds that the object of so-called erroneous cognition is not erroneous at all (*akhyātivāda*). Silver is neither apprehended erroneously nor is it illusory; rather, it is simply true, as there are two cognitions present, one perceptually grasped and one remembered. The commentator uses a series of metaphors to defend his argument and then concludes that the poet of the *Naiṣadhīya* consciously prepared verse 6.51 to reflect the Prābhākara-mīmāṃsā view.[32] Satisfied that he has identified Śrīharṣa's embedded reference, by way of conclusion, Cāṇḍupaṇḍita reconnects the philosophical idea with the narrative situation by integrating alternative explanations of the words he has already glossed with his hypothesis that this verse reflects the view of Prābhākara-mīmāṃsā:

> Both Damayantī and Nala embraced each other in actuality, though seeing each other as if they were in different places. Where? In the midst of their false embrace. That there is an illusory union of the two here would ordinarily be accepted. In this case, however, it has actually happened. It follows that even though being in front of each other, they understood each other to be as if in a mistaken location on account of a superimposition of one form onto another. The meaning is this—Nala may at some point have had the experience of a true embrace somewhere. And Damayantī also experienced embraces with her friends. That experience alone is what is remembered in this shared space.
>
> Therefore, both are real—the perceptual knowledge of embracing each other and the memory consciousness of embrace. Neither are false. Therefore, the embrace of the couple is real, for the memory-consciousness cannot be logically opposed. And this is the uniform stance of the Prābhākara-mīmāṃsā school. Also, there cannot be a repetition in meaning of the synonymous words *anyonya*, *paraspara*, and *mitha* [all meaning "each other" or "mutually"]. First, *anyonya* signifies the embrace experience in the past. The next word *paraspara* refers to the memory-consciousness with respect to what is in front of them. The final word *mitha* points to the union of

> the perceptual and memory-consciousness with respect to so-called illusion posited by other philosophers; it designates the notion established by the Prābhākara school of thought and fulfills its proposition that, in every way, the two truly embrace each other.[33]

Through a sophisticated analysis, Cāṇḍupaṇḍita has claimed to decode Śrīharṣa's magical fusing of idea and image in the description of a significant emotional experience in the poem. One gets the feeling here, however, that Śrīharṣa's verse merely provides him a pretext to fulfill his own intuitive hypothesis about the *Naiṣadhīya* and, correspondingly, to carry out his self-appointed task of delivering a scholarly interpretation based on that hypothesis. His diligent commentary compels the sensitive reader to at least pursue the argument carefully, to see for himself if the possibility is, in the first case, legitimate and, second, if the author might have (at least unconsciously) intended it.

OVERINTERPRETING THE *NAIṢADHĪYA*

No such ambivalence about the probability of an interpretation seems justifiable for polyvalent readings after the sixteenth century. The hermeneutic gestures of Nārāyaṇa are, I suggest, clearly not meant to convince the reader of the probability of his multiple interpretations. Nārāyaṇa rather, like an Oulipo poet of contemporary times, thrives on possibilities of interpretation under the guidance and dual restraints of Sanskrit grammar and cultural convention. I give here an example, from Nārāyaṇa's commentary on *Naiṣadhīya* 1.40, to clarify the distinction I make between the pointed interpretive practices of Cāṇḍupaṇḍita and those of Nārāyaṇa. Unlike the nine interpretations gleaned from Nārāyaṇa's commentary on *Naiṣadhīya* 1.1, this one only yields two. Here is translation no. 1 (the standard one) based on Nārāyaṇa's commentary and shared by all other commentaries of the poem:

> After hiding from her two closed eyes
> and also from her heart,
> closed by the silence of external sense organs,
> that great secret Nala,
> who had never been seen earlier,
> was shown to her by Sleep.

Damayantī is asleep and deep in her dreams. As she has not yet met Nala, Sleep personified as an intimate friend introduces him to her. Here is a reconstruction of the original Sanskrit with Nārāyaṇa's gloss of each term:

> Closed/from the eyes/closed by the silence of the external organs of sense/ even from the heart/and/after hiding/that lord of the earth, i.e., the king/ never seen/great secret/by sleep/to her/was shown.

> nimīlitāt/akṣi-yugāt/bāhyendriya-mauna-mudritāt/hṛdo 'pi/ca/saṃgopya/ sa mahīpatiḥ/kadāpy avīkṣitaḥ/mahat rahasyaṃ/nidrayā/asyāḥ/adarśi

Here is translation no. 2:

> Great Nala, become my husband!
> Live outside of Kaliyuga's reach and
> stay away from those who inflict pain on others.
> Be different than those who, through ignorance,
> remain silent of others' virtues.
> You of mysterious beauty,
> be one who has contact with those who have realized Viṣṇu!

Here, Damayantī speaks directly to Nala, as a lover to a beloved as he departs for an extended stay away from her. Here is how Nārāyaṇa resegments some of the relevant word divisions of the verse to reorder the syntax and to arrive at this desired interpretation:

> akṣi-yugāt/bāhya/nidrayā/indriya-mauna-mudridāt ahṛdo 'pi/mahan/ adarśi-saṅga/api/akadāpy avīkṣitaḥ/sa/rahasyama/mahī-patiḥ/syāḥ

> from Kaliyuga/Be outside!/because of ignorance/not acknowledging the virtues of others by staying silent/Great Nala/one who has contact with those who have realized Viṣṇu [represented by the letter "a"]/also/ unseen by those who inflict pain on others/O you of mysterious beauty/ my celebrated husband/Become!

At the end of this radical reorganization of the verse's elements, Nārāyaṇa understates: "That's enough!" (*ity alam*). Taking stock here of Nārāyaṇa's exercise in *overinterpretation*, we can first note the impediments he had to face: sticking to the plot (the verse had to be about Nala and Damayantī), adhering to the rules of grammar, and bringing sensitivity to the propriety of the context. To overcome these obstacles, he brings forth an array of remarkable tools: exploiting the double meanings (*śleṣa*) available through homonyms; creatively breaking up word boundaries; relying on secondary and tertiary meanings of words or significance specifically created by special dictionaries, like the "Lexicon for Single Phonemes" (*ekākṣarakośa*). One assumes that, from a narrative point of view, Nārāyaṇa had to judge whether it is sensible to think that Damayantī would utter these words (translation no. 2). On one level, they do express the immense love and desire for well-being she feels toward Nala; on another level, her admonition to Nala to be wary of Kali, who will eventually break up their marriage, is also contextually appropriate here. Furthermore, consonant with the broader premise of his commentary—that Śrīharṣa's favored divinity is Rāma, the seventh *avatāra* of Viṣṇu—invoking Viṣṇu in this verse also makes sense for Nārāyaṇa. Thus, it is clear that if one accepts the notion that Nārāyaṇa's intellectual milieu demanded such sophisticated exegetical achievements, replete with charm and surprise (*camatkāra*) and extreme in their ability to stretch the forms of language and thought, then interpretations like these do not ring false or seem excessive.

CONCLUDING OBSERVATIONS

Pierre Bourdieu has compared the practice of literary criticism to a "well-regulated ballet, in which individuals and groups dance their own steps, always contrasting themselves with each other, sometimes clashing, sometimes dancing to the same tune, then turning their backs on each other in often explosive separations, and so on, up until the present time" (Bourdieu 113). While perhaps too dramatic a metaphor to describe premodern critical scholarship on *Naiṣadhīya*, the materials we have to work with do invite the question of how hermeneutics change over time in Sanskrit literary culture. This chapter has argued that the thirteenth-century commentators of *Naiṣadhīya* faced the task of making an exciting new work available to their courtly audiences. Their own scholarship on the poem, therefore, was unfettered by received ideas about the poem but also, therefore, unsatisfactorily equipped to provide a global perspective on the multiple possibilities available to interpret the *Naiṣadhīya*. I largely attribute the coherence and univocal nature of their hermeneutic position to this fact.

Later commentators like the sixteenth-century Nārāyaṇa, writing in a context where the *Naiṣadhīya* was already seen as a canonical work, produced (or rather, were able to produce) commentaries that were willfully polyvalent, keen to overinterpret, and even self-contradictory. Whereas the early commentators generally interpreted through one prism of Śrīharṣa's composition, the later commentators attempted to assimilate a perceived totality of Śrīharṣa's vision, which allowed for the negation of absolute validity to any single interpretive hypothesis. No wonder then that these later commentaries set the tone for allegorical and "religious" readings outside of the formal Sanskrit commentary. These later documents aim to relive the scene, as it were, and rewrite the *Naiṣadhīya* through the lens of supernatural accomplishment, something Śrīharṣa himself claims to have relied upon to inspire his poem.

Mallinātha and his cohort—in the middle period—perhaps prefigured the developments of the sixteenth century or perhaps they already had access to such commentaries in their own time and reacted unhappily to them. By this time, the canonical *mahākāvya* had high pedagogical status and was an important site for contestation among professional scholars. To give multiple interpretations, where one interpretation was no better than the other, likely seemed excessive to them and clearly caused some consternation. The impression that Mallinātha's commentary gives is that Śrīharṣa's poem functioned as one among several other canonical poems in need of a commentary suitable for students; unlike the commentaries of Vidyādhara, Cāṇḍupaṇḍita, and Nārāyaṇa, whose efforts are guided by Śrīharṣa's own agenda, his commentary seems to be more guided by the general requirements of *mahākāvya* studies in pedagogical contexts. I imagine that the idea that interpretations could be unpredictable (Cāṇḍupaṇḍita) and brazen (Nārāyaṇa), but not outright wrong, rankled commentators like Mallinātha, who was seemingly more concerned with getting it right than allowing for wrongheaded, if not grammatically wrong, interpretations. Why? Because the abuse (as he sees it) of tropes, by making them wander away from convention, opens up a closed normative tropological system that gives Sanskrit literature a specific identity; commentators who read for too much nuance have a perceptual disorder, as it were, that effectively *kills* the text (as Mallinātha implies in entitling his *Naiṣadhīya* commentary as The Enlivener) or at least kills what the text is supposed *to do* for a culture, which apparently is to contribute to its steady self-propagation. Or could it be that *overly close* readings, like Nārāyaṇa's, dull (kill?) the readers' own vital drive toward refining their own ability to distinguish nuance in Śrīharṣa's language? From this perspective, Mallinātha's pedagogical preference is for a clear surface reading that pays sufficient attention to a verse's minutiae over and above a deeper reading that draws perception away from the text's literal meanings. Such a preference might underlie a theory of reading that summons the reader to experience and articulate for herself a text's potency for nuance.

In conjunction with their role as links between the poet and audience, it is important to remember that commentaries constitute traditions of interpretation, as Paul Griffiths explains, and generally revolve around issues of authority, hierarchy, community, and tradition.[34] As such, the hermeneutic efforts of the *Naiṣadhīya*'s Sanskrit commentators have, by and large, determined the appreciation and grounds for inquiry suitable to the text, exerting interpretive control through a host of strategies. While their general adherence to normative forms of exegesis circumscribes the range of interpretive choice they provide, some of the *Naiṣadhīya* commentators successfully create a space for other types of reading—the allegorical, for example—that evolved eventually into full-fledged interpretive traditions in their own right. The case of Nārāyaṇa's *Prakāśa*, the vastly popular sixteenth-century commentary, is instructive here. In addition to his commentary being invariably read alongside Śrīharṣa's poem in modern times, it is also an early source for popular allegorical readings of the text (see chapter 5). That being said, most commentaries on *Naiṣadhīya* are the work of scholars trained in specific disciplines (*śāstra*). Each commentator brings to the forefront, therefore, a series of relevant adjunct texts from a carefully constructed textual hierarchy to clarify or bolster his position. The Sanskrit exegetical tradition is, as Robert Goldman explains, a highly "literate intellectual culture of reference" where the commentary constitutes merely the superstructure for the multiple genres that actually construct the text.[35] The citations of certain texts available in *Naiṣadhīya* commentaries reflect the ways in which the text may have been constructed in a given historical context or literary milieu. Commentators' choice of quotation informs the texts that were being read and studied at the time, what types of knowledge were in currency, and the kinds of approaches that were accepted as legitimate in the understanding of texts. It turns out, therefore, that, like the *Naiṣadhīya* itself, each *Naiṣadhīya* commentary constitutes traditions of multiple, hybrid, and heterogeneous texts marked by a distinctive historicity, nuanced critical sensibilities and paradigms, and complex hermeneutic desires.

4 ◈ STRUGGLES OVER THE TEXT

THE PREVIOUS chapter made the argument that *Naiṣadhīya*'s diverse interpretive careers closely followed a pattern of changing reception contexts within which formal commentaries were produced. Thus, I suggested in outline a set of relationships over the span of seven centuries between interpretive practices and shifting attitudes toward the *mahākāvya*'s function in particular reading contexts. This chapter follows a similar strategy, but rather than focusing on the interpretation of *Naiṣadhīya* from a literary-critical perspective, it directs attention to the ways in which practices of editing—especially during and after the fifteenth century—inform and illuminate aspects of the reception of the poem. Commentators' editorial decisions, I argue, mesh in insightful ways with their hermeneutic attitudes and interpretive practices. Their text-critical determinations effectively generate information about the *Naiṣadhīya*'s reception in ways that exceed a calculus of variants or a record of emendations. Most significantly, arguments over variant readings and emendations reflect divergent perspectives among the commentators about Śrīharṣa's style and authorial intentions, perspectives that profoundly informed commentators' critical apprehension of the work. Like the various interpretive modes discussed in the previous chapter, text-critical arguments distilled past attitudes about the poem and shaped, in turn, the inheritance of the *Naiṣadhīya* among later generations of readers.

Most prominent among their editorial tasks is to settle on a perfect text, one that is filtered of any faulty accretions or subtractions. I suggested earlier that on account of its enterprising experiments with language and imagery, the *Naiṣadhīya* is a catachrestic text *par excellence*. As such, even well-read commentators of Sanskrit *kāvya* are often left wondering if they are reading a correct form or not. This frequently leads them to engage in arguments about identifying the *correct* reading or simply the *best* reading. Such debates became a defining feature of the *Naiṣadhīya*'s textual history. The result of these arguments, concludes Handiqui, is that: "A study of the [*Naiṣadhīya*'s] commentaries reveals a bewildering mass of variant readings and there is probably no other poem of the *kāvya* period which presents so many of them."[1] It could be the case that as the earliest *mahākāvya* commentaries are only available since about the tenth century, variant readings of poems before this time have not come down to us. Nevertheless, as Handiqui suggests, *Naiṣadhīya* commentators frequently cited variant readings they had either rejected as wrong or passed over as inferior; sometimes, they sparingly emended the text altogether if they presumably believed it had been miscopied by a scribe or perhaps interpolated by someone other than the author. As I discuss in the section that follows, however, until the twentieth century, rarely do commentators explicitly call for the text to be emended even if they might have believed Śrīharṣa himself had committed a technical *doṣa*, a literary transgression, by using the wrong word or exceeded poetic decorum by repeating a similar idea over the course of two or more verses.

Fixing a definitive version of the text also has proved to be an enduring challenge to *Naiṣadhīya*'s commentators, as has the problem of the poem's *extent*—unresolved questions about whether Śrīharṣa's original work has come down as an unfinished text. Several early commentators as well as some modern scholars believe that it is an incomplete text. Others, such as Vidyādhara and Nārāyaṇa, while acknowledging the arguments of unnamed critics who believed otherwise, put forth a compelling case in support of the poem's extent as it currently stands. The lack of consensus among early readers about the authoritative text of the *Naiṣadhīya* is staggering, and separating what authentically belongs to Śrīharṣa's poem from what was mistakenly added or interpolated has been a matter of great contestation. A comparative analysis of these different readings helps us, at least, to identify lineages of reading communities from the thirteenth to sixteenth centuries, some inflected by the region from which they emerge but others notably transcending regional markers. We can deduce, for example, that Cāṇḍupaṇḍita and Vidyādhara generally agree and are followed in their readings by fourteenth-century commentator Īśānadeva and seventeenth-century commentator Jinarāja. The fact that readings from the three commentators from Gujarat (Cāṇḍupaṇḍita, Vidyādhara, and Jinarāja) agree supports a thesis of regional text-lineages; however, their agreement with the Vārāṇasī-based Īśānadeva's readings, only one-half century removed from the two earlier Gujarati commentators (Vidyādhara and Cāṇḍupaṇḍita), suggests a wider network of manuscript transmission.[2] Nārāyaṇa (sixteenth century), Mallinātha (fifteenth century), and Narahari (fourteenth century) often agree on readings, although Mallinātha's text sometimes differs in distinctive ways from all the others.[3] We can also be certain that there were other readings available even before Vidyādhara's and Cāṇḍupaṇḍita's commentaries that do not get picked up by any other commentators afterward.[4] In my own citations and translations of the *Naiṣadhīya*, I have opted to use sixteenth-century Nārāyaṇa's text-with-commentary because it is the latest of the printed versions, contains many of the variants used by earlier commentaries, and is the base text used by K.K. Handiqui, A.N. Jani, and most other twentieth-century scholars in their writings on the poem.

IS THE *NAIṢADHĪYA* FLAWED?

Unsurprisingly, one of the many synonyms in Sanskrit for a scholar (*paṇḍita*) is *doṣajña*: "one who recognizes faults." The scholastic acumen (*pāṇḍitya*) demonstrated by most *kāvya* commentaries places a great deal of emphasis, therefore, on grammaticality and linguistic decorum (*sādhutva*). Microscopic analysis of linguistic usage, in fact, constitutes the most important function of Sanskrit commentaries. The *Naiṣadhīya* tradition exhibits an ideal case study to examine the extent to which Sanskrit intellectual life fixated on the ideal of *sādhutva*. Pollock argues that the impulse to guide literary correctness among Sanskrit intellectuals extends to a more general "cultural-political problematic of correctness (*sādhutva*)," which itself is "generated from within the discourses and histories of grammars, the grammaticized language usage of *kāvya*, and the symbiotic ties of both grammar and *kāvya* with kings, courts, and larger polities."[5] Building on the logic of *sādhutva*, if we accept that one of the functions of canonical works is to serve as a model of literary excellence, it is not surprising that the *Naiṣadhīya*'s popularity as a textbook for literary training in institutional pedagogical contexts was intimately tied up with arguments about its virtues—and flaws. A cluster of scholarly essays in Hindi and Sanskrit from the twentieth century speaks to the endurance of this discourse. For example, Sāhityācārya Parameśvarānanda Śāstri of the Oriental College in Jalandhar (Panjab) argues in a 1948 essay that Śrīharṣa's commission of literary faults (*doṣa*) is actually the *Naiṣadhīya*'s "sixth virtue"; another Hindi essay from 1952 by R.N. Bhatt plays on the famous Sanskrit aphorism that asserts that "poets cannot be goaded into conformity" (*niraṅkuśāḥ kavayaḥ*) to argue against critics who find fault with Śrīharṣa's unconventional poetry.[6] Another essay discusses the poem's "aesthetic propriety" (*aucitya*) from the point of view of its *doṣas*.[7]

The fact that Sanskrit commentators since the fifteenth century have been eager to dispel controversies in their remarks on *Naiṣadhīya* confirms the prevalent existence of hostile or potentially hostile responses to the poem's appreciation as a work of high literary merit. In fact, intensive scrutiny of the poem's perceived *doṣas* becomes a long-standing appendix to any study of the *Naiṣadhīya* tradition and is woven into the anecdotal history of the poem's reception. Remembered narratives of critics chiding Śrīharṣa's iconoclasm probably reflect a reality of the mixed reception given to the *Naiṣadhīya*'s literary usages and choices. For example, a popular account (*lokokti*) that has wide circulation (and is definitely anachronistic) locates Śrīharṣa as the nephew of the poetics master Mammaṭa. According to the story, Mammaṭa regrets that he did not have the *Naiṣadhīya* in front of him when he composed his chapter on *doṣa*; had he known about the poem, he would not have had to scour other poems for examples to put in his book.[8] Indeed, Śrīharṣa does not seem too concerned with the customary "rules" and conventions of *mahākāvya*. Sanskrit commentators who sympathetically identify with Śrīharṣa have noticed this and are quick to come to his defense against the critics. Sixteenth-century *Naiṣadhīya* commentator Rāmacandra Śeṣa points out, for instance, at the end of the first canto of his *Bhāvadyotanika* (Explaining the Sense) commentary that "even if Śrīharṣa does not describe the conventional topics of the genre (introduction of the seasons, mountains, flower plucking, water sports, wine drinking, amorous games, etc.), it should not raise any controversy about whether this poem is a *mahākāvya* or not."[9] Rāmacandra then cites the renowned poetics master Daṇḍin's *Kāvyādarśa* (1.20) to bolster his argument that leaving out some conventional aspect or other does not ruin a poem.[10]

In an important way, therefore, the historiography of the *Naiṣadhīya* tradition that I have laid out, to trace retrospectively the fact of the poem's canonicity today through secondary literature on it from the past eight centuries, participates in a larger ongoing debate in Sanskrit intellectual culture about what poetry *is*, and especially what *good* poetry is. Generally, this question fell into the purview of the discourse on poetics (*alaṅkāraśāstra*). However, I contend, we can also draw insights from monitoring the nature of debates going on in the *kāvya* commentaries (even concerning a single verse), which, owing to the fact that many of the commentators are also trained in formalist poetics, may amount to similar (if not the same) results articulated by the *alaṅkāraśāstra*. The differences between the two evaluative traditions, however, reflect the divergent agendas underlying their sets of practices. As far as I can tell, commentaries in the premodern period were not written on texts that were thought to be problematic or inferior to other works. Commentaries on the *Naiṣadhīya*, therefore, are premised on the notion that the work represents an exemplary ideal of the *mahākāvya* genre and the culture it reflects. The *alaṅkāraśāstra*, however, sees a defined set of *rules* as defining *mahākāvya* culture and, therefore, when elucidating a totalizing prescription that identifies *doṣa* in literary works, the *alaṅkāraśāstra* treatise and its commentator may exemplify *any* given poet's (even a highly esteemed poet's) verse for its transgressive quality. Contrarily, however, the *kāvya* commentator, who has an intimate relationship with the poem he is commenting on, will usually not *explicitly* point to a flaw in the poet's verse. The commentator's criticism, rather, will be more oblique, with either strategic neglect or a gentle form of emendation being the preferred means of critique.

Three examples will elucidate the variety of commentarial response on *doṣa* in the *Naiṣadhīya*. The first comes from twentieth-century commentator Haridāsa Siddhāntavāgīśa, whose suggested emendation to what he fears might be a *doṣa* in Śrīharṣa's poem is conveyed in a way that is atypical of the practices of earlier *Naiṣadhīya* commentators. The second example here takes up the case of seventeenth-century commentator Gāgābhaṭṭa (Viśveśvara). Gāgābhaṭṭa was not only a *Naiṣadhīya* commentator but also a major commentator on an influential twelfth-century *alaṅkāraśāstra* text entitled the *Candrāloka* (Moonlight).[11] In his commentary on the *Candrāloka*, Gāgābhaṭṭa's gloss on a particular *doṣa* leads him to draw an example from the *Naiṣadhīya*, thus providing us with a glimpse into another side of the critical enterprise and the freedoms and restrictions respectively associated with commentaries on *alaṅkāraśāstra* and *kāvya*. The third example comes from Gadādhara's fifteenth-century commentary. Gadādhara repudiates the practice of emending the poem's verses without due consideration of the poem's broader tendencies and aesthetic. His response constitutes an interesting, and perhaps unique, premodern perspective on the propriety of certain editorial decisions that have since become standard.

EMENDING THE POEM

As late as the twentieth century, Haridāsa Siddhāntavāgīśa's commentary and translation of *Naiṣadhīya* (completed in the 1930s) contains numerous identifications of Śrīharṣa's counternormative expressions and even goes so far as to offer emendations. In this aspect, as I suggest above, Haridāsa's practice resonates more closely with that of writers and commentators of *alaṅkāraśāstra* than with premodern *kāvya* commentators. For example, Haridāsa notices a problem in verse 9.90 of the *Naiṣadhīya* where he sees what is, to his mind, an infelicitous consonantal harshness with the use of the disagreeable "ra" in place of a softer phoneme. Emending Śrīharṣa's expression "*vilambase jīvita kiṃ* drava drutaṃ" ("Oh life, do you still hang on? Go away quickly!"), Haridāsa suggests "*vilambase jīva kim* āśuniḥ sara," which, more or less, means the same thing but avoids, according to the commentator, the obstruction of the verse's primary emotional tenor of love-in-separation (*vipralambha-śṛṅgāra*) with the harsh sound "ra." Other less than desirable poetic usages in general that commentators frequently cite are summarized in the *Sāhityadarpaṇa*: sound quality that is not easy on the ear, an inappropriate or vulgar implication, ineffective execution of trope, unintelligibility, ambiguity, vagueness, using obsolete words or meanings whose context suggests other meanings, inexpressiveness, obscurity, distasteful suggestion, and indecency in terms of provoking shame or inauspiciousness.[12]

Faults in composition are usually characterized as some kind of technical failing of grammatical norms or linguistic effect (*śabda*). Otherwise, they are usually expressed either in terms of being detrimental to the meaning (*artha*) and emotional tenor (*rasa*) or, as in several cases with the *Naiṣadhīya*, on account of their being some violation of poetic conventions (*kavi-saṅketa*) or popular notions (*prasiddhi*). One *Naiṣadhīya* commentator, the seventeenth-century Viśveśvara (better known as Gāgābhaṭṭa), in his commentary *Rākāgama* (The Approach of the Full-Moon Day) on Jayadeva Pīyūṣavarṣa's celebrated twelfth-century poetics manual *Candrāloka* (Moonlight), frequently uses *Naiṣadhīya* verses to exemplify figures of speech but, in some notable cases, to exemplify cases where the poet could have avoided criticism for his usage by doing things differently. For example, Gāgābhaṭṭa sees a flaw in Śrīharṣa's word construction (*pada-doṣa*) in verse 1.2. He argues that it has "a seed of being flawed" (*dūṣakatā-bīja*) because it obscures the clarity of the image intended by the poet. First I give Śrīharṣa's text and translation of 1.2, followed by Gāgābhaṭṭa's proposed emendation:

rasaiḥ kathā yasya sudhāvadhīraṇī nalaḥ sa bhūjānir abhūd guṇā 'dbhutaḥ/
suvarṇa-daṇḍaika-sitātapatrita-jvalat-pratāpāvali-kīrti-maṇḍalaḥ//

Nala was the husband of the earth, the king,
a man whose virtues were astounding.
He left a line of blazing splendor
that served as the golden staff
and an orb of fame
that was the single white royal umbrella.
His stories, filled with many *rasas*,
excel the divine nectar.

In order to remove the perceived *pada-doṣa* in Śrīharṣa's rendering, Gāgābhaṭṭa alters the verse as follows:

rasaiḥ kathā yasya sudhāvadhīraṇī nalena tenāśu kṛtaṃ mahī-bhujā /
jvalat-pratāpāvali-kīrti-maṇḍalaṃ suvarṇa-daṇḍaika-sitāta-patritam //

Nala, ruler of the earth,
made the orb of his fame—
with its line of blazing splendor—
serve as his single white umbrella and golden staff.
His stories, filled with many *rasas*,
excel the divine nectar.

Here, Gāgābhaṭṭa dissolves Śrīharṣa's *bahuvrīhi* compound because he believes that, as it stands, the compound confuses what is being predicated and what is being modified. He correctly identifies that *suvarṇa-daṇḍaika-sitātapatrita* ("a single white royal umbrella and a golden staff") modifies the description of Nala as *pratāpāvali-kīrti-maṇḍala* (that Nala who had an "orb of fame with a line of blazing splendor"). Gāgābhaṭṭa's version, accordingly, separates the elements in the compound and reorients the grammatical subject (the instrumental case *mahi-bhujā* for the nominative case *bhū-jāniḥ*) more clearly to capture the poet's intended sense.[13]

While he averts the perceived *pada-doṣa*, the emendations Gāgābhaṭṭa suggests in the second, third, and fourth quarters of the verse essentially mute the dazzling alliterative effects Śrīharṣa's verse achieves. Thus, the assonance created by the repetition of the phoneme *bhu/bhū* in the second quarter of Śrīharṣa's verse (*sa bhūjānir abhūd guṇā 'dbhutaḥ*) is lost in Gāgābhaṭṭa's reworking, as is the sound effect of the third and fourth quarters by creating two compounds and reconfiguring the original order of the words to replace the sonically effective singular one in Śrīharṣa's text (*jvalat-pratāpāvali-kīrti-maṇḍalaṃ* and *suvarṇa-daṇḍaika-sitāta-patritam* for *suvarṇa-daṇḍaika-sitātapatrita-jvalat-pratāpāvali-kīrti-maṇḍalaḥ*). Two points can be made here. First, Gāgābhaṭṭa's remarks illuminate the kind of immersion a Sanskrit commentator has in the broader literary culture of the source poem. Along with the poet and the scribe, the commentator clearly played an important intermediary role in not only being a reader of the text but also having an important part in *writing* the text. He thus feels comfortable suggesting emendations to the text as long as they are consonant with improving the poem's stature among literary critics. Here, therefore, the production and consumption of the text, its *writing* and *reading*, do not constitute distinctive realms for him.

The second significant issue is that of the critique that such editorial work opens itself up to, whereby the commentator violates one aspect of the poet's probable aesthetic intentions ultimately to satisfy the *commentator's* aesthetic intentions for the poem. Gāgābhaṭṭa disciplines Śrīharṣa's verse by bringing it into line with a more grammatically acceptable usage. His remark, therefore, from a strictly logical point of view, is well taken. However, the commentator's version effectively strips Śrīharṣa's original of its alliterative expressivity and also minimizes the complexity that the poet strives to achieve in this and many other verses of his poem. The *effect* of the verse on the audience is fundamentally altered by the emendation, despite the fact that the basic semantic sense is kept intact.

COUNTERCRITIQUES TO EMENDATION

It is also clear, however, from some strident critiques against this practice that not all commentators approved of emending the poet's work without due caution. The fifteenth-century commentator Gadādhara is an excellent example of such a commentator, as revealed by his extensive discussion about text-critical practices concerning the first two verses (1.1 and 1.2) of the *Naiṣadhīya*:

That Nala was a treasure-house of resplendence,
a great and dazzling festival,
the orbit of whose fame is represented by
the white royal umbrella.
Drinking in the stories of this earth protector,
even gods do not care as much for the divine nectar.

Nala was the husband of the earth, the king,
a man whose virtues were astounding.
    He left a trail of blazing majesty
    that served as the golden scepter,
and an orbit of fame
    that was the single white royal umbrella.
His stories, filled with many *rasas*,
excel the divine nectar.

We notice here that the first and second verses are strikingly similar from a structural, semantic, and stylistic point of view. In fact, the basic sense is virtually the same: to hear stories about Nala trumps even the desire to feed on ambrosia. Commentators, however, who have been disciplined by poetics prescriptions to find fault with repetitions of words and redundancy of ideas (*punar-ukti*), were clearly troubled by verses that seem to repeat the same idea in a slightly different way (even more troubling for them, perhaps, is that these are the first verses of the poem!). We know this because Gadādhara, two centuries after the first commentaries on *Naiṣadhīya* emerged, felt the need to articulate a feisty defense of the poet's usage against those who, citing it as an interpolation, wanted to edit out the second verse altogether.

What follows here is Gadādhara's exposition. He first differentiates the first verse from the second one in order to offer an explanation for the apparent discrepancy:

> In desiring to compose this poem, this poet's first thought must have been: "What heroic king existed in this world, who was stoic and yet charming? I will make such a person the hero of my story, which will surpass even the taste of nectar. Because he was thinking about this again and again for a long time and devotedly practicing the *cintāmaṇi mantra*, it is said that an answer flashed forth. And having telepathically received the first verse beginning with the phrase "Drinking in," he composed the poem out loud. The point of all this is to say that in doing so, the poet is saying: "I crown as the hero of this story a king named Nala, who in the Golden Age was adorned with virtue upon virtue."[14]

In attempting to establish that the second verse (1.2) is not a repetition of the first verse (1.1), Gadādhara then argues that the first verse satisfies the requirement of being an invocatory verse to spread auspiciousness (*maṅgalācaraṇa*) while the second verse deals with the subject matter of the poem (*vastu-nirdeśa*). As discussed earlier, the presupposition is that texts on poetics typically prescribed that the first verse either be a *maṅgalācaraṇa* or a *vastu-nirdeśa*. It is probable that some critics during Gadādhara's time argued that the first and second verses both served the identical purpose of *vastu-nirdeśa*, and, therefore, either the poet is guilty of repetition or the second verse must be an interpolation. Gadādhara methodically deconstructs this argument in defense of the poet's usage by first providing a summary of the various opinions on the matter:

> In the second verse, beginning with the words "stories filled with many *rasas*," the poem's subject matter (*vastu-nirdeśa*) is indicated. The poet reiterates the same meaning, indicated in the first verse, in a different style. Some, however, say that the first verse itself presents the story's subject matter and that the second verse is a variant reading. Others say that this second verse supplements the idea from the previous verse, but that they share a singular purpose. Calling it a variant reading only means that the idea in the first verse is established because of the second verse. It is akin to the notion that a kisser becomes a kisser after there is a kiss. This is the line of thinking, then: the phrase "husband of the earth" (*bhūpāla* or *bhūjāni*) in the second verse is a synonym for "earth protector" (*kṣiti-rakṣin*) in the first verse. In both phrases, the second element of the compound predicate essentially indicates the word *king*, which is the subject of the story. That king from the past was Nala, drinking in whose stories even gods do not care much for the divine nectar. Thus the second verse supports the first.[15]

Here, Gadādhara cites three different opinions, either of his own creation or those expressed by actual commentators: first, that the second verse is a roundabout repetition of the first and, therefore, can be safely eliminated; second, that 1.2 is an equally valid variant reading that can be exchanged for 1.1; or third, that 1.2 is a continuation of 1.1 and, therefore, should be semantically understood as a single verse. The first two opinions are straightforward. Gadādhara skillfully explains the third opinion by saying that 1.1 and 1.2 relate and share a single meaning as two kissers relate in the act of kissing, that the two verses are different but become a unit when they encounter each other.[16] Thus, both verses share the intention of being a *vastu-nirdeśa*, or mentioning of the subject matter (i.e., King Nala). Gadādhara further elaborates on the anonymous commentator's view by citing that the specific mention of the concept "king" described as protector (*rakṣin*) in 1.1 and husband (*jāni*) in 1.2 signals a unity of purpose: to tell the story of King Nala.

Now, Gadādhara moves to his own opinion, which is an extension of the latter discussion: that the poet could not logically sustain the desired expression in a single verse and so divided it into two verses, whereby 1.1 primarily fulfills the role of being an invocatory verse, while 1.2 touches upon the subject matter. Therefore, he concludes, both verses are necessary, and the poet's usage should not be faulted:

> The name of the hero is already provided for (*anūdyatva*) in the ancient story literature (*purāṇa*)—"There was a king named Suratha." It is provided in poetic texts (*kāvya*)—"There was a king of the mountains named Himālaya." A name is also used in ordinary expressions—"In the town of Kāmpilya, there was a brāhmaṇa named Viṣṇuśarman." And so, here in the second verse (1.2), it reads "There was a king named Nala." However, if one holds Nala to be a predicate (*vidheyatva*) in 1.2 that does not indicate the subject matter of the poem, then it would be inauspicious, so to speak. On the other hand, if there is a specified predicate too closely joined to a related word in the utterance, then there would immediately arise an ambiguity whose deciphering would produce a great deal of stress on the reader.
>
> Therefore, a predicate dissimilar from the one in 1.2 has been employed in 1.1, whereby the uselessness of nectar to the gods has been conveyed as the predicate, that is to say, the cause for the gods' disregarding of nectar is the presence of Nala stories. Sensing that this idea might be misconstrued, the poet has purposefully extended the expression of his desired meaning in 1.2—under the guise of a variant reading. And, therefore, in doing this, the gifted poet exhibits the profound maturity of his poetic efforts. Otherwise, why would this all-knowing poet not embed in a single verse the primary subject matter in an uncontroversial and normative manner? My comments are based on my own learning and common sense. Only the poet knows the secret truth of the matter. A devoted reader only gives his own opinion.[17]

Gadādhara's comment at the end, that the poet could have made things easier, suggests that he too is intuitively uneasy with Śrīharṣa's usage but, upon reflection on the matter, finds it justifiable. His explanation is in keeping with the legendary notion that even the mention of the

Nala story (the predicate of 1.1, according to Gadādhara) drives away all inauspiciousness.[18] The last bit in Gadādhara's comments again reveals a formulaic reverence toward the text shared by many Sanskrit commentators. Overall, however, his meta-critical discussion is an unusual occurrence in Sanskrit commentary writing. It provides us with a glimpse into an important aspect of text-critical practices in early-modern India and sheds light on the nature of oral debate during this period that must have occasioned these formal exegetical statements.

As Gadādhara's comments suggest, compared with other *mahākāvya*, text-critical scholarship on the *Naiṣadhīya* has shown an inordinately strong inclination to emend or erase perceived repetitions in received versions of Śrīharṣa's poem. Commentators use various expressions to highlight an alleged interpolation or cite textual difficulties. For example, regarding certain verses (7.87, for example), Cāṇḍupaṇḍita says, "Some do not read this verse" (*kecid imaṃ ślokaṃ na paṭhanti*), whereas Jinarāja writes that "this verse is a variant reading of the preceding one and others do not even read it" (*pāṭhāntaram idam. evam anye 'pi na paṭhanti*). Nārāyaṇa says: "Even though it is a variant verse, it is generally commented upon" (*iti ślokāntaram api vyākhyāta-prāyam*).[19] Commentators also remark on the absence of certain verses in some manuscripts, as they seemingly have an awareness of alternate readings in other manuscripts.[20] Scribes are also invested in the process of forming a critical text of their authors.[21] All of these editors, however, walk a fine line. While open to emendation, they are also wary of falsifying their poet's usage without due consideration. While they are judicious in doing so, in the process of settling upon a valid reading, occasionally the *Naiṣadhīya* commentators necessarily engage in acts of emendation that could be contested. Such acts point to a complex understanding of author and text and an awareness of their potential to influence subsequent readings of the text. Once they perceive that some undesirable textual usage must have been interpolated, commentators swiftly eliminate, alter, or at the least draw attention to their inherited reading.

Gadādhara's comment, however, is a warning to his fellow commentators. Often, in their zeal to emend perceived flaws, along the lines of their *alaṅkāraśāstra* training, commentators (like in the case of Gāgābhaṭṭa discussed earlier in this chapter) fail to take notice of Śrīharṣa's unconventional stylistic tendencies. For example, throughout the *Naiṣadhīya*, Śrīharṣa characteristically exhausts his imaginative conceits, either by clothing them in new language or by elaborating on their multiple possibilities. This often leads him to repeat the same thought in a different way over the span of two verses. From the point of view of a rigid poetics, however, the *Naiṣadhīya* is to be faulted for this urge to repeat and for a series of other violations of normative poetic practice. Jani, who synthesizes a series of these breaches of grammaticality in Śrīharṣa's poem ranging from unaccounted-for forms to irregular compounds to incorrect declensions, demonstrates the persistence of the *alaṅkāraśāstra*'s influence on literary criticism in the modern period.[22] The poet himself shows awareness of this fact about his poem and, in characteristic fashion, includes a verse (22.82) that chides fussy critics to accept that popular custom frequently overrules the presumptuous rules of prescriptive grammar:

> Popular usage of words by poets (*loka*)
> upstages the vanity of grammarians,
> as actual usage trumps the rules governing it.
> So it is that the word for "moon" is *śaśin*,
> because it supposedly harbors a rabbit (*śaśa*).
> The moon is not called an "antelope" (*mṛgin*)
> even though many say it possesses spots
> that resemble those of an antelope (*mṛga*).

The point here is that, according to grammar, the same grammatical suffix should apply in the case of both "moon" and "antelope." Popular usage, however, trumps grammatical prescription. Nārāyaṇa explains that Śrīharṣa's point here is that grammar should be *subservient* to popular usage, as logic dictates that a counterproposition would lead to a host of unwanted fallacies (*doṣa*).[23] Clearly, this is not a perspective universally shared by many of the grammarian-scholars who comment on his poem. Nārāyaṇa suggests that Śrīharṣa means *himself* when he refers to "popular usage" (*eṣaḥ kavir lokaḥ prabhuḥ*). Again, in the ninth canto (9.37), through Damayantī's words to Nala (disguised as a messenger), Śrīharṣa makes a reference to the attitude a commentator has for the author, perhaps making a subtle plea for sensitivity on the part of his own critics:

> I am merely a mortal woman.
> How can I give a fitting response to the eloquent gods?
> You should be like a commentator,
> not an adversary, of this series of aphorisms,
> the words spoken by me.

Śrīharṣa's awareness of criticism swirling around his work marks an important moment in the history of the genre. While he is poised to use the massive resources of a developed poetic and linguistic tradition, Śrīharṣa has also inherited the burdens of centuries of convention and tired metaphor, some of which he naturally and self-consciously transgresses, renovates, or completely reimagines.

As Gadādhara implies, however, commentators often do not see it this way and challenge their inherited readings, without necessarily saying anything unseemly about the poet. Another illuminating example of this phenomenon, along with the critical debate it spawns, concerns verses 10.41 and 10.42. The commentators' handling of these two verses is especially instructive of the Sanskrit exegete's diverse text-critical practices around issues of suspected interpolation. During Damayantī's husband-choosing ceremony (*svayaṃvara*), Śrīharṣa imagines that the gathered kings collectively expressed their envy for Nala in a mocking tone. He explains this thought across two verses. Both verses play on the words for ordinal numbers "first," "second," and "third" (*prathamā, dvitīyā, tṛtīyā, ādya, dvaita, tṛtīyatā*):

10.41:

The jealous kings belittled him under the pretext of praising him:
"Has the new (*prathama*) moon itself incarnated onto the earth?"
"Is he a second (*dvitīya*) god of love?"
"Is he a third (*tṛtīya*) Aśvin?"

10.42:

Those jealous ones exaggeratedly praised him:
"He is the original (*ādya*) incarnation of the moon on the earth."
"This youth is a second (*dvaita*) god of love."
"He is a third (*tṛtīyatā*) embodiment of the (two) Aśvins."

Both verses ostensibly share the same code: jealous kings sarcastically identifying Nala as undeserving of the high regard others have of him. Both cite the kings' strategy of saying one thing and meaning another: praising Nala superficially but expressing their underlying contempt. The two verses reveal subtle differences, however, on three different levels. First is on the most obvious level of diction: the use of different words to describe identically the kings' expression of Nala's uniqueness (in 10.41: *prathama/sudhāṃśu*, *dvitīyā/smara*, and *tṛtīyā/dasra*; in 10.42: *ādya/vidhu*, *dvaita/rati-vallabha*, and *tṛtīyatā/nāsatya*). The second level is structural: Whereas the kings frame their insincere praise for Nala in the form of questions in 10.41, they make declaratory statements in 10.42. The third level is semantic. In 10.41, Śrīharṣa explicitly states that the kings "belittled him" under the pretext of praising him, while in 10.42 the verbal surface only implies the kings' contempt, which can be inferred from their affected, exaggerated praise for Nala.

The reaction of the commentators to these two verses is varied. The existence of verse 10.42 is not even acknowledged by commentators Vidyādhara and Jinarāja, presumably on the grounds that it is an interpolation. Cāṇḍupaṇḍita very briefly comments on verse 10.42 and makes no mention of its repetitive theme, explaining simply that both verses are expressions of "false praise" (*vyāja-stuti*). Nārāyaṇa is clearly not happy with the second verse's inclusion in his inherited text, patiently offering a spare remark on it (on the word *dvaitam* meaning "second") and then swiftly concluding that "this verse is redundant because of its expressing a previous meaning" (*ayaṃ ślokaḥ gatārthatvāt punar-uktaḥ*). The commentator Mallinātha's gloss on this verse bears some reflection. Mallinātha seems, at first, to distinguish 10.42 from 10.41 by reading in the last quarter of 10.42 "*kila matsaraiḥ*" instead of "*kṛta-matsaraiḥ*." If it is "*kṛta-matsaraiḥ*," then little doubt remains that Śrīharṣa is simply rephrasing the same idea from the previous verse, that the jealous kings are mocking Nala. However, by suggesting that the word *kila*, which commonly expresses contempt, is synonymous here with *khalu*, which implies certainty (*taiḥ stutaḥ kila stutaḥ khalu*), Mallinātha seems to be opening up the possibility that the kings are actually praising Nala, thus adding the suggestion that Nala's greatness compels even enemies to respect him. It is notable that none of the commentators ask why anyone would possibly interpolate the second verse here.

SCRIBAL INTERVENTIONS

Mallinātha's concluding comment on verse 10.42, however, which is redacted in two alternative versions, reveals a curious perspective that very assiduously attempts to spare the poet from the charge of being repetitive. One reading (in the Krishnadas Academy edition) of his gloss concludes that "even though [this verse] is a repetition of the previous verse, *because the poet wrote it*, it is a correct, established reading just like the prior verse is established as correct" (*pūrva-ślokena punar-uktam api kavinā* **likhitatvāt** *sthitaṃ pūrva-vat*). A second reading of Mallinātha's gloss reads that "even though [this verse] is a repetition of the previous verse, *on account of the poet's greed*, it is a correct, established reading just as the prior verse is established as correct" (*pūrva-ślokena punar-uktam api kavinā* **kavi-lobhāt** *sthitaṃ pūrva-vat*).[24] By the poet's "greed" in the second reading of Mallinātha's gloss, one assumes that Mallinātha understands the poet to be trying to milk too much from his conceit by extending it over two verses.

It is perhaps indicative of the interrelational fluidity of the *mahākāvya*'s textual tradition that a scribe, whose provenance is uncertain, thought better to change the reading of Mallinātha's comment, from "*kavi-lobhāt*" ("on account of the poet's greed") to "*kavinā likhitatvāt*" ("because the poet wrote it") or vice versa. Goodall and Isaacson reflect on similar types of "text confusion" in a note on Vallabhadeva's commentary on Kālidāsa's *Raghuvaṃśa* 1.83 (*prasraveṇa* for *prasnavena*), where they write that such confusion perhaps resulted from "the paleographic similarity of the two words or from mental association" and ultimately led to various scribal modifications to make sense of the terms. The case here is slightly more difficult to attribute to either of these causes, however, and requires some other explanation.[25] One point is certain: scribes who copied the manuscripts of *Naiṣadhīya* commentators frequently express their own intelligence, editorial or generally scholastic, to bring about or reinforce a plausible reading whenever necessary. For instance, a scribe of an early fifteenth-century manuscript of Cāṇḍupaṇḍita's commentary adds lengthy discussions to the manuscript on topics ranging from grammar to astronomy to poetics, presumably to fill in gaps left by the otherwise diligent exegesis of Cāṇḍupaṇḍita; the scribe is identified as Joshi Narapati, an Audicya brāhmaṇa who apparently copied the commentary "for the study of Mahannārāyaṇa and others, including the sons of the minister Bhābhala of the Nāgara caste."[26] Joshi Narapati's manuscript contrasts with another very old manuscript (1386 CE) of Cāṇḍupaṇḍita's commentary, composed by a scribe who was not a professionally trained scholar at all but rather a self-described "weapons dealer" (*silāra-sarapha* = *śiloha-śarāpha*); this manuscript, which, according to J. Jani, contains no additional material, was copied for the study of a certain Malik Mufarriha (Farḥat al-Mulk) at Vejalpur. Farḥat al-Mulk was a governor of Gujarat during the late-fourteenth century and apparently a student and patron of Sanskrit literature.[27] Similarly, at the end of the nineteenth canto, a scribe of Īśānadeva's commentary (different from the one noted above that supplies missing sections from other commentaries) remarks that a folio is missing in the manuscript of the last six verses (19.61–66) and that he wrote it up himself with the help of his teacher Vyāsa Kālidāsa.[28] Examples such as this shed insight into the readership of the *Naiṣadhīya* during these early centuries of its history and about the transmitting agents and the commissioning milieu within which they operated. We glean complex processes of textual criticism that involve a symbiotic relationship between the foundational text, its commentaries, and the scribal practices that govern their preservation.

Returning to the above example, regardless of the "correct" reading of Mallinātha's comment, the two versions highlight dual tensions in the commentator's (or scribe's) consciousness—whether to tolerate perceived flaws in the text or to rationalize the poet's genius—and the attempt to reconcile the two by offering criticism while also trying to construct a perspective imputed to the poet. In other words, the options are that the audience should accept the two verses as genuine because Śrīharṣa wrote them *or* that one should accept the two verses as genuine because it happens to be the poet's style to repeat ideas. Looking at this example objectively, one may simply conclude that Śrīharṣa is playing with the same idea using different nominal items and syntactical constructions. Most of the commentators, however, seem unable to accept this position. On a certain level, there may be reason to sympathize with them. In a poem with as much wordplay as the *Naiṣadhīya*, it is indeed difficult to pin down a "correct" text when one reading may *seem* accurate but is actually not *necessarily* accurate. Educated in the science of poetics, commentators seem to have reacted with intolerance toward any kind of apparent redundancy from one verse to the next. They, therefore, resorted to labeling a suspect verse as interpolated and removed it altogether or called it a variant reading in their own preferred way. Many commentators before the sixteenth century also resisted celebrating the poem's proclivity toward polyvalence. These and many other text-critical decisions of the commentators appear ultimately as strained efforts to fix the character of the poem. They aim to discipline the poem, primarily making it amenable to their trained expectations rather than to accept it the way it is and instead adjust their expectations of it.

IS THE *NAIṢADHĪYA* COMPLETE?

Another important feature of the text-critical discourse about the *Naiṣadhīya* are arguments that the poem is unfinished. Fixing the extent of the poem is an editorial decision that has dominated the attention of both earlier commentators and contemporary scholars. Spanning twenty-two cantos and some 2,760 verses, the *Naiṣadhīya* is one of the longest *mahākāvyas* available in Sanskrit literature, with only Ratnākara's *Haravijaya* and Vimaladevagaṇi's *Hīrasaubhāgya* being longer. Yet, some readers are distressed by the fact that Śrīharṣa ends the poem where he does, with Nala describing the moonrise to Damayantī. Sometimes their dissatisfaction has been source-critical, finding Śrīharṣa's logic in adapting the Nala theme to his *mahākāvya* lacking the appropriate closure. Others have cited internal evidence to suggest that the poem was meant to continue on but was stopped short for some reason or other. Yet others have made claims to seeing or hearing of a lost set of verses and cantos that somehow failed to enter the mainstream redaction of the poem. Some have themselves supplied what they gather to have been the unfinished project of Śrīharṣa. These kinds of critical reactions resonate with similar debates about other classic *mahākāvyas* as well, most notably Kālidāsa's *Raghuvaṃśa* and *Kumārasambhava*.[29]

For most of the *Naiṣadhīya*'s early commentators, twenty-two cantos seem to have been enough to serve what they see as Śrīharṣa's artistic vision. In the thirteenth century, Vidyādhara apparently was reacting to circulating debates about the extent of the *Naiṣadhīya* during his time by making the following observation in the preface to his commentary:

> One may ask why Śrīharṣa has ended his poem at a particular point in the Nala narrative when it would have been more appropriate to tell the entire story the way it is told in the *Mahābhārata*. Fine, this perspective has merit. But a poem is meant to attract an audience and a poet follows his own emotions to attract the hearts of his readership. And this is the part of the Nala narrative that Śrīharṣa found most attractive. Therefore, he ends his poem where he ends it.[30]

For Vidyādhara and most *Naiṣadhīya* commentators, arguing against Śrīharṣa's choices and the integrity of his composition seems to have made little sense. Sixteenth-century Nārāyaṇa notably remarks at the end of the first canto (1.144) that "this poem's favored word (*aṅka*) is *ānanda* (spiritual bliss) because the poet uses the word in the final verses of all the cantos." He follows up this comment by introducing one of the final verses of the poem (22.148) with the short sentence, "Now Śrīharṣa desires to end the poem by having the benedictory blessing come from the mouth of his hero." Indeed, verse 22.148 takes the form of Nala's benediction to the moon:

> The glorious moon is a big round pot
> with thousands of holes made by the demon Rāhu,
> a many-toothed machine that relentlessly gnaws at it.
> From the holes of that golden pot-moon flow moonbeams—
> cool, glistening, like nectar.
> May that divine moon be for our happiness at the festive time,
> when marriage is consecrated with spiritual bliss—
> when Rati the beloved bride joins with Kāmadeva the love god,
> on whose bow sit arrows made of flowers.

The end of Nārāyaṇa's commentary on this verse again focuses on the use of the word *ānanda* ("spiritual bliss") and explains why Śrīharṣa ends his poem where he does, as Vidyādhara did several centuries earlier:

> By employing the word *ānanda* ("spiritual bliss") in the context of the benediction "May the divine moon be for our happiness," Śrīharṣa signals the end of the *Naiṣadhīya*. Although the second half of Nala's story may be narrated in the *Mahābhārata*, it lacks *rasa* by describing the fall of the hero. Poetry is supposed to culminate in joy for a receptive audience. Here, because the second half of the story is marked by the presence of a disruption of *rasa*, Śrīharṣa does not depict it.[31]

According to Nārāyaṇa, because the last verse is benedictory in nature (the use of the word *ānanda*) and appropriate to Śrīharṣa's overarching aesthetic intentions (the focus on the *śṛṅgāra rasa*), the poem ends here.[32]

While Nārāyaṇa and Vidyādhara before him represent many commentators' acceptance of where Śrīharṣa ends his poem, many contemporary scholars reject their conclusions. A.N. Jani, for example, points to Śrīharṣa's own suggestion of future events found in the *Mahābhārata* version and sees the introduction of the character Kali in the seventeenth canto of the *Naiṣadhīya* as strong evidence to suggest an incomplete text.[33] He also mentions another report that, on the basis of an "old list of some manuscripts published by Muni Jinavijayaji," some have speculated on the existence of an extensive (though lost) commentary by Kamalākaragupta, reputed to be Śrīharṣa's grandson; the claimed existence of this commentary indicates for Jani a temptation to "conjecture that it might be dealing with the sequel [of the *Naiṣadhīya*] also, which is lost to us at present."[34] Jani also reports some "fantastic" stories of twentieth-century Sanskrit paṇḍitas who claimed to have seen manuscripts or passages from a lost text:

> N.K. Bhaṭṭācārya informs us that Pt. Rāmagopāla Smṛtibhūṣaṇa of Banaras had witnessed with his own eyes a manuscript of the sequel in Uriya character with an Uriya pupil of his named either Dāmodara or Rudranārāyaṇa (he did not recollect which) and that he remembered two verses (one in full and the other in part) from that sequel. The same scholar refers to the late revered MM Rākhāladāsa Nyāyaratna who too used to quote a half verse that, according to him, belonged to the *Naiṣadha* but is not found in the extant poem.[35]

Another theory rests on an anachronistic and confused account by a nineteenth-century commentator named Acyutarāya, who claims in his auto-commentary on a text called the *Sāhityasāra* (Essence of Literature) that Śrīharṣa's *Naiṣadhīya* had one hundred cantos. Jani clarifies, however, that Acyutarāya, conflating details found in a sentence from Mammaṭa's *Kāvyaprakāśa*, mistakenly "ascribes the authorship of the *Naiṣadhīya* to some Dhāvaka," a poet who meditated on the *cintāmaṇi mantra* and, according to Acyutarāya, sold the poem to a King Harṣa by first changing the epilogue verses of each *Naiṣadhīya* canto to read the king's name. Acyutarāya is clearly confusing the detail from the *Kāvyaprakāśa*, where a certain poet named Dhāvaka (probably synonymous with Bāṇabhaṭṭa) is said to have earned riches from his patron, King Harṣa of Kanauj (seventh century CE).[36] Quoting much of Acyutarāya's commentary on the subject, A.N. Jani rejects the claim but still holds to his contention that the *Naiṣadhīya* is incomplete: "This tradition at least proves that the *Naiṣadhīya* had more than twenty-two cantos if not exactly one hundred."[37] Other indications that the text might be incomplete are often couched in the fact that there are also original creative texts written by later poets to perhaps fill the perceived void left by Śrīharṣa's version of the Nala narrative, works such as Vandārubhaṭṭa's seventeenth-century *Uttaranaiṣadha*.

Much of the logic behind the search for lost traditions of "the rest of the *Naiṣadhīya*" is conveyed in philological terms but seems to be largely grounded in an impulse not to accept Śrīharṣa's dismemberment of the "original" *Mahābhārata* narrative of Nala's life into a few select episodes. We can infer that this unease with the extent of the *Naiṣadhīya* must have been a very early type of response to Śrīharṣa's poem as the early Sanskrit commentators, like Vidyādhara, as well as the later Nārāyaṇa, seem to feel compelled to answer charges of an incomplete text. They are at pains to demonstrate the integrity of the poem and that Śrīharṣa's choice to end his narrative with the rising and setting of the moon at the end of the married couple's honeymoon is significant and emotionally fulfilling. While not squarely joined to their efforts to determine a critical text, the commentators naturally wonder about the motivations behind a poet's choice to modify a venerated narrative tradition like the *Mahābhārata*. In the case of the *Naiṣadhīya*, their explanations seem to be solely framed around aesthetic concerns. Nārāyaṇa, like Vidyādhara, argues that had Śrīharṣa continued the traditional narrative of Nala and Damayantī as recorded in the *Mahābhārata*, the poet would have in effect violated his own purpose (stated in the epilogue verse to the first canto) for writing the poem: to explore the *śṛṅgāra rasa* in an unprecedented and artful manner.

CONCLUDING OBSERVATIONS

As an extension of their role as interpreters, the editorial tasks of Sanskrit commentators are important to consider for students of the *mahākāvya*. Indeed, the poem's reception hinges as much on the final form of the text as it does on the ultimate function its interpretation plays in any given reading community. Text-critical decisions are guided by, and play a major role in guiding, attitudes about the poem and its poet's style. The *Naiṣadhīya* tradition, especially as it develops from the fifteenth century onward, proves to be an excellent case study for this relationship between the hermeneutic and the editorial functions of the commentator precisely because, as discussed in this chapter, no other *mahākāvya* has as many variant readings as the *Naiṣadhīya*. Furthermore, the majority of *Naiṣadhīya* commentators did not agree on a fixed text at various moments. That a relatively late *mahākāvya* like the *Naiṣadhīya* would present so many variant readings seems to be a somewhat unexpected phenomenon, as it is usually older texts with widespread use or broken lines of transmission that present the kinds of textual difficulties faced by commentators of Śrīharṣa's poem. Nevertheless, the diversity of arguments among *Naiṣadhīya* commentators concerning Śrīharṣa's text—about where to smooth over perceived inconsistencies or to leave the inherited reading alone—presents us with an interesting glimpse into the editorial practices of Sanskrit scholars in the second millennium.

Accepting or rejecting certain readings over others implies, as Pollock explains, a "logic of variation" of which we currently have an imperfect understanding as it pertains to most Sanskrit works; nevertheless, he continues, "as for what constitutes the correct or best reading and the criteria for establishing it, scholars then as now differed—and they differed, then as now, on the basis of principles and not whim":

> One of the earliest extant commentators on *kāvya*, Vallabhadeva (fl. 950, Kashmir), often chose a reading on the principle of difficulty and the antiquity such difficulty suggests: "This must be the ancient reading precisely because it is unfamiliar." Or he might combine principles of antiquity and aestheticism: "The old reading in this verse is more beautiful." Yet authenticity has its limits for Vallabha; like other commentators, he will rewrite a verse in order to save his author from a supposed solecism. . . . Generally editor-commentators sought to establish as coherent and authoritative a text as they could on the basis of the materials available to them (*āgata*) rather than conjectured (*kalpita*). Such practical criteria have something to tell us about the model of textuality at work: Some readings are not only objectively more beautiful (*ramya*) than others, or contextually more sensible (*yukta*) or more clearly what is intended by the author (*vivakṣita*), but are also older or more original (*jarat*; *ārṣa*); some may clearly be corruptions (*apapāṭha*) and in need of emendation (*śodhana*), and some are just as clearly interpolations (*prakṣipta*) and must be rejected. Text critical practices of this sort are common among commentaries on not only epics but also *kāvya*.[38]

It may have been the case that older commentators had sources that we no longer have access to (other commentaries, various manuscripts of the poem, knowledge of other works by the poet, etc.) to justify their choice in giving privilege to one reading over another. Perhaps they operated, as Pollock suggests, on the basis of text-critical principles that called for choosing a reading on the basis of its conformance to some defined hierarchy; for example, that a shorter reading (*lectio brevior*) is preferable to a more difficult reading (*lectio difficilior*). Or, it is plausible that commentators made text-related decisions in accordance with emic aesthetic principles, such as *aucitya* (aesthetic propriety) or *rasa*. Unithiri suggests such an understanding by citing the following unattributed statement:

> A modern researcher aims at finding the original reading, irrespective of its grammatical correctness or incorrectness, or relative propriety or impropriety. Ancient Sanskrit commentators, on the other hand, insisted on the choice of the best reading from the available variants, because their emphasis was only on the propriety of a reading in relation to Rasa.[39]

Regardless of the theoretical principles under which they make text-critical observations, the decisions and justifications *Naiṣadhīya* commentators settle on reflect their broader understandings of the text's nature that transformed over time.

While other Sanskrit *mahākāvya* traditions surely present different challenges to editor-commentators, this chapter has shown two problems that have particularly vexed *Naiṣadhīya* commentators since the fifteenth century.[40] Both are peculiar to the *Naiṣadhīya* and, therefore, have become as much part of the poem's reception for centuries as the various types of interpretive modalities described in the previous chapter. The first is managing contradictions between their own expectations as scholars of literature and the poet's distinctive style to repeat ideas across a span of verses. In that Śrīharṣa's practice seems at odds with customary expectations, the second issue is related to the first; rather than the poet's use of language, however, the point of contention centers around the narrative extent of the *Naiṣadhīya*. The first speaks to the poem's excess and the second one to the poem's insufficiency.

The *Naiṣadhīya* commentators' philological approach, in fact, reflects the two axioms for a "new philology" that Spanish philosopher José Ortega y Gasset developed in his essay "The Difficulty of Reading" (1959:1): "Every utterance is deficient—it says less than it wishes to say"; "Every utterance is exuberant—it conveys more than it plans." In his discussion of Ortega y Gasset's axioms, Becker explains: "The modern philologist seeks meaningful interpretations between the inherent deficiencies and exuberance of the texts he studies."[41] As philologists, the *Naiṣadhīya* commentators take on the onus to address both the "deficiencies" and "exuberances" in Śrīharṣa's language. Their ultimate aim is not necessarily to commandeer the direction of the poem's reception but rather to pragmatically steer the audience to an informed position to receive the work with all of its hidden richness and muted insufficiencies.

5 ◈ SECONDARY WAVES OF READING

If the fifteenth-century commentaries consisted mostly of debates about the *Naiṣadhīya*'s textual authenticity and extent, we see in the sixteenth century a shift in attitudes toward the poem. A more or less stable text tradition now established, sixteenth-century commentaries reflect less a culture of competition over fixing the text's interpretation and more an articulation of the poem's semantic polyvalence. Eventually, these exegetical stirrings toward seeking multiplicity in Śrīharṣa's language use led to full-fledged allegorical readings of the *Naiṣadhīya*. These two hermeneutic urges—to *overinterpret* and to *allegorize*—inform related but nevertheless different features of the *Naiṣadhīya* tradition. The commentaries of Nārāyaṇa and Śrīdhara, both from the sixteenth century, were presented in chapter 3 as examples of a peculiar kind of *overinterpretation*. To yield a level of semantic multiplicity unavailable in earlier commentaries, these works utilized well-developed exegetical techniques to convert surface meanings in the poem to more textured forms of significance. These techniques to bring about more than a single significance to words, sentences, and whole texts—broadly understood under the rubric of *śleṣa* (literally, "conjunction" or "embrace")—are described by Bronner as allowing *kāvya* commentators to "re-creat[e] the text thoroughly," where "each new reading yields not so much a different meaning of a given text as a new parallel text with its own set of signifiers."[1] Thus, for example, we saw (in chapter 3) the ways in which Nārāyaṇa used *śleṣa* to reconfigure in radical ways the expected meaning of verse 1.40. Offering alternative ways of resolving the coalescence of sounds across word boundaries (*sandhi*), relying on technical vocabulary and less common usages of otherwise common words, and staying close to the narrative and emotional registers of the situation within which the verse appears, Nārāyaṇa's exegesis essentially remained within the strictures of what the grammatical and generic conventions implied by Śrīharṣa's words would allow.

Śleṣa, however, is different from allegory, in that it does not seek point-to-point correspondences between two levels of meaning available from the surface text's signifiers.[2] Bronner explains the difference:

> Allegorical interpretations typically retain the original set of signifiers and their syntactic relations while explaining the main signifiers, especially the nouns, as encoding a second and symbolic level. A *śleṣa* reading, by contrast, typically involves a metamorphosis of the entire utterance—nouns, verbs, and prepositions—in a way that creates a new sentence with a new vocabulary, a new syntax, and, obviously, a new meaning.[3]

The key point here is that whereas *śleṣa* creates parallel texts, allegory maintains a singular one underscored by a shift in attitude toward its ultimate significance. Also important to recognize is that *śleṣa* may be put in service of allegory and, as in the *Naiṣadhīya*'s case, is often used to justify the poem's essentially allegorical nature. In this chapter, therefore, I present a snapshot of both types of critical engagements (*śleṣa* readings and allegory) as they distinctively relate to historical reading communities of the *Naiṣadhīya*. The first section focuses on how commentators constructed a discrete *śleṣa*-centered reading strategy for the poem built around an episode from the thirteenth canto known as the *Pañcanalīya* (The Episode of the Five Nalas), what Bronner calls the "most famous occurrence of a *śleṣa* section in a poem." This episode (selectively translated later) features Sarasvatī introducing Damayantī to her divine and human suitors—all appearing as Nala and one of whom she must choose—through verbal puzzles built on *śleṣa*. Bronner explains that this chapter in the poem serves as a "meditation on the similarity between the king and the divine—an issue that stands at the heart of *śleṣa* experimentation from the start."[4] Manuscript catalogs confirm the existence of these twenty-two verses composed in the *vasantatilaka* meter as a separate text known as the *Pañcanalīya*.[5] Nārāyaṇa is the first commentator to call the episode by the name *Pañcanalīya*.[6] It seems likely, therefore, that some time in the sixteenth century, it became recognized as a work worthy of studying in its own right, probably as the most prominent treatment of an episode within a plot utilizing *śleṣa* practices.

The second section also addresses the ways in which *śleṣa* reading strategies operated among literary communities of *Naiṣadhīya*—not, however, to create parallel texts but rather to produce a univocal allegorical narrative of the poem. Although it is likely that the seeds of reading the *Naiṣadhīya* as a spiritual allegory began sometime in the sixteenth century (if not earlier), by the nineteenth century, we can unmistakably identify reading communities that chose fundamentally to read *Naiṣadhīya* as a spiritual allegory. In this regard, this chapter discusses two distinct manifestations of this trend. One concerns post-sixteenth-century Sanskrit commentaries' contribution to reading *Naiṣadhīya* allegorically, and the other recapitulates contemporary accounts of reading practices from the nineteenth and twentieth centuries that see the *Naiṣadhīya* as either an allegory of Advaita Vedānta, which maps an individual's movement from a world of diversity and individuation toward a consciousness of universal nonduality, or as a gradual unfolding of the *cintāmaṇi mantra*, the realization of which confers enormous creative powers to the yogi. As shown earlier, Śrīharṣa notably highlights both Advaita and the *cintāmaṇi mantra* at various points in the *Naiṣadhīya*. Though they sometimes have historically distinct trajectories in the reception of *Naiṣadhīya* among "religious" readers, both also converged at some point to fortify the impression for some audiences that the *Naiṣadhīya* was indeed, fundamentally, an allegory and could be read simultaneously as both an Advaita and Tāntrika allegory.

COMMENTARY ON THE "FIVE NALAS" EPISODE

The *Pañcanalīya*'s importance in the reception history of the *Naiṣadhīya* cannot be overemphasized. It is the one chapter of the poem that is consistently remembered today by those who have even a faint acquaintance with Śrīharṣa's poem. One is impelled to assume that these twenty-two verses from the thirteenth canto were abstracted as a separate work by the sixteenth century precisely because they highlighted, in a nutshell, Śrīharṣa's extraordinary command of the Sanskrit language and *śleṣa* technique. Indeed, a verse from the fourteenth canto explicitly links the special powers of a poet with the ability to express double meaning.[7] The *Pañcanalīya*'s popularity may also rest on the fact that it *requires* commentary fully to appreciate the parallel texts being created by the poet. All but one of the twenty-two verses refer to one of the four Vedic gods

(Damayantī's suitors disguised as Nala) in simultaneity with the actual human king Nala or vice versa; the final verse—in a remarkable crescendo to the episode—narrates a description of all five characters at once. In total, out of the eighteen, five verses apparently refer to Indra,[8] and four apparently describe Agni, Yama, Varuṇa, and Nala, respectively. The eighteenth verse (13.34) narrates all five together. As apparent from the length of their discussion, commentators obviously relished this episode, and its transmission as a discrete text may have served its use as a pedagogical tool for students of *mahākāvya.*

To give an idea of the kind of interpretive difficulty Damayantī encounters, along with the reader, in Sarasvatī's puzzling descriptions of each of the four divine suitors—Indra, Agni, Yama, and Varuṇa—I translate here several verses from the *Pañcanalīya*. Mallinātha economically explains the *śleṣa* involved in each, juxtaposing the parallel readings in linear fashion. Nārāyaṇa, by contrast, sets apart the one reading (describing the god) from the other (describing Nala); this permits him to elucidate, in Nārāyaṇa's characteristic fashion, alternative ways of reading the *śleṣa*. The translation that follows reflects the points where Mallinātha's and Nārāyaṇa's commentaries converge. Where relevant, I provide Nārāyaṇa's alternative explanations to demonstrate the ways in which his commentary sees these verses as a site for deeper reading. The other commentaries I consulted more or less follow Mallinātha and Nārāyaṇa's gloss. Here is the first verse (13.3) that ostensibly describes Indra, king of gods:

REFERRING TO INDRA

Excellent woman, what shall
I say about him? His power
defeated the demonic enemy Bala.
He was assisted by Ganeśa and Viṣṇu,
whose splendor on the battlefield
took the form of the demons' fear.

REFERRING TO NALA

Excellent woman, what shall I say
about the son of Vīrasena?
Defeating powerful enemies,
his bravery combines with the
aromatic discharge streaming
down the faces of his army of war
elephants, to generate a special
splendor on the battlefield.

This verse sets the tone for the rest of the episode: The clever linguistic play that allows for the *śleṣa* leads to some rather awkward details that, while not defiant of cultural logic, certainly stretch the imagination.

For example, here Śrīharṣa depicts Ganeśa as a warrior on a battlefield, an unlikely scenario elsewhere in Sanskrit literature. It is also not totally clear how the scent from the secretions of rutting elephants (translators often use the word "ichor") mixes with Nala's bravery to add a distinctive splendor to the field of battle. Nārāyaṇa offers an alternative interpretation to explain the context for Ganeśa and Viṣṇu's assistance to Indra: that their presence did not so much cause fear to the demons as it removed the gods' fear of demons.[9] After five consecutive verses describing Indra, the poet's voice enters (13.8) and explains to the audience that Damayantī could not form a conclusion, neither with her eyes nor with her ears, about whether Sarasvatī was referring to Indra or to Nala.

And so she moved on to Agni, the god of fire. Here is the second of the four verses (13.11) uttered by Sarasvatī to describe the god:

REFERRING TO AGNI	REFERRING TO NALA
[Listen], pretty-eared girl: His flames skillfully swallow firewood, out of which ashes are born. These ashes serve as the body powder even of an ascetic like Lord Śiva.	[Listen], pretty-eared girl: Through many battles, and through the force of his arms, he emerges as the source of an empire. Rival kings come under his fold, and his prosperity garners respect among the very rich and the abject poor.

In this verse, Nārāyaṇa interprets the appellation "pretty-eared girl" (*rucirakarṇi*) as indicating that Damayantī has beautiful ears to listen carefully (*sāvadhānā bhava iti vyajyate*) so as not to choose Agni; if she does not choose carefully, Nārāyaṇa makes explicit, all she will get is ashes or become ashes herself. Nārāyaṇa also alternatively interprets the final line of the text describing Nala as garnering "envy" (*īrṣyā*) from the rich and the poor alike, not love and respect. After the fourth verse describing Agni, the poet tells us (13.14) that Damayantī's confusion about who the true Nala was itself took the form of a *śleṣa*: she could not tell if Sarasvatī had just described Nala or "Not-Nala" (*anala*; also another name for Agni).

Leaving her confusion unattended to for a moment, the princess moves on to the third divine suitor, Yama, the god of death. The following is the second verse (13.17) of the four describing Yama:

REFERRING TO YAMA

It is heard that Saṃjñā, the wife of
the sun, is his mother. Nowhere
is Chāya (another wife of the sun)
named as his mother. Whose life-
breath does this Yama not take
away? It is this very Yama who duly
performed austerities.

REFERRING TO NALA

His bearing and very name
confer well-being to friends.
Such unique beauty cannot be
found anywhere else. To whom
is he not a friend? With self-
control and clean living,
he performed austerities.

Here both Mallinātha and Nārāyaṇa explain that the word *saṃjñā*, which refers to the name of the sun's spouse given in Purānic lore, can mean both "name" and "behavior" or, as I have translated, "bearing." Śrīharṣa cleverly inserts technical vocabulary from the *Yogaśāstra* (the discipline of Yoga) in the text referring to Nala. Here, *yama* does not mean the god of death but the practices of self-control (avoiding violence, avoiding lying, etc.), and *niyama* does not mean "duly" but the practices of clean living (observing purity, remaining content, etc.). Nārāyaṇa adds an interesting detail: in addition to Nala's "unique beauty," the word *chāyā* could also mean, according to the commentator, "a unique style" (*rīti*) of administering to the public welfare.[10] After Sarasvatī concludes the series of four verses describing Yama, the poet again gives voice (13.20) to Damayantī's exasperation with Sarasvatī's *śleṣa* utterances; repeatedly being given a description of both a god and Nala at the same time is, she says, like "crushing a thing already crushed" (*piṣṭa-peśanam*).

Finally, Sarasvatī arrives at the last of the four divinities, the god of waters, Varuṇa. Here is the last of the four verses (13.25) describing him:

REFERRING TO VARUṆA

Look at the river Śona, ministering to
his feet, and the river Sarasvatī,
who constantly waits on him.
Beautiful one, serve the Lord
of Waters! What body of water
is not devoted to him?

REFERRING TO NALA

Look at the rosy complexion of
his feet. The Goddess of Learning
is always present in him. Beautiful
one, serve this lord of the earth!
Who, seeking wealth, is not
devoted to him?

After Sarasvatī concludes with this description of Varuṇa (Nala), the omniscient narrator enters to highlight how *śleṣa* draws out the cryptic quality of the text. A paraphrase of this verse (13.26) reads as follows: "One may acknowledge that it is not unusual that Damayantī was thrown into a maelstrom of doubts regarding who was Nala and who was Varuṇa; but it is really amazing that Varuṇa and Nala also found themselves wondering who Damayantī was!" Nārāyaṇa teases out all of the internal doubts that Nala and Varuṇa experience: Nala's doubt was that Damayantī will choose Varuṇa himself, because he is standing there disguised as Nala; Varuṇa's doubt was that Damayantī may or may not choose him. However, Damayantī, Nārāyaṇa argues, is clear on the matter. Unlike the two males, she is intelligent (*caturā*) and understands *śleṣa* and "crooked speech" (*vakrokti*), and therefore, her doubts will slowly be removed. Recognizing this quality about her, Nala also grows confident that she will understand the situation and eventually choose him; Nārāyaṇa also attributes this confidence to Varuṇa, who also thinks Damayantī will choose him.[11]

After passing by Varuṇa, the goddess of wisdom now comes to the human king Nala and describes him in four verses, each verse also respectively narrating a description of Indra, Agni, Yama, and Varuṇa. Seeing Damayantī still perplexed, as she knew Nala contained the qualities of all four divinities but was not singularly any one of them, Sarasvatī concludes the *Pañcanalīya* with a sharp exhortation for her to now pick the real Nala, who is, in fact, standing right in front of her (13.34):

> Learned lady,
> it cannot be that you do not identify
> **the protector of the earth (*dharājagatyā*)**—
> he is divine but not a god,
> so why not choose him?
> **He is obviously not a reed (*nala*).**
> If you pass him over,
> it would be a calamity.
> Who else are you going to pick?

This verse elicits several pages of exegesis in Nārāyaṇa's commentary. Even the generally succinct Mallinātha is forced to divide up his commentary on this verse into five parts, dealing with each parallel text (*pakṣa*) describing the four Vedic gods and ultimately Nala. The *śleṣa* in this verse primarily focuses on the multiple interpretations available for two elements of the verse (in **boldface** above): the exocentric nominal compound (*bahuvrīhi*) *dharājagatyā* and the tricky wordplay on Nala's name (*nāyaṃ nala*), both of which can be distributed across five separate verses to indicate not only Nala but also the four Vedic deities. As my translation of this verse above indicates, I have suggested that given the context, it is explicitly about Nala. I will now briefly summarize the ways in which the commentaries of Mallinātha and Nārāyaṇa explain the verse to mean Indra, Agni, Yama, and Varuṇa. Other commentaries generally supply some form of what these two commentators give. In general, both agree on the most likely interpretation, with Nārāyaṇa offering a few alternative ones that Mallinātha does not entertain. Here are the meanings that they both agree upon:

ON *DHARĀJAGATYĀ*

Indra: "That one who gives protection by hurling the mountains" [*dhara* = mountains; *aja* = hurler (*ajati* = he hurls); *gati* = protection].[12]
Agni: "That one with a goat for a vehicle who gives protection" [*dhara* = vehicle; *aja* = goat; *gati* = protection].
Yama: "That one whose mode of transport is a buffalo" [*dhara* = mountains; *aja* = hurler (*ajati* = he hurls using hooves (*khura*) and horns) *śṛṅga* = buffalo; *gati* = mode of transport].[13]
Varuṇa: "The one who gives shelter to animate things born on the earth" [*dharā* = earth; *ja* = those who are born (*jāyante*); *gati* = shelter in the sense of giving life in the form of water].
Nala: "The one who protects the people of the earth" [*dharā* = earth; *jagatī* = people; *pati* = protector].

Both commentaries, then, seem to agree with these senses of the compound word *dharājagatyā*. Nārāyaṇa adds for Indra that his "protection" (*gati*) takes the form of his thunderbolt weapon (*vajra*). For Yama, he uses the technique of supplying a dropped letter (*akṣara-cyuta*) to render *dharājagatyā* as *dharmarājagatyā* ("taking the form of the king of Dharma"). Finally, with respect to Varuṇa, he renders *dharā-ja* ("born from the earth") as meaning "medicinal herbs" (*auṣadhi*) and *gati* ("protection, vehicle, path") as "water" (*udaka*), which is the vehicle that bears and moves the earth.

In the first part of his gloss on this verse (13.34), Nārāyaṇa explains that Śrīharṣa marks Damayantī as a "learned" woman (*viduṣī*) to highlight the fact that "she is skilled in ascertaining the cleverness of double-meaning expressions" (*śleṣokti-cāturī-parijñāna-cature*). In a way, the commentator himself must identify with Damayantī, charged as he is with the task of identifying the cryptic double-meanings in the poet's/Sarasvatī's utterances. Bronner explains Damayantī's task as a model reader of Sarasvatī's statements as follows: "The gods will become visually distinguishable from Nala, thus allowing Damayantī to make her choice, only if she can solve the linguistic puzzle Sarasvatī has presented. Sarasvatī's *śleṣa*, then, is not just the literary vehicle of the canto; it is the main event of the chapter, if not the poem as a whole."[14] By extension, the commentator, as a trained *śleṣa* reader, wields great power over shaping the poem's understanding. Y. Bronner, in fact, speculates that "*śleṣa* readers were empowered, perhaps more than any other group of readers in human history, to regenerate and mold a text at will."[15] Indeed, as he suggests in his discussion of this era, it is possible to demonstrate that by the sixteenth century, the hermeneutic desire to draw out multiple meanings from *kāvya* becomes a sort of obsession among poets and commentators.[16]

Notably, the *Pañcanalīya* episode and, on the whole, the power that *śleṣa* poetry gives to the trained specialist reader (i.e., commentator) over and above the learned general reader has continued to disturb many twentieth-century critics of *Naiṣadhīya* and of *śleṣa-kāvya* generally. Keith, for example, writes that "[i]t is a consolation to reflect that, even had [Damayantī] known Sanskrit, she would not have been able without a comment to understand what was said by the goddess."[17] Dasgupta and De offer a similar statement, again, betraying what I believe to be a misplaced sympathy for Damayantī: "[I]t certainly sets a perplexing task to poor Damayantī, to whom the verses perhaps would not be intelligible forthwith without a commentary."[18] Both opinions about Damayantī's initial inability to understand the *śleṣa* hit the right point—that commentary is essential to this kind of literary enterprise—but misread, I believe, the relationship of Sarasvatī and Damayantī, which is not one between a deliberately mystifying poet and a naïve reader but, more likely, between a learned poet (or commentator) and an *ideal* reader (or student). Neither Śrīharṣa nor the Sanskrit commentators depict Damayantī as a helpless bystander; rather, they consistently describe her as "learned" (*viduṣī*) and able to identify *śleṣa*. In this regard, I agree with Bronner, who reads the entire *Pañcanalīya* as a "metapoetic statement" where "Sarasvatī represents the poet, Damayantī the reader of the text, and the five Nalas its heroes."[19] To my mind, the networks of reading practices that converged in the analysis of the *Pañcanalīya* may explain why commentators, in their capacity as teachers, abstracted it as a set piece worthy of separate attention and study.

THE BEGINNINGS OF AN ALLEGORICAL TRADITION

The *Pañcanalīya* (13.34 and 13.35) culminates with Damayantī lost in a sea of confusion. The verse that immediately follows (13.36) suggests that a deeper metaphysical problem underlies the inability of the princess to choose her *true* husband in the face of the four *false* ones. Here is how the poet crystallizes Damayantī's dilemma:

> Confronted by four ways of seeing the world,
> [it exists, it does not exist, it both exists and does not exist,
> it does not exist and it does not not exist],
> people doubt a fifth alternative, the Truth of Oneness.
> Damayantī could not believe in the one real Nala
> as she gazed upon the set of four false ones.

In terms of the plot, Damayantī is here put in the precarious position of identifying, and to risk misidentifying, the real Nala in the midst of four false Nalas. However, in a variant of 13.36 read by several commentators, including Mallinātha, *Nala* is the one who is shrouded in doubt:

> Confronted by four ways of seeing the world,
> [it exists, it does not exist, it both exists and does not exist,
> it does not exist and it does not not exist],
> people doubt a fifth alternative, the Truth of Oneness.
> The real "fifth" Nala, indecisive in his mind,
> could not believe in himself in the presence
> of the four other Nalas vying to win Damayantī.

The two readings, which hinge on variations in only two syllables,[20] lead to different interpretations of the simile and the context within which it operates—either Damayantī could not determine the real Nala or Nala could not be certain he would obtain Damayantī. But the broader significance remains uniform: that in the face of four compelling alternatives, both the king and the princess doubt the "fifth" element—the Truth of each other. Despite the fact that the real Nala is standing right in front of her among four false Nalas, Damayantī is having a crisis of faith and cannot recognize the true love of her life, while Nala doubts if Damayantī will ever choose him. This quandary is comparable, Śrīharṣa explains, to those who cannot recognize the Truth when they are confronted with falsehoods masquerading as truths. The Truth for Śrīharṣa is nondual (*advaita*)—the fifth alternative (*pañcama-koṭi*)—and beyond the scope of the fourfold set of propositions that bind others to the world of falsehoods; these four ways of understanding the nature of existence (*catuṣkoṭi*) are the notions that something exists, that something does not exist, that it both exists and does not exist, and that it does not exist and does not not exist.[21]

Many readers regard the metaphysical problem presented in this verse—determining the truth in the midst of errors and falsehoods—to be the central theme of the *Naiṣadhīya*. Commentaries on this verse, before and after the sixteenth century, are clearly governed by an *a priori* understanding of Śrīharṣa (author of the *Khaṇḍanakhaṇḍakhādya*) as a proponent of a nondualist (*advaita*) interpretation of the *Upaniṣads*, that indeed all diversity is ultimately false and there truly is *only one* entity. For readers after the sixteenth century, as we shall see in the final section of this chapter, the *advaita* component informs the entire *Naiṣadhīya*'s verbal surface, which they see as populated with expressions that operate on multiple levels of understanding that relate to the central philosophical problem of distinguishing appearance from reality. In this vein, for them, the *śleṣa* of the *Pañcanalīya* would radically dramatize this archetypal struggle to distinguish what is true and real from what is false and unreal. In the context of the narrative action of the poem, Damayantī and Nala risk losing each other; for the reader and commentator, the risk lies in misunderstanding the verbal play of the poet and failing to see its philosophical implications; and for the religious reader, who elucidates the very structural core of the poem as an *advaita* allegory, the entire salvific potential of the poem may be lost if the clues are not appropriately deciphered. Phyllis Granoff writes of the *Naiṣadhīya*'s allegorical tradition in her study of Śrīharṣa's *Khaṇḍanakhaṇḍakhādya*:

> [*Naiṣadha* has been read as an] allegory, with Nala as the soul, or *paramātman*, and Damayantī as the aspirant yearning for union with Brahma, and thus for *mokṣa*. . . . [This notion] is not entirely unfounded. There are several indications that Nala is not to be regarded as an ordinary mortal. One may divide them into two groups: (A) Verses in which it is directly stated that Nala is the highest God, Śiva; and (B) Verses in which Nala is described with words which might apply equally to Brahma, and those in which Damayantī's approach to Nala is portrayed in terms of the standard Vedānta methods of reaching oneness with the Ultimate Real.[22]

This kind of allegorical reading is not taken up at great length in the Sanskrit commentaries. Indeed, no available Sanskrit commentary rewrites the romance of Nala and Damayantī as one might expect an Advaita philosopher to do, reading the union of the two lovers as individual souls (*jīvātman*) realizing each other's Oneness (*para-brahman*) after deep reflection and meditation.

In the sixteenth century, Nārāyaṇa suggests an allegorical significance to the *Naiṣadhīya* but does not sustain this interpretation throughout his commentary. Thus, he merely states in his preface that Śrīharṣa, in the opening verse to his poem (discussed earlier in chapter 3), "mysteriously seeds his benediction by paying homage to his preferred deity Rāma, lord of the Raghus" (where Nala is read as Nara). While it is clear that Nārāyaṇa is partial to a Vaiṣṇava perspective and sympathetic to Advaita Vedānta, his commentary only occasionally reveals an explicit allegorical practice, a point I take up in the next section. By and large, commentators like Nārāyaṇa can be seen as merely laying the groundwork for later allegorical readings—in two important ways. First, by identifying and recapitulating Advaita doctrines in Śrīharṣa's verses, they drew attention to this important aspect of Śrīharṣa's work. Thus, in their notes on 13.36, many of the commentators—from Cāṇḍupaṇḍita and Īśānadeva to Mallinātha, Jinarāja, and Nārāyaṇa—unpacked the fourfold *catuṣkoṭi* as representative of several rival doctrines of Advaita (i.e., Sānkhya, Nyāya, Mīmāṃsā, Bauddha, and Jaina) in various configurations vis-à-vis their perspectives on the reality of existence and the plurality of selves.[23] In doing so, their diverse arguments arguably lent the *Naiṣadhīya* the character of a foundational philosophical text like the *Yogasūtra* or the *Vedāntasūtra*, intellectually assimilated into a world of commentary and subcommentary that yields debate, conjecture, and new syntheses of developed principles. Engaging in philosophical debate with each other, the commentators depended on their deep familiarity with points of doctrine in terms of definitions, subtle distinctions of language and thought, relevant examples, and a host of hierarchical texts that, in conjunction with their own training, culminated in refined arguments. Although many of the schools of Indian philosophy are amply represented in the poem's images, Advaita doctrines garner the most references.

The second mode through which commentaries stimulated later interest in reading *Naiṣadhīya* allegorically along Advaita lines was through the practice of converting conventional surface meanings into polysemic expressions using *śleṣa* techniques, which we saw in chapter 3, for example, in the form of Nārāyaṇa's and Śrīdhara's analysis of the first verse of the *Naiṣadhīya*. Both commentators read the opening verse to refer not only to gods (the most available surface meaning) but also to scholars, kings, divine serpents, elephants, and so on.[24] This hermeneutic urge gained momentum in the sixteenth century and, while not yet strictly allegorical, focused on semantic transformations of Śrīharṣa's language that, I argue, must have had an influential role in encouraging reading communities to interpret *Naiṣadhīya* as allegory.

Just as an invitation to read the *Naiṣadhīya* as an Advaita allegory begins with Śrīharṣa's own overt indications and their extrapolation by commentators beginning with Cāṇḍupaṇḍita, the desire to read the poem as a Tāntrika allegory built around the significance of the *cintāmaṇi mantra* also apparently originates with Śrīharṣa's allusions to the mantra and his commentators' analysis of its import in the *Naiṣadhīya*. As briefly discussed in chapter 1, later readers give credence to the notion that the mantra that Śrīharṣa says he meditated upon (1.145c) was an especially powerful source for aspiring poets, as its mastery would lead to abundant creative capabilities. There is a wide reverence for some form of the *cintāmaṇi mantra* in Śaiva, Vaiṣṇava, Bauddha, and Śākta religious cultures, with each explaining the mantra differently and associating with it a different deity.[25] Śrīharṣa alludes to this mantra in three verses in the *Naiṣadhīya*,[26] the first of which (14.88) I repeat here:

> Remember and repeatedly chant, King,
> that hidden mantra of mine.
> It has no form and represents
> the form of the Lord called Śiva,
> who is pure and moon-endowed,
> and who is Whole but twofold,
> on account of being joined by two aspects.
> Let this mantra grant you success!

Elaborated upon at length, the basic meaning that both Nārāyaṇa and Mallinātha give is that this verse describes Lord Śiva and explains the *cintāmaṇi mantra*'s definition as *auṃ hrīṃ aum*.[27] According to Nārāyaṇa, the embedded mantra *hrīm* contains in itself Śiva's name (*hara* minus the vowels); the "moon" in the verse refers to the moon on Śiva's head as well as the nasalization marker (*anusvāra*) in the mantra. Furthermore, Nārāyaṇa reconfigures the components of the verse using *śleṣa* and secondary senses to come up with the following reading: that the verse mentions Sarasvatī's own form (*svarūpa*); that it refers to both Śiva and the goddess Śakti (as Pārvatī) separately as well as conjointly in the form of the bigendered divinity Ardhanārīśvara; that it refers to goddess Lakṣmī and Viṣṇu together or Śiva and Viṣṇu; and finally, that it crucially refers to the Tāntrika goddess Bhuvaneśvarī, visualized in a bigendered form and taking the form of the *cintāmaṇi mantra*.[28] Although Nārāyaṇa does not elaborate on the last of these intriguing interpretations, some later readers read the entire *Naiṣadhīya* in relation to a Tāntrika elucidation of the *cintāmaṇi mantra* as it particularly relates to the goddess Bhuvaneśvarī.

COMMUNITIES OF ALLEGORICAL READERS IN THE TWENTIETH CENTURY

Based on such evidence from extant commentaries after the sixteenth century and on the comparable reception histories of other important *kāvya* works that received allegorical readings at the hands of commentators, it is plausible to surmise that at some point during the sixteenth and seventeenth centuries, allegorical readings of *Naiṣadhīya* became popular. As no substantial Sanskrit commentaries on *Naiṣadhīya* dating to the eighteenth century have been found yet, we have little direct evidence from this period to suggest the existence of reading communities that favored a radically allegorical interpretation of the *Naiṣadhīya*. However, judging by accounts about teachers of the *Naiṣadhīya* during the past two hundred years, we can piece together a history of allegorical reading that very likely existed over the past four centuries.

The reading of literary texts as religious allegories has a well-developed history in South Asia. The proliferation of devotional cultures during the middle centuries of the second millennium alongside an efflorescence of commentary writing on Sanskrit *kāvya* may partially account for the growth of allegorical readings during this period.[29] The epics are the primary locus of such readings with Nīlakaṇṭha's seventeenth-century *Bhāratabhāvadīpa* (Light on the Inner Significance of the *Mahābhārata*) as a prime example, in addition to the numerous examples from the Śrīvaiṣṇava commentators of the *Rāmāyaṇa*.[30] There are also notable *kāvya* works that receive allegorical treatment, where a conventional reading is decoded to convey an esoteric sense. For example, sixteenth-century commentaries on Jayadeva's *Gītagovinda*, which fuse eroticism with longing for union with the divine; Ravicandra's commentary on the *Amaruśataka* (undated), which reads erotic love and renunciation in the same linguistic register; Rāghavabhaṭṭa's famous reading of Kālidāsa's *Abhijñāna-Śākuntalam* (seventeenth century); and Pūrṇasarasvatī's late-fourteenth-century *Rasamañjari* commentary on Bhavabhūti's *Mālatīmādhava* are other examples.

The earliest explicit reference to an allegorical reading of the *Naiṣadhīya* comes from the late nineteenth century in the form of a Sanskrit drama, entitled *Dhīranaiṣadham*, composed by a celebrated Benares scholar named Rāmāvatār Sharma (1877–1929), who taught for years, among other places, at Central Hindu College in Benaras and at the University of Patna. Sharma apparently wrote this play at the early age of fifteen to facilitate the staging of the *Naiṣadhīya* among his fellow students of Sanskrit. According to Baldev Upadhyay's account, "Pandit Rāmāvatār Sharma was very fond of Kālidāsa and Śrīharṣa, the author of the great *mahākāvya Naiṣadhīyacarita*." "He regarded," Upadhyay continues, "the verses of the *Naiṣadhīya* as mantras. Even while examining the answer-books of students at the University of Patna, he was known to be chanting verses from the *Naiṣadhīya*."[31] Two more recent volumes—both written in Telugu, one with a Hindi translation and the other with an English preface—also corroborate that there must have been lineages that read the *Naiṣadhīya* allegorically from at least the middle- to late-nineteenth century. One of these volumes recalls a teacher (and his teacher's teacher) who taught the *Naiṣadhīya* as a fusion of Advaita and Tāntrika philosophy. The other extensively draws point-to-point correspondences between Śrīharṣa's verses and Advaita or Tāntrika significances based on a received oral tradition.

Jayaseetarama Sastry, in the preface to his book *The Elements of Darśanas in Śrīharṣa's Naiṣadha* (1987), recalls:

> As a student, I had an opportunity to read the *Śṛṅgāra Naiṣadha*, a Telugu translation [of the *Naiṣadhīya*] by Śrīnātha. My father used to say—"*Naiṣadha* is full of references to various *śāstras* [b]ut Śrīnātha did not pay much attention to those *śāstric* points; he has only translated this *kāvya* as a *śṛṅgāra kāvya*. . . ." When I was going through *Naiṣadha*, in search of various points connected with different *darśanas* [philosophical schools], I found that the Vedānta *darśana* was maintained by the poet throughout the work and I started to struggle with the text to prove my thesis. I felt that I might get some light thrown on the subject if I met Brahmarṣi Śrī Rāghavanārāyaṇa

> Śāstri Gāru, an erudite scholar, reputed poet and a great Tapasvin [a practitioner of various types of austerities] in Andhra Pradesh. Encouraged by my parents, I went to Śrī Śāstri Gāru and requested him to clear up my doubts regarding the subject and show a path by which to proceed. Śrī Śāstri Gāru had gracefully conceded to my humble request saying—"Ever since I was 19 years of age, I had a desire to write a commentary on the *Naiṣadhīya* with a Vedāntic Interpretation. It remained a desire only. When I mentioned it to your father, he said that he would write an *Uttaranaiṣadham*. He also could not write it. It is interesting that you also should get a similar idea. Let us study the *Naiṣadha*."[32]

Sastry's memoir recalls his guru's conviction that Śrīharṣa's poem possessed a unified and coherent Vedāntic core, reiterated by other students of Śrī Rāghavanārāyaṇa Śāstri Gāru. The recollection of Gollaudi Venkata Rama Sastry, a retired judge of the high court of Hyderabad, makes clear that the idea of reading Vedānta and Śrīvidyā *tāntrika* philosophy (a devotional system dedicated to the goddess Lalitā or Bhuvaneśvarī) into Sanskrit *kāvya*, especially with respect to the *Naiṣadhīya*, was not unusual but extremely common in the early twentieth century:

> My Guruji [Brahma Sri Tadepalli Raghava Narayana Sastry Garu of Chandolu village in Guntur District in Andhra Pradesh] is a Vedāntin in theory as well as practice. He adopts what he preaches. He is a true Karmayogi [a person who dedicates his actions and their results to God], always immersed in prayers to God and attaining the Samadhi state [one-pointed meditative absorption] very often. In view of his multifarious scholarly achievements and Vedāntic approach he could dive deep into the latent meaning of many *kāvyas* and expound the inner meaning therein. One of the *kāvyas* in which he evinced such keen interest was the *Naiṣadhīyacarita*, which is often described as *naiṣadham vidvadaushadham* ["a medicine for the learned"].
>
> Even in his nineteenth year he could bring out the real meaning of the said *kāvya*, its Vedāntic aspect and its close affinity with Śrīvidyā Tantra, on account of his profound knowledge and practice of Srīvidyā Upāsana [devotional practices]. Shriharsha has himself indicated that the real meaning and purpose of his *kāvya* is not patent but latent and none should approach to arrive at it except through the assistance of proper Master (guru). . . . This *kāvya* deals indirectly (*vyaṅgya*) with words imparting Sahasrāra in the beginning and at the end of the *kāvya*. Hence the real meaning is what the poet

> intended to imbed into it by using words capable of different interpretations. My knowledge of Sanskrit is very limited and the above gist of the *kāvya*'s *vyaṅgyārtha* [suggested meaning] is what I could gather from what little I learned about it. Even with this little learning of a *mahākavi* like Shriharsha I feel proud and am obliged to my Guruji for expounding its real meaning, its Vedāntic aspect and its close inter-relationship with Śrīvidyā.[33]

This passage highlights the fundamental premises of this particular teacher's reading of the *Naiṣadhīya* and directs our attention to the legacy of particular Sanskrit commentators in this respect: those who emphasized these facets of the work. First is the importance of Vedānta in constructing the interpretation of the poem's central themes and characters. Second is the close connection with the Śrīvidyā *tāntrika* tradition.

Jayaseetarama Sastry's basic thesis, in paraphrasing the teachings of his guru, focuses on imbuing the poem's characters and events with Vedāntic significance. Thus, the golden goose (*haṃsa*) who conveys Nala's love to Damayantī and vice versa comes to represent for Sastry the transcendent Truth (*paramātman*) in some places in the *Naiṣadhīya* and, in other contexts, the life breaths (*prāṇa* or *jīva*). Nala and Damayantī's apprehension of the bird comes to be allegorically converted to the process by which an individual seeker realizes the *paramātman*. As might be expected, following Nārāyaṇa and other Sanskrit commentators, Sastry's Vedāntic conversion of the *Naiṣadhīya* begins with verse 1.1. He writes:

> If Nala were to be an ordinary *kṣatriya* king this description [verse 1.1.] is to be taken as a mere hyperbole. But this verse contains a special hidden meaning. As per the etymological explanation, the word "*kṣiti*" (*kṣīyate, naśyatīti kṣitiḥ*) means 'the body.' The protector of the body (*kṣiti-bhṛt*) is the Ātman only, and that which has entered into it as the Jīvātman. [Nala's] story is the compilation of the Vedānta (Upaniṣadic) sentences. Nectar may give *devatva* (godhood) but *amṛtatva* (salvation, permanent freedom from birth and death) can be obtained only through the Upaniṣadic Vidyā [esoteric knowledge]. If Nala is identical with the Supreme Being, then only his story can be *sudhāvadhīraṇī* (surpassing Nectar).[34]

Whereas Nārāyaṇa and Śrīdhara understood terms such as *kṣiti-rakṣin* as "kings," "divine snakes," or as the "destruction of Kali," the esoteric reading of Sastry's guru sees the compound expression as the *ātman* itself; that is, the "protector (*rakṣin*) of the body (*kṣiti*)." Sastry goes on to present numerous other examples that reorient the figure of Nala or the *haṃsa* as *parabrahman*. *Naiṣadhīya* 1.117, where the *haṃsa* first appears, is a particularly good example. Here is a translation of the verse:

> Near a pleasant pool
> which had appropriated some of the ocean's loveliness,
> Nala awakened to the presence of a spectacular golden *haṃsa*
> stirring nearby, intent on seeking out
> the indistinct cooing of a female *haṃsa*
> desirous of love-play.

Nārāyaṇa reads esoteric significance in Nala's initial apprehension of the *haṃsa*. He comments that in seeing the golden *haṃsa*, Nala is like a yogi perceiving the *paramātman* that is described in the *Upaniṣads*. Furthermore, he explains, the pleasant pool that the bird swims in is actually the body, while the female *haṃsa* is rendered as the illusory energy (*śakti*) of a mistaken reality (*māyā*).[35]

Seshendra Sharma, a contemporary Telugu author of a commentary on *Naiṣadhīya* called *Svarṇahaṃsa* (The Golden Haṃsa), asserts that Śrīharṣa must have consciously intended this meaning in 1.117 and cites as evidence the aorist usage of the verbal root *budh* (*abodhi*), literally meaning "to awaken" or "to realize," in the sense of "seeing."[36] Thus, for Sharma, Nala's first sight of the *haṃsa* was really a moment of profound "awakening" for him, in a spiritual sense. He puts forward numerous such readings as examples to demonstrate the ways in which Śrīharṣa prompts the Vedānta-oriented commentator to unleash staggering displays of hermeneutic virtuosity. Nārāyaṇa's commentary on verses 3.3 and 3.4 is exemplary in this regard. These verses, translated earlier in chapter 1, are repeated here:

> The way that vow-observant yogis lead their minds
> away from the world,
> toward the singularly indescribable Truth—
> that is how Damayantī's friends were:
> their eyes were led away
> from other distractions
> to that one indescribably beautiful *haṃsa*.

The way the mind's fluctuations become still
in the yogi's own body
so that the mind can approach the Soul within,
that's how Damayantī plunged into stillness:
the desire to catch with her hand
the bird stirring nearby
was a cautious effort, out of both fear and respect.

Picking up on Nārāyaṇa's analysis, both Sastry and Sharma note Śrīharṣa's careful use of the words *haṃsa*, *eka* (the one), and *nirupākhya-rūpa* (unutterable beauty), which for them refer to both the bird and to Brahman.[37] While the connection between the bird and Brahman is introduced in 3.3, the next verse (3.4) connects the relationship of Damayantī and the bird with that of the spiritual seeker and Brahman, respectively. Nārāyaṇa provides the correspondences through two clever etymologies. First, he converts the past participle *sannihitam,* usually understood as a frozen form meaning "near," by dividing it up into three components, as if it were a compound word. He takes the first prefix "*sam*" to nominally mean "by the virtuous ones" (*sad-bhis*) such as Manu; the prefix "*ni-*" he takes to mean "fully" (*nitarām*); and the past passive participle "*hitam*" in the sense of "meditated upon" (*dhyātam*). Thus, Nārāyaṇa explains this verse in the sense of "yogis fully meditating on the activities of mind that proliferate within Brahman, which resides inside or near the body." Alternatively, he understands the compound as signifying that "for the virtuous ones" (*sad-bhyas*), the exceedingly (*nitarām*) good thing (*hitam*) is that which is desired (*iṣṭam*), which for them is the Absolute (*paramātman*); and it is that which they desire to understand.[38] Cāṇḍupaṇḍita offers virtually the same interpretation.[39]

Alongside the application of Vedānta hermeneutics to the *Naiṣadhīya*, reading the contents of the entire *Naiṣadhīya* along the lines of Śrīvidyā thought has been the most visible allegorical reading strategy. While the importance of the *cintāmaṇi mantra* dominates this stream of commentary writing, which, from all of the examples I have been able to locate, seems to constitute a regional tradition developed in Andhra Pradesh, other features of the poem are also translated into Śrīvidyā language. Thus, for example, while Nala is a seeker of *brahman* or *parabrahman*, Sastry posits Damayantī as representative of the special power of esoteric knowledge (*vidyāśakti*); when Śrīharṣa compares Damayantī to Lakṣmī and likens her to the crescent moon resting on the head of

Śiva in verse 2.19, it reflects, according to Sastry's reading, a direct reference to the *pañcadaśi-mantra.*[40] The Śrīvidyā regards as supremely efficacious the complex fifteen-syllable mantra (*pañcadaśi*) that represents the transcendent form of goddess Lalitā or Bhuvaneśvarī.[41] Sastry stunningly renders Śrīharṣa's head-to-toe description (*nakha-śikha-varṇana*) of Damayantī in the seventh canto (mentally recounted by Nala) as a description of the *vidyāśakti* in the form of *kūṭatrayātmikā*, literally "she who consists of three peaks (*kūṭa*)."

These three "peaks," connected with the power of speech (*vāg-bhava-kūṭa*), desire (*madhya-kūṭa* or the *kāma-rāja-kūṭa*), and power (*śakti-kūṭa*), are mapped onto the three sectors of Damayantī's body: from her hair to her chin; from the neck to downy line above her navel; and the rest of the lower body. Sastry's reading of verse 7.96, for example, where Nala notes that the sage Bhṛgu takes refuge in Damayantī's breasts, Nārada her face, and Vyāsa her thighs, is decoded by the author as follows:

> Doubts of mine about this verse were cleared up after Śrī Sāstri Gāru explained the hidden meaning of the verse. Here, Bhṛgu is the seeker of *aiśvarya* [power], worshipping the *madhyakuṭa* [desire], Nārada who is interested in praising *paramātman*, worships *vāgbhavakuṭa* [speech]. Vyāsa, the seeker of *jñāna* worships *śaktikuṭa* [power]. He is the author of the *Brahmasūtra* and has brought out in it the essence of the *Upaniṣads*. However great they may be, each one of them is connected with one *kuṭa* only where as *vidyāśakti* is the combination of all the three *kuṭas*. That is the reason why they are bewildered regarding her complete form. Many *upāsakas* [devotees] are interested in *aiśvarya*, some of them are interested in *vāk siddhi* [special powers of speech] and only a few of them are interested in salvation. While changing the order of the three *kuṭas*, Śrīharṣa wanted to suggest this point.[42]

Similarly, Nala's becoming invisible by virtue of the gods' plan to sneak him into the women's quarters past the security staff is connected with the supernatural power of invisibility, which only great yogis attain.[43] Every element is likewise converted to fit an allegorical significance. Thus, the twenty-second and final canto of the poem, a lengthy description of the rising moon, opens with a statement (22.1) that Nala, longing to kiss his beloved's red lips upon seeing the setting sun, "arrived" (*avāptavān*) at the "seventh floor" (*saptama-bhūmi-bhāga*) of the "palace" (*saudha*) to see Damayantī. Sastry sees special significance in, what is to his mind, Śrīharṣa's curious mention of the "seventh floor":

> The description of the moon has connections with the *candrakalā khaṇḍa* [the domain of the moon-digit, where the part is the whole]. The *bījākṣara* [seed syllable] '*śrīṃ*' is meditated upon in the *sahasrāra cakra* [the seventh subtle energy-wheel at the crown of the head]. There are six *cakras* [subtle energy-wheels in the body] beginning with *mūlādhāra* [the root *cakra* at the base of the spine]. *Sahasrāra* is the seventh one. The twenty-second canto employs words such as "*avāptavān*" and "*saudha*," which means "the place of *sudhā*, i.e., *amṛta*." That is the *saudhā* where Bhaimī [Damayantī] lives. That is on the seventh floor, which Nala reached. Examine how significant each word is here. The phrase "*bhaimī-dhara*" literally means that which "bears Bhaimī." How awkward this meaning is! In such places, one is forced to go up to the suggested meaning.[44]

Although no earlier Sanskrit commentary makes much of any of these marked words, such as *saudha* for "palace" or *avāptavān* for "arrived at," these allegorical readings of *Naiṣadhīya*, by contrast, focus squarely on the esoteric possibilities of Śrīharṣa's peculiar usages.

CONCLUDING OBSERVATIONS

The growth, and eventual formalization, of allegorical engagements with the *Naiṣadhīya* was a "secondary wave" of reading that came about during a mature phase in the development of the poem's receptive tradition, when its wide popularity among Sanskrit literati was already established. Weighing the available evidence, we can conclude that the *Naiṣadhīya* entered this phase sometime in the sixteenth century. The fact that Nārāyaṇa is the first to call this section *Pañcanalīya*, for example, and that we know it was written up and transmitted as a work separate from the *Naiṣadhīya* as a whole, encourages me to refer to commentaries on it as a "secondary" type of engagement that works in conjunction with the evolution of succeeding allegorical reading strategies that also abstract themselves from an organically whole literary text. Readers from this point forward feel comfortable dismembering the poem, along the lines of the episodes that make it up, in service of more fruitfully using it to teach or to think through nonlinear ways. Thus, the *Pañcanalīya* section serves as an ideal lesson in the virtuosity of *śleṣa* practices; unlike other examples of *śleṣa*, where commentators seem to instigate the double-readings, with the *Pañcanalīya* the poet has facilitated for the commentators a situation that calls for *śleṣa* reading strategies within the plot itself. Likewise, various episodes artfully stitched together by Śrīharṣa are purposefully disaggregated so that they can function as separate units conducive to allegorical readings. Thus, for example, Nala's mental description of Damayantī's body is reconfigured as a description of the metaphorical body of *vidyāśakti*, consisting of three "peaks"; Nala's movement through the seven floors of Damayantī's palace takes on the significance of ambrosial fluid moving up the subtle energy channels; and so on.

Many of the historiographical trends of *Naiṣadhīya* hermeneutics, identified in earlier chapters, also hold true here. With respect to the *Pañcanalīya*, Cāṇḍupaṇḍita, for example, only engaged with those verses in this section that stimulate his urge to bring out the philosophical implications of Śrīharṣa's verse. Mallinātha efficiently explicated the *śleṣa* woven into the *Pañcanalīya* by the poet but, true to form, did not provide more than is necessary. Nārāyaṇa, like Śrīharṣa, fond of seeking a surplus of meanings wherever he can locate it, clearly relishes both the *Pañcanalīya* and the exploration of allegorical significances in the poem. Allegorical understandings of the *Naiṣadhīya* after the sixteenth century were, as I argued here, deeply influenced by works such as Nārāyaṇa's, especially sharing with him their emphasis on Śrīharṣa's linguistic polysemy. The allegorical readings I discussed in this chapter were also informed, I believe, by the store of legends about *Śrīharṣa* and the *Naiṣadhīya* that had gradually accrued from the thirteenth century onward. In the next chapter, I introduce these various legends of the poem and flesh out another major component of the *Naiṣadhīya* tradition.

6 ◈ LEGENDS OF THE *NAIṢADHĪYA*

Allegorical readers of the *Naiṣadhīya* take it for granted that Śrīharṣa's virtuosity is a supernatural gift. They inherently trust the indications given by the poet in his own words: that he realized *Brahman* in meditation (22.153) and that his poem is a product of the *cintāmaṇi mantra* (1.145). Likewise, as discussed in earlier chapters, by the fifteenth century the literary practices associated with the *Naiṣadhīya*'s attention to philosophical allusion also inform well-established understandings of the poem and its poet. Up to this chapter, both of these literary-historical phenomena—the emergence of allegorical readings pre–sixteenth century and the consolidation of interpretive prisms through which the *Naiṣadhīya* is read, understood, and discussed—have been discussed strictly in terms of the genre of the Sanskrit commentary. This chapter focuses on another important development in the formation of the *Naiṣadhīya* tradition, one that takes shape in the mid-fourteenth and fifteenth centuries and exerts tremendous influence on virtually all understandings of the poem's history thereafter: the emergence of a store of anonymous, quasi-historical verses, stories, or "hearsay" (*kimvadantī*, literally "what they say") and textualized "biographies" (*prabandha* or *carita*) from "treasuries of stories" (*kathākoṣa*), semi-historical narratives composed in Sanskrit that are seemingly about the historical Śrīharṣa and the *Naiṣadhīya* but, in fact, are legends that combine new details told in anecdotal form with information drawn from antecedent sources like the commentaries.

These *prabandhas* are usually in prose (with a few verses interspersed) and, aside from being engaging works that have their own literary merits, constitute narratives that perform multiple critical and historical functions in the formation of the *Naiṣadhīya* tradition. For example, they reflect on and enhance already established understandings of the *Naiṣadhīya*'s aesthetic and its poet's special stature as a remarkable poet, philosopher, and yogi. With the absence of any corroborative sources, all of these legendary narratives—while perhaps based in some fact intrinsically embedded in the text or part of an oral tradition available to them—are ultimately structured around anecdotal, semi-historical, and pseudo-biographical data crafted to suit a credible legend of the poet and text. In this way, textual criticism and unresolved curiosities are artfully inserted into provocative, though unlikely, literary histories. Historical readers want to know about the poet's personal biography (where he was from, who his patron was, how he came to compose the poem, what his ultimate fate was as a court poet) as well as issues concerning the poem's transmission and reception (when and how the poem gained celebrity, where it was initially composed, where and through what channels it traveled, whether or not it was uniformly received in all critical circles). Some of these questions, as we shall see, are raised and briefly examined by the *Naiṣadhīya* commentaries. Their interventions are made to explain, for example, some of what the *Naiṣadhīya*'s auto-account has already framed for these early readers (the poem's "difficulty" and its association with the *cintāmaṇi mantra*, for instance) and also matters left unstated by the poet: its noncustomary linguistic style and usage, and the shadowy history of its transmission and recognition among different communities. Where Śrīharṣa places himself historically as part of the Gāhaḍavāla court and draws links between his poem and his other accomplishments as a spiritual *sādhaka* and philosopher, the early commentators provide more comprehensive, and often conflicting, "histories" of the poet.

Here, I especially highlight the introductory paratexts (*avataraṇa*) of thirteenth-century commentator Cāṇḍupaṇḍita and fifteenth-century Gadādhara, both of whom have interesting things to say about the poet and the poem's history and critical reception. Most of the other curiosities, however, are left for the works of Rājaśekharasūri (fourteenth century) and Vidyāpati (fifteenth century) to sort out. Both of these story collections (largely, but not exclusively, in prose) devote sustained attention to the *Naiṣadhīya* and its poet, extending the narratives introduced in the Sanskrit commentaries and, in essence, establishing their own parallel tradition of commentary on the Sanskrit *mahākāvya*. Rather than focusing on its verbal forms and literary themes, however, their "commentary" is on the *Naiṣadhīya*'s history of production, transmission, and critical reception. These orally circulated stories are fascinating entry points to think about how once-obscure poets emerge to popular acclaim in South Asia and the ways in which the historical imagination of Sanskrit audiences memorializes their legacy. The subject that interests me most here, however, concerns the intersection of textualized biographical legends and literary criticism. Śrīharṣa is the subject of sets of narratives that posit him as a supernaturally gifted poet and philosopher, a master yogi, a man of extraordinary memory and language facility, an inhabitant of Kashmir and alternatively Benares or Bengal, an elite member of the Gāhaḍavāla court at the end of the twelfth century, and, as I discussed earlier, the unlikely nephew to the celebrated poetics master Mammaṭa. Each of these narratives (however anachronistic or implausible) makes a point that one might label literary-critical or literary-historical. Some speculate on the poet-philosopher's origins, others on the ontology of his genius to compose. Some speak to the verses of the *Naiṣadhīya* and serve as commentaries to them, while another merely fleshes out an imagined life history of the author.

COMMENTATORS EXPLAIN THE *NAIṢADHĪYA*'S ORIGINS

Inference may be said to be
the primary trope of this poem. It alone shines.
The poem's rasa is delivered
both directly and indirectly—and it is superb.
Figures of speech and rasa make a poem,
like the combination of milk and nectar.
It is worthy of being clutched
by a learned man or god, in a firm embrace.[1]

Gadādhara, fifteenth-century commentator

Before beginning their close textual analysis of the *Naiṣadhīya*, two traditional Sanskrit commentators give the appearance of providing a received biography of Śrīharṣa. Cāṇḍupaṇḍita (thirteenth century) inaugurates the legend of the *Naiṣadhīya* with the following details from his preface to the poem (1.1):

> Unable to bear pitying glances, the poet Śrīharṣa desired to compose the impenetrable *Khaṇḍanakhaṇḍakhādya* as a response to the philosopher

> Udayana, who had defeated his father Śrīhīra during the course of logical debate. Reduced to harboring this single vengeful thought, he was simultaneously overwhelmed by an impulse to fulfill the traditional goals of human life (*puruṣārtha*): sensual pleasure, material prosperity, and the meeting of social and religious obligations. This being the case, upon first seeing the river Gaṅgā in Vārāṇasī, the land where ultimate freedom is won, he sought to strike a balance between the call of action and religious duty. In Vārāṇasī, he experienced a vision of the supreme *Brahman*. By seeing in front of him a treasure of golden coins resembling Mount Meru, he proceeded to fulfill the aims of a well-lived, prosperity-filled life.[2]

Cāṇḍupaṇḍita goes on to say that Śrīharṣa spent the next sixteen years making sensual pleasure his servant (*kiṅkarī-kṛta-kāma-puruṣārthā*), spending time with young, beautiful women. Having satisfied the call of worldly life, he then composed a text on logic to cut to pieces (*khaṇḍaśaḥ khaṇḍitavān*) the arguments of his father's antagonist, the logician Udayana, one of the most famous names in the history of Indian philosophy and a recurring figure in the *Naiṣadhīya* tradition whose connection to the poem's history will be treated separately later.[3] The philosophical logic of the *Khaṇḍanakhaṇḍakhādya* being too difficult for most readers, Cāṇḍupaṇḍita continues, led Śrīharṣa eventually to compose a poem predominantly infused with the erotic *rasa* that would be sure to please the critics.[4]

Inaugurating the history of speculation about Śrīharṣa as poet and philosopher, Cāṇḍupaṇḍita's account conveys two noteworthy points. First, it reinforces ideas already available from Śrīharṣa's "autobiography": that the poet Śrīharṣa was also a philosopher of considerable stature, that he composed a "difficult" poem, and that the religious man Śrīharṣa had achieved some kind of gnostic revelation. Cāṇḍupaṇḍita's additions to these details mark the second notable feature of his account: that Śrīharṣa's spiritual career reached fruition in Vārāṇasī, that his challenging philosophical contribution was the product of a deeply felt vengeance toward his father's rival Udayana, and that his life at court (as a worldly man) was part of a broader project to fulfill all of the normative aims of Vedic life. Each of these accretions to the "historical" record solicits attention because they are nowhere to be found in the poet's information about himself: that Śrīharṣa was in Vārāṇasī; that within the eleventh- or twelfth-century scholarly subcultures of the Gāhaḍavāla court, a revenge scenario implicating Śrīharṣa's father Śrīhīra and Udayana was unfolding; and that Śrīharṣa—self-defined as a yogi and recipient of great literary powers—decided to live a life of court poet in order to fulfill his normative *dharma*. Here, the idea of Śrīharṣa as a genius with innate poetic powers merges with Śrīharṣa the poet in historical time. The realities of court life stir the imagination of Śrīharṣa, compelling the poet to produce a tangible work of literature that functions in a very real social context.

Corroborating Cāṇḍupaṇḍita's account to some extent but providing new and alternate details, the fifteenth-century commentator Gadādhara, in the preface to his commentary on the first verse, explains:

> There was a king named Govindacandra in Vārāṇasī, like Indra in his capital city of Amarāvatī. Among the numerous scholars in his court, all of them well decorated with learning, Śrīharṣa emerged as the jewel. When it became known that he composed the *Khaṇḍanakhaṇḍakhādya*, certain scholars—who thought themselves equal to a forest of juicy mango trees when it came to composing poetry—became jealous of Śrīharṣa. These jealous pandits quietly sneered at Śrīharṣa every time he entered the assembly: "Oh, look, here comes that dry Śamī tree of logic" and "Oh, the desert stands before us." One day, Śrīharṣa took notice of their secretive comments to each other and tried to figure out what was going on. Someone close to him told him what some of these petty scholars were saying about him. In order to silence them, Śrīharṣa openly announced his intention to compose a *mahākāvya* called *Nalacarita* [*Naiṣadhīyacarita*] that, he declared, would be like an ocean that could not be crossed with an ordinary boat. He would offer it directly to the king as a gift. After he acted on his declaration, the king was so happy with Śrīharṣa that he honored him with two seats and two *pān* (betel leaf): one signifying his mastery of logic and one for his skill as a poet. He also was given the title of *kavipaṇḍita*—"poet-scholar."[5]

Clearly, Gadādhara's account takes its clues from Cāṇḍupaṇḍita's historicization of Śrīharṣa but, significantly, differs in one important aspect. Cāṇḍupaṇḍita explicitly states that Śrīharṣa wrote the *Khaṇḍanakhaṇḍakhādya* to avenge the logician Udayana's insult to his father Śrīhīra; however, because even well-trained scholars found that text too difficult to digest intellectually, he wrote the love poem *Naiṣadhīya* to deliver difficult ideas in a more attractive and charming form.

Gadādhara, however, picks up on the code of rivalry between two logicians (Śrīhīra and Udayana) found in Cāṇḍupaṇḍita's account and reimagines an entire assembly of scholars mocking Śrīharṣa for his philosophical work. In Gadādhara's narrative, Udayana is no longer present. Neither is Cāṇḍupaṇḍita's notion that the *Naiṣadhīya*'s very reason for being was to serve as a palatable medium to transmit complicated ideas. Gadādhara instead envisions Śrīharṣa's project in writing the *Naiṣadhīya* as a sharp rebuttal to a charge that he *could not* write poetry, that he was simply a "dry" philosopher. The decisive detail in Gadādhara's passage above—that Śrīharṣa was equally honored as poet and *paṇḍita*—is again drawn from Śrīharṣa's admission of being honored with two *pān* and two seats (22.153, cited in chapter 1). While it is not clear that the two *pān* (or the seats) signify anything more than the esteem in which Śrīharṣa was held by the king of Kanauj, Gadādhara makes the inference that the two *pān*—and, according to his interpretation of verse 22.153, the two seats—offered by the king imply Śrīharṣa's brilliance as both poet and philosopher. Gadādhara provides a rational gloss for a fact that seems to have astonished *Naiṣadhīya* audiences throughout its receptive history: that one and the same person could possibly compose both the *Khaṇḍanakhaṇḍakhādya* and the *Naiṣadhīyacarita*.

Especially noteworthy to take away from these accounts from the Sanskrit commentators are three significant features that become staple discussion points for later noncommentarial narratives of Śrīharṣa and the *Naiṣadhīya*. First is the fact that both commentators base their speculative narratives about the poem's origins on details provided by the poet. Thus, while Cāṇḍupaṇḍita draws attention to Śrīharṣa's "vision of the supreme *Brahman*" (*Naiṣadhīya* 22.150), Gadādhara repeats the detail about Śrīharṣa's being honored by the King of Kānyakubja (*Naiṣadhīya* 22.153a). Second, both narratives notably place Śrīharṣa in Vārāṇasī; as we shall see below, later readers will locate the poet in Kashmir, Bengal, and, of course, Kanauj. The third feature concerns the presence of a rival philosopher Udayana or, in Gadādhara's case, a rival set of jealous pandits that are surrogates for the lone logician. Udayana (or collectively, the pandits) provoke Śrīharṣa to vengeance and inspire him to write the *Naiṣadhīya*. Cāṇḍupaṇḍita assumes the anachronistic rivalry between Śrīharṣa and Udayana, who predates the poet by at least a century, while Gadādhara chooses not to mention the logician by name at all.

NAIṢADHĪYA IN THE PROSE NARRATIVES OF THE FOURTEENTH CENTURY

Presumably having Cāṇḍupaṇḍita's account before him, the fourteenth-century Jain author Rājaśekharasūri first elaborates, in his *Prabandhakośa* (Treasury of Prabandhas), the narrative given by the thirteenth-century commentator. The *prabandha* genre of western India, composed largely within Jain literary milieus and written in Sanskrit from the thirteenth century onward, comprises collections of quasi-historical narratives about well-known poets and kings.[6] Rājaśekharasūri's *Prabandhakośa*, in a biographical narrative entitled *Harṣakaviprabandha* (The Story of the Poet Harṣa), offers the following details about Śrīharṣa:

> There was a king of Vārāṇasī named Govindacandra. His son was Jayantacandra. The father gave over the kingdom to the son and went off to meditate and prepare for the next world. In Jayantacandra's court, there were many scholars. One was Hīra, whose learned son was Śrīharṣa. While Śrīharṣa was still a boy, his father Hīra lost face when he was defeated in debate by one of the king's other court scholars. Sunk in a mire of shame, he bore a sharp enmity. At the time of his death, Hīra addressed Śrīharṣa: "Right in front of the king, some scholar defeated me in debate. This burns me deeply. If you are a true son of mine, then you will avenge me in the assembly." Śrīharṣa replied: "So it will be." Hīra went to heaven. Śrīharṣa deputed his familial duties to his relatives and went abroad to study. Very quickly, Śrīharṣa became expert in the various sciences: logic, poetics, music, mathematics, astronomy, gemology, Veda (*mantra*), and grammar. For a full year he stayed on the bank of the river Gaṅgā, attentively meditating on the *cintāmaṇi mantra* given to him by his spiritual teacher. The goddess Tripurā herself appeared and granted him a special power: the unfailing command of Speech.
>
> Armed with this power, first Śrīharṣa attended royal scholarly conferences, confounding one and all with abstruse allusions to various academic topics. Even though he was now profoundly learned, being unintelligible to others terribly frustrated him. Śrīharṣa again invoked the goddess Speech: "Mother, my immense learning is a curse. Make me comprehensible." The goddess advised him: "So be it. In the middle of the night, pour water on your head and, then, eat some yogurt. After that, go to sleep. That will induce the elemental humor *kapha* and dull your intellect a bit." And so it transpired. Śrīharṣa became intelligible. He composed hundreds of texts, among them

> the *Khaṇḍanakhaṇḍakhādya*. He accomplished what he wanted and came to Vārāṇasī, where he lived on the outskirts for a while before being introduced to Jayantacandra.[7]

Rājaśekharasūri's account has become the standard conception in the awareness of the *Naiṣadhīya* tradition for most contemporary readers and emphasizes Śrīharṣa's own admission that the *Naiṣadhīya* is an outcome of deep meditative practice and the fruit of the *cintāmaṇi mantra*. It seems likely in this passage that Rājaśekharasūri is assimilating Cāṇḍupaṇḍita's details with his own idea that it was Govindacandra's son Jayantacandra that was the official patron of the poet. He maintains Cāṇḍupaṇḍita's suggestion that Śrīharṣa was especially connected with Vārāṇasī and also reiterates the notion that he received his special powers to compose texts there. Unlike Cāṇḍupaṇḍita, however, Rājaśekharasūri does not name Udayana as Śrīhīra's rival. The detail about Śrīharṣa's incomprehensibility—before undergoing the unusual remedy prescribed by the goddess to correct his deficiency (or rather, his oversufficiency)[8]—seems again rooted in the "difficulty" code established by the poet and nurtured by later commentators, beginning with Cāṇḍupaṇḍita.[9]

Furthermore, while the accounts of Cāṇḍupaṇḍita and Gadādhara merely outline a process to explain the origins of Śrīharṣa's two celebrated texts, Rājaśekharasūri fleshes out the scenario under which both texts were produced. While completing a clever panegyric verse for Jayantacandra (Śrīharṣa's putative royal patron) that simultaneously praises the king's heroism and a beauty,[10] Śrīharṣa notices his father's enemy (*pitṛ-vairin*) from the corner of his eye (*sa-kaṭākṣam*) and fires the following verse at him:

> When I compose,
> Goddess Speech (my eloquence)
> plays in equal measure:
> with the supple stuff of stanzas *and*
> with conceptually complicated conundrums.
> If a woman loves her man, making love is the same
> whether on a soft, quilted bed,
>   or on the weed-grassy ground.[11]

Here, Śrīharṣa's double vision as a poet and philosopher is invoked as a sharp rejoinder to those critics at court who might have questioned his intellectual versatility. It also suggests Śrīharṣa's salty style, his unabashed mingling of unlikely metaphors and his pugnacious tone of challenge to both the keepers of inherited tradition and to rival contemporaries. The stanza, therefore, does the work both of mimicking the poet's composition and of reproducing, in pithy form, a major vector of the *Naiṣadhīya*'s literary reception among its scholastic communities. It also, of course, completes Śrīharṣa's vengeance against the here-unnamed Udayana. Awed by this sharp flash of confidence and wit and acknowledging Śrīharṣa's flair for composing poetry and his aptitude for arguing logic, the story goes, Hīra's rival (Udayana) admits defeat instantaneously. Jayantacandra then duly honors Śrīharṣa with a title.

THE *NAIṢADHĪYA*'S EARLY TRAVELS TO KASHMIR

Having spruced up Cāṇḍupaṇḍita's and Gadādhara's details regarding Śrīharṣa's evolution as a philosopher, Rājaśekharasūri now expands his narrative of the *Naiṣadhīya*'s history into the realm of more formalized structures of literary criticism and textual dissemination, explaining first how Śrīharṣa's poem initially gained approval among the learned critics of Kashmir:

> One day, the king excitedly urged Śrīharṣa: "Best of Poets, King of Speech, write a jewel of a poem." And so, Śrīharṣa wrote the extraordinary *Naiṣadhīya mahākāvya*, full of sublime emotion, suggestive and profound. He presented it to the king, who said: "This is excellent! Go at once to Kashmir and show it to the scholars there. Leave it there in the hands of the goddess, who herself lives in that holy spot. She throws away unworthy compositions as one would a heap of dust. But, if it is good, she will nod her head and bring the composition close to her heart. Flowers will rain from above." Under the patronage of the king, Śrīharṣa went to Kashmir and placed the text in Sarasvatī's hand. . . . She hurled it far away.[12]

According to Rājaśekharasūri, Sarasvatī explains her displeasure with Śrīharṣa's poem by citing verse 11.66 of the *Naiṣadhīya*. Sarasvatī finds it offensive that Śrīharṣa, in this verse, describes her as a wife of Viṣṇu. Śrīharṣa justifies his verse to her by citing a somewhat obscure passage from the *Purāṇas* that corroborates his allusion.[13] He assuages Sarasvatī's anger to the extent that she accepts his explanation. However, while in

Kashmir, when Śrīharṣa asks the literary scholars at court for an audience with the king, their jealousy leads them to dupe Śrīharṣa into waiting until the king's time frees up. Śrīharṣa bides his time near a well of a temple along a river chanting a mantra to Rudra. Months pass while his supplies grow thin. While at the temple, according to Rājaśekharasūri's account, the poet witnesses a heated dispute between two women who had come to draw water from the well about who gets the water first. The police come and cart both women away to the magistrate. Witnesses to the quarrel are sought. The two women remember somebody chanting near the well of the temple. Śrīharṣa is brought in to the king himself for questioning:

> Śrīharṣa says, "I am a foreigner. I have no idea what local language (*prākṛta*) these two women were speaking. I can only reproduce the words they were using." The king replies, "Speak, then." Sequentially, Śrīharṣa repeats the dialogue the women had. Astonished, the king says, "Ah, what a mind! What a memory!" First attending to the legal matter with the women, the king then addresses Śrīharṣa: "Who are you, learned man?" Śrīharṣa tells him about himself and explains: "I've been mistreated by your petty scholars." The king summons his pandits and rebukes them.[14]

According to Rājaśekharasūri, Śrīharṣa then bitterly castigates the pandits himself, with a verse found at the end of the twenty-second canto (22.150, cited in chapter 1):

> Beautiful women take hold of a young man's imagination.
> They cannot be appreciated by prepubescent boys.
> My sweet verses delight learned connoisseurs.
> Why should I care of disparagement from insipid critics?

The Kashmiri king's scholars, shame-faced, review Śrīharṣa's poem and give their wholehearted approval. Śrīharṣa returns to a delighted Jayantacandra, who then makes arrangements for the dissemination of the *Naiṣadhīya* (*prasṛtaṃ naiṣadhaṃ loke*). The details in this passage take on significance for later readers that cite it to demonstrate that Śrīharṣa was not a Kashmiri.

While Śrīharṣa confirms his poem's approval by the scholars of Kashmir (verse 16.131 of the *Naiṣadhīya*), Rājaśekharasūri's novel elaboration in the *Prabandhakośa* initiates the first of a series of discursive threads relating to Śrīharṣa's connection with Kashmir. The most interesting of these identifies the Kashmiri writer on poetics Mammaṭa as Śrīharṣa's disappointed maternal uncle. The source of Mammaṭa's disappointment: that had he known about the *Naiṣadhīya* before he wrote his chapter on defects in poetry, he would not have had to scour other poems for examples to put in his book.[15] For instance, from the example given above (verse 11.66), the specific "fault" (*doṣa*) for which Śrīharṣa is guilty in citing Sarasvatī as the wife of Viṣṇu is misrepresentation by consciously supplanting a well-known usage with an obscure one (technical Sanskrit term: *aprasiddhadoṣa*), in this case violating the popular understanding of Sarasvatī's being Brahma's wife by citing her instead as Viṣṇu's wife. A topic discussed earlier in light of commentators' editorial anxieties, Śrīharṣa's poem was especially infamous in certain circles of Sanskrit literary culture for its questionable linguistic, tropic, and thematic choices. His bold strokes were welcomed by some, while for others they represented an undesirable breach of normative *kāvya* standards regarding taste, propriety, and aesthetic effect. The circulating stories linking Śrīharṣa with Mammaṭa may reflect a historically significant critical perspective that Śrīharṣa's boldness (*prāgalbhya*) as a poet has never been universally admired by all audiences, making the *Naiṣadhīya*'s inclusion the most contentious of all within the traditional scheme of the five great classics of the *mahākāvya* tradition (*pañcamahākāvya*).

Critics for centuries reiterate the notion that Śrīharṣa in many places in his poem deviates, to ill effect, from Mammaṭa's wooden view, that the best poets steer clear of wayward usages in terms of linguistic and poetic convention while doing their best to deck their work, within moderation, with effective tropes and linguistic sound effects (*tad adoṣau śabdārthau saguṇāv alaṃkṛtī punaḥ kvāpi*). The *Naiṣadhīya* is often flagged, from this perspective, as a notorious specimen of bad taste masquerading as innovative style. The flagrant anachronism of linking Śrīharṣa and Mammaṭa notwithstanding, this narrative informs the understanding of *Naiṣadhīya* among many readers of the poem for the past several centuries. Narratives like this function as the performance of literary criticism on the one hand and also as a means to satisfy historical curiosities unaddressed elsewhere on the other. The *Naiṣadhīya* is famous among Sanskrit *littérateurs* as an astonishingly innovative piece of art. Perhaps in its immediate context and certainly during the decades that follow, this fact of its newness clearly did not please all audiences.

THE *NAIṢADHĪYA*'S ARRIVAL IN GUJARAT

Rājaśekharasūri's details about the initial rejection and eventual acceptance of the *Naiṣadhīya* in Kashmir may also reflect a historical memory of the literary-critical debates that must have gone on around Śrīharṣa's poem during the thirteenth and fourteenth centuries, if not earlier. Or, quite simply, these narratives reflect one stream of the *Naiṣadhīya*'s historical reception and transmission, much as another story (the *Hariharakathā*) in the *Prabandhakośa* explains how the earliest commentaries of the *Naiṣadhīya* came to exist in Vāghela-administered Gujarat during the mid-thirteenth century. According to this story, the *Naiṣadhīya* traveled to Gujarat along with Śrīharṣa's own relative, Harihara. The account goes that Harihara, a wealthy and learned descendant of Śrīharṣa, came from Gauḍadeśa to the court of Vīradhavala, which was located in Dhavalakka (modern Dholakā, near Ahmedabad). There, Vīradhavala's minister Vastupāla organized a literary gathering where Harihara recited verses from the *Naiṣadhīya* to the astonishment of the gathered poets and scholars. According to Rājaśekharasūri's account, Vastupāla immediately asked to borrow Harihara's personal manuscript of the poem and had it copied overnight:

> At night, Vastupāla hires a scribe to draft a new manuscript. Binding it with tattered cords and dusting it up with a musty powder, he leaves it on the shelf. In the morning, he returns the manuscript to Harihara and says, "Here, take your copy of the *Naiṣadha*." As Harihara takes it, the minister continues, "I just remembered that this text was also in our collection. Take a look for yourself." After a suitable delay, the "new" copy is brought out and, sure enough, leafing through it, Harihara discovers that indeed it is a copy of the *Naiṣadhīya*, beginning with the first verse "Having drunk whose stories . . ."[16]

Harihara good-naturedly acknowledges Vastupāla's cleverness. Thus begins, according to this account, the history of the *Naiṣadhīya* in Gujarat. The chronology of this story (if not the details, necessarily) matches the manuscript record, as the earliest reported manuscript of the *Naiṣadhīya* dates to the mid-twelfth century in a palm-leaf manuscript found in northern Gujarat (Pāṭan).

We also know, of course, that the first known commentary on the *Naiṣadhīya* (Vidyādhara's *Sāhityavidyādharī*) was produced in Vīradhavala's court in the early thirteenth century (discussed in chapter 2). Rājaśekharasūri, a little more than a century later, seems to give us, in this probably fanciful narrative about Harihara, a prehistory to

Vidyādhara's commentary—the only verifiable material evidence we have of the early presence of the *Naiṣadhīya* in Gujarat. Whether or not Harihara was a descendant of Śrīharṣa and came with this manuscript is uncorroborated elsewhere. The basic fact remains that outside of what can be gleaned from the poem itself and the scanty information in the early commentaries, very little absolutely compelling information is available about Śrīharṣa's commissioning milieu and the *Naiṣadhīya*'s manuscript transmissions.

One of the more fascinating aspects of this story, however, is what it says about the hybrid reality of the process of textual transmission and the social world of exchange in which the *Naiṣadhīya* operates as a material object. On the one hand, there is the actual physical materiality of the manuscript being copied down by Vastupāla's scribe. On the other hand, there is the broader "immaterial" world of the *Naiṣadhīya*'s oral transmission and its role in an imagined literary culture of "great poems" or "new poems" that operates largely within a frame of symbolic exchange and reciprocity. Furthermore, Rājaśekharasūri's linkage of minister Vastupāla's archiving activities with the *Naiṣadhīya* fortifies several widely held notions about the *Naiṣadhīya* tradition's putative historicity: that Śrīharṣa may have been born in Bengal (his supposed grandson Kamalākaragupta is said to have written a long commentary on the poem and, of course, Harihara from the above narrative is also thought to be a relative) and that the earliest transmission of, and documented critical attention to, the *Naiṣadhīya* occurs in Gujarat.

THE *NAIṢADHĪYA* IN GAUḌA COUNTRY

While the *Prabandhakośa* recollects the *Naiṣadhīya*'s transmission stream in Kashmir and Gujarat, another well-known Sanskrit source of the *Naiṣadhīya*'s possible transmission history comes from the fifteenth-century *Puruṣaparīkṣā*, a collection of well-crafted, quasi-historical vignettes authored by the Maithili poet and storyteller Vidyāpati. In a story called *Medhāvikathā* (The Man of Amazing Memory)—which is actually about a learned scholar-ascetic named Koka who possessed a remarkable memory—Śrīharṣa makes a memorable appearance. Here, Vidyāpati acknowledges Śrīharṣa's relationship with the city of Vārāṇasī but ultimately places the poet in the Gauḍa region (the modern Indian states of Bengal, Assam, Orissa, and part of eastern Bihar): "There was a learned poet named Śrīharṣa from the Gauḍa region. He composed a poem called the *Nalacarita*, which he took with him to Vārāṇasī to present to a conference of scholars."[17] Vidyāpati recounts the history of the *Naiṣadhīya* after it was composed by the poet and imagines Śrīharṣa to have self-doubt about the legitimacy of his creation:

> Only a captivating poem
> filled with rasa,
> fashioned with imaginative tropes,
> and thoughtfully expressed,
> confers Fame upon poets.
> Otherwise . . . it becomes a laughing matter.
> Gold is tested in fire,
> a poem by learned critics.
> What is a poet to do
> with a poem that the critics do not like?[18]

Thus beset with this nagging concern that his poem will not be well received, Śrīharṣa goes to Vārāṇasī to test his poem out on the learned authorities there. In Vārāṇasī, he meets a learned scholar-ascetic named Koka who, Vidyāpati informs us, was turned away from the pleasures of the world and absorbed constantly in meditation. Śrīharṣa, the account goes on to say, follows Koka to the banks of the Gaṅgā (specifically at the Maṇikarṇikā *ghāṭ*) where he goes daily to perform his ritual bath. While shadowing the old scholar, day after day, Śrīharṣa recites the *Naiṣadhīya* to him. After many days, frustrated that Koka demurs from any kind of comment at all, Śrīharṣa blurts out:

> Sir, I've worked very hard on this *mahākāvya*. I've come a long way to have this poem examined by a great mind like you, you who are from the same country as I am. I keep reciting this poem, waiting to hear your opinion. You don't have any criticism nor any praise for it. It seems that you have not even been listening.[19]

Shaken out of his silence, Koka responds:

> How could I not have listened! I do not want to say anything specific until I have heard the whole thing, until I've judiciously analyzed it and understood the sound and sense in their proper contexts. I've been listening to the verses and I've committed them to memory. If you don't believe me . . . then listen.[20]

Vidyāpati concludes this narrative with Koka reciting the entire *Naiṣadhīya* (up to the point that Śrīharṣa had recited to him). Śrīharṣa is delighted and praises Koka for his incredible memory, which was the main point being demonstrated by Vidyāpati in this particular story. Koka then proceeds to expound point by point the effective and ineffective literary usages in the poem (*guṇa* and *doṣa*) and then (presumably exhausted by the young poet's persistence) sends Śrīharṣa home.

To substantiate this point, "[h]ow the written, the performed, and the memorized interacted to give Sanskrit literary culture its unique character," Pollock recounts Vidyāpati's story of Śrīharṣa's presenting his poem to Kokapaṇḍita for approval. Pollock's commentary on the significance of this narrative is germane to the point of Sanskrit poetry's commitment to both the written and to the oral dimensions of the literary experience:

> The undoubted importance of writing in creating and transmitting the literary work, the continuing commitment to memory as a pedagogical value, and the undiminished centrality of performance in the publication and consumption—the copresence of such factors throughout the long history of Sanskrit literary culture suggests how complex was the status of literacy in premodern South Asia, and how unfamiliar to modern sensibilities.[21]

The early readers of *Naiṣadhīya* seem to have been aware of the changes unfolding in Sanskrit literary culture and the particular role their poem was playing in this world. In sorting out what the poet may have intended from what the text actually says to them, independent of the author's intentions, it may be that narratives such as these conflate the two features by having the poet participate in a world they imagine and feel to be true. The legend, therefore, gives coherence to the readers' expectations about the *Naiṣadhīya* tradition.

ŚRĪHARṢA'S EXIT

Vidyāpati's account ends with the final approval of the *Naiṣadhīya* as worthy of dissemination and fame. Having been given the seal of approval by Koka, Śrīharṣa and his poem can now safely be brought into conversation with the other great poems of Sanskrit tradition. Whereas this fact—the establishment of the *Naiṣadhīya* as a classic text worthy of being included in the canons of Sanskrit literature—completes the purpose of reconstructing a history of the *Naiṣadhīya* and its poet for Vidyāpati and the early commentators, the desire for closure to Śrīharṣa's biography leads Rājaśekharasūri to deliver a rather unsavory coda to the *mahākavi*'s activity as court poet to Jayantacandra and ultimately his demise at the hands of the Gāhaḍavāla monarch's queen. The odd narrative implicates Śrīharṣa in scandalous imbroglios and power struggles that eventually lead to his exile. Clearly unfolding within a context of court intrigue in Gāhaḍavāla king Jayantacandra's court (and involving the king's second wife), this narrative sheds light on the transitional role played by a poet-at-court during the late-twelfth century.

The story begins with Śrīharṣa away from court. During this time, Jayantacandra's minister Padmākara has gone to King Kumārapāla's court in Gujarat (to Aṇahilapura), where he is strangely overcome by the sight of a beautiful *sārī*, covered by dark honey bees (as if they were hovering around a Ketakī tree). The minister asks the washerman to lead him to the house of the woman to whom this *sārī* belongs. When Padmākara sees this beautiful woman, who is a courtier's widow named Sūhavadevī, he asks Kumārapāla's permission to bring her back to Vārāṇasī, after taking a tour with her to the Somanātha temple. Once she is married to Jayantacandra, Sūhavadevī—described as proudly fancying herself a learned woman—expresses a wish to be called the *kalā-bhāratī*, that is to say, the very personification of skill in the arts. Once she recognizes that Śrīharṣa has a similar title, as the *nara-bhāratī* (Bhāratī, or Eloquence personified, among men), her jealousy gets the better of her and she summons him:

> "Who are you?" Śrīharṣa replies, "I am one who knows all the arts (*kalāsarvajña*)." The queen counters: "Then make me a pair of slippers." What could this mean, Śrīharṣa thought? If I say I don't know how to do it because I am a twice-born man, then I will be exposed as not being all-knowing; [if I do it, my caste position will be degraded]. Śrīharṣa accepts the challenge and fashions for her a pair of shoes made of bark, as a skilled cobbler would. Dejected by the whole experience, however, he takes his leave of the queen, informs the king of her machinations, [tenders his resignation], and withdraws to the banks of the Gaṅgā river where he becomes an ascetic.[22]

Thus concludes Rājaśekharasūri's story of Śrīharṣa: a broken man at the end of his career, humiliated in the context of a bizarre power play at court. Rājaśekharasūri's specificity strikes a note of authentic historical detail, a hallmark of the *prabandha* genre, but there is very little to authenticate this strange narrative. The historicity of the details notwithstanding, the totality of Rājaśekharasūri's account in the *Prabandhakośa*, as also the brief account of Śrīharṣa in Vidyāpati's *Puruṣaparīkṣā*, strikes a remarkably consistent tone with respect to the characterization of the *Naiṣadhīya*'s poet: a polymath who is defiant, impulsive, and uncompromising in his literary and philosophical practice.

THE ŚRĪHARṢA–UDAYANA–MAMMAṬA CONNECTION

Consonant with what we have seen thus far, matching up the *Naiṣadhīya*'s poet in some kind of intellectual grudge match with major personalities from the history of Sanskrit philosophy and literary criticism also appears as a recurring motif in the Śrīharṣa legend cycle. On the most basic level, this makes perfect sense as Śrīharṣa authors both a work on philosophy that breaks with an earlier stream of normative thought and a poem that stretches the limits of the then-mainstream grammars of poetic description and analysis. In both cases, his work squarely faces up to the logical arguments of Udayana the philosopher and more obliquely to the customary values of Mammaṭa, especially regarding what passes for effective linguistic and tropic shaping in poetry. Certainly no chronological reckoning can situate Śrīharṣa, Udayana, and Mammaṭa in the same temporal frame, as the authors cited above do. Both Udayana and Mammaṭa precede Śrīharṣa: the first by almost two centuries and the second by at least one. However, their juxtaposition by the guardians of collective memory like Cāṇḍupaṇḍita and then by Gadādhara and Rājaśekharasūri does reflect an actual thread in the history of Indian philosophy and Indian literary criticism. It seems likely that Śrīharṣa's defense of Advaita logic in the *Khaṇḍanakhaṇḍakhādya* against the views expressed in the logician Udayana's famous texts (*Lakṣaṇāvalī* and *Nyāyakusumāñjali*) compels readers like Cāṇḍupaṇḍita to conflate their historical proximity. Reiterating what was said above, in addition to their possible Kashmiri connection, the circulating stories linking Śrīharṣa with Mammaṭa may reflect a historically significant critical perspective that Śrīharṣa's boldness (*prāgalbhya*) as a poet has never been universally admired by all audiences, making the *Naiṣadhīya*'s inclusion the most contentious of all within the traditional scheme of the five great classics of the *mahākāvya* tradition (*pañcamahākāvya*).

It is appropriate here briefly to consider another crucial literary-historical perspective to the Śrīharṣa–Udayana–Mammaṭa connection. It seems very plausible that the Śrīharṣa–Udayana and Śrīharṣa–Mammaṭa narratives seek to provide a credible ontology for the fact that the works of Śrīharṣa, Udayana, and Mammaṭa share a common function in the circumscribed world of the traditional Sanskrit school system (*pāṭhaśālā*). As I mentioned earlier, writing a commentary on any one of these three works—Udayana's *Nyāyakusumāñjali*, Mammaṭa's *Kāvyaprakāśa*, or Śrīharṣa's *Naiṣadhīyacarita*—immediately conferred upon the scholar the title of *mahāmahopadhyāya*, Sanskrit pedagogical culture's equivalent of a modern university professorship.[23] Perhaps this formulation itself reflects the fact that these three works have the most extant commentaries written on them in their respective genres: logic, poetics, and *mahākāvya*. As a final comment here, one may also speculate that stories anachronistically linking Mammaṭa and Śrīharṣa in the anecdotal histories have something to do with the fact that the unprecedented production of commentaries on *Kāvyaprakāśa* and *Naiṣadhīya* seems to flourish simultaneously in the manuscript chronologies of both works. The legends that build around these three authors bear a striking resemblance. Portraits of all three authors emphasize their pugnacious character, reflecting perhaps the sharp dialectical tone of their works. Udayana, for example, is frequently seen as a lively combatant with Buddhist scholars.[24]

Similarly with Mammaṭa, in addition to his sarcastic jibe at his "nephew" Śrīharṣa, there are legends that mark him as an acerbic defender of conservative views about literary criticism. In this light, one may reasonably speculate that the stories of Kashmiri pandits initially repudiating the *Naiṣadhīya* and the anachronistic criticism of Mammaṭa perhaps reflect debates about what texts were "proper" to include in the nascent canons of *mahākāvya* being formed during the period. Recent scholarship on the formalist poetics of this period has pointed to the possibility that those very scholastic exercises aimed at evaluating and providing models to account for the varieties of trope and theme in the *mahākāvya* were themselves transforming in light of the emergence of works like *Naiṣadhīya*, which were instrumental in reformulating and reforming existing modes of poetic expressivity. As discussed earlier, post-Śrīharṣa manuals on poetics (such as the works of Jayadeva Pīyūṣavarṣa and Appayadīkṣita), along with commentaries on these works, were clearly guided by the tropic innovations of texts like *Naiṣadhīya*. Appayadīkṣita quotes the most

Naiṣadhīya verses in his poetic works, thirteen in the *Kuvalayānanda* and thirty-two in the *Citramīmāṃsā*.

From a related but less historically pregnant perspective, crafting such detailed narratives that uniquely situate Śrīharṣa as excelling equally as philosopher and poet may simply reflect an urge on the part of audiences to articulate their astonishment about the poet's versatility. It may also signal an acknowledgment of another broad stream of the historical reception of *Naiṣadhīya*: the enduring discourse that Śrīharṣa's expansive abilities were largely the product of his extraordinary spiritual attainments, an idea explicitly seeded in the verses of the poem itself. In this way, the imaginative details given by Cāṇḍupaṇḍita and Gadādhara—about Śrīharṣa's conscious decision to achieve yogic power to defeat his father's rival—and Rājaśekharasūri's amplification of these details to suggest Śrīharṣa's frustration about receiving *too much* power from the goddess of learning serve ultimately to satisfy audiences' unresolved curiosity: How indeed could one person be so proficient at two extremely difficult tasks? The answer these narratives provide: Śrīharṣa composed these two difficult texts to justify his own claim to omniscience, a power drawn from his own extensive spiritual practice. The final detail given by Rājaśekharasūri—the humbling of a proud Śrīharṣa by a queen who wishes to supplant his position as resident genius—reinforces, on the one hand, how closely tied to Śrīharṣa's identity is this claim to omniscience and, on the other hand, provides the only fitting denouement available to such persons: a sudden withdrawal, out of dispassion and disgust, to Vārāṇasī where, as the archetype holds, yogis and traditional pandits retire to wait patiently for their impending death.

CONCLUDING OBSERVATIONS

Historians and scholars of society and religion in India have for a long time noticed the wide circulation of premodern narratives about poets, poet-saints, and other literary figures. While recent scholarship in these fields has grown more sophisticated in interpreting premodern "life narratives,"[25] usually they have been relegated to the stuff of legend or quaint narrative. Most histories of Sanskrit literature, for example, have attempted to assess the "veracity" of stories current about Sanskrit poets, but, almost as a rule, they conclude that as these stories are unfit to settle conventional chronological issues, their value for the scholar is virtually nil.[26] The traditional Sanskrit term for these accounts (*kimvadantī*) translates to something like "unconfirmed reports" or "hearsay." A few recent scholarly attempts have begun to read these quasi-biographical documents in the contexts that they were probably designed for—as narrative modes that do the work of literary criticism and literary history. The collective record of the *Naiṣadhīya* and Śrīharṣa reveals a peculiar type of historical reckoning in terms of source and strategy. One narrative rests on the edifice of another, with each subsequent source applying strategic hermeneutic procedures on its predecessor whereby fundamentally inherited details about the poem and the poet—usually from the poem itself—are selectively interpreted, modified, reinforced, redirected, or radically altered in service of carefully considered literary-historical motives.

Many of these textualized legends of Śrīharṣa seem to be rooted in oral traditions composed, as Sandesara writes about the *Prabandhakośa*, "on the basis of historical traditions preserved and transmitted through the *vṛddha-paraṃparā* or line of teachers."[27] One may also think of the artistic vignettes about Śrīharṣa and the *Naiṣadhīya* as short critical essays about a certain individual or community's creative impressions about poet, text, and the tradition of the text. V. Narayana Rao writes about the historicity of these narratives in the following way:

> Although rejected by recent literary historians as historically unreliable, these legends, honored by tradition, have a value similar to literary criticism, and they are worth considering as serious representations of the collective wisdom of the literary community.[28]

The narratives recounted above, from the prefaces of the early commentators and in the developed vignettes of the *prabandha* literature, are, above all, imaginative reconstructions of both a received and studied historical consciousness of past events and processes. Where to place Śrīharṣa's home occupies these commentators, for example, and the lack of consensus—arguments are made for Kanauj, Varanasi, Kashmir, Bengal, and Orissa—may simply reflect that the poet's activity while alive, and the content of the work itself, takes in the sweep of multiple regional experiences. Many legends of Sanskrit poets circulate through what Shulman and Narayana Rao have called the "*cāṭu*" verse tradition. According to these authors, *cāṭu* stanzas imitate the "original" poet's voice so well that they are often attributed to historical poets. In fact, however, they themselves collapse historical time and function as a kind of "displacement through identification, which allows for incisive commentary upon or criticism of great poets' works through innovative imitation."[29] Transmitted orally, at some point textualized, *cāṭus* are attributed to a historical author but in fact are composed in the manner or in the style of the historical author to epitomize some characteristic stylistic or thematic aspect. Other types of legendary reflections are captured in what are sometimes called "treasuries of stories" (*kathākoṣa*), collections of *textualized* narratives that emerge in South Asia during the second millennium. The short vignettes of poets (and king-poets, in the case of the eleventh-century Bhoja) begin fully to emerge in the thirteenth and fourteenth centuries. Many of them appear in genres like the *prabandha*, of which Rājaśekharasūri's *Prabandhakośa* is a fine example. Others appear in didactic collections such as Vidyāpati's *Puruṣaparīkṣā* or in the prefaces (*avataraṇa*) of Sanskrit commentaries on *mahākāvya*.

Unfortunately, it is usually difficult to contextualize these biographical accounts. Why were they composed? How were they used? What kind of history do they reflect? While some famous Sanskrit authors are more or less established under the patronage of certain historical kings (Bhavabhūti and Bilhaṇa, for example), there are others whose "biographies" are almost entirely shrouded in legend. Bhartṛhari, for example, has been received by readers for centuries as wholly outside of a historical orbit and embodied only through stories recounting his ambivalence for life as king and monk, narratives clearly structured around understanding his logic for writing one hundred verses each about love, worldly life, and detachment. Legends have made the Sanskrit *mahākavi*, perhaps beginning with Vālmīki himself, participate in various scenarios or made to utter various statements that reveal aspects of the literary processes of production and reception in South Asia unavailable from any other types of sources. These narrative forms often support, reinforce, or reform a poet's *aura* or some particular literary-critical understanding of his work and its relationship to a larger literary tradition. The impression of a great poem as a product of an author-less master (or of an author of extraordinary genius) is often initiated by the historical poet himself in his work and certainly reinforced by his commentators and critics. Certainly, such is the case with Śrīharṣa.

The relationship between poet and biographer in light of constructing a "voice" becomes, therefore, essential to the way the poem lives in the consciousness of audiences over the span of centuries. How useful are the fifteenth- and sixteenth-century documents cited in this chapter toward reconstructing an *emic* conception of literary reception and history? If many of these stories illuminate the overlapping author functions that collectively constitute a poet's "voice," what historical processes do these legends reflect in terms of shaping the construction of this voice? The range of historical response available in these legends often reveals that what we might call the poem's "reception" constitutes more than simply a loose network of colorful impressions and readings about the works and their authors. Rather, the *effect* created by the cumulative history of readings seems to have a crucial influence on the role the poem must have played historically and continues to play today. Many of the legendary stories of canonical Sanskrit poets are well known to literary communities in South Asia, if not always textually corroborated.

7 ◈ THE TRADITION EXPANDS TO THE REGIONS

The future of a text—the conventions and the world-views it will help to form and consolidate—is just as much a part of its history and its contribution to history.[1]

Franco Moretti

In the late-fourteenth and fifteenth centuries, the *Naiṣadhīya* tradition enters into a mature phase. In addition to quasi-biographical narratives and professional commentaries, we additionally observe two significant developments. One of them is the transformation of the *Naiṣadhīya*'s status, from a text inviting critical comment to a canonical work indispensable to a literary culture's self-understanding. The second development, coeval with and profoundly related to the *Naiṣadhīya*'s popularity among learned audiences in South Asia, is the advent of regional-language translations of the poem. This chapter offers a glimpse into the complex world of the *Naiṣadhīya* translation and, in particular, explores the ways in which these translations represent both continuities with earlier commentarial engagements with the *Naiṣadhīya* and, at the same time, divergent forms of literary practice that transform what the poem comes to mean to literary audiences.

I use the term "translation" in this chapter to refer to a wide range of texts that *consciously* look to the *Naiṣadhīya*'s verses or its style to render a partial, more or less complete, or oblique conversion of Śrīharṣa's poem. Those works that translate the poem into a regional language I refer to here as "interlingual" translations. Those works written in Sanskrit, but *consciously* translating Śrīharṣa's linguistic usages and thematic choices in a new idiom, I call "intralingual" translations.[2] Both of these types of works, I argue, show strong affinities to Sanskrit commentaries on the

Naiṣadhīya and are, indeed, indebted to, and in conversation with, them. With approximately fifty known Sanskrit commentaries on the poem and multiple translations and adaptations, the *Naiṣadhīya* stands apart from most other *mahākāvyas.* Also telling is the number of creative works written by known or attested commentators of *Naiṣadhīya.* Grappling with the diversity of linguistic usage and other such textual difficulties in the poem, the *Naiṣadhīya* presents special challenges to its medieval commentators and translators. Foundational Sanskrit poems, Sanskrit commentaries on them, regional language translations and their commentaries, and newer Sanskrit and regional-language works fundamentally tied to their older sources occupy a shared space in medieval and early modern India in ways that have perhaps escaped notice in a milieu that privileges each of these source types as semi-autonomous developments of literary culture. Despite its richly well-traveled record, it seems unlikely, however, that the *Naiṣadhīya* tradition—with its wide dispersion of commentaries, biographical narratives, translations, and literary-critical documents—is fundamentally different from other popular works of literature in South Asia in this regard.

Furthermore, similar to the ways in which a range of documents mushroom around Śrīharṣa and his poem (commentaries, hagiographies, pseudepigrapha, translations), the regional-language translators/authors and their poems also attract commentators, legend makers, and translators. Observing these translations (and the histories of their reception) alongside the *Naiṣadhīya* and its "afterlife," therefore, reveals the extent to which these works constitute and inspire parallel traditions of aesthetic creation and literary historiography that become stable components of many of South Asia's literary cultures. In effect, then, these translations—commentaries on the Sanskrit poem *and* creative works in their own right—become subjects of their own critical traditions of reception. As such, their histories resemble the *Naiṣadhīya*'s.

A HISTORICAL SURVEY OF *NAIṢADHĪYA* TRANSLATIONS

Śrīharṣa's *Naiṣadhīya* left a deep impression in the subcontinent's literary cultures from the thirteenth to twentieth centuries. And, in turn, we can say that the changes transpiring in the linguistic situation of late-twelfth-century South Asia left a stamp on the *Naiṣadhīya.* One notices, for instance, numerous usages in the verses of the *Naiṣadhīya* that exhibit the ways in which twelfth-century Sanskrit was linguistically interacting with the emerging regional languages of the time. While it is often highlighted that Śrīharṣa mines the Sanskrit dictionaries (*kośa*) to render some thousand difficult and obsolete words in his poem, the numerous contemporary (*samakālika*), local (*deśīya*), and newly minted (*navya*) words brought into the Sanskrit idiom by Śrīharṣa have yet to be accounted for in histories of South Asian language. It is likely that the *Naiṣadhīya*'s conscious recognition of the emerging influence of regional South Asian languages and their peculiar literary predilections correspond to its meteoric dissemination among and wide use by regional-language authors in all genres. The distinctive twelfth-century Sanskrit usages in *Naiṣadhīya* show the period's growing proximity among the linguistic worlds of Sanskrit and regional languages.

A.N. Jani gives several examples of newly minted Sanskrit expressions in *Naiṣadhīya* that correspond to common contemporary usages in Gujarati and Marathi. For example, the phrase "*katham āsyaṃ darśayitāhe*" ("How can I show my face") in *Naiṣadhīya* 5.71 and 20.49 could be rendered in Gujarati as "*kevi ṛte moḍhuṃ batāvuṃ*" or verse 9.41's "*navīnam aśrāvi tavānanād idam*" ("This is something new I'm hearing from your mouth") in modern Gujarati would be "*navuṃ sāmbharyuṃ tamāra moḍhāṃ thiṃ*" (Jani 1957: 241ff). Jani's list of idioms is supplemented by new types of diction in Śrīharṣa's Sanskrit, reflective of profound contact with late-medieval India's regional languages.[3] For instance, in describing the moon's activity of destroying pining lovers in *Naiṣadhīya* 4.62, the poet uses the word *vyasana* in the sense of "general habit," uncommon in Sanskrit before this time and a primary sense of the word in many modern regional languages. Another interesting "modern" use (in *Naiṣadhīya* 3.8) is of the Sanskrit root *lag* in the sense of "following" (commentator Nārāyaṇa, for example, glosses *lagati* with *cacāla*).[4] Similarly, Śrīharṣa's awareness and use of vernacular meters is another potential avenue for exploration.[5]

Commentaries on *Naiṣadhīya* reveal the extent to which the regional languages of South Asia entered the domain of the high Sanskrit *kāvya*. Very often in medieval and early-modern *Naiṣadhīya* commentaries, one finds commentators labeling diction directly inserted from the regional languages as *bhāṣaśabda* or *deśyaśabda*, sometimes speculating on the particular region as well. A.N. Jani (1957:241), for example, notes unprecedented usages from the "popular language" such as the word *iṅgāla* in *Naiṣadhīya* 1.9, *biruda* in *Naiṣadhīya* 11.37, and *dhoraṇi* in *Naiṣadhīya* 15.49. All of these words are either labeled as "regional" by commentators (Nārāyaṇa calls '*iṅgāla*' a *bhāṣaśabda* that means "charcoal," while Mallinātha brands it *deśyaśabda*) or, alternatively, well-attested Sanskrit words are presented as synonyms (Jinarāja, for example, glosses *iṅgāla* with the normative *aṅgāra*). Sometimes, commentators give remarkably specific information about a given regional word or expression. Nārāyaṇa, for example, in locating the origins of the word *ḍimba* (in *Naiṣadhīya* 22.51) says that in Gauḍa language, *ḍimba* or *lalaḍimba* is the word for "a toy top" (*bhramaraka*), while in the languages of Kānyakubja and Mahārāṣṭra (Nārāyaṇa's country), the word is *bhaṃvarā*.[6]

Starting backwards, we can identify at least a dozen complete translations of the poem into modern Indian languages during the late-nineteenth and twentieth centuries.[7] These translations usually accompany some edition of the Sanskrit text and are primarily prose works that resemble the paraphrases offered by traditional Sanskrit commentaries; this era also saw several poetic summaries of the poem written by Sanskrit scholars, such as Kṛṣṇarāma's *Sāraśataka* and A.V. Narasiṃha Chari's nineteenth-century *Āryanaiṣadha*.[8] Strikingly similar to the case of commentarial production on the *Naiṣadhīya* during the eighteenth and early-nineteenth centuries, there seems to have been very little in the way of translation projects on the *Naiṣadhīya* during this period. The only work from the eighteenth century (1769), in fact, is the *Kāvyakalānidhi* (Treasure-house of the Arts of Poetry), poet Gumāna Mishra's unfinished verse translation of the poem in Brajbhāṣā.[9]

The seventeenth century presents an entirely different story. During this century, a series of important works can be identified as not only translations of the *Naiṣadhīya* but also as foundational works in their own right. In his survey of translations and adaptations of the Nala story, Unni cites the works from Keralite Sanskrit poets from the seventeenth century as being either modeled on *Naiṣadhīya* (Karuṇākara's *Nalacandrodaya*, or The Moonrise of Nala) or intended as a continuation of it (Vandārubhaṭṭa Mādhavan Aṭithiri's *Uttaranaiṣadhīyacarita*, or The Later Adventures of Nala); other works, like the anonymous *Nalacaritaprabandha campū*, are direct translations.[10] Also from this century is Unnayi Variyar's *Nalacharitham Attakkatha*, on which is based the script for the performance of the quintessential Kathakali dance-drama *Nalacarita*; much of the first day's performance (out of seven) relies on Śrīharṣa's version of the Nala story. The famous Kathakali text (*attakatha*), according to N.P.

Unni, is "one of the best, if not the best, of original literary productions in Malayalam . . . the only one of its kind in the whole range of *kathakali* literature and unsurpassed."[11] Marathi poet Raghunātha Paṇḍita's *Damayantīsvayaṃvara* (Damayantī's *Svayaṃvara*) frankly admits the poem to be a commentary on the *Naiṣadhīya* in its preface.[12] Another *mahākāvya*, entitled *Pratinaiṣadha* (Each and Every Nala), is attributed to *Naiṣadhīya* commentator Śrīvidyādhara; while the commentary is no longer extant, according to Jani, the poem was "written under Shah Jahan's reign in the seventeenth century."[13] The seventeenth-century Gujarati poet Premānand's *Nalākhyān* reflects his predecessor's Bhālaṇ's translation of the same name much in the way that Bhālaṇ's composition does the *Naiṣadhīyacarita*.[14]

Some scholars believe that the seventeenth-century Sanskrit poet Bhānubhaṭṭa's *Haihayendracarita* (dealing with the hero Kārtavīryārjuna from the *Viṣṇupurāṇa*) is modeled on the *Naiṣadhīya* as well.[15] A.N. Jani cites Caṇḍa's opening of the seventeenth-century *Pṛthvīrāja Rāso* to indicate Śrīharṣa's influence on the Brajbhāṣā poet's own work (*naraṃrūpa paṃcamma śrīharṣasāram / nalairāya kaṃṭhaṃ dinai śuddhahāraṃ //*).[16] The most celebrated translation from this era is the *Lāvanyavatī*, a poem by Upendra Bhañja in the Oriya *chautisa* tradition (lyrical ballad narratives). This poem, which is only obliquely a translation of the *Naiṣadhīya*, recasts the hero as Chandrabhānu, prince of Kārṇāṭaka, and the heroine as the eponymous Lāvanyavatī, a Sinhala princess. Ananta Tripathy Sharma, who has translated the *Lāvanyavatī* into Sanskrit, writes of the poem:

> *Lāvanyavatī* can be taken as the choicest sample of Upendra Bhañja's poetry: rich with imagery, consummate artistry and superb music, enlivened with the touch of rare poetic genius. In it, music and poetry fuse into a happy blend. . . . Since the *kāvya* was a venture to emulate the far-famed *Naiṣadhīya* of Śrīharṣa, which constituted a terror of the Sanskrit scholars of the country for more than 700 years with its extraordinary scholarship, intricate expressions and with verses having more than one, two or three meanings in many cases, a clear understanding of the *Lāvanyavatī* even in the Oriya original presupposes a study of Śrīharṣa.[17]

The *Lāvanyavatī* and two other works (the *Vaidehīvilāsa*, or Sītā's Playful Gestures; and *Koṭibrahmāṇḍasundarī*, or Beauty for the Ages) by Upendra Bhañja constitute a trilogy of Oriya classic works that, like the *Naiṣadhīya*, are standard works for students of Oriya literature. What is especially noteworthy, however, is that in addition to the fact that the *Lāvanyavatī* consciously strove to emulate the *Naiṣadhīya*, the fate it shared in Oriya literary circles for the past three hundred years also follows a trajectory familiar to the *Naiṣadhīya*'s reception among Sanskrit scholars.[18]

Though conferred the title of "emperor of poets" (*kavisamrāṭ*) by admirers, Bhañja apparently attracted bitter critics as well. Intriguingly similar to the narratives of Śrīharṣa and the *Naiṣadhīya*, Sharma explains that Bhañja's poetry was revolutionary in its effect on the "apathy traditional Sanskrit Pandits held for the Oriya language due to the absence of scholarly poetical works like the *Naiṣadhīya*." "It was commonly felt," he adds, that before Upendra Bhañja, "a poet with the talents of Bhāravi, Māgha, and Śrīharṣa was yet to be born to accept the challenge of the entire group of traditional pandits of those days and to vindicate the glory of the Oriya poets at the highest academic levels of the country."[19] Like Śrīharṣa, Upendra Bhañja is also reputed to have achieved his poetic prowess through meditation on a mantra, specifically the *rāmatāraka mantra*,[20] and was challenged by unsympathetic Oriya pandits to undergo several ordeals to establish the merits of his work; he won over all of them and, because he could give a dozen interpretations to his own verses, he was commonly referred to as *Puruṣabhāratī* (Sarasvatī in male form).[21] Again reminiscent of the *Naiṣadhīya*'s reception, Bhañja's poetry has been especially criticized by some twentieth-century critics for its frankness in treating sexual themes and its consistently difficult-to-understand language. For example, Guruprasad Mohanty (1924–2004), popularly known as Guru Prasad, summarized the reception of Upendra Bhañja among (unappreciative) contemporary audiences: "Upendra Bhañja means a woman and a dictionary."[22]

The great translations of the *Naiṣadhīya* from the fourteenth, fifteenth, and sixteenth centuries faced a reaction similar to Upendra Bhañja's among both contemporaries and later scholars. Some in the twentieth century spoke, for example, of the grand sixteenth-century Tamil translation of Śrīharṣa's poem *Naiṭatam* by poet Ativīrarāma Pāṇṭiyaṉ (aka Aḻakar Perumāḷ) as "almost unreadable." Zvelebil describes the poem, which was once a staple of Tamil literary education, as "an intoxicating drug" and attributes the famous saying associated with this poem to his own feeling about the poem: *Naiṭatam pulavark kauṭatam* (*Naiṭatam* is the drug of poets).[23] This characterization of the poem, perhaps consciously, echoes a traditional saying about the *Naiṣadhīya* (cited earlier): that it is a "medicine/tonic" for scholars (*naiṣadham vidvad-auṣadham*). David Shulman speaks in detail of the *Naiṭatam*'s translation practices and offers insight into the historical importance of this poem to Tamil education:

> Less than a century ago, Ativīrarāma's masterpiece, the *Naiṭatam* . . . was the foundation of a Tamil education, one of the most widely known and often reprinted of all classical Tamil works. . . . It was also always considered among the most difficult of classical works. The principle was, it seems, that once a child had mastered the *Naiṭatam*, with its archaic morphology and diction, its intricate *alaṅkāras*, its metrical virtuosity, and its high *kāvya* themes and *topoi*, then he or she would be able to read anything in Tamil. The usefulness of all this erudition, condensed into a single long work (1172 verses), must have outweighed the slight embarrassment of teaching so many overtly erotic verses to children.[24]

Shulman explains that "for all its close adherence to the Sanskrit prototype, the *Naiṭatam* is an utterly new work, organized differently from its model and embodying an expressivity all its own." Indeed, one may transplant this statement as well to describe the great *creative* translations of Śrīharṣa's poem from the fourteenth and fifteenth centuries, especially Bhālaṇ's fifteenth-century Gujarati poem *Nalākhyān* and the fourteenth-century masterpiece *Śṛṅgāranaiṣadham* (*Naiṣadhamu*), the first *bona fide* translation of the *Naiṣadhīya* composed by the great Telugu poet Śrīnātha, often called *sarvabhauma* ("king of poets").[25]

Before looking more closely at these two works by Bhālaṇ and Śrīnātha, which are truly translations of the *Naiṣadhīya*, two other works from the thirteenth century merit attention. First is the poem *Rukmiṇīsvayaṃvara* (*Rukmiṇī's Svayaṃvara*), a work that may be the earliest-known creative composition consciously tied to the *Naiṣadhīya* tradition (1292–1293). Its poet Narendra (or Narīndra) was an early and central figure of the *Mahānubhāva* sect, a devotional movement founded by Cakradhara in the late mid-thirteenth century (in what is now Maharashtra). A.N. Jani explains that the poem's "descriptions of the love of Kṛṣṇa and Rukmiṇī, of the assembled kings at the *svayaṃvara*, of the love-lorn condition of Rukmiṇī and of the measures taken by her friend to counteract it, and finally, of the physical charms of Rukmiṇī and Kṛṣṇa are modeled upon the *Naiṣadhīya*."[26] Tulpule offers some interesting examples from this work, in addition to relating several fanciful anecdotes about its composition, giving credence to this poem's strong connections with the *Naiṣadhīya*. Here is a passage from his description of the poem:

> [Narendra] seems to have been attempting a *mahākāvya* in Marāṭhī on the lines of Sanskrit *mahākāvyas* . . . His pen-pictures are a rare combination of the real and the imagined as can be seen from the following sketch of Rukmiṇī pining for Kṛṣṇa:
>
> "Lying with her left hand placed under the head,
> She had kept her right hand on the heart,
> So as not to allow Lord Kṛṣṇa to escape from it."
>
> Narendra had a keen aesthetic sense and introduced an ornate style which was imitated by the successive narrative poets of his [Mahānubhāva] sect.[27]

The example that Tulpule cites here bears an unmistakable resemblance to a series of verses from the beginning of the fourth canto of the *Naiṣadhīya*, where Śrīharṣa fancies Nala to reside in Damayantī's heart. Here is a verse, for example, I translated in chapter 1 (4.11):

> Just imagine the pain produced by a small splinter
> entering the sole of the foot?
> What to say of a mountain—the lord of the earth, Nala—
> entering the soft-bodied Damayantī's heart and staying lodged in there?

The series of verses that follow this one explain how Damayantī's eyes were so fixed on the recesses of her heart (where Nala was) that they could not see what was right in front of her (4.12), how her face drooped down to her chest in sadness but brightened on account of it because it was closer to Nala who, again, was in her heart (4.13), and so on. Clearly, Narendra is replicating the playful aesthetic, if not the specific images, of these verses in his own poem.

More intriguing, however, are the hagiographical narratives of the *Rukmiṇīsvayaṃvara*'s composition that, remarkably, mimic the ones we have about the *Naiṣadhīya* from the middle of the thirteenth century. Tulpule writes about a narrative found in the *Smṛtisthala*, a collection of (anonymous) biographical anecdotes in a proto-Marathi language from the early fourteenth century:

> The anecdote about the creation of the *Rukmiṇī-svayaṃvara* . . . is interesting. It seems that the two brothers of Narendra were also poets and when they recited their own poems on the episodes from the *Mahābhārata* and

> the *Rāmāyaṇa* respectively in the court of Rāmadeva Yādava, Narendra, who was present there and who had already heard about Cakradhara and his teachings, rebuked them for not singing the glory of Śrīkṛṣṇa instead. On being challenged by them to try for himself, Narendra composed then and there 1800 *ovīs* [a Marathi verse form, where the first line rhymes with the next two] on the episode of Kṛṣṇa's marriage with Rukmiṇī that the king liked so much that he asked for their authorship in exchange for a sumptuous royalty to the composer. Narendra, however, being a poet with self-respect, rejected the royal offer and taking home the manuscript of his poem, copied about half of it with the help of his two brothers and returned the original to the king the next morning. It is thus that this *Rukmiṇī-svayaṃvara* in its present form looks incomplete, containing only 879 *ovīs*, the completion of which was later attempted by not one but many unknown authors.[28]

I quote this passage at length because we see in it several important parallels from the biographical accounts given of Śrīharṣa and the *Naiṣadhīya* in the various works discussed in the previous chapter. First is the notion that the *Rukmiṇīsvayaṃvara* was composed in response to a challenge that the poet, Narendra, could not write a *kāvya* that was not explicitly devotional. Second is that the poem that we currently have is incomplete and, therefore, subject to the need for later authors to complete it. Finally, there is the narrative about the *Rukmiṇīsvayaṃvara*'s transmission and use, with a reference to the poet himself copying the manuscript overnight with the help of his brothers. While all three features of this narrative do not exactly correspond to the narratives discussed earlier concerning the *Naiṣadhīya*, the echoes are certainly there: Śrīharṣa writing the *Naiṣadhīya* as a response to the challenge given him by jealous paṇḍitas; the *Naiṣadhīya*'s legendary "incompleteness"; and minister Vastupāla's clever copying (again, overnight) of Harihara's manuscript so as to preserve it for the Vāghela king's royal library. As both sets of quasi-historical accounts (Cāṇḍupaṇḍita's preface to his *Dīpikā* commentary, the *Smṛtisthala*, and Rājaśekharasūri's *Prabandhakośa*) appear sometime in the mid-thirteenth and early-fourteenth centuries and repeat similar details about their respective authors, we may infer that these secondary accounts grew in popularity simultaneously while assuming that the stories about Śrīharṣa and the *Naiṣadhīya* were probably models for those fashioned about Narendra and the *Rukmiṇīsvayaṃvara*.

The final text that deserves comment in this historical survey is the thirteenth-century Sanskrit *mahākāvya Sahṛdayānanda* (Pleasure for the

Connoisseur) by Kṛṣṇānanda, poet and reputed commentator of the *Naiṣadhīya* from Orissa. While his commentary is no longer available, the poem itself is well known and well received by texts on poetics like the *Sāhityadarpaṇa* (A Mirror on Literature), which cites verses from it. I cautiously treat the *Sahṛdayānanda* as a partial intralingual translation of the *Naiṣadhīya* even though it is not usually understood as a "translation" but rather an important *mahākāvya* in its own right. It is, of course, that but, as I will show, this *mahākāvya* also shows the ways in which intertextuality, commentarial consciousness, and translation practices merge in interesting ways during the early centuries of the second millennium, making it difficult to disaggregate them into discrete categories of analysis.

COMMENTARY AND THE INTERLINGUAL TRANSLATION

The range of remarkable transformations happening after the twelfth century in terms of Sanskrit literary culture's relationship with regional-language literary cultures is a subject that has only recently garnered acute attention.[29] Established forms of literary composition, prevailing exegetical practices, and new creative genres such as the regional-language translation begin to share spaces in a literary culture marked by complex intersections and convergences that linked the efforts of multilingual poets with professional pedagogues and wider audiences for literature. Interlingual and intralingual translations of the *Naiṣadhīya* reveal a deep familiarity with the methods and procedures of the Sanskrit commentary on the poem and, consequently, represent a new kind of exegesis on the *Naiṣadhīya*, one that operates alongside the traditional Sanskrit commentary to enrich the poem's stature among the literary and pedagogical cultures of the regions. These translations, therefore, not only represent inaugurating moments in the literary history of regional languages but also reflect philosophical shifts in attitudes toward literature in general, embodying debates and ideas forged in pedagogical contexts and reproduced in new creative forms. Most germane to the subject of this book is that they should be seen as cornerstones of the *Naiṣadhīya* tradition's growth and, undoubtedly, a major reason for the tradition's enduring presence in South Asia's literary cultures.

Among the multiple literary reworkings of this masterpiece in South Asia's regional languages, two notable examples that demonstrate the richly interwoven textures of commentary writing and translation in premodern India are Bhālaṇ's fifteenth-century Gujarati work *Nalākhyān* and Śrīnātha's Telugu *Śṛṅgāra-naiṣadham* (or *Naiṣadhamu*) from the late-fourteenth century. While not implying that these two works are, in any way, commentaries on the *Naiṣadhīya*, I argue that there is a commentarial *consciousness* in their translating practices. With the composition of the *Nalākhyān*, Bhālaṇ inaugurates a new genre of Gujarati literature known as the *ākhyān*, a form that transports metrically tight, but thematically loose, verse composition (*pada-mālā*) into a formal narrative (*ākhyān*) dimension with clear boundaries or links (*kaḍavu*).[30] In rendering the Nala episode of the *Mahābhārata* into old Gujarati, Bhālaṇ explicitly clarifies the great epic as his source text while *implicitly* engaging with, in an obviously intertextual relationship, the *Naiṣadhīya*. While Bhālaṇ mentions his chief intertext to be the Nala episode found in Vyāsa's *Mahābhārata*, it is clear that Śrīharṣa's *Naiṣadhīya* is the most important source text for his depiction of Nala's life up until his union with Damayantī. Notably, Bhālaṇ mentions neither the *Naiṣadhīya* nor Śrīharṣa and, therefore, does not consider his work to be a translation of the *kāvya*. A close look at his work, however, discloses to what extent his Gujarati rendering of the Nala story lexically and syntactically coincides with the paraphrases found in Sanskrit commentaries on the *Naiṣadhīya*.

In the fourth *kaḍavu* [canto, literally "link of a chain"] of the *Nalākhyān*, Bhālaṇ combines two of Śrīharṣa's descriptions of Nala's outstanding character (details found in *Naiṣadhīya* 1.14 and 1.16) and constructs a passage of six verses that condenses and reorders the semantic content of Śrīharṣa's verses. In *Naiṣadhīya* 1.13, Śrīharṣa suggests that Nala was more powerful than the sun. In verse 1.14, he continues with this theme:

> Whenever the thought comes to the Creator
> that *those two* are redundant
> in the presence of Nala's brilliance and eminence,
> he draws a circle around them to cross them out—
> that's the illusive halo around the sun and the moon.

Here there is an implicit comparison of the sun and moon with King Nala's magisterial qualities: powerful brilliance, associated with the sun, and the ubiquitous celebrity enjoyed by the moon. The complex image combines several desires on the part of the poet: to praise Nala profusely, to create correspondences between Nala and the radiant orbs in the sky, to draw attention to the infrequent optical phenomenon of the halo that sometimes forms around these orbs, and finally to fancy the Creator as a sort of amanuensis (a scribe or a merchant) and his creation a manuscript or accounting book in need of occasional correction through crossing-out or, in this case, circling the mistake. Here is how Bhālaṇ renders Śrīharṣa's verse into Gujarati, spreading out the image over three stanzas:

> On rainy days, sometimes a halo appears behind the sun and the moon.
> This inspired an imaginative thought in the great poet's mind.
>
> Seeing Nala's brilliance in the sun and Nala's eminence in the moon,
> the Creator deliberated with himself, "Which sun and moon are real?
> Which ones are false?"
>
> And then, just as a merchant catches a mistake in his accounting book and
> draws a circle around it, so too did Brahmā put a halo around the sun
> and moon.[31]

We notice here that Bhālaṇ's verse expands Śrīharṣa's terse, compacted expression into three verses that flow together. Simultaneously, he collapses the themes of the original verse into metrical couplets (*doha*) to mirror the aesthetic concision of the *Naiṣadhīya* and also to replicate, though not necessarily reproduce, the stylistic condensation of Śrīharṣa's semantic intentions.

But he also adds or changes several important linguistic and thematic features not found in his source text. It is here, I argue, that Bhālaṇ reveals a consciousness akin to the Sanskrit commentators. First there is Bhālaṇ's statement that the site of the natural phenomenon "inspired an imaginative thought in the great poet's mind." Mallinātha, in explaining this verse, writes:

> The trope here is *apahnuti* (concealment, denial) as the scribal mark—not the putative subject of the image (the halo)—is superimposed onto or blocks the image of the halo, the putative subject. Earlier writers on poetics say that it is another trope known as *sāpahnavotprekṣā* (poetic fancy through dissimulation/concealment): a "cancelling mark" (*kuṇḍalanā*) is imagined to exist around the sun and moon under the pretext of a halo, and this has to be understood implicitly because no explicit words (such as "like") point to this trope.[32]

Whereas Mallinātha's commentary takes recourse here to the poetics discourse on trope (*alaṅkāraśāstra*) to cite the imaginative element of the image—alluding to the technical figure of concealment (*apahnuti*), for example—Bhālaṇ makes explicit that the poet had an "imaginative thought" and then goes on to make unambiguous the correspondence between Nala and the luminous orbs ("Seeing Nala's brilliance in the sun and Nala's eminence in the moon").

Next Bhālaṇ adopts a diagnostic approach to Śrīharṣa's language (frequently used by commentators like Nārāyaṇa) by reorienting the structure of the verse into an internal dialogue to explore multiple meanings or layers buried beneath the obvious lexical units of meaning. Thus, he writes: "Seeing Nala's brilliance in the sun and Nala's eminence in the moon, the Creator deliberated with himself, 'Which sun and moon are real? Which ones are false?'" Finally, the most glaring change made by Bhālaṇ is his explicit interpretation of Śrīharṣa's verse that he imports into his own couplet: the idea that "just as a merchant catches a mistake in his accounting book and draws a circle around it, so too did Brahmā put a halo around the sun and moon." While Śrīharṣa merely implies the metaphor of the merchant (or scribe) in saying about the Creator that "he draws a circle around them to cross them out," the *Naiṣadhīya* commentators (like Bhālaṇ) make explicit the basic sense that Śrīharṣa seeks to suggest. Here, for example, is how Mallinātha glosses Śrīharṣa's metaphor: "On the pretext of creating a halo, the Creator is actually making an indicatory mark to cancel the redundancy of the sun and the moon—just like a scribe or an author to erase an extra syllable or letter."[33] By specifying and analogizing the nature of the Creator's scribal work with that of a merchant who goes over his account books at the end of the business day ("just as a merchant catches a mistake in his accounting book and draws a circle around it"), Bhālaṇ creatively exploits the source text's inherent invitation for polyvalent interpretation. Whereas the Sanskrit commentators almost unanimously explain the scribe's convention as the intertext that makes the analogy clever, Bhālaṇ converts the coded scribe/manuscript metaphor to merchant/accounting ledger without losing anything from the original conceit but yet, presumably, adding something illustrative for his immediate audience.

This mode of extending an inherited commentarial consciousness with his own is apparent throughout Bhālaṇ's text and suggests that, like the commentators, his own attitude as a translator and creative artist tends both toward extending the source poem's semiotic potential and, simultaneously, toward displacing it with his own. The passages from the *Naiṣadhīya*'s Sanskrit commentaries paradigmatically reveal the commentator's tendency to unravel, reconstruct, supplement, and ultimately expand on the artistic ellipsis the Sanskrit poet has manufactured to veil and obstruct unambiguous understanding. In the examples given above, each commentator unravels the carefully arranged paratactic syntax of Śrīharṣa's composition in order to reconstruct an easy assessment of the poet's main image: that it was the Creator's intention in producing the occasional optical event of the halo around the sun and moon to speak to the redundancy of these orbs, as Nala excels both in the very qualities for which they are known. This halo is then imagined as the scribal custom of putting a circle with a pen around the items one wants ultimately to cross out or erase, the implication being that sometimes the Creator sets up the sun and moon to require cancellation, as they are unnecessary in the presence of Nala. The commentaries also supply, where necessary, the implications the poet skillfully leaves out. Śrīharṣa does not explicitly mention the Creator as a scribe nor does he spell out the correspondence between Nala and the celestial bodies in the sky. The three commentators only *explicitly* elucidate the actual scribal act implied by Śrīharṣa's mention of the cancelling mark (*kuṇḍalanā*). When Bhālaṇ translates this verse from the *Naiṣadhīya* in three stanzas (4.10–12), therefore, he seems to bring to his expression an explanatory consciousness reflected in commentarial practice.

Similar in some ways to Bhālaṇ's project is the grand work of fourteenth-century Telugu poet Śrīnātha. However, of the two, to study the ways in which a skilled translator in early premodern India was, at once, a first-rate poet and an astute commentator and critic, the text most worthy of attention is Śrīnātha's *Śṛṅgāra-naiṣadham*, or, as it is commonly called, the *Naiṣadhamu*. Like Bhālaṇ's *Nalākhyān*, the *Naiṣadhamu* marks important "firsts" in the history of regional-language literary cultures. As Bhālaṇ inaugurates the *ākhyān* in Gujarati, Śrīnātha's work is a model poem of the *prabandha* genre in Telugu, integrating as it does verse structures into a single, coherent narrative with clear movements and breaks. As significant is the fact that the *Naiṣadhamu* is the first known translation of a Sanskrit *mahākāvya* into a regional Indian language. Whereas Bhālaṇ effectively translates Śrīharṣa's verses here and there, Śrīnātha seems to be the first explicitly to assert his path-breaking enterprise to translate a Sanskrit *mahākāvya*. Śrīnātha, near the end of his composition

(*Naiṣadhamu* 8.202), provides a statement of his translation's methodology, rendered as follows by Narayana Rao and Shulman:

> The erotic poem made by the great Bhaṭṭa Harṣa, who traveled paths unseen by other poets, is here rendered into Telugu in a way that makes use of the special features of the language, to touch the hearts of the wise—following the sound of the text, aiming at the poet's intention (*abhiprāya*), keeping the poetic feeling (*bhāva*) in view, supporting the mood (*rasa*), embellishing the figures of expression (*alaṅkāra*), taking care of propriety (*aucitya*) and avoiding impropriety (*anaucitya*), closely obeying the original. This Telugu *Naiṣadhamu* will last as long as the moons, the stars, and the sun.[34]

At least from the point of view of reproducing the "poet's intention" and avoiding improper interpretations, Śrīnātha's statement above echoes more or less something a Sanskrit commentator might articulate. In fact, one tradition (discussed in chapter 2) identifies the Telugu poet Śrīnātha as himself a Sanskrit commentator on the *Naiṣadhīya*.

Like a commentator, Śrīnātha wants to make the original accessible to his audience and, therefore, pays careful attention to Śrīharṣa's willful misappropriation of words and syntax. As a translator and creative artist he, however, tries to reproduce as much of the sound and idea of the original without voiding his ambition to produce a distinctive work that will "last as long as the moons, the stars, and the sun." The principles he lays out for himself here include that, where appropriate, he will try to reproduce Śrīharṣa's usages without subverting the Sanskrit poet's narrative choices nor his intended complexity of expression. In other places, Śrīnātha is liberal in his impulse to emend the source text where there is perceived linguistic, aesthetic, or moral impropriety. The Telugu poet also condenses the *Naiṣadhīya*'s lengthy cantos by collapsing several verses (sometimes as many as six) into one single verse, essentially pruning what is Śrīharṣa's penchant for *exergasia*—to exhaust a single theme—in verse after verse with lush description or extravagant references to an array of cultural intertexts. And there are several other such "rules" of translation that Śrīnātha imposes upon himself in the *Naiṣadhamu*.[35]

Take, for example, his treatment of *Naiṣadhīya* 19.60 in the eighth canto of the *Naiṣadhamu*. Both of these verses are virtually untranslatable without resorting to a lengthy exposition about Sanskrit grammar. Semantically, they are virtually identical. However, the few changes that Śrīnātha makes are worth discussing in light of the mediating influence of the Sanskrit commentaries on this verse. Here are the two verses, beginning with the *Naiṣadhīya* 19.60 and followed by *Naiṣadhamu* 8.19:

> ***iha*** *kim* ***uṣasi*** *pṛcchāśaṃsi-kim-śabda-rūpa-*
> *pratiniyamita-vācā vāyasenaiṣa pṛṣṭaḥ* /
> *bhaṇa* ***phaṇi-bhava-śāstre tātaṅaḥ sthāninau*** *kā-*
> *viti vihita-tuhī-vāg-uttaraḥ kokilo'bhūt* // 19.60

> ***prātaḥkālamu*** *vāyasaṃbu* ***paṇināpatyoktaśāstraṃbulo***
> ***tātaṅsthānulu*** *ceppuḍ' ĕvvi? Yanu candaṃb' ŏppa kau kau yanan* /
> *cāturyaṃb' alarāran uttaramu vispaṣṭaṃbugā kokila-*
> *vrātaṃb' iccĕ tuhī tuhī yani gṛhārāmapradeśaṃbulan* // 8.19

First, a few words about the context of this verse and its meaning: The nineteenth canto of *Naiṣadhīya* provides a lengthy description of morning. Although the newly married King Nala is already awake and doing his morning prayers elsewhere, his royal panegyrists (*vaitālika*) gather to awaken him. In verse sixty of this *sarga*, the poet fancies a vignette of two birds in rapt conversation. A crow apparently asks a question to a cuckoo bird, who then fashions a reply in his own bird language. Śrīharṣa imagines a connection between the inarticulate matinal chatter of these birds and homophonous morphemes in a Pāṇinian *sūtra* and wonders if perhaps the two birds might be having a spirited morning discourse about grammar. The Sanskrit verse is framed in a melodious fifteen-syllabic meter (*mālinī*) while the Telugu verse is in a lengthier nineteen-syllabic one (*śārdūlavikrīḍita*).

The basic sense here is that in the morning at dawn, one may wonder if a crow—in repeatedly employing some declensional form of the Sanskrit word for "what" (*kimśabdarūpa*)—is in fact asking about the two substituted forms optionally replaced by the Pāṇinian affix "*tāt*," the answer to which is delivered by the cuckoo bird to the crow.[36] Could their dialogue be enacting, the poet mischievously wonders, the technical terminology found in texts on grammar? In essence, then, as the Sanskrit commentaries on the verse make clear, the crow is cawing something like "*kau kau*" ("which two" "which two") and the cuckoo is whistling back with "*tuhī*" "*tuhī*." Clearly, a verse like this proves very difficult to render in any language other than Sanskrit, intricately tied up with technical issues of Sanskrit grammar as it is. Unsurprisingly, both Śrīharṣa's and Śrīnātha's stanzas mean essentially the same thing: two birds in conversation, the one asking the other (in the poet's imagination) about a technical point of grammar. The semantic parallelism between the two is conspicuous and unsurprising, as Śrīnātha fashions his poem in the shadow of a well-formulated translation scheme that he works out in the preface to his composition. The superficial parallelism in meaning between the two verses aside, however, worthy of scrutiny here are the places where Śrīnātha chooses not to mimic the *Naiṣadhīya*'s diction. It is in these variant expressions that one may cite the role played by the hermeneutic consciousness of Sanskrit commentaries on the *Naiṣadhīya* in informing the creative choices of Śrīnātha. Comparing these two verses it again becomes evident that the rich academic discourse that accompanied the Sanskrit sources had an important function in mediating the dialogue between the Sanskrit source and the regional-language translation (the relevant phrases are in **boldface** in the text cited above and below).

The very first word of the verse, for instance, finds Śrīnātha collapsing the Sanskrit ***iha uṣasi*** with ***prātaḥkālamu*** ("in the morning"). This resembles—revealingly—the gloss of virtually every Sanskrit commentator on the verse, where *prabhāte* or *prātaḥ-kāle* paraphrases Śrīharṣa's *iha uṣasi*. Śrīnātha translates with the closely resonant Telugu *prātaḥkālamu*. Next, we notice that Śrīnātha chooses to retain the core of Śrīharṣa's playful verse by citing in his verse the Pāṇinian affix-marker *tātaṅ* while notably emending the most common reading of ***phaṇibhavaśāstra*** with ***paṇināpatyoktaśāstram***. Śrīnātha's choice reflects a significant commentarial antecedent and, therefore, proves noteworthy here. There is a disagreement among the early Sanskrit commentators about the correct reading of *phaṇibhavaśāstra* in the verse. All commentators, except Cāṇḍupaṇḍita, seem to favor the reading that indicates Patañjali's *Mahābhāṣya* (that is to say, "the *śāstra* produced by '*phaṇi*' or Śeṣanāga," i.e., Patañjali, the second-century BCE commentator of the great grammarian Pāṇini [fourth century BCE]).[37] The thirteenth-century commentator Cāṇḍupaṇḍita, however, insists that one should emend the wrong reading of *phaṇibhavaśāstre* to *paṇibhavaśāstre* and take the reference here to mean Pāṇini's *Aṣṭādhyāyi* itself.[38] Regardless of the correctness of the textual quibble, Śrīnātha chooses to supersede the most common reading and side with the less likely interpretation by rendering the source text's *paṇibhavaśāstra* with his own *paṇināpatyoktaśāstra,* remarkably following Cāṇḍupaṇḍita's explanation *paṇino'patyam*.

While there is no attempt here to link Śrīnātha with Cāṇḍupaṇḍita (or any other Sanskrit commentator) historically, it is likely that Śrīnātha is aware, along with the Sanskrit commentators, of the technical issues of grammar involved with this verse, and clearly this grammatical consciousness informs his own creative choices. Furthermore, we may observe the most marked parallel between the Sanskrit commentaries and Śrīnātha in the second and fourth quarters of his verse. Śrīharṣa merely suggests the actual sounds of the birds being repeated again and again by indicating that the crow used some form of the Sanskrit word *kim* and the cuckoo's response was *tuhī*. The Sanskrit commentators unpack their poet's implication by staging the dialogue explicitly. Cāṇḍupaṇḍita renders the crow's repeated cawing as "*kim kim*" and the *kokila*'s repetitive reply being "*tuhī tuhī*," while Nārāyaṇa has the crow abrasively repeating "*kau kau*" while the cuckoo croons "*tuhī tuhī*" ("which two" "which two"; "*tu* and *hi*" "*tu* and *hi*").[39] Śrīnātha apparently shares Nārāyaṇa's view and instantiates the commentary-like gloss into his own verse. And so, rather than merely implying the sounds as Śrīharṣa does, Śrīnātha downloads the entire commentarial expansion into his verse.

Unlike Bhālaṇ, Śrīnātha chooses not to reorient the details of this verse into a prosaic, explanatory mode. His translation seeks both to reproduce Śrīharṣa's image and imaginative analogy and to echo the rhythms of Śrīharṣa's verse. In this way, he negotiates a more facile comprehension for the reader—by expanding the implied dialogue between the two birds—but does not take the moment out of its immediate context by explaining the fancy the way a Sanskrit commentator might. Mallinātha, for example, summarizes verse 19.60 after glossing its lexical terms in the following way:

> The indistinct sounds of morning birds awakens an imaginative thought in the poet who, imagining the crow to say "*kau*" and the cuckoo "*tuhī*," fancies the previously recounted question-and-answer dialogue between the crow and the cuckoo. The idea here is built on the fact that birds, such as the crow, warble when the morning comes.[40]

Bhālaṇ implies in his preface that he is composing for an audience of largely Gujarati speakers, among whom there may be many with a good knowledge of Sanskrit; his prosaic explanation, therefore, closely follows the kind a commentator like Mallinātha might provide.[41] Śrīnātha's translation, however, seems clearly to be meant for highly learned Telugu audiences and Sanskrit scholars alike. Indeed, his work inspired its own sets of Telugu commentaries.[42] Śrīnātha's self-admitted task is to create a unique work that will nevertheless "obey" the original. Chief among his strategies to avoid misrepresenting or violating the aesthetic pleasure of the original text is to emphasize, as Narayana Rao and Shulman note, "an explicit focus on the *sounds* of the original (*śabdam 'anusārinciyunu*)."[43] In this regard, Śrīnātha differs from Bhālaṇ in terms of the ways in which the two translators incorporate the functions of commentary into their work.

While both take up strategies familiar to the Sanskrit commentary, in terms of condensing or expanding or restructuring their source, Bhālaṇ contentedly translates the source along the lines of a traditional commentary's conceptual understandings, without trying to make his poem sound or resonate like Śrīharṣa's. Śrīnātha intends, in contrast, to capture the peculiar force of Śrīharṣa's "sound" and thereby produces a far more dazzling feat of translation. One can say that Bhālaṇ is content with translating the *idea* whereas Śrīnātha strives also to reproduce the *expression* of the *Naiṣadhīya*'s verses. It is also noteworthy to add that the Telugu poet consistently produces a "second-order" reframing of the *Naiṣadhīya*, one that reproduces the specificity of Śrīharṣa's diction and simultaneously highlights, in a Telugu idiom, the Sanskrit original's intentions to be, at turns, complex and playful.[44]

COMMENTARY AND THE INTRALINGUAL TRANSLATION

It appears that, at least in part, regional language translations like the *Nalākhyān* and the *Naiṣadhamu* serve the function of Sanskrit commentaries without necessarily supplanting their continued production in certain academic or institutional contexts. Translations like Bhālaṇ's render the Sanskrit text's dense poetic tropes, language, and syntax comprehensible and accessible for local audiences that include both the Sanskrit and non-Sanskrit literati. Where Bhālaṇ's translation seeks some form of dynamic equivalence with Śrīharṣa's poem, giving primacy to the Sanskrit text's content, Śrīnātha seeks both a formal semantic and morphological equivalence with its source text. His translation condenses, expands, and makes more accessible the source text—all commentarial practices and aims—but goes further in many cases not only to reproduce the sonic and semantic effects of the Sanskrit source into a new regional idiom but also to refine and enhance it. Alongside this trend of regional-language translations working in tandem with the Sanskrit commentaries as conduits of

Sanskrit literary production for diverse audiences, another kind of work also invites attention in this regard: the *intralingual* translation.[45] One remarkable example from the Nala tradition, from the thirteenth century, is Orissa poet Kṛṣṇānanda's *Sahṛdayānanda*.[46] This poem appeals to the Sanskrit reader's previous experience of listening to (or reading) the *Naiṣadhīya* and, in reproducing word clusters and images used by Śrīharṣa, it relies on meta-linguistic reference to create a wholly new equivalence with its source text. An interesting conjecture, cited in numerous places including by Krishnamachariar himself, holds Kṛṣṇānanda (like Śrīnātha) to have himself written a Sanskrit commentary on the *Naiṣadhīya* as well. If this commentary did exist, it could be considered one of the earliest on the poem, contemporaneous with Cāṇḍupaṇḍita's.

In his Hindi introduction to the text, Vachaspati Dvivedi provocatively surmises that Kṛṣṇānanda's *Sahṛdayānanda* might not have survived the centuries were it not for its relationship with the *Naiṣadhīya*.[47] The number of examples in *Sahṛdayānanda* that reflect processes we observe in *Naiṣadhīya* commentaries (amplification, abbreviation, selective paraphrase) are, even from a brief study of this text, numerous. The few critics who have looked at the *Naiṣadhīya* and the *Sahṛdayānanda* together do not explore the source/commentary angle any further, however, than citing its possible connection. Instead, they cobble together a set of similarities and differences that exist between the two works, starkly noting the divergence in style and texture. Dvivedi, for example, writes that in Śrīharṣa's verse, naturalness of expression is compromised by the burden placed on the poem by excessively complicated conceits.[48] He contrasts Kṛṣṇānanda's verse as favorable to Śrīharṣa's in the following characteristics: there is "naturalness" to his descriptions; unlike Śrīharṣa's poem, he writes, there is little flashy "artistry" and showing off in Kṛṣṇānanda's; also, there is no forcing of sound effects like alliteration (*anuprāsa*) and repeated phoneme "twinning" (*yamaka*); finally, the *Sahṛdayānanda* does not cross the line between "poetry" (*kāvya*) and "scholarship" (*śāstra*), and there are no abstruse allusions inaccessible to the "ordinary" reader.[49]

Steering clear of typical comparisons between the two works' structural, thematic, and stylistic approach to rendering the Nala story, the following examples emphasize the intersection of a "translating" and "commentarial" consciousness evident in Kṛṣṇānanda's composition. Like Bhālaṇ (and unlike Śrīnātha), Kṛṣṇānanda never explicitly mentions

Śrīharṣa. Both Bhālaṇ and Kṛṣṇānanda, however, do pay their homage to the "great poet," which may reasonably be taken to refer to Vyāsa, to Śrīharṣa, or to both. Though neither Bhālaṇ's nor Kṛṣṇānanda's poems are openly acknowledged as translations—as Śrīnātha's is—both are informed by distinct hermeneutic practices and the impulses that guide them. The translating consciousness of the *Sahṛdayānanda*, as would be expected, differs from the regional language translations in significant ways. Unlike Bhālaṇ and Śrīnātha, there is no "non-Sanskrit" audience for whom the poet translates the verses from the *Naiṣadhīya*. In actuality then, calling it a translation signifies more its relationship to Sanskrit commentaries on the *Naiṣadhīya* (and to other classic *mahākāvyas*, as is shown later) than to the actual source text. It is clear that in several places, Kṛṣṇānanda reproduces Śrīharṣa's diction directly into his verse, while in most cases he paraphrases—in the ways Bhālaṇ and Śrīnātha do—a *Naiṣadhīya* commentary-like gloss and inserts it skillfully into his own work.

Take, for example, the famous scene where Nala first encounters the gold *haṃsa* bird (*hiraṇmaya-haṃsa*) that will shortly become his go-between with Damayantī. *Naiṣadhīya* 1.117 (translated in chapter 5 and repeated here) and 1.118 describe the scene as follows:

payodhi-lakṣmīmuṣi keli-palvale riraṃsu-haṃsī-kalanāda-sādaram /
sa tatra citraṃ vicarantam antike hiraṇmayaṃ haṃsaṃ **abodhi** *naiṣadhaḥ* //1.117

Near a pleasant pool
which had appropriated some of the ocean's loveliness,
Nala awakened to the presence of a spectacular golden *haṃsa*
stirring nearby, intent on seeking out
the indistinct cooing of a female *haṃsa*
desirous for love-play.

priyāsu bālāsu rata-kṣamāsu ca dvipatritaṃ pallavitaṃ ca bibhratam /
smarārjitaṃ rāga-mahī-ruhāṅkuraṃ miṣeṇa cañcvoś caraṇa-dvayasya ca//1.118

For his beloveds—submitting to their arousal—
he was bearing a pair of leaves with tender shoots,
in the guise of his red beak and feet,
born of Love
and sprouts of Passion's red tree.

The most marked word (in boldface above and below) in the first of these verses is "awoke," which in Śrīharṣa's text is the aorist form *abodhi*, a word that Sanskrit commentators gloss with any number of terms conveying the more logical meaning of "saw"; that Nala *saw* the bird. Mallinātha and Cāṇḍupaṇḍita, for example, gloss *abodhi* with the perfect form *dadarśa*[50]—the very same word used by Kṛṣṇānanda in *Sahṛdayānanda* 1.60:

mukhe priyāyāḥ praṇayānubandhād bālaṃ mṛṇālāṅkuram arpayantam /
sarojinī-patra-niṣaṇṇam ekaṃ hiraṇmayaṃ haṃsam asau **dadarśa** // 1.60

Nala saw a *haṃsa* made of gold: sitting on the leaf of the lotus, serving his beloved's mouth fresh lotus sprouts, out of love.

While keeping the metrical resonance of the source exactly intact to create a formal equivalence, the replacement of the suggestive usage of the marked verb signifying "[spiritual] awakening" (*abodhi*) to a more literal gloss of "seeing" (*dadarśa*) suggests a commentator's touch and also deflates the Vedāntin Śrīharṣa's allusive connection of the gold *haṃsa* and the *ātman*, which, in allegorical readings of *Naiṣadhīya*, Nala "awakens" to when he confronts it.[51] Kṛṣṇānanda, unlike later modern commentators, seems uninterested in the Advaita resonance of Nala's encounter with the bird.

In addition to the pregnant replacement of the word *abodhi* with *dadarśa*, *Sahṛdayānanda* 1.60 also collapses the two involved descriptions of Nala's first sighting of the *hamṣa* in *Naiṣadhīya* 1.117 and 1.118 with a single verse that manages to carry virtually verbatim a portion of the source text with an important divergence that reflects a commentator's pointed intervention. What Nala sees in the *Sahṛdayānanda* after recognizing the male *haṃsa* is only one beloved of the bird; the Nala of *Naiṣadhīya* sees two. On the surface, this may merely reflect an aesthetic choice (making singular Śrīharṣa's pluralization). More likely is that Kṛṣṇānanda's imagery reflects a creative choice made by a poet with a commentator's awareness of the complex idea embedded under the surface of Śrīharṣa's language. The *Naiṣadhīya* verses present quite a complicated image upon whose sense the commentators do not agree. Nārāyaṇa's idea seems to be that there are two beloveds—one experienced in lovemaking and one relatively inexperienced. The *haṃsa*, therefore, gives tender lotus sprouts to the young one whom he loves less than the experienced beloved, to whom he gives the lotus leaves. Kṛṣṇānanda seems to focus only on the young beloved, making it a point that the *haṃsa* placed the sprouts directly in her mouth implicitly with his own mouth—giving her, as Nārāyaṇa suggests, something akin to a loving kiss.[52] He does not pluck the leaves for a second beloved but merely sits on the lotus leaf. Mallinātha echoes this explanation and cites the verse as exhibiting a suggestive force that is built on complex tropic structure (*alaṅkāra-dhvani*); he lists at least four complex semantic tropes (*arthālaṅkara*) in the verse: metaphor (*rūpaka*), concealment (*apahnuti*), hyperbole (*atiśayokti*), and poetic fancy (*utprekṣā*). To reduce the complexity and yet keep the most charming suggestion in Śrīharṣa's verse intact—that the male *haṃsa* effectively kisses the female as he delivers the stalk into her mouth with his mouth—Kṛṣṇānanda astutely abbreviates the image to say only that the bird served "his beloved's mouth" out of love.

By and large, the practices of commentators to either expand or contract serve to inspire in Kṛṣṇānanda's poem a creative prompt rather than an explanatory one. The *Sahṛdayānanda* tends not to mimic the specific imagery of the *Naiṣadhīya*'s conceits (as we see in the two regional language poets) but rather echoes its tone—playful, prone to piling one trope upon another, and deeply referential (to itself and to cultural intertexts)—without generating the renowned complexity of Śrīharṣa's composition. Thus, for instance: he suggests Śrīharṣa's clever etymology of Damayantī's name by providing one of her father Vīrasena or of Nala (compare *Naiṣadhīya* 2.18 with *Sahṛdayānanda* 1.24); he has Kāmadeva describe Damayantī's beauty from head to toe (*nakha-śikha-varṇana/padādi-keśānta*) in a few verses rather than Nala's elaborate mental description of Damayantī in canto seven of *Naiṣadhīya*; or he replaces the famous "lament of the *haṃsa*" verses from the *Naiṣadhīya* (*haṃsa-vilāpa*) with similar ones addressed to a monkey Nala encounters and frees out of compassion while hunting (*Sahṛdayānanda* 1.56); and so on and so forth. Kṛṣṇānanda's consciousness of the *Naiṣadhīya*'s tone and texture is found everywhere in the early cantos of the *Sahṛdayānanda*, as is his deep awareness of the possibilities that exegetical modalities of expression hold to further his creative aims. The following verse from the second canto of *Sahṛdayānanda* (2.56) reflects the ways in which the poet Kṛṣṇānanda channels Kṛṣṇānanda the commentator:

> So slender he made that delicate Damayantī's waist
> that he feared it might snap.
> And so, right afterwards, the Creator
> protected it with three golden harnesses—
> conjured as the three flesh-folds around her midsection.

Kṛṣṇānanda's clever verse stands as a sequel thematically to *Naiṣadhīya* 2.34 and 2.35, and its form creatively contracts Śrīharṣa's *exergasia* in form (only one verse)—something commentators often do by simply ignoring the second verse as repetitive (*punar-ukta*) and, therefore, superfluous—and simultaneously expands Śrīharṣa's invocation of the corporal phenomenon of three folds on the belly (*trivali*) through an etymological analysis familiar to commentarial modes of observation.[53] In 2.34, Śrīharṣa imagines the Creator sculpting Damayantī's body with four fingers on the front and the thumb in the back: the four fingers produce three thin folds of flesh above her naval (*trivali*) and the thumb fashions the arched curvature of her back; in 2.35, Śrīharṣa fancies the indentations left by the four fingers squeezing her waist to be the three flesh-folds and the decorative gold chain women wear around their waist:

> Made beautiful was the midsection
> of Dama's sister by the Creator's fist
> around her belly: three flesh-folds
> squeezed out between the spaces of the four fingers;
> the arch in the lower back made by the thumb's indentation.
>
> Is someone curious about the midsection of Dama's sister?
> Is he measuring it with a fist?
> The four fingers holding it appear
> with three folds and a decorative gold chain.

Kṛṣṇānanda takes the imagery from both *Naiṣadhīya* verses but creates a wholly novel image: the three folds (and the gold chain) from Śrīharṣa's verses are converted in his verse to be three gold harnesses meant to protect her delicate waist. The creator, Kṛṣṇānanda implies, fears Damayantī's waist to be too fragile and so, under the pretext of the *trivali*, he fashions three golden belts to protect her body from breaking. Kṛṣṇānanda is playing on the related words *vali* (fold or wrinkle) and *valaya* (decorative belt or the old-fashioned "girdle"). Mallinātha unpacks the grammatical implication of this move in Śrīharṣa's text, which Kṛṣṇānanda is also clearly aware of, that the compound *trivali* (three folds of flesh) can be unpacked and the word *vali* can be pluralized to *valaya*.[54] The play lies in the fact that the term *valaya* itself is a noun that means "belt or decorative girdle." Once again, Kṛṣṇānanda's creativity—the verse is beautifully alliterated—fuses the word games played by poet and commentator.

CONCLUDING OBSERVATIONS

In the case of Bhālaṇ, Śrīnātha, and Kṛṣṇānanda, the point is not that the poets were necessarily reading commentaries on the *Naiṣadhīya* and "translating" them. Even if the tradition that Śrīnātha and Kṛṣṇānanda wrote commentaries on the *Naiṣadhīya* is not accurate, the point here is that these poets' work is nevertheless informed by a consciousness that is somewhat, if not thoroughly, imbued by the Sanskrit commentaries on Śrīharṣa's poem. While Sanskrit commentaries continued to be produced for specialized contexts even after the emergence of translations as functional commentaries on Sanskrit *kāvya*, in some measure the latter provided a more uninhibited space for rhetorical exploration. As these translations themselves entered into a pedagogical space occupied traditionally by Sanskrit commentaries, it is probable that something akin to what Copeland argues as conflicts between the claims of rhetoric and grammar in the academic discourses of the European Middle Ages could have arisen in a South Asian context, within the theoretical systems of textual production and textual interpretation that collectively compose Sanskrit literary discourse (*sāhityaśāstra*). As a commentary on the original, the regional-language translations emphasize the rhetoric of the source text. The latent translating animus of formal commentarial acts, however, is often buried in its attention to the details of grammar and the task of pedagogy. Unlike the Sanskrit commentary's ambivalent underplaying of its assumption of the authority of the source text, the translation allows for more freedom to transact this authoritative move. Whereas the commentator's ostensible service to the source text is a *sine qua non*, the translator can choose to be faithful or to emend radically, as each of the poets discussed above do. In light of their role in academic institutions, commentaries often have little leeway to veer from their conformance to the style and substance demanded from the contexts of their production.

The very fact that regional-language poets thought seminal Sanskrit texts to be "translatable"—especially a challenging poem like the *Naiṣadhīya*—is remarkable. It implies a belief in their accessibility to non-Sanskrit audiences, challenging the notion that Sanskrit texts were untranslatable and thereby fixed in their static, canonical perches. Generally, the translation into a regional language was a creative act first and only then a commentary. However, the commentator was free to provide multiple explications and to let his inventiveness wander, either in the circumscribed world of grammatical possibility or through the invocation of wide cultural reference. The translator could generally only make one choice. These poets' exegetical interests not only lay in the accessible transference of the Sanskrit masterpiece for Sanskrit and non-Sanskrit audiences but also include practices to "clean up," where necessary, the excesses or deficiencies of the master Sanskrit poet. The very textual characteristics that mark the Sanskrit commentary constitute an oblique mechanism for displacing the text. The translation of the Sanskrit text into the regional language, however, represented not so much a displacement of the authoritative source text as much as an appropriation of the hermeneutic function and perhaps the very form of the academic discourse that mediated the source text with the translation. The resultant creative text then functioned as both new source and repository of hermeneutic practice. *Naiṣadhamu* and *Nalākhyān*, as much as they purported to rewrite the *Naiṣadhīya*, also served as commentaries on it. They themselves were, inevitably, the subjects of their own commentarial tradition.

With the emergence of new literary cultures in South Asia, Sanskrit commentaries inevitably began to share their functions with regional-language translation. Translators, in turn, absorbed and adapted commentarial practices for their own creative purposes. One important tactic appears to have been the adoption of the Sanskrit commentary's surface text and/or its itinerant compositional strategies. Thus, for example, syntax is often reordered into a standard prose order; synonyms are strategically inserted for explanatory or creative effect; and meanings implied or suggested in the original are unpacked and expanded in the reformatted commentary or translation. Other standard practices of commentators are, as expected, dropped by translators: citations from texts on lexicography (*Amarakośa*, etc.) and grammar (Pāṇini's *sūtras*), for instance; identification of particular *alaṅkāras*; and, most visibly, multiple readings or interpretations for any given lexical or semantic unit in the root text. Another important feature usually found in both Sanskrit commentaries and regional-language translations is the inclusion of a pointed preface. In that commentators and translating poets are tense about how successful they are in rephrasing or representing their source text, their introductory remarks reveal a strikingly similar relational attitude. Both, at turns, affirm their loyalty to the original's intent and profusely praise the Sanskrit poet. Sensing that they are rewriting the original—the commentators through a special kind of paraphrase and the translator through an audacious presumption that a classic original can be somehow replicated and even, perhaps, reformed in another language—the commentator and the translator unsurprisingly find themselves apologetic.

There are many more examples one can cite from the *Sahṛdayānanda*, as from *Nalākhyān*, *Naiṣadhamu*, and other translations of *Naiṣadhīya*, to visualize a conscious process of complex *kāvya* translation that transpired during the middle centuries of the second millennium CE, involving not only the Sanskrit source text but also the implied commentarial theories and actual practices that attended that source. Toward this end, this chapter has attempted to contribute to the ongoing conversation on the subject of "vernacularization" in South Asia and the important role a poem like the *Naiṣadhīya* played in that conversation.[55] By culling several passages from two interlingual, regional-language translations of the *Naiṣadhīya* and complementing them with passages from an intralingual translation in the form of a Sanskrit poem called *Sahṛdayānanda*, the aim has been to explore the level of intimacy these creative texts share with the hermeneutic documents that serve and preserve the Sanskrit source poem. The tentative argument here has been that commentaries on poems like the *Naiṣadhīya* mediated the conversation between the creative texts of Sanskrit literary culture and the new regional-language literatures that blossomed after the thirteenth century. Commentaries also supplied techniques, functions, and a creative logic all their own to these new literary cultures and inevitably became secondary themselves as they shared with regional-language translations the function of being bearers of Sanskrit literary culture to new audiences, precisely for whom the translations were designed.

CONCLUSION

How do I measure the depth of this poem called Naiṣadhīya?
It is a palatial abode for limitless meanings, concealed and remote.
There are many, many radiant jewels in the middle of the earth.
It is the rare digger who can locate the entire quarry of diamonds.[1]

Gadādhara, fifteenth-century commentator

Because of the drops of water flowing fast
from the streams of the sibling of the Khaṇḍanakhaṇḍakhādya,
we detect the sprouts of delight by their characteristic flowers,
well-watered and in bloom, growing without interruption.
We know that such is the delight of the connoisseur:
hair standing on end, moistened with rasa that slowly builds.[2]

Viśveśvara [Gāgābhaṭṭa], seventeenth-century commentator

THIS BOOK has ostensibly been about *one* poem. But it has argued that the study of one poem—with a long reception history—requires that attention be given to dozens, if not hundreds, of other works that constitute its *tradition*. This tradition of a text entails not only a repertoire of genres—like the formal commentary, narrative legends, and translations—but also an *effect* that audiences inherit, enhance, and transform through history. What we experience today in reading a work from the twelfth century, therefore, bears the stamp of centuries of engagements by literary communities that found it necessary to respond to, remember, and teach such a work. In the case of my study of the twelfth-century poem *Naiṣadhīyacarita*, I found that the learned commentators of the poem from the thirteenth to the twentieth centuries were an especially significant community of readers that needed to be better understood. Chapters 2, 3, 4, and 5, therefore, brought attention not only to the commentators' specific scholarly contributions to the poem's understanding but also to the specialized hermeneutic practices they helped shape over several centuries. The final two chapters, while also very much concerned with commentarial practices, introduced genres other than the commentary. Chapter 6 treated the narratives and legends that retrospectively attempted to fill out a biography of the poet and the poem. These works, I argued, functioned as oblique forms of premodern criticism and history that complicate our understanding of literary culture in South Asia in ways that still require more reflection from scholars. Chapter 7 showed the extent to which the *Naiṣadhīya* figures into the literary histories of many other works composed in multiple South Asian languages. In this chapter, I attempted to show how a work that was widely adapted, imitated, and translated for at least five hundred years completes the *Naiṣadhīya*'s trajectory. From a twelfth-century Sanskrit poem composed in the Gāhaḍavāla courts of northern India, it evolved into a widely influential South Asian work that resonated with generations of artists throughout the subcontinent.

REVIEWING THE *NAIṢADHĪYA* TRADITION

Seventeenth-century commentator Gāgābhaṭṭa, in the introduction to his commentary on the *Naiṣadhīya*, wrote that of all the poets, past and present and yet to come, only Śrīharṣa could make claim to "ascend the literary throne of all quarters of the country."[3] Truly, by the fifteenth century, as I recounted in chapter 2, commentators from virtually every corner of premodern India had written a commentary on the *Naiṣadhīya*. The diversity of engagement with the poem contributed to its ascent to legendary status and, consequently, to its place in the "Great Works" canon of Sanskrit literature. Perhaps signaling a change in literary consciousness, the *Naiṣadhīya*'s *afterlife* began not with its early commentators but with the author himself. Śrīharṣa's self-conscious awareness of his own powers as a poet and of his poem's originality is displayed sporadically throughout the *Naiṣadhīya* and especially in the autobiographical verses found at the end of each canto. His "voice" and his multiple authorial functions as poet, logician, yogi, and as an elite member of court carry a strong presence in the work itself, expanding, as one would expect, to hyperbolic proportions at the hands of later admirers and critics. This marked a rather new understanding of the canonical Sanskrit poet, a contrast from what was expected of the usually anonymous and unassuming *mahākavi*.

James Porter, with reference to the construction of European antiquity's classical ideal, writes that: "Classicism is not a spontaneous effect but a practiced gesture, repeated over historical time, and a cultivated attachment; it is learned, not discovered; it comes secondhand."[4] That Śrīharṣa himself guided—or taught—his audience in how to think about the *Naiṣadhīya* was evident in the verses of the poem itself. We saw this especially in the four verses at the end of the poem (cited at the end of chapter 1), which presented for readers an explicit insertion of an authorial identity that marked a historical location for the text's production and an idea of how it was initially produced and received. The first commentators of the *Naiṣadhīya* immediately seized on the novelty the poem seemed to offer and lent their own voice to constructing *Śrīharṣa* and *Naiṣadhīya* as symbolic effects. As chapter 2 discussed in detail, these early reading communities of *Naiṣadhīya* seemed eager to discipline the poem into structured interpretive frameworks. And so, for example, Vidyādhara in the mid-thirteenth century read the poem largely through a lens of its literary excellence while his near-contemporary Cāṇḍupaṇḍita insisted that the poem needed the perspective of a learned philosophical mind. While these early readings emphasized the need for specialist training fully to appreciate the *Naiṣadhīya*, they still viewed the poem as largely *open* in terms of establishing rubrics for its exegesis. Later readers increasingly rendered the poem more and more in need of elucidation, foregrounding their mediating role and reinventing the poem as either an object of critical scrutiny or of congenial identification.

Changing course somewhat from the early commentators of the thirteenth century, the fourteenth and fifteenth centuries spoke more to the poem's *value* and inaugurated a culture of commentary writing that highlighted what might have been a contentious sanctioning process among professional scholars. As I discussed in chapter 4, commentaries from this period struggled over text-critical issues such as the fixing of correct readings and the extent of the text. In their foregrounding the primacy of text criticism in exegesis, these commentators reflected a reading culture's critical temperament and practice that was serious about establishing grammatically and stylistically normative forms and fixed on demonstrating the depth of its commitment to guide present and future readers through the foundational source text. The *Naiṣadhīya*'s canonization, as a fifth and final work that effectively closed the *pañcamahākāvya* formulation, rested largely on the poem's usefulness in institutional settings of education.

The *Naiṣadhīya* seems to have become a fixture in the *mahākāvya* curriculum as early as the fifteenth century, as many of the prefaces to the commentaries from this period attest. The poem both confirmed and disrupted familiar expectations of the *mahākāvya* genre through its conceptual and linguistic complexity. Its special role in the crystallization of a Sanskrit *mahākāvya* tradition during the fifteenth century, therefore, placed it squarely in discussions of literary canon formation in South Asia, in critical ways that, for later generations, exceeded a study of the text itself. Unlike modern notions of canon, the *pañcamahākāvya* canon seemed less about conveying all-purpose excellence and more about the function each of the five works served in the way of being inspirations, guides, and successful measures of the genre's potential. The *Naiṣadhīya*'s canonical claim, it seems, rested largely on its being an artistic model that represents a decisive development in literary consciousness and practice. Although not necessarily a model poem along the traditional lines of *alaṅkāraśāstra* calculations about ideal *mahākāvya*, it nevertheless was at the center of interplaying interests involved in fixing literary standards.

Alongside its canonization in the fourteenth and fifteenth centuries was the emergence of remarkable narratives attached to memories of its creation, transmission, and reception. During this middle phase of the *Naiṣadhīya*'s history as a subject of critical analysis, as I argue in chapter 6, documents that one might label biographical in nature emerged to perform the tasks of literary criticism and literary-historical contextualization that were ill-suited to the purposes and structures of the formal commentary. Works like Rājaśekharasūri's fourteenth-century *Prabandhakośa* and Vidyāpati's fifteenth-century *Puruṣaparīkṣā* established some of the more memorable legends of the poet Śrīharṣa and the *Naiṣadhīya*. These quasi-historical narratives simultaneously provided the *Naiṣadhīya* tradition with an aura of historicity while also pointing to new forms of literary awareness and criticism outside of the realm of *alaṅkāraśāstra*'s evaluative paradigms. These works often built on details found in the prefaces of Sanskrit commentaries, which extended, amplified, and complicated the poet's self-history of authorship and text creation. Both the commentaries and the legend-making narrative works sought to extrapolate even more than the poet told us, fusing the poem's self-delivered details within a literary-critical or hagiographical context. In their accounts, there was an attempt to capture the immediacy of Śrīharṣa as a "new" poet and yet an impulse to distance him and the *Naiṣadhīya* from the immediacy of their own historical circumstances, conferring upon the poet and text a certain "universal" effect. Their critical temperament reflected their gaze back at the past but also the continuity between their understanding and the frames built into and perceived by the text itself.

Also developing during this middle phase was the notion that the *Naiṣadhīya* ought to be understood as a product of and a code for spiritual realization, a strategy that required an intuitive identification of the reader with the text. Indeed, as I presented in chapter 5, an undercurrent of allegory runs through the *Naiṣadhīya*'s reception from the beginning, first inspired by the poet himself and taken up in the thirteenth century by the commentator Cāṇḍupaṇḍita and then again by Nārāyaṇa in the sixteenth century; it was only in the twentieth century, however, that a full textual articulation of this aspect of its history found voice in printed sources from traditions of allegorical reading in contemporary Andhra Pradesh. Esoteric readings of the *Naiṣadhīya* coexisted with scholastic treatments the poem received for much of its history after the sixteenth century. The dramatic and inconsistent reversals of taste and critical appraisals that marked its history from the thirteenth to twentieth centuries demonstrate the changes that aesthetic ideologies undergo within different environments of literary reception. These shifts also, however, serve to highlight the historical process at large for canonical texts with a long reception history: one cannot clearly map a continuous *Naiṣadhīya* tradition along a linear path of development nor can one assert that the changing features of that tradition are disconnected sets of new beginnings.

This unpredictability becomes especially evident when we consider the ways in which this particular Sanskrit poem served a crucial function in the burgeoning literary cultures of South Asia's regions after the fourteenth century. Along with translations of the poem's language and its ideas was the wholesale transference of the *Naiṣadhīya*'s prestige and privilege. As individual commentators enjoyed the benefits conferred upon them (such as, for example, the title of *mahāmahopadhyāya*) for writing a *Naiṣadhīya* commentary, the reception of translations of the poem in local literary contexts, I explained in chapter 7, also appropriated the *Naiṣadhīya*'s symbolic capital. Thus, for instance, Śrīnātha's *Naiṣadhamu* was, like its inspiration, an integral part of a "five classics" model in Telugu culture, as was Ativīrarāma Pāṇḍiyar's sixteenth-century *Naiṭatam* for Tamil literature. Both the translations themselves and the critical cultures within which they resided, therefore, carried on the legacy of the *Naiṣadhīya* in the regions of South Asia. They also, in some measure, demythologized the canonical Sanskrit poem; after all, translating the text into a regional language signified a turn away from granting the Sanskrit author the aura of an irreproducible originality and, therefore, untranslatability that he once may have enjoyed.

The *Naiṣadhīya*'s reception history proves that, over time, it has both enjoyed a privileged status as well as endured turbulent waves of criticism. Critics and commentators throughout the past eight centuries have been *ambivalent* about the poem—profusely honoring or deriding it, at various turns. The lack of consensus about the work has also rendered ambivalent its ultimate destiny within the canons of Sanskrit literature; however, its status as a *classic* has never been in doubt perhaps because, as Altieri suggests, "most literary texts matter because of the properties they hold in tension."[5] Śrīharṣa's was a voice that was not often appreciated by Sanskrit scholars who wrote literary histories in the early twentieth century. Still, it often appeared that premodern and modern audiences reading the *Naiṣadhīya* were responding to a similar *effect* the poem had on them, and that they were only at variance in the value they ascribed to it.

THE FUTURE OF STUDYING THE PASTS OF LITERARY TEXTS IN SOUTH ASIA

As a representative of a literary tradition that for centuries was both a site of contestation and a celebration of a particular kind of aesthetic and intellectual engagement with Sanskrit culture, the *Naiṣadhīya* was an integral part of what had become a "*Naiṣadhīya* effect." My sense is that every work of literature that has passed through centuries of critical review and institutional use has a life story worth telling and has impressed upon generations of audiences a similar kind of effect. Unfortunately, outside of perhaps the great Sanskrit epic *Rāmāyaṇa*, we have very few, if any, biographies of South Asian texts. We know very little about their poets, their early reading communities, the modes through which they were historically read and used, the contexts where they became fixtures, the literary offspring they produced, and the emotional power they held or still hold for a culture that values them. This book has aimed to be such a biography in hopes that, imperfect though it is, it may serve as one kind of model to approach other venerated texts of South Asia.

Works of literature like the *Naiṣadhīya* that have attracted diverse audiences across centuries will naturally have a distinctive history all their own. It is only when we attend to each of these works' specific histories, therefore, that we can commence to produce more comprehensive—and more interesting—histories of literature that study important works through a comparative lens. Histories of South Asian literature have generally neglected this perspective. A case in point is that two centuries of modern scholarship on Sanskrit literature have yet to produce monographs about the literary traditions of individual Sanskrit works. While I chose to make a case study of the *Naiṣadhīya*, a remarkable example of a Sanskrit classic that has had a rich and textured reception history, it is clear that other works with a comparable or even older history deserve their own studies along these lines. Only then, perhaps, can we begin fully to understand how South Asian literary communities received and experienced important works. While the texts of formal poetics (the *alaṅkāraśāstra*) have provided much valuable information about the reception of literature among historical audiences in South Asia, other genres like the commentary and the biographical *prabandha* need to be given their due in future studies, as does the role that translations and a translating consciousness played in regional-language adaptations of classical-language texts.

As I suggested in the introduction, certain literary critics from the past century perceived works like the *Naiṣadhīya* as finite medieval texts that modern readers could *respond* to but, being sealed off temporally and culturally, could not *contribute* to its further understanding. These works, therefore, could only remain, as Dasgupta and De cynically put it in a passage I cited earlier, as part of a "cult of style" that once may have been popular among "scholars of a traditional type" but could no longer speak to the modern temperament.[6] The impression that statements like this leave is that the diversity of engagements with older works stopped at a given point, and modern scholarship, now clearly distinguished from the contributions of earlier audiences, superseded a centuries-old literary tradition in a negative, rather than productive, spirit of criticism. Only the *paṇḍitas* who continued to read Sanskrit texts along with their older commentaries could thus claim to be the successors of past generations of readers. While this may have been the overarching situation in the recent past, there seems nothing fixed or inevitable about it in the near future.

Today, scholars of classical South Asian texts—and readers encountering these works either in the original or in translation—have shown that older works are still capable of yielding thought-provoking, if not potentially transformative, aesthetic experiences to audiences now separated by many centuries from older classics. With a more comprehensive understanding of how these works were read in earlier times, it is my hope that scholars and general readers of literature in South Asia today will come to enrich their own encounter with important works from the past. In doing so, perhaps they too will feel compelled to add to a text's *tradition* by offering new perspectives or perhaps reforming—and even resisting—earlier ones.

APPENDIX 1: SANSKRIT TEXT OF CITATIONS FROM COMMENTARIES AND NARRATIVES

EXCERPTS FROM CHAPTER 2

1.1 [Anonymous scribe of Vidyādhara's commentary]

līlā-dyotita-gūḍha-bhāva-subhagālaṅkara-vṛndānvitā / saṃsevyā sumano-varair
nava- rasa-prollāsinī śobhanā // citta-secanake nalasya carite baddhās-padā yā
sadā / ṭīkā kānti-guṇānvitā jayati sā sāhitya-vidyādharī //

1.2 [Cāṇḍupaṇḍita]

ṭīkāṃ yady api sopapatti-racanāṃ vidyādharo nirmame / śrīharṣasya tathāpi na tyajati sā gambhīratāṃ bhāratī // dik kūlaṅka-ṣatāṃ gatair jala-dharair udgṛhyamāṇaṃ muhuḥ / pārāvāram apāram ambu kim iha syāj jānu-mātraṃ kvacit //

1.3 [Īśānadeva]

ye 'laṃkāra-vivecane kutukinaḥ śrīharṣa-saṃkīrtite / kāvye 'smin svayam eva te vidadhatu prajñā-vilāsaṃ budhāḥ // ṭīkāṃ vā bahuśo vicāra-jaṭilāṃ paśyantu vidyā-dharīṃ / tad-vācyā na vayaṃ hi tasya karaṇe prāyo na jātodyamāḥ // satāṃ mude naiṣadha-ṭippaṇaṃ mayā viracyate śaiva-matānusāriṇā / mādhukarīṃ samāśritya vṛttim etad ihārjitam mayā tapasvinā tasmād alaṃ kāvya-vidāṃ hāsaiḥ // sarvo' pi kāvyam upajīvya karoti śāstra-vyākhyāṃ guror api mayā'nukṛtā tadeyam / vidvān sa yāti narakaṃ khalu yaḥ prasiddhyai svīyāṃ vadan para-kṛtiṃ pratibhāti loke //

1.4 [Bhavadatta / Bhavadeva]

asty eva samprati mahākavibhiḥ praṇītā / nānārtha-bodha-madhurā vivṛtis tv anekā // teṣāṃ tad atra tu samā na tathā mamaiṣā . . . vaktuṃ sudhīr api gurūṇ anupāsya yasya śaknoti kiñcid api naiva rahasyam asya. kāvye śramo'tra vivṛtau kavi-paṇḍitasya mohāya kintu mama saṃprati bālakasya . . . tathāpi bālyāc capalatvam uccair atra pravṛtto'smi vidhātum etām / ṭīkām yathāvad vidhuro'pi kāvye. bālasya kiṃ kṛtya-vidhau vicāraḥ //

1.5 [Mallinātha]

kṣudra-vyākhyā-viṣārtānāṃ śrīharṣa-kavi-sadgirāṃ / ujjīvanāya jīvātur jīyād eṣa mayā kṛtaḥ //
nāmūlaṃ likhyate kiñcin nānapekṣitam ucyate / ihānvaya-mukhenaiva sarvaṃ vyākhyāyate mayā //

1.6 [Cāritravardhana]

śrīharṣair yamaka-muraja-sarvatobhadra-pramukhān bandhān arthāpuṣṭikarān anādṛtyārtha-puṣṭikaro 'nuprāsābhidhā-śabdālaṅkāraḥ prāyaḥ prayuyaje.

1.7 [Śrīdharasūri]

viśveśvarākhya-dvija-puṃgavena sarvajña-saṃjñena tathā 'pareṇa /
vyākhyātam etat khalu naiṣadhīyaṃ kāvyaṃ vibhinnārtham avistareṇa //
karomi tāccakaravaṃ kariṣye kāvyaṃ rasa-syandi mano 'nukūlam /
tathāpi lokā "dṛta-naiṣadhīya-kāvyārtham udbodhayituṃ yatiṣye //

1.8 [Śrīdharasūri]

veda-vyākaraṇāśrayaḥ sukavitā-vedānta-tarka-smṛti-cchando 'laṃkṛti-kāvya-nāṭaka-purāṇāmnāya-śaivāṃbudhiḥ / jyotis-tantra-sumantra-nīti-bharata-śrī-yoga-vaidyāṅgabhūḥ vidyā-śrīdhara-paṇḍito vijayate śrīmarkibhaṭṭānvaye //

1.9 [Lakṣmaṇabhaṭṭa]

karomi naiṣadha-vyākhyām anyā-dṛṣṭa-pathānugām / santi yady api sad-vyākhyā budhānāṃ naiṣadhe śatam. tathāpy amuṣyā vaidagdhīṃ kecid vijñātum īśate //

1.10 [Rāmacandra Śeṣa]

salila-krīḍāyā avarṇane' pi na mahākāvyatva-bhaṅga-prasaṅgaḥ . . . nyūnam apy atra yaiḥ kaiścid aṅgaiḥ kāvyaṃ na duṣyatīty uktatvāt.

1.11 [Jinarāja]

evam-vidhāḥ jina-matonnati-kārakāḥ samasta-tarka-vyākaraṇa-cchando 'laṅkāra-kośa kāvyādi-vividha-śāstra-pāriṇo naiṣadhīya-kāvya-saṃbandhī jinarājīvṛtty ādy aneka-navīna-grantha-vidhāyakāḥ.

1.12 [Premacandra]

anyāsu bhāva-bahulāsu sadarthikāsu ṭīkāsu ced iha bhaved viphalaḥ prayāsaḥ / sadbhis tathāpi mṛdu-bodha-vibodhanārthaṃ jātodyamo 'ham iha mat prati nāvabudhyai //

1.13 [Haridāsa Siddhāntavāgīśa]

prācīnām analaṅkṛtiṃ gata-rasāṃ lupta-śriyaṃ durgamā nirbhāvāṃ viguṇāṃ viśeṣa-vikalāṃ ṭīkāvalīṃ varjayan / navyāṃ bhavyatamāṃ nitānta-sugamāṃ sālaṅkṛtiṃ ṭīkām imām //

1.14 [Śrīnātha]

praṇamya maulinā vandyān sampradāya-vidaḥ sataḥ / tyājyaṃ tyājyam asad-vākyaṃ sad-alpam api likhyate // ye sad-artham ajānanto vṛthā-vacana-vistaraiḥ / dūṣayanti kaveḥ kāvyaṃ dhik tān paṇḍita-māninaḥ // yadi khaṃ karaṭo gatvā sindhor upari kāyati / tat kim sa vetti gāmbhīryam ratnāni ca tadāśaye //

EXCERPTS FROM CHAPTER 3

1.15 [Vidyādhara]

aṣṭau vyākaraṇāni tarka-nivahaḥ sāhitya-sāro nayo vedārthāvagatiḥ purāṇa-paṭhitir yasyānya-śāstrāṇy api / nityaṃ syuḥ sphuritārtha-dīpa-vihitājñānānvakārāṇy asau vyākhyātuṃ prabhavaty amuṃ suviṣamaṃ sargaṃ sudhīḥ kovidaḥ //

1.16 [Narahari]

na mama mati-vilāso vāsanābhyāsa-jo vā // vividha-bahu-nibandha-skandha-saṃvāhanaṃ vā // taralayati mano me kevalaṃ naiṣadhīyaṃ / caritam akhila-loka-ślokanīyaṃ kaveś ca // samutsahe gūḍha-rasārtha-sāraṃ vigāhituṃ kāvyam idaṃ jaḍo 'pi / ajāta-dantā api khaṇḍa-golaṃ kutūhalād ākalayanti bālāḥ // pramādāśaktyāder iha mahati gaṃbhīra-gahane satām / apy arthānāṃ kvacid api nibandho 'pi na bhavet // athāpy asmād etan na khalu mama doṣāya nikhilaṃ / samuccettuṃ śaktaḥ ka iva jaladhau ratna-nicayam //

1.17 [Gadādhara]

kaver asya svarga-prabhu-guru-garīyastara-mateḥ / pramāṇāc chāyāsu prakṛtir abhiviśrāmyati muhuḥ / na me tu vyutpatteḥ paricitir iha prāyikatayā hy ato vyatyāse 'pi kvacidapi na vācyo 'smi sudhiyaḥ //

1.18 [Rāmacandra Śeṣa]

sa brahmā caturānanaḥ sa bhagavān īśo 'pi pañcānanaḥ sa skandaś ca ṣadānanaḥ sa phaninām īśaḥ sahasrānanaḥ / yat-padyārtha-viśeṣa-varṇana-vidhau neśāḥ vayaṃ tatra ke yad-vyākhyāyi tathāpi kiñcid akhilaṃ tac-cāpalaṃ kevalaṃ //

1.19 [Gāgābhaṭṭa]

grantheṣv etat pareṣu pratana-nava-budha-vyākhyayānāvilānāṃ śabdālaṃkāra-koṣādi-kaviṣaya-para-grantha-vikhyāti-bhājām / ślokānām atra kāvye sakala-kavi-kulālaṅkṛter asmad-uktau nodbhāvyaṃ paunar-uktyaṃ tvidam akhila-samāhāra-mātrodyatatvāt //

1.20 [Cāṇḍupaṇḍita on *Naiṣadhīya* 1.1]

tataś ca śāstrārambhe nirvighnena grantha-samāptaye śrotṝṇāṃ maṅgala-caraṇāya śiṣṭācāra-paripālanāyā 'dhikṛtābhīṣṭādidevatābhyo namas-kāraḥ pratipādyaḥ. sa ca na kṛtaḥ. yato nalasya puṇya-ślokatvāt tat-saṃkīrtanād aghaugha-vighaṭṭanāt kuto vighna-nighnatā? tathā pṛthu-sahasrārjuna-bharata-nala-prabhṛtīnāṃ smaraṇaṃ parama-maṅgala-hetuḥ ato maṅgalācaraṇam apy asti. tathā ca śiṣṭācāro 'pi nala-damayantī-kīrtanaṃ kali-nāśanam iti. ato grantha-kāraḥ prathamaṃ nalam eva varṇayan maṅgalācaraṇam āracayati—

sa nalo nāma raja āsīt. kiṃviśiṣṭaḥ. mahasāṃ pratāpānāṃ rāśiḥ. tathā mahān ujjvalaś ca kāntyā. athavā mahair utsavair ujjvalaḥ. etad eva maṅgala-sūcanam. kiṃbhūtaḥ? sitac-chatritaṃ kīrti-maṇḍalaṃ yena sa tathā. etena kīrti-pratāpa-kamanīyatānāṃ nidhānam. yasya kathā upākhyānāni nipīya. pīṅ pāne 'sya prayogaḥ. budhā vidvāṃsaḥ sudhām api amṛtaṃ sūktaṃ vā tathā tena prakāreṇa na ādriyante. kiṃ bhūtasya? kṣiteḥ pṛthivyāḥ rakṣiṇaḥ pālayituḥ.

atha ca budhāḥ devā amṛtaṃ nādriyante, tat-kathā-śravaṇāt. etena cakravartitvaṃ maṇḍale sūcitam. athavā mahasāṃ rāśir iva śrīsūrya iva āsīt. mahair utsavair vā ujjvalaḥ. ujjvalaḥ śṛṅgāraḥ pradhāno dhīralalita-nāyakatvān nalasya. atha vā yasya kathā nipīya kṣiti-rakṣiṇo nṛpās tathā sudhāṃ pṛthivīm api nādriyante.

1.21 [Vidyādhara on *Naiṣadhīya* 1.1]

atra śloke 'nuprāsaḥ śabdālaṅkaraḥ. sudhā-kathayor aupamye pratīte sati sudhān ādaratvena kathādhikya-pratipādanād vyatireko 'rthālaṅkāro 'pi. anyac ca nala-sūrya-varṇanayoḥ prākaraṇikā 'prākaraṇikayoḥ śliṣṭa-padopanibandhe śleṣālaṅkāro 'pi. sūryeṇa sahābheda-pratipādanād rūpakaṃ. tasmāt tila-taṇḍula-nyāyenātra saṃkara iti vidyā-dhara-viracita-sāhitya-vidyādharī.

1.22 [Mallinātha on *Naiṣadhīya* 1.1]

(A)

atha tatrabhavān śrīharṣa-kaviḥ kāvyaṃ yaśase 'rthakṛte vyavahāra-vide śivetara-kṣataye. sadyaḥ paranirvṛtaye kāntā-sammitatayopadeśa-yuje ity ālaṃkārika-vacana-prāmāṇyāt kāvyasthānaika-śreyaḥ-sādhanatvāc ca kāvyālāpāṃś ca varjayed iti tan niṣedhasyāsat-kāvya-viṣayatāṃ paśyan naiṣadhā-khyaṃ mahākāvyaṃ cikīrṣuś cikīrṣitārtha-vighna-parisamāpti-hetoḥ. āśīr-namaskriyā vastu-nirdeśo vāpi tanmukham ity āśīr ādy any-atamasya prabandha-mukha-lakṣaṇatvāt kathā-nāyakasya rājño nalasya itivṛta-rūpaṃ maṅgalaṃ vastu nirdiśati nipīyeti.

(B)

nipīyeti. yasya kśiti-rakśiṇaḥ kśamā-pālakasya nalasya kathām upākhyānam. nipīya nitarām āsvādya pīṅ svāde ktvo lyab-ādeśaḥ na tu pibateḥ na lyap iti pratiṣedhādītīvāsambhavāt. budhās taj-jñāḥ surāś ca jñātṛ-cāndrisurā budhā iti kṣirasvāmī. sudhām api tathā yatheyaṃ kathā tadvad ity arthaḥ nādriyante sudhām apekṣya bahu manyante iti yāvāt. sitac-chatritaṃ sitac-chatraṃ kṛtaṃ sitātapatrīkṛtam ity arthaḥ, tat kṛtāv iti ṇyantāt karmaṇi ktaḥ. kīrti-maṇḍalaṃ yena saḥ mahasāṃ tejasāṃ rāśiḥ ravir iveti bhāvaḥ. mahaiḥ utsavaiḥ ujjvalaḥ dīpyamāno nitya-mahotsava-śālīty arthaḥ. maha uddhava utsava ity amaraḥ. sa nala āsīt.

(C)

atra nale mahasāṃ rāśir iti kīrti-maṇḍale ca sitac-chattratva-rūpasyāropāt rūpakaṃ kathāyāś ca sudhāpekṣayā utkarṣāt vyatirekaś cety anayoḥ saṃsṛṣṭiḥ. taduktaṃ darpaṇe rūpakaṃ rūpitāropād viṣaye nirapahnave iti. ādhikyam upameyasyopamānān nyūnatā 'thavā. vyatireka iti mitho 'pekṣayaiteṣāṃ sthitiḥ saṃsṛṣṭir ucyate iti ca. asmin sarge vaṃśasthaṃ vṛttaṃ jatau tu vaṃśastham udīritaṃ jarav iti tallakṣaṇāt.

1.23 [Śrīdhara on *Naiṣadhīya* 1.1]

atra pūnya-ślokena nala-rūpa-viśiṣṭa-vastu-nirdeśena nirvighna-grantha-samāptir ity abhiprāyeṇāha—sa nala āsīt ity anvayaḥ. pṛthvādīnāṃ smaraṇam api sakalābhīṣṭa-hetuḥ kiṃ punaḥ kīrtanam iti. kimviśiṣṭo nalaḥ. mahasāṃ rāśiḥ pratāpānām āśrayaḥ. yadvā—mahasāṃ tejasāṃ rāśiḥ sūrya iva sthitaḥ. luptopamā luptotprekṣā vā. etena sa eva tejasvī sūryavat nānya iti vyaṅgyam. sa kaḥ.

yadvā arthāntarāṇi brūmaḥ budhā vivekinaḥ kṣiti-rakṣiṇo bhūpālāḥ yasya kathāḥ nipīya sudhāṃ vasudhām api tathā nādriyante atra vasudhā-śabdena varṇa-cyuti-nyāyena va-kāra-lopo draṣṭavyaḥ. uktañ ca cūḍāmaṇau—ananta-śayanaś-śāntaḥ kṣīrāmbho-nidhi-madhya-gaḥ. śaṅkha-cakra-gadā-padma-dhārī-pathir ūpāsyatām iti atra strī-varṇa-lopaḥ strī-patīr iti padaṃ tathātrāpīti asya kathāṃ śrutvā rājānaḥ bhuvo guṇaṃ jānanto 'pi vasudhām avamatya svayaṃ vasudhā-rakṣitvaṃ tyajantīty anenāsya mahā-puruṣatvaṃ dyotitam.

athavā kṣitiṃ dhāraṇena rakṣantīti kṣiti-rakṣiṇaḥ kula-parvatā dig-gajendraś ca gṛhyante te 'pi sudhāṃ suṣṭhu dhānaṃ dhāraṇaṃ tām api tathā nādriyante nalas tv anāyāsena bhuvaṃ bibharti parantu paramāyāsā ity ātmano dhāraṇaṃ nindantīty arthaḥ anena śaurya-dhairyādayo guṇā varṇitāḥ. kṣiti-rakṣi-śabdena ananto vāpi gṛhyante tal-liṅga-samavāyāt kṣiti-rakṣiṇo nāgāḥ te sudhāṃ kṣīram api tathā nādriyante. pīyūṣa-kṣīrayos sudhā ity abhidhāna-ratna-kośaḥ. asya kathā-rasa-śravaṇāt teṣām āhārecchāpi na bhavatīty anenāsya īśvarāṃśatvam aṅkuritaṃ nāgāṃ īśvara-priya-hārecchā-rahitās tam eveśvaraṃ sevanta iti prasiddheḥ.

athavā yasya kṣiti-rakṣiṇaḥ kathā nipīya budhā vibudhā devāḥ sudhām api tathā nādriyante atra varṇa-cyuti-nyāyaḥ devā api yatkathām ākarṇya sudhayāpi kim iti tām avadhīrayantīty anenāsya mahā-bhāgyatvādayo darśitā mahasi svamahimni jvalati prakāśata iti mahojvalaḥ paramātmā sa kasmin pratiṣṭhitaḥ mahasāṃ tejasāṃ rāśiḥ koṭi-sūrya-saṅkāśaṃ ravi-tejomayatvāt evaṃ-bhūtas sa paramātmanā nalo 'bhūt abhaṅgura-svarūpasya tatvaṃ yuktānāṃ viṣṇuḥ pṛthivī-patir iti vacanāc ca siddham matsya-kūrma-varāhādy avatāra-viśeṣeṇa kṣiti-rakṣiṇo yasya kathām avatāra-kathām iti anyat samānaṃ.

yadvā nalo nāma mahasāṃ rāśiḥ sūrya āsīt nilīyata iti nalo mahob-his tejobhir jvalati bhāsata iti mahojvalaḥ sahasra-kiraṇatvāt ādityāj jāyate vṛṣṭer annaṃ tataḥ prajāḥ ity etad vā rakṣiṇo bhū-loka-sthasya prāṇivṛndasya rakṣiṇaḥ mañcāḥ krośantīty ukte yathā mañca-sthāḥ puruṣā lakṣyante tathā atra apīti. ādityo vā eṣa etan-maṇḍalam (??)

(anta)tapat(īr?)īty ādinā vedo vāgīyamāṇād iti sitac-chatravad ācarat kīrti-yuktaṃ maṇḍalaṃ yasyeti vigrahaḥ anena sūrya-rūpaka-cchalena māṅgaliko 'rtho 'bhihitaḥ. athavā mahojvalo maheśaḥ nalo nāma maheśo 'bhūt kāla-kūṭa-grahaṇādinā jagad-rakṣiṇaḥ chatra-śabdāt tat-karotīty ādinānantā(?). niṣṭhā—sitena guṇena chatritaṃ maṇḍalī-kṛtaṃ kīrtīnāṃ maṇḍalaṃ samuho yena.

athavā mahe kāntānāṃ krīḍotsave ujjvalaḥ śṛṇgāra-sarvasva-bhūtaḥ candro lakṣyate nalo nāma candro 'bhūt yaduktaṃ mahā-kavinā kālidāsena—dilīpa iti rājendur induḥ kṣira-nidhāviva (??) iti mahaḥ prakāśaḥ sad-rūpa-tejaḥ (?) sarvātma-sūktiṣu iti durgā-tantre (?) 'bhihitatvāt mahasāṃ prakāśānāṃ sad-rūpasya vā rāśir nidhiḥ tasya sakalena adhīśatvāc ca kṣiti-rakṣiṇo jagad-ānanda-karasya kalā tathā vṛtti-rūpā tat-pānecchayā devās sudhām api tathā satyam avadhīrayati tatheti satyārdhe sitac-chatravad ācarantīti kīrtir eva maṇḍalaṃ evam asya śṛṇgārāmṛtam yasya prabandhasyābhimato 'bhihito 'sya kāvyasya kṣoma-kṣamatvād atraiva śloke anye 'pi bahavo 'rthas sambhavanti te grantha-gaurava-bhayān na kathyante.

1.24 [Nārāyaṇa's preface to *Naiṣadhīya* 1.1]

cikīrṣitasya granthasya nirvighna-samāptyarthaṃ śiṣṭācāra-pariprāptam āśīr namas-kriyā vastu-nirdeśo vāpi tanmukham iti maṅgalācaraṇaṃ kartavyam iti grantha-kṛc-chrīharṣa-nāma kavir gūḍhaṃ sabīja-raghunāthābhīṣṭa-devatā-namaskāra-rūpaṃ maṅgalam ācarati. anye tu 'viśiṣṭa-vastunirdeśa-lakṣaṇaṃ maṅgalam ity āhuḥ.

1.25 [Cāṇḍupaṇḍita on *Naiṣadhīya* 6.51]

tau damayantī-nalau mithaḥ parasparaṃ tathyaṃ satyam evābādhyaṃ pariṣasvajāte. kva—āliṅgitālīka-paras-parānta āliṅgitaṃ yad-alīkaṃ parasparaṃ tasyāntaḥ madhye. alīkāliṅgana-madhye satyam āliṅganaṃ jātam. athavā āliṅgitālīka-paras-param antaścittaṃ yat-pariṣvaṅge iti kriyā-viśeṣaṇaḥ tathya viśeṣaṇaḥ vā. gṛhītālīka-bhaimī-cittena nalena satya-bhaimī āliṅgitā. alīka-nalāviṣṭa-cittayā bhaimyā ca satya-nala āliṅgitaḥ. atra hetu-garbhaṃ viśeṣaṇam. kiṃ kurvāṇau—anyonyam any-atravat anya-pradeśe sthitāv iva īkṣamāṇau vilokayantau. kva—paras-pareṇa adhyuṣite'py āśrite'pi deśe. ekatra sthitāv api satyāv api tau.

yathā nityaṃ bhrāntyā mithyāliṅganam anubhavataḥ tathaivātmānaṃ bhrāntyāliṅgitaṃ manyete sma. paraṃ bhrāntir api yasmāt bhrānti-kāle satyeva bhavati. yathā svapnaḥ svapna-vyavahāra-kāle satyaṃ paścāt bādhyo bhavati, tathālīkāliṅganam api tat-kāle satyaṃ paścāt bādhyam. yathā ca śukti-rajataṃ tat-kāle satyaṃ paścāt bādhyam. param ayaṃ viśeṣaḥ. bhrāntyā dṛśyamānasya śukti-rajatāder īdṛṣaṃ bhayaṃ bhavati, yad idaṃ kṣaṇena yadi bādhyaṃ bhaviśyati tadā mama rajata-prāptir na bhaviśyati. atra tu satyāliṅgane 'pi bhrāntyāliṅgana-sadṛṣī pratītir jñātā.

atra vādināṃ vipratipattiḥ. sat- khyāti-vādī sāṅkhyaḥ. bhrāntau śukti-mastake yad-rajataṃ khyāti pratibhāsate tat sadeva kvāpi vidyamānam eva. asat-khyāti-vādī bauddhaḥ. śunya-vādī mādhyamikaḥ. asad eva śunyaṃ rajataṃ bhrāntyā khyāti. anyathā-khyāti-vādī naiyāyiko bhaṭṭaś ca. anyathā vartamānaṃ rajataṃ bhrānti-dośa-vaśāt purovarti-deśe śukti-mastake anyathā khyāti. yatas tasya mate abhāvo 'pi bhāvātmakaḥ. iha bhū-tale ghaṭo nāsti ity ukte ghaṭābhāvo nāma bhūtale na tu sarvathābhāvaḥ. tathā idaṃ rajatam ity arthaḥ. bhrāntau nedaṃ rajatam ity anena bādhaka-jñānena anyathābhāvāmātraṃ bādhyate na tu rajatam. tathā anirvacanīya-khyāti-vādī vedāntī. idaṃ rajataṃ san na bhavati bādhyatvāt. tathā asadapi na bhavati.

pratīyamānatvāt. tathā sad-asad api na bhavati bhāvābhāvayoḥ parasparaṃ virodhāt. na ca sad-asadbhyām aparaḥ prakāro 'sti. tasmāt kenā pi prakāreṇa nirvaktum aśakyatvāt anirvacanīyaṃ rajataṃ khyāti. akhyāti-vādinaḥ prābhākarāḥ. idaṃ rajataṃ na khyāti na prātibhāsikaṃ bhāti. kiṃtu satyam eva, yad ete grahaṇa-smaraṇa-vijñāne satye. tathā hi vaṇig-vīthyādau kāntā-kaṅkaṇādau ca gṛhītaṃ sat cākacikyādi-śveta-bhāskaratvādi-sādṛśyāt pūrvānubhava-saṃskārodbodhe sati śukti-mastake tad eva rajataṃ smṛtam. tato dvayam api satyam. idaṃ purovarti satyaṃ rajatam. pūrvānubhavāt smṛtaṃ tad api satyam. ayaṃ ca ślokaḥ prābhākarābhiprāyeṇa kavinā kṛtaḥ.

anyonyam anyatravad īkṣamāṇau tau damayantī-nalau mithaḥ paras-paraṃ tathyaṃ pariśasvajāte. kva—āliṅgitasya alīkasya paras-parasya antar-madhye. yal loke saṃpratipannam idaṃ paras-paraṃ mithunam alīkāliṅgitaṃ tasmin tathyaṃ paras-param āliṅgitaṃ babhuva. yad āropitarūpeṇa paras-pareṇa adhyuśite 'pi puro-vartini deśe anyonyaṃ jānantau. ayam arthaḥ—tat pūrvam anyatra deśe nalena kvāpi satyāliṅganam anubhūtaṃ gṛhītam. damayantyā ca sakhībhiḥ sahāliṅganam anubhava-gṛhītam. tad evedam adhyuśita-deśe smṛtam. ato 'nyonyāliṅgana-grahaṇa-jñānaṃ smaraṇa-jñānaṃ cobhayam api tathyam eva, na tu mithyā. atas tathyo mithaḥ pariśvaṅgaḥ smaraṇa-jñānasya abādhitatvāt iti mīmāṃsakaika-deśināṃ prābhākarāṇām āśayaḥ. ato'nyonya-paras-para-mithaḥ-śabdānām apaunar-uktyam. anyonya-śabda ekaḥ pūrvānubhūtāśleṣa-vācī. aparaḥ paras-para-śabdaḥ puro-vartini deśe smaraṇa-jñāna-vācakaḥ. tṛtīyaḥ apara-vādināṃ saṃpratipannām alīkatāṃ bhrānti-saṃjñām anūdya grahaṇa-smaraṇa-jñānayor ekatra melakaḥ. caturtho mithaḥ-śabdaḥ prābhākara-siddhānta-siddhaṃ pratijñāṃ pratipādayati. ataḥ sarva-prakāreṇa tathyaṃ mithas tau pariśasvajāte.

EXCERPTS FROM CHAPTER 4

1.26 [Gāgābhaṭṭa's *Rākāgama* 1.2]

atra pratāpāvali-kīrti-maṇḍaloddeśena suvarṇa-daṇḍaika-sitātapatritatvaṃ vidheyaṃ tac ca samāsāntargatam. na ceha vidheyasya kriyā-viśeṣaṇatvāt samāsenetara-viśeṣaṇatvenāvagatasya kriyā-viśeṣaṇatvānupapattir dūṣakatā-bījam . . .

1.27 [Gadādhara on *Naiṣadhīya* 1.1 and 1.2]

(A)

prathamataś cāsya kaveḥ kāvyam idaṃ nirmātum icchataḥ—ko 'atra jagati tathā-vidhaḥ khalu dhīra-lalitaḥ kṣiti-patir abhūd yam aham iha jita-sudhā-rasa-kathaṃ kathā-nāyakaṃ karomīti. bhūyaś ciraṃ cintayataḥ samyag upāsitasya cintāmaṇi-mantrasya prasādād yaḥ kilā 'rtho 'ntaḥ prāsphurat sa eva nipīyetyādāv ādima-śloke bahir upanibaddhaḥ. yo 'yam evaṃguṇa-gaṇālaṅkṛtaḥ kṛta-yuge nalo nāma kṣiti-patir āsit tam aham iha kathāyāṃ nāyaka-pade 'bhiṣekṣyāmīti cātra tātparyārthaḥ.

(B)

rasaiḥ kathetyādau dvitīya-śloke tu vastu-nirdeśa-rūpatayā tam evārthaṃ bhaṅgyā kavir ayam anūktavān . . . kecit tu prathama-ślokam eva vastu-nirdeśa-pratipādakam āhur dvitīyaṃ tu pāṭhāntaram. mukha-rūpasya pūrva-ślokasyaikārthatvena pratimukha-rūpatayā cumbanāc cumbako 'yam ity apare. tac ca pāṭhāntara eva samāviśatīti tenaiva tat-kāryam avāpyate. atra pakṣe ca bhū-pāla-paryāyasya kṣiti-rakṣiṇa iti vidheya-padasyottarārdhe nirdeśo yuktaḥ. yasya kathāṃ nipīya budhās tathā sudhām api nādriyante sa tathā-vidhaḥ khalu nalo nāma kṣiti-patiḥ pūrvam āsīd iti. kathā-vastu-nirdeśo hi viśeṣaṇasya vidheyatvam.

(c)

nāmnas tv anūdyatvam eva yathā purāṇe suratho nāma rājā kāvye himālayo nāma nagādhirājo 'sti loke 'pi kāmpilye nagare viṣṇuśarmā nāma brāhmaṇo babhuva ity ādi. atraiva ca dvitīya-śloke nalo nāma rasā-jānir abhūd iti. nalasyaiva tv atra vidheyatve vastu-nirdeśatvaṃ vimṛsyamānam asamañjasam iva syāt. yathā kathaṃcit pada-sambaddhena vidheyānūdya-krama-yuktim āpādyamāne tu prathamata eva kliṣṭa-kalpanā khalv atīvodvega-jananī bhavet. prathama-śloke vidheyānūdya vaisadṛśyaṃ budhānāṃ sudhāyām anādara-hetor anupādānān nirhetutvaṃ ca dūṣaṇam āśaṅkamānaḥ kavir ayaṃ tasyaivārthaṃ dvitīya-śloke pāṭhāntarāpadeśena sa-yuktikaṃ kṛtvā pratyapīpadat. evaṃ ca śrīmatā 'nena nijasya kavi-karmaṇaḥ khalu prauḍhīḥ pradarśitā. anyathā kavir ayaṃ sarvajñaḥ sad-vastu-nirdeśa-paraṃ saguṇaṃ nirdoṣaṃ cātraikam eva ślokaṃ kiṃ na vidadhyāt. iti mayā yathā-śrutaṃ yathā-mati ca vyākhyātam. nijaṃ rahasyaṃ tu kavir eva veda. vyākhyāna-viśeṣaṃ tu sahṛdaya iti.

1.28 [Nārāyaṇa on 22.82]

tasmād ativyāptyādi-doṣād vyākaraṇa-mūla eva loka-prayoga iti niyamo na yuktaḥ. lakṣyam uddiśya lakṣaṇa-pravṛttiḥ na tu lakṣaṇam uddiśya lakṣya-pravṛttir iti. tasmāt prayoga-mūlaṃ vyākaraṇam iti vyākaraṇāl loka eva prayoge balīyān iti bhāvaḥ.

1.29 [Vidyādhara's preface to 1.1]

nanu mahābhārate nalopākhyānasyaiva vaktum ucitatvāt śrīharṣeṇopākhyānaikadeśe kāvya-viśrāntiḥ kathaṃ kṛtā. sakala-nalopākhyānasyaiva vaktum ucitatvāt. satyam. kāvyaṃ hi sahṛdaya-hṛdayānām āvarjakaṃ bhavati. hṛdayāvarjakaṃ ca kāvyaṃ sva-rasena kriyate. tatra ca punar aitihye eka-deśe sarasatvaṃ dṛśyate. tatraivānenāpi viśrāntiḥ kṛteti bhāvaḥ.

1.30 [Nārāyaṇa on 22.148]

ānanda-padena tuṣṭaye 'stu ity āśiṣā ca grantha-samāptiṃ dyotayati. mahābhāratādau varṇitasyāpy uttara-nala-caritrasya nīrasatvān nāyakānudaya-varṇanena rasa-bhaṅga-sad-bhāvāc ca kāvyasya ca sahṛdayāhlādana-phalatvāc cātrottara-caritraṃ śrīharṣeṇa na varṇitam ity ādi jñātavyam.

EXCERPTS FROM CHAPTER 5

1.31 [Nārāyaṇa on 13.3]

yasya raṇa-śrīḥ senācarī-bhavantau sainikau bhavantau yāv ibhānana-dānavārī gaṇeśa-nārāyaṇau tayor vāsenādhiṣṭhānena kṛtvā janitā kṛtā asurabhīr daitya-bhayaṃ yayā. asurebhyo devānāṃ yā bhīḥ tasyā īraṇaṃ kṣepaṇaṃ tena yā śrīḥ sā yasya janiteti vā.

1.32 [Nārāyaṇa on 13.17]

chāyā rītiḥ loka-paripālanam ity artha iti vā. asyeva jagat-pālanaṃ ko 'pi na karotīty arthaḥ.

1.33 [Nārāyaṇa on 13.26]

mat-sandehād enaṃ bhaimī bhajed iti nala-bhrāntiḥ. nala-saṃdehān māṃ bhajed iti varuṇa-bhrāntiḥ. varuṇa-vāci-śabda-sadbhāvāc chleṣa-vakroktyādi-jñāna-caturā bhaimī varuṇaṃ na variṣyatīti niścayena nala-bhrama-nāśaḥ. nale 'nuraktā bhaimī mat-pratipādaka-śabda-sadbhāvān māṃ na variṣyatīti niścayena varuṇa-bhrama-nāśa iti vā.

1.34 [Nārāyaṇa on 14.88]

ha-kāra-rephayor uccāraṇārthaṃ yad akāra-dvayaṃ tad-rahitaṃ "hra" iti vyañjana-mātra-ha-kāra-repha-mayam ity arthaḥ. tathā senduṃ ī ca induś ca tābhyāṃ saha vartamānam. ī-kāreṇa ardha-candreṇa ca yuktam. tathā—sakalaṃ kalā anusvāras tat sahitam hrīṃ-kāra-rūpam ity arthaḥ . . . asmiñ chloke ṭīkāntara-kṛto bahūnāṃ śaiva-vaiṣṇavādi mantrāṇām uddharo vijñeyaḥ. atra grantha-vistara-bhiyā kaṣṭa-kalpanayā ca noktaḥ.

1.35 [Nārāyaṇa on 1.117]

atha ca vistaratvāt samudra-tulye vināśitvāt palvala-tulye śarīre vicarantaṃ haṃsaṃ paramātmānaṃ kaścid yogī paśyati. riraṃsur haṃsī śaktiḥ tasyāḥ kala-nāde sādaraṃ. hiraṇmayatvaṃ hiraṇmayaḥ puruṣaḥ (Chāndogya 6.6) iti śruteḥ.

1.36 [Nārāyaṇa on 3.34]

yathā muner yogino mānaso vṛttir vyāpāraḥ svikāyāṃ tanau carantaṃ sadbhir manv ādibhir nitarāṃ hitaṃ dhyātam . . . sadbhyo vā tebhya eva nitarāṃ hitam iṣṭaṃ haṃsaṃ paramātmānam ādara-yuktena atiśayena abhiprāyeṇa grahītukāmā sati niścalatāṃ prāpnoti.

1.37 [Cāṇḍupaṇḍita on 3.34]

yathā manaso vṛttir mano-vyāpāraḥ svakīya-tanau śarīre sannihitam antaś carantaṃ haṃsam ātmānam ādara-yuktena āśayena antaḥkaraṇena grahītukāmā jñātum icchur niścalatāṃ dhyāna-paratāṃ jagāhe.

EXCERPTS FROM CHAPTER 6

1.38 [Cāṇḍupaṇḍita 1.1 (preface)]

(A)

prathamaṃ tāvat kavir vijigiṣu kathāyāṃ svapitṛ-paribhāvukam udayanam atyamarṣaṇatayā kaṭākṣayaṃs tad-grantha-granthīn udgrathithayituṃ khaṇḍanaṃ prāripsuś caturvidha-puruṣārthair abhimānam anavadhīyamānam avadhīrya mānasam ekatānām āninàya. tathā ca śrīvārāṇasyāṃ mukti-kṣetre 'nubhūta-parabrahma-svarūpe gaṅgā-darśanādinā dharma-karma-madhya-madhyāsīno dṛṣṭi-puraḥsthita-svāyatta-meru-śikhara-sama-sauvarṇa-niṣka-rāśi-darśanena vaśīkṛtārtha-puruṣārthaḥ kṛtārthaḥ.

(B)

ṣoḍaśa-varṣābhir yauvanvatībhir apūrva-lāvaṇya-sampattibhiḥ snānodvartana-bhojanādy upacāra-caturābhiḥ pramadābhiḥ paricaryamāṇatayā kiṅkarī-kṛta-kāma-puruṣarthāḥ, evaṃ caturbhir api puruṣārthair anākṣipta-hṛdayatayā granthaṃ nirmāya tad-granthān khaṇḍayan yuktibhiḥ khaṇḍaśaḥ khaṇḍitavān.

(C)

tatra ca karkaśa-tarkodarkatvāc chṛṅgārādi-rasa-pradhānānām āparitoṣāṃ sambhāvya tad-āvarjanāya rasa-pradhānaṃ kāvyam idaṃ cakāra.

1.39 [Gadādhara 1.1 (preface)]

vārāṇasyām govindacandro nāma rājā babhuva. yathā 'stīndro 'marāvatyām. tasya sabhāyāṃ bahavaḥ paṇḍitā babhūvuḥ. maṇḍitāḥ sad-guṇaughena. teṣu ca sarveṣu śrīharṣaḥ parṣan-maṇḍanam. yaḥ kila kṛtavān khaṇḍanam . . . taṃ ca yathāvasaram anusarantaṃ nṛpa-saṃsadam apare matsariṇaḥ prathamopagatāḥ sāhitya-rasāla-taru-vanaṃ manyāḥ parasparā ''sya vīkṣā-puraḥsaram upahasanti sma prativāsaraṃ saṃprāpto 'yam tarka-śamī-taru-rupa-sanniveśaḥ sākṣān marur eva deśa iti. ekadā tu sahasopasthitena tena te liṅgair ulliṅgitāḥ svam anusandhāya dhyāyantaḥ kimapi visadṛśaṃ gūḍham. pṛṣṭaś ca kaścana tat-samīpa-vartī svāptaḥ kim eteṣāṃ duṣṭādinām īdṛśa-viceṣṭitam iti. kathitaṃ ca tena tat-sarvaṃ tasmai yathāvad ānupurvyā. atha 'sau vidvān abhimānavān kilai-tat kimapi śṛṅgāra-rasa-dhāma nala-carita-nāma samudravad anāvyaṃ mahākāvyaṃ vinirmāya nyavedayat tasmai nṛpāya pratyakṣa-devāya. tataś ca vidvān eṣa viśeṣa-viduṣas tasmāt suprasannāt tarka-vediṣv ekaṃ sāhitya-vediṣv ekam iti sabahumānam āsana-dvayaṃ labhate sma. tāmbūla-dvayaṃ ca kavi-paṇḍita iti ca nāmāntaraṃ lebhe.

1.40 [Rājaśekharasūri (from the *Harṣakaviprabandha*)]

pūrvasyāṃ vārāṇasyāṃ puri govindacandro nāma rājā . . . tat-putro jayantacandraḥ. tasmai rājyaṃ dattvā pitā yogaṃ prapadya para-lokam asādhayat. . . tasya rājño bahavo vidvāṃsaḥ. tatraiko hīra nāmā vipraḥ. tasya nandanaḥ prājña-cakravartī śrīharṣaḥ. so 'dyāpi bālāvasthaḥ. sabhāyāṃ rājakīyenaikena paṇḍitena vādinā hīro rāja-samakṣaṃ jitvā mudrita-vadanaḥ kṛtaḥ. lajjā-paṅke magnaḥ. vairaṃ babhāra dhārālam. mṛtyu-kāle harṣaṃ sa babhāṣe. vatsa amukena paṇḍitenāham āhatya rāja-dṛṣṭau jitaḥ. tan me duḥkham. yadi sat-putro 'si tadā taṃ jayeḥ kṣmāpa-sadasi. śrīharṣeṇoktam om iti. hīro dyāṃ gataḥ. śrīharṣas tu kuṭumba-bhāram āpta-dāyādeṣv āropya videśaṃ gatvā vividhācārya-pārśve 'cirāt tarkālaṅkāra-gīta-gaṇita-jyotiṣa-cūḍāmaṇi-mantra-vyākaraṇādīḥ sarvā vidyāḥ sasphurāḥ prajagrāha. gaṅgā-tīre suguru-dattaṃ cintāmaṇi-mantraṃ varṣam apramattaḥ sādhayāmāsa. pratyakṣā tripurā 'bhūt. amoghādeśatvādi varāptiḥ. tadādi rāja-goṣṭhīṣu bhramati. alaukikollekha-śikharitaṃ jalpaṃ karoti yaṃ ko 'pi na budhyate. tato 'tividyayā 'pi lokāgocara-bhūtayā khinnaḥ punar bhāratīṃ pratyakṣīkṛtyābhaṇat. mātaḥ atiprajñā 'pi doṣāya me jātā. budhyamāna-vacanaṃ māṃ kuru. tato devyoktam. tarhi madhya-rātre 'mbhaḥ klinne śirasi dadhi piba. paścāt svapihi. kaphāṃśāvatārāj jaḍatā-leśam āpnuhi. tathaiva kṛtam. bodhya-vāg āsīt. khaṇḍanādi-granthān paraḥśatāñ jagranthaḥ. kṛta-kṛtyībhūya kāśīm āyāsīt. nagara-taṭe sthitaḥ. jayantacandram ajijñapat.

1.41 [Rājaśekharasūri (verse from the *Harṣakaviprabandha*)]

sāhitye sukumāra-vastuni dṛḍha-nyāya-graha-granthile tarke vā mayi saṃvidhātari samaṃ līlāyate bhāratī / śayyā vāstu mṛduttara-cchadavatī darbhāṅkurair āstṛtā bhūmir vā hṛdayaṅgamo yadi patis tulyā ratir yoṣitām //

1.42 [Rājaśekharasūri (from the *Harṣakaviprabandha*)]

(A)

ekadā mudā nṛpeṇoktaḥ—kaviśa vādīndra kiñcit prabandha-ratnaṃ kuru. tato naiṣadhaṃ mahākāvyaṃ baddhaṃ divya-rasaṃ mahā-gūḍha-vyaṅgya-bhāra-sāram. rājñe darśitam. rājñoce—suṣṭhutamam idam. paraṃ kāśmīraṃ vraja. tatratya-paṇḍitebhyo darśaya. bhāratī-haste ca muñca. bhāratī ca tatra pīṭhe svayaṃ sākṣād vasati. asatyaṃ prabandhaṃ haste nyastam avakara-nikaram iva dūre kṣipati. satyaṃ tu mūrdha-dhūna-pūrvaṃ suṣṭhy ity ūrikaroti. uparitaḥ puṣpāṇi patanti. śrīharṣo rāja-dattārtha-niṣpanna-vipula-sāmagrīkaḥ kāśmīrān agamat. sarasvatī-haste pustakaṃ nyāsthat. sarasvatyā dūre kṣiptaṃ tat.

(B)
vaideśiko 'ham. na vedmi kimapy ete prākṛta-vādinyau brūtaḥ. kevalaṃ tān śabdān vedmi. rājñoktam—brūhi. tat-krama-stham eva tad-bhāṣita-prati-bhāṣita-śatam abhihitam anena. rājā camatkṛtaḥ—aho prājñā. aho avadhāraṇā. dāsyor vādaṃ nirṇāya yathā-sambhāvaṃ nigrahānugrahau kṛtvā prahitya śrīharṣam apṛcchad rājā—kas tvam evaṃ medhira-śiromaṇiḥ. śrīharṣeṇoktaṃ sarvaṃ kathānakaṃ svam. rājan paṇḍita-kṛta-daurjanyāt tava pure duḥkhī tiṣṭhāmi. samyak pāramparya-jño rājā paṇḍitān āhūyāvādīt—dhiṅmūḍhāḥ. īdṛśo 'pi ratne na snihyate.

1.43 [Rājaśekharasūri (from the *Hariharaprabandha*)]

rātrau sadyo lekhaka-niyogibhir lekhitā navīnā pustikā. jīrṇa-rajjvākṛta vāsa-nyāsena dhūsarīkṛtya muktā. prātaḥ paṇḍitāya pustikā dattā. gṛhyatāṃ tad idaṃ svaṃ naiṣadhaṃ. gṛhitā paṇḍitena pustikā. mantriṇā nyagādi asmākam api kośe kilāstīvedaṃ śāstram iti smarāmaḥ. vilokyatāṃ kośaḥ. yāvad vilambenaiva kṛṣṭā navīnā pratiḥ. yāvac chodyate tāvan nipīya yasya kṣiti-rakṣiṇas kathā ityādi naiṣadham udaghaṭiṣṭam.

1.44 [Vidyāpati (from the *Medhāvikathā*)]

(A)
babhūva gauḍa-viṣaye śrīharṣo nāma kavi-paṇḍitaḥ. sa ca nalacaritābhidhānaṃ kāvyaṃ kṛtvā tat-kāvyaṃ darśayituṃ paṇḍita-maṇḍalīm uddiśya vārāṇasīṃ jagāma.

(B)
rasavan-māna-saṃgrāhi guṇālaṅkāra-saṃyutam / kavīnāṃ yaśase kāvyaṃ hāsyāyān yac ca jāyate // agnau parīkṣyate svarṇaṃ kāvyaṃ sadasi tad-vidi / kiṃ kaves tena kāvyena sadbhir yan nānugamyate// [Puruṣaparīkṣā 1.10.2–3]

(C)
tatra ca koka-nāmānaṃ paṇḍitaṃ śrāvayāmāsa . . . śrīharṣas tu tam anugacchan paṭhati praty aham tad uttaraṃ kimapi nāpnoti. ekadā śrīharṣeṇoktam—ārya mahākāvye kṛta-śramo 'ham. tat-parīkṣārthaṃ

tvām uddiśya buddhyā svadeśīya-vātsalyena ca mahato dūrād āgato 'smi . . . bhavān na nindati na cābhinandati. tan-manye karṇam eva nārpayatīti.

(D)

koka uvāca—āhaḥ katham ahaṃ karṇaṃ nārpayāmi. kiṃ tu sampūrṇaṃ śrutvā śabdārthayor ūhāpohena sandarbha-śuddhiṃ jñātvā viśeṣaṃ vakṣyāmi. anayā vāsanayā na kimapi vacmi. kāvyaṃ tu mayā karṇe kṛtaṃ manasi dhāritaṃ ceti. yadi bhavān na pratyeti tadā śṛṇotu.

1.45 [Rājaśekharasūri (from the *Harṣakaviprabandha*)]

atrāntare jayantacandrasya padmākara-nāmā pradhāna-naraḥ śrī-aṇahilapattanaṃ gataḥ. tatra saras-taṭe rajaka-kṣālitāyāṃ śāṭikāyāṃ ketayām iva madhukara-kulaṃ nilīyamānaṃ dṛṣṭvā vismito 'prākṣīd rajakam—yasyā yuvater iyaṃ śāṭī tāṃ me darśaya. tasya hi mantriṇas tat-padminītve nirṇayasthaṃ manaḥ. rajakena sāyaṃ tasmai tad-gṛhaṃ nītvā tām arpayitvā tat-svāminī sūhavadevi-nāmnī śālāpati-patnī vidhavā yauvanasthā surūpā darśitā. tāṃ kumārapāla-rāja-pārśvād uparodhya tad-gṛhān nītvā somanātha-yātrāṃ kṛtvā kāśīṃ gataḥ. tāṃ padminīṃ jayantacandra-bhoginīṃ akarot. sūhavadevir iti khyātim agāt. sā ca sa-garvā viduṣīti kṛtvā kalābhāratīti pāṭhayati loke. śrīharṣo 'pi narabhāratīti paṭhyate. tasya tan na sahate sā matsariṇī. tvaṃ kaḥ. śrīharṣaḥ—kalāsarvajño 'ham. rājñyā 'bhāṇi—tarhi mām upānahau paridhāpaya. ko bhāvaḥ—yady ayam na vedmīti bhaṇitaṃ dvijatvāt tarhy ajñaḥ. śrīharṣeṇāṅgīkṛtam. gato nilayam. taru-valkalais tathā tathā parikarmitaiḥ sāyaṃ lolākṣaḥ san dūra-sthaḥ svāminīm ājūhavat . . . . rājānam api tat-kṛtāṃ kuceṣṭāṃ jñāpayitvā khinno gaṅgā-tīre saṃnyāsam agrahīt.

EXCERPTS FROM CHAPTER 7

1.46 [Mallinātha on 1.14]

(A)

atra prakṛtasya pariveṣasya pratiṣedhenāprakṛtasya kuṇḍalanasya sthāpanāt apahnutir alaṅkāraḥ . . . prācīnās tu pariveṣa-miṣeṇa sūryā-candramasoḥ kuṇḍalanotprekṣaṇāt sāpahnavotprekṣā.

(B)
evaṃ kaitavaṃ chalaṃ tasmāt bhānoḥ sūryasya vidhor api candrasya ca kuṇḍalanām atiriktatā-sūcaka-veṣṭanam ity arthaḥ karoti. adhikākṣara-varjanārthaṃ lekhakādivad iti bhāvaḥ.

1.47 [Cāṇḍupaṇḍita on 19.60]

vāyaso hi prātaḥ kiṃ kim iti śabdaṃ karoti. sa ca pṛcchā-vācakaḥ . . . tuhī tuhī iti śabdaṃ prātaḥ pikaḥ karoti.

1.48 [Mallinātha on 19.60]

pakṣi-prabhṛtīnām avyakta-dhvanī yasya cetasi yad udeti sa tathaiva manaḥ-kalpitaṃ prakāśayati. evaṃ ca kavir ayaṃ tadā kāka-dhvaniṃ kāv iti kokila-dhvaniṃ ca tuhīti kalpayitvā kāv iti tuhīti ca kāka-kokila-kūjitena pūrvokta-praśṇottaratvam utprekṣate. prabhātaṃ jātaṃ kākādayaḥ pakṣiṇaḥ kūjantīti bhāvaḥ.

1.49 [Nārāyaṇa on 1.118]

smarārjitam kāmotpannaṃ rāgo ’nurāgas tal-lakṣaṇo rāga-mahīruho vṛkṣas tasyāṅkuraṃ bibhrataṃ yathā-kramaṃ dhārayantam . . . bālāsu priyāsu cumbanādi-vyāpāraḥ.

1.50 [Mallinātha on 2.34]

tadapi cet karaṇa-sāmarthyāt trivalaya iti bahuvacana-prayoga-darśane sthitaṃ gati-mātraṃ na sārvatrikam iti pratīmaḥ.

APPENDIX 2: ENCOMIA (*PRAŚASTI*) TO ŚRĪHARṢA AND THE *NAIṢADHĪYA*

2.1

Playfully broken are the tusks of that mad elephant,
that group of Cārvākas who hold that
only perception leads to true knowledge.
The attack is executed by the hands of a lion,
whose human form is Śrīharṣa.
These actions of his are well-known in the world.[1]

[Varadarāja Paṇḍita]

2.2

Glory to Nala, the jewel in the crown of all kings!
To praise him makes everything auspicious.
A collection of the pearls of Nala's fame,
Śrīharṣa's elegant poem confers a special delight.[2]

[Gopinātha Ratha]

2.3

After adopting a superb path,
a path untrodden by other poets,
and initiated by his own pioneering steps,
the poet Śrīharṣa—the glorious Harṣa—
strides about gloriously.[3]

[Gadādhara]

2.4

In technical matters of philosophy, Sarasvatī
became the *Khaṇḍanakhaṇḍakhādya.*
In the world of poetry, she became the *Naiṣadhīya.*
These two works represent the sun and the moon
and are sung about everywhere.
Scholars—competitive soldiers—
bent on defeating their rivals, and pushing their own ideas
on the battlefield of scholarship, adore Śrīharṣa
for his pungent and sweet qualities.
With the *Khaṇḍanakhaṇḍakhādya*, he is pungent.
Sweet he is in the *Naiṣadhīya.*[4]

[Gadādhara]

2.5

It has the syllable Om as its ornament.
Admired by all the critics,
its elegant expressions sparkle.
It is simply beautiful, to the extent that
its superb sequence of words
gives pleasure to the goddess of Beauty.
The delight it gives to the heart lingers long.
Truly, it serves as a means to accomplish the aims of life.
Śrīharṣa's poem is a scripture *par excellence.*
Ah, so dear to connoisseurs of poetry,
how intense is its brilliance![5]

[Śrīdhara]

2.6

To whose heart does Śrīharṣa not give pleasure?
Entertaining through his poetry,
he is a hill that playfully sways in the waves
of the nectar of rasa.
Attractive with his philosophizing,
he is a craggy mountain churning the sea

with deeply penetrating arguments,
a boatman skilled enough to cross the ocean
of both schools of Mīmāṃsā![6]

[Rāmacandra Śeṣa]

2.7

Śrīharṣa, king of poets, has produced an extraordinary composition:
The stage for her play is the peak of the palace of the learned heart.
The activity backstage is the fashioning of novel sentiments.
Her friends are the expressive manifestations of *rasa*.
Her skillful acting is the careful use of words.
Naiṣadha—Nala—is the husband she has chosen for herself.[7]

[Viśveśvara (Gāgābhaṭṭa)]

2.8

A union of sound and sense,
elegantly bound up within choice meters,
is its powerful roots.
The range of logical arguments
makes for a beautiful roof of rough *śiphā* branches.
Śrīharṣa's expressive words are the flowers,
and its sole fruit is *śṛṅgāra*, ripe and glistening with lots of *rasa*.
What can excel this great medicinal plant?[8]

[Śrīdhara]

2.9

Going through inferior poems of other poets
has led many to mental strain.
These works aggravate the mind's *doṣas*
and cause an unhealthy imbalance.
May the poetry of Śrīharṣa,
the lord of the family poets,
be a rejuvenating medicine!
Drink it up with your ears![9]

[Gāgābhaṭṭa]

2.10

Inference may be said to be
the primary trope of this poem. It alone shines.
The poem's *rasa* is delivered
both directly and indirectly—and it is superb.
Figures of speech and *rasa* make a poem,
like the combination of milk and nectar.
It is worthy of being clutched
by a learned man or god, in a firm embrace.[10]

[Gadādhara]

2.11

How do I measure the depth of this poem called *Naiṣadhīya*?
It is a palatial abode for limitless meanings, concealed and remote.
There are many, many radiant jewels in the middle of the earth.
It is the rare digger who can locate the entire quarry of diamonds.[11]

[Gadādhara]

2.12

Because of the drops of water flowing fast
from the streams of the sibling of the *Khaṇḍanakhaṇḍakhādya*,
we detect the sprouts of delight by their characteristic flowers,
well-watered and in bloom, growing without interruption.
We know that such is the delight of the connoisseur:
hair standing on end, moistened with *rasa* that slowly builds.[12]

[Gāgābhaṭṭa]

NOTES

INTRODUCTION

1. I am thinking of David Smith's work on the *Haravijaya* and Indira Peterson's book on the *Kirātārjunīya* [David Smith, *Ratnākara's Haravijaya: An Introduction to the Sanskrit Court Epic* (Delhi: Oxford University Press, 1985); and Indira Visvanathan Peterson, *Design and Rhetoric in a Sanskrit Court Epic: The Kirātārjunīya of Bhāravi* (Albany: State University of New York Press, 2003)].
2. See especially the third volume of Ricoeur's *Time and Narrative* for a discussion of the distinction [Paul Ricoeur, *Time and Narrative*, vol. 1–3, tr. K. McLaughlin and D. Pellauer (Chicago: University of Chicago Press, 1984)].
3. The poem is also called *Naiṣadhacarita* or, as I will be calling it from here onward, the *Naiṣadhīya*.
4. Georg Bühler, "Age of Śrīharṣa," *JBBRAS* 10 (1875): 33.
5. S.N. Dasgupta and S.K. De, *History of Sanskrit Literature*, vol. 1 (Calcutta: University of Calcutta, 1947), 325; 330.
6. In this regard, colonial-era scholarship on the *Naiṣadhīya* echoes what recent scholarship on other Sanskrit works has attempted to address: the often-negative valuations stamped on the aesthetic trends of post-Kālidāsa poetry. Especially relevant in this regard are Yigal Bronner's analysis of the Western bias against complex, double-meaning (*śleṣa*) poetry [Yigal Bronner, *Extreme Poetry* (New York: Columbia University Press, 2010)] and Lawrence McCrea's article on Māgha's *Śiśupālavadha*, which aims to redirect the conversation of Māgha's aesthetic aims away from the perspective of nineteenth- and twentieth-century critics of Sanskrit poetry [Lawrence McCrea, "The Conquest of Cool: Theology and Aesthetics in Māgha's *Śiśupālavadha*" in *Innovations and Turning Points: Toward a History of Sanskrit Literature*, ed. Yigal Bronner, David Shulman, and Gary Tubb (Dehli: Oxford University Press; forthcoming)].
7. In the case of Sanskrit literary culture, pseudepigrapha usually take the form of verses falsely attributed to a famous poet that, in most cases, come from the pens of later poets attempting to mimic or reproduce the style of the master poet.
8. While this book focuses on an important literary work's *reading* communities, a separate study could emphasize the visual and performance communities that form

around works like the *Naiṣadhīya*, somewhat along the lines of Philip Lutgendorf's exemplary case study of the ways in which the *Rāmāyaṇa* of Tulsidās has been received and perpetuated by audiences through performance [Philip Lutgendorf, *The Life of a Text: Performing the Rāmcaritmānas of Tulsidas* (Berkeley and Los Angeles: University of California Press, 1995)].

9. See especially Jauss's essay [Hans Robert Jauss, "Literary History as a Challenge to Literary Theory" in *Toward an Aesthetic of Reception*, tr. Timothy Bahti (Minneapolis: University of Minnesota Press, 1982)]. See also Stephanie Trigg's book on the reception history of English poet Geoffrey Chaucer [Stephanie Trigg, *Congenial Souls: Reading Chaucer from Medieval to Postmodern* (Minneapolis: University of Minnesota Press, 2002)].
10. Iser writes about the effect a text has on the reader and the implications it holds in critical attitudes toward literature: "Now if the reader and the literary text are partners in a process of communication, and if what is communicated is to be of any value, our prime concern will no longer be the *meaning* of the text . . . but its *effect*. Herein lies the function of literature, and herein lies the justification for approaching literature from a functionalist standpoint" [Wolfgang Iser, "The Act of Reading" in *Critical Theory Since 1965*, ed. H. Adams and L. Searle (Tallahassee: Florida State University Press, 1986), 360]. See also Iser's book *The Implied Reader* (1972, trans. 1974) and Fish's collection of essays *Is There a Text in This Class* (1980).
11. See section 2.1 of appendix 2 for Sanskrit text.
12. *Khaṇḍa-khādya* can be translated as "edible pieces" but also may refer to an Āyurvedic potion. An unwieldy translation of *Khaṇḍanakhaṇḍakhādya* may also be something like "a disease-curing tonic (*khaṇḍa-khādya*) that systematically smashes (*khaṇḍana*) the logic of opponents." Another common translation for the strange term *khaṇḍa-khādya* is "sweets" or the archaic "sweetmeats."
13. Formerly known also as Mahodaya, modern Kanauj is located in the center of the Indian state of Uttar Pradesh. Kānyakubja was the focal point of several important royal dynasties from the seventh century CE and became for several centuries, as Stein notes, "the emblem of the cakravartin in northern India" [Burton Stein, *A History of India* (Malden, Mass.: Wiley-Blackwell Press, 1998), 124]. Kanauj, under the Gurjara-Pratīhāra empire (sixth through eleventh centuries), was also a center of learning and a home for several important Sanskrit and Prakrit poets, the most well known among them being Rājaśekhara Yāyāvarīya in the tenth century.
14. Though the Gāhaḍavāla dynasty's founding is attributed to Yaśovigraha (1042–1070 CE) and his son Mahīcandra (1071–1089), the first available inscriptions only date from the reign of Candradeva (1090–1103), the first Gāhaḍavāla king to establish control over Kānyakubja. Candradeva was followed by his son Madanapāla (1104–1113 CE), who was, in turn, briskly succeeded by Govindacandra (1114–1155 CE), the most successful of the Gāhaḍavālas—in terms of expanding his empire to include the important places of Ayodhya, Vārāṇasī, Kuśikā, and Indrasthānīyaka; repelling the incursions of various rivals, including the Pālas from the east and the Yāmīnī sultāns from the west; and fashioning his imperial domain as a center of learning where we know that at least one of the most important works of medieval *dharmaśāstra* emerged, the legal digest (*nibandha*) entitled *Kṛtyakalpataru* of Govindacandra's minister Lakṣmīdhara. For a summary of arguments about Śrīharṣa's date, see A.N. Jani, *A Critical Study of*

Śrīharṣa's Naiṣadhacaritam (Baroda: Oriental Institute, 1957), 121–129. Many of the details about the history of the Gāhaḍavāla dynasty are drawn from Roma Niyogi's work on the subject [Roma Niyogi, *The History of the Gāhaḍavāla Dynasty* (Calcutta: Calcutta Oriental Book Agency, 1959)].

15. Lakṣmaṇasena himself is reputed to have been the patron of Sanskrit poets such as Umāpatidhara, Dhoyi, Jayadeva, and Govardhana and of significant projects such as the anthology of Sanskrit poetry known as the *Saduktikarṇāmṛta* compiled by Śrīdharadāsa. Śrīharṣa is cited as the author of several verses from this anthology, the significance of which is discussed in the concluding chapter of this volume.
16. The most famous of the Gāhaḍavāla kings, Jayacandra (Jayaccandra, Jayantacandra)—often associated with the appellations Jāichand, Jaichand Rai, or the Rāi of Banaras—is memorialized as the great rival of both the Cāhamāna king Pṛthvīrāja and his ultimate vanquisher Muhammad Ghūri in numerous texts from the late medieval period. These texts include Vidyāpati's *Puruṣaparīkṣā* (The Examination of the Man) and Jain Sanskrit poet Nayacandrasūri's *Rambhāmañjarīnāṭaka* in the fifteenth century. [Nayacandrasūri, incidentally, compares himself to the "immortal Śrīharṣa" in his *Rambhāmañjarī*, as a poet who can create extraordinary poetry (*lokottara*) that is both graceful in sound and striking in image (*lālityam amarasyeha śrīharṣasyeva vakrimā / nayacandrakaveḥ kāvye dṛṣṭaṃ lokottaraṃ dvayam //*).] Two other works are *Firishta's History* (*Tarikh-i-Firishta*) and Cānd Bardāi's epic *Pṛthvīrāja Rāso* in the seventeenth century.
17. Niyogi, *History of the Gāhaḍavāla Dynasty*, 207–208.
18. For Watve's ideas about Śrīharṣa's patron and the connection with Pṛthvīrāja, see Jani, *Critical Study of Śrīharṣa's Naiṣadhacaritam*, 259. The seventeenth-century Brajbhāṣā text *Pṛthvīrāja Rāso* provides the most detailed portrait of Jayacandra as it not only recounts a romanticized military rivalry between the Gāhaḍavāla king and Pṛthvīrāja but also provides a detailed account of Pṛthvīrāja's secret attendance at Saṃyogitā's *svayaṃvara*. According to this narrative, Pṛthvīrāja elopes with Saṃyogitā, reinforcing Jayacandra's enmity with Pṛthvirāja and thus making it possible for the Yāmīnī sultans to gain hegemony over both their kingdoms. In Hindi, therefore, to be called a "Jaichand" is to be understood as a traitor to one's family or nation.
19. *karkoṭakasya nāgasya damayantyāḥ nalasya ca ṛtuparṇasya rājarśeḥ kīrtanaṃ kalināśanam* (*Mahābhārata*, *Vanaparva* (Book Two)].
20. V. Narayana Rao and David Shulman, "Nala: The Life of a Story" in *Damayantī and Nala: The Many Lives of a Story*, ed. Susan Wadley (New Delhi: Chronicle Books, 2011).
21. See note 19.
22. See section 2.2 of appendix 2 for Sanskrit text.

1. THE *NAIṢADHĪYA*'S AESTHETIC

1. See section 2.3 in appendix 2 for Sanskrit text.
2. One may tentatively compare the *mahākāvya* genre to the *epyllion* ("little epic" in Greek) or to literary (or secondary) epics in European languages like Milton's *Paradise Lost*, Spencer's *Faerie Queen*, or Dante's *Inferno*.

3. See Siegfried Lienhard, *A History of Classical Poetry: Sanskrit, Pali, Prakrit* (Wiesbaden: Otto Harrassowitz, 1984), 163ff.
4. David Smith has published a monograph on the poem [David Smith, *Ratnākara's Haravijaya: An Introduction to the Sanskrit Court Epic* (Delhi: Oxford University Press, 1985)].
5. Michael Hahn has worked extensively on this poem [Michael Hahn, "Appendix" in *Śivasvāmin's Kapphiṇābhyudaya or the Exaltation of King Kapphiṇa*, ed. Gauri Shankar (New Delhi: Aditya Prakashan, 1989), i–xxxvi].
6. For a good translation and discussion of Daṇḍin's definition of *mahākāvya*, see Indira Viswanathan Peterson, *Design and Rhetoric in a Sanskrit Court Epic: The Kirātārjunīya of Bhāravi* (Albany: State University of New York Press, 2003), 8ff.
7. Peterson suggests that these "topics of a *mahākāvya* are not mere items on a list, but coherent, viable arenas of composition for the poet and enjoyment for the connoisseur" (Peterson, *Design and Rhetoric*, 18). Outside of these rather conventional contours of the shape Sanskrit poets give to a *mahākāvya*, Sanskrit writers on poetics rarely explore in their works the critical issues that contemporary readers consider relevant to a fuller appreciation of why certain episodes from the great epics are chosen by the poet, what social or political commentary accompanies their choice, or if there is a particular literary design that marks the work as a whole.
8. See E. Röer (ed.), "*Naiṣadhīyacarita* of Śrīharṣa with Premacandra Tarkavāgīśa's Commentary (Cantos 1–11) and Nārāyaṇa's Commentary (Cantos 12–22)" in *Biblioteca Indica* (Calcutta: Asiatic Society, 1836–1855), 327.
9. See G.C. Jhala, "The *Naiṣadhacarita* of Śrīharṣa—A Linguistic Study," *Journal of Oriental Institute Baroda* 22.2 (1973): 157.
10. K.K. Handiqui, *Naiṣadhacarita of Śrīharṣa: English Translation with Notes*, 2nd ed. (Poona: Deccan College, 1965), xi–xv.
11. See section 2.4 in appendix 2 for Sanskrit text.
12. Śrīharṣa mentions this in the epilogue verse to the sixth canto (*NC* 6.113c). The compound *khaṇḍa-khādya* could refer to either a sweet dessert or to a medicinal tonic used to cure diseases. The word *khaṇḍana* has the sense of "smashing" or "refuting" something, especially, in Śrīharṣa's case, the logic of those with whom you disagree.
13. All citations from the *Naiṣadhīya* are taken from the 1998 edition (with Nārāyaṇa's commentary) prepared by Śivadatta Sharma [Śivadatta Sharma, *Naiṣadhacaritam: Śrīmannārāyaṇaṭīkayā* (Lucknow: Uttarapradeśa Saṃskṛta Saṃsthāna, 1998)].
14. This is a well-known definition found in numerous Advaita Vedānta texts: *abhinna-nimittopādāna-kāraṇam brahma*. Śrīharṣa's dialectical strategy in the *Khaṇḍanakhaṇḍakhādya* to deconstruct the very bases of epistemological definitions through demonstrating their internal contradictions leads to a conclusion that *all definitions are untenable* (*sarvāni lakṣaṇāni anupapannāni*) and that Truth is free of negatability (*bādhitatva*), is self-illuminating (*svaprakāśa*), and is beyond the logical flaws intrinsic to all philosophical propositions about Truth. See Stephen Phillips's comprehensive work [*Classical Indian Metaphysics* (Chicago: Open Court, 1995)] and Phyllis Granoff's classic study [*Philosophy and Argument in Late Vedānta: Śrīharṣa's Khaṇḍanakhaṇḍakhādya* (Dordrecht, Holland: D. Reidel Publishing Company, 1978)] for a thorough discussion of Śrīharṣa's seminal contribution to the development of post-twelfth-century Indian philosophy.

15. Maya Tevet-Dayan has an especially perspicuous analysis of this episode from the *Naiṣadhīya* [Maya Tevet-Dayan, *Divine Language Incarnate: The Poetic Metaphysics of Śrīharṣa's Naiṣadhīya-carita* (Tel Aviv: Faculty of Humanities, Tel Aviv University, 2010)]. See also B.N. Goswamy's classic work [B.N. Goswamy, *Pahari Paintings of the Nala-Damayanti Theme* (New Delhi: National Museum, 1995)].
16. See section 2.5 of appendix 2 for Sanskrit text.
17. B.K. Matilal's essay entitled "Skepticism and Mysticism" eloquently brings out this connection in Śrīharṣa's philosophy [B.K. Matilal, "Skepticism and Mysticism," *Journal of the American Oriental Society* 105, no. 3 (July–Sep. 1985): 479–484].
18. On the wide appearance of this mantra in various religious traditions of early India, see Handiqui, *Naiṣadhacarita of Śrīharṣa*, 580.
19. Tevet-Dayan (*Divine Language Incarnate*, 199ff) comprehensively discusses the role of Sarasvatī and the *Naiṣadhīya*'s discourse on Speech generally.
20. Moritz Winternitz, *History of Indian Literature* (New Delhi: Motilal Banarsidass, 1966), 64.
21. See section 2.6 of appendix 2 for Sanskrit text.
22. Śrīharṣa again compares the fame of Damayantī with the fame of this particular style of poetic composition in 14.91.
23. A.N. Jani, *A Critical Study of Śrīharṣa's Naiṣadhacaritam* (Baroda: Oriental Institute, 1957), 145.
24. *sapīteḥ saṃprīter ajani rajanīśaḥ pariṣadā parītas tārāṇāṃ dina-maṇi-maṇi-grāva-maṇikaḥ / priye paśyotprekṣā-kavibhir-abhidhānāya suśakaḥ sudhām abhyuddhartuṃ dhṛta-śaśaka-nīlāśma-caṣakaḥ // Naiṣadhīya* 22.144.
25. The tradition of putting four (or sometimes five) verses at the end of a given *mahākāvya*, giving information about the poet and the poem, becomes common after the seventh century (see, for example, the *Bhaṭṭikāvya*, *Jānakīharaṇa*, *Śiśupālavadha*, and *Haravijaya*).
26. *āvaktrendu tad-aṅgam eva sṛjataḥ sraṣṭuḥ samagras tv iṣāṃ koṣaḥ śoṣam agād agādha-jagatī-śilpe 'pi nālpāyitaḥ / niḥśeṣa-dyuti-maṇḍala-vyaya-vaśād īṣal labhais (?) tat-tanū-śeṣaḥ keśa-mayaḥ kim andha-tamas astomair abhūn nirmitaḥ //* [Cited in A.N. Jani, *Critical Study of Śrīharṣa's Naiṣadhacaritam*, appendix 12: 48].
27. *īṣan nāsā-nikocaḥ khara-mukhara-mukha-prekṣaṇaṃ hāsa-leśaḥ svābodhād aprasāda-dhvananam asad avadyokti-helāvahelā / mauna-vyāsaṅga-vārtāntara-para-ruciraś loka-pāṭhādayas te soḍhavyāḥ ke kiyantaḥ śiva śiva kavitve kucchalā matsarāṇām //* [Cited in A.N. Jani, *Critical Study of Śrīharṣa's Naiṣadhacaritam*, appendix 12: 49].
28. Among them include Śrīdharadāsa's *Saduktikarṇāmṛta* (c. 1206) and Bhagadatta Jalhaṇa's *Sūktimuktāvalī* (c. 1257). See A.N. Jani, *Critical Study of Śrīharṣa's Naiṣadhacaritam*, 48–54: appendices 12 and 13 for a complete list of citations. The appearance of *Naiṣadhīya* verses in anthologies—and unique works like the anonymous *Vasantavilāsa* of the fourteenth century—remains fairly consistent up until the seventeenth century: *Subhāṣitaratnākara* and *Subhāsitaratnabhāṅḍāgara* (c. fifteenth century); Gadādharabhaṭṭa's *Rasikajīvana* (c. 1670); and Veṇidatta's *Subhāṣitapadyaveṇi* (c. seventeenth century).
29. *kuc-giri caḍi ati thakit hvai calī ḍīṭhi muṃh-cāḍ / phiri na ṭarī pariyai raho giri cibuk ko gāḍ //* [Cited in Amarnath Jha, *The Veiled Moon: Translations of Bihārī's Satsai* (New Delhi: ICCR, 1973), 66].

30. Iser writes about the *effect* a text has on the reader and the implications it holds in critical attitudes toward literature: "Now if the reader and the literary text are partners in a process of communication, and if what is communicated is to be of any value, our prime concern will no longer be the *meaning* of the text . . . but its *effect*. Herein lies the function of literature, and herein lies the justification for approaching literature from a functionalist standpoint" [cited from Iser's essay entitled "The Act of Reading" in *Critical Theory Since 1965*, ed. H. Adams and L. Searle (Tallahassee: Florida State University Press, 1986), 360].
31. Yigal Bronner, *Extreme Poetry* (New York: Columbia University Press, 2010), 11. Bronner (*Extreme Poetry*, 9–13) devotes several pages of his book on double-meaning poetry (*śleṣakāvya*) to delineate the bias against post-Kālidāsa poetry in Sanskrit among critics of the nineteenth and twentieth centuries, who saw works like Māgha's and Śrīharṣa's as excessively ornamented and often degenerate of the *kāvya* "ideal." Recently, Lawrence McCrea's essay (forthcoming) on Māgha's *Śiśupālavadha* has also attempted to rescue Māgha from colonial-era criticism of the poem's aesthetic goals [L. McCrea, "The Conquest of Cool: Theology and Aesthetics in Māgha's Śiśupālavadha" in *Innovations and Turning Points: Toward a History of Sanskrit Literature*, eds. Y. Bronner, D. Shulman, and G. Tubb (Delhi: Oxford University Press; forthcoming)]. On this era's bias against Sanskrit prose poetry, particularly of the prose master Bāṇabhaṭṭa, among these very same critics, see Robert Hueckstedt, *The Style of Bāṇa: An Introduction to Sanskrit Prose Poetry* (Lanham: University Press of America, 1985), 3–22.
32. Recently, in the context of discussing twentieth-century engagements with Sanskrit literature and especially with Kālidāsa, Simona Sahwney has suggested that "Kālidāsa has to be safeguarded, as it were, from the general image of classical Sanskrit poetry, precisely because the subsequent fall of Sanskrit poetry is a necessary part of its narrative." See Simona Sahwney, *The Modernity of Sanskrit* (Minneapolis: University of Minnesota Press, 2009), 166.
33. K.C. Chatterji, "Some Notes on the *Naiṣadhcarita* of Śrīharṣa," *Calcutta Oriental Journal* 3, no. 6 (1936): 155.
34. W. Yates, "Review of the *Naiṣadhacarita*," *Asiatic Researches*, vol. XX (1836): 318–337 [cited in A.N. Jani, *Critical Study of Śrīharṣa's Naiṣadhacaritam*, 234].

2. EIGHT CENTURIES OF COMMENTARY

1. Sheldon Pollock, "Sanskrit Literary Culture from the Inside Out" in *Literary Cultures in History: Reconstructions from South Asia*, ed. Sheldon Pollock (Berkeley: University of California Press, 2003), 80.
2. I have primarily used Sanadhyashastri's edition of Mallinātha's commentary, published by Krishnadas Akademi Press (1984–1987); Śivadatta Sharma's 1998 edition of the *Naiṣadhīya* with Nārāyaṇa's commentary; and J. Jani's 1997 edition of the poem with Cāṇḍupaṇḍita's commentary. See the bibliography for complete citations of all editions used.
3. For a discussion on, and practical description of, the formulaic nature of Sanskrit commentaries on *kāvya*, see especially J.A.F. Roodbergen, *Mallinātha's Ghaṇṭāpatha on Kirātārjunīyah, I-VI: Introduction, Translation, and Notes* (Leiden: Brill Publishers,

1984), and Gary Tubb and Emery Boose, *Scholastic Sanskrit: A Manual for Students* (New York: American Institute of Buddhist Studies, 2007).

4. Sheldon Pollock, *The Language of the Gods in the World of Men* (Berkeley: University of California Press, 2006), 83.
5. Rājaśekharasūri's narrative is partially translated and discussed in chapter 6. For more details about Vastupāla and his milieu, see Sandesara (1953).
6. Vidyādhara tells us in the colophon of his commentary to the second canto of the *Naiṣadhīya* that he was the son of Rāmacandra Bhiṣak and Sītā. For further details, see A.N. Jani, *A Critical Study of Śrīharṣa's Naiṣadhacaritam* (Baroda: Oriental Institute, 1957), 77, fn. 281.
7. The manuscript from which this verse comes is from the nineteenth century (no. 415 at the Bhandarkar Oriental Research Institute, Pune) and is described by K.K. Handiqui, *Naiṣadhacarita of Śrīharṣa: English Translation with Notes*, 2nd ed. (Poona: Deccan College, 1965), xxiv–xxv. See section 1.1 of appendix 1 for Sanskrit text.
8. Cāṇḍupaṇḍita mentions this in the preface to his commentary on *Naiṣadhīya* 1.1. See Jaydev Jani, *Naiṣadhamahākāvya with Cāṇḍupaṇḍita's Commentary* (Jodhpur: Rajasthan Oriental Research Institute, 1997), xiv–xxxxix, for other details Cāṇḍupaṇḍita gives about the *Naiṣadhīya* and his own commentary on it.
9. See J. Jani (*Naiṣadhamahākāvya with Cāṇḍupaṇḍita's Commentary*, xvii; 43) for more details about the colophons of Cāṇḍupaṇḍita's *Dīpikā*.
10. For further details, see Jaydev Jani's preface to the critical edition of Cāṇḍupaṇḍita's *Dīpikā* (J. Jani, *Naiṣadhamahākāvya with Cāṇḍupaṇḍita's Commentary*, xx).
11. See section 1.2 of appendix 1 for Sanskrit text.
12. See Handiqui (*Naiṣadhacarita of Śrīharṣa*, xix–xxii) for a complete list of citations found in Cāṇḍupaṇḍita.
13. Kṛṣṇānanda from Orissa is said to have written a commentary on the *Naiṣadhīya*. His well-known *Sahṛdayānanda*, a Sanskrit *mahākāvya* from the thirteenth century, clearly demonstrates his familiarity with Śrīharṣa's poem. I discuss this poem as an "intralingual translation" in chapter 6. Two other commentaries from the thirteenth century include one from Śrīdatta, whom A.N. Jani dates between 1275 and 1310 (A.N. Jani, *A Critical Study of Śrīharṣa's Naiṣadhacaritam*, 68–69), and Vaṃśivādana Śarma, whose colophon places him around the same time (A.N. Jani, *A Critical Study of Śrīharṣa's Naiṣadhacaritam*, 75–76).
14. See section 1.3 of appendix 1 for Sanskrit text. Īśānadeva pugnaciously adds a parting comment defending the originality of his work, however limited it might be: "A scholar who for the sake of celebrity shows the world the work of another by saying that it is his—such a scholar certainly goes to hell."
15. Īśānadeva's textual readings and interpretations generally follow Vidyādhara's commentary. See A.N. Jani (*A Critical Study of Śrīharṣa's Naiṣadhacaritam*, 49) for further details.
16. A.N. Jani (*A Critical Study of Śrīharṣa's Naiṣadhacaritam*, 58–59), among others, also identifies Vidyāraṇya (head of the Śriṅgeri monastery from 1377 to 1386), author of such works as *Pañcadaśi* and *Sarvadarśanasaṃgraha*, as a potential commentator on *Naiṣadhīya* itself, being the teacher of Narahari. No evidence of such a commentary exists, however.
17. Sukhdev Sharma writes about Narahari's commentary: "The *Dīpikā* (on the first seven cantos) contains in all 556 quotations or references. Out of these 556, in the

case of 536 quotations it mentions the source by name, from which they have been taken. It is only in the case of 20 references where it does not mention the source by name and therefore the hunt is to be made to trace them" [Sukhdev Sharma, "A Critical Estimate of Narahari's Commentary on NC," *The Mysore Orientalist*, Oriental Research Institute, Mysore, vol. 9 (1976): 7]. Sharma lists some of Narahari's textual citations, many of which represent not only texts popular during the fourteenth century but also works now lost.

18. Handiqui (*Naiṣadhacarita of Śrīharṣa*, xxxi, fn. 61) favors Gode's opinion that Narahari's commentary arrived in Kashmir during the reign of "Sikandar the Idol-breaker," who was king of Kashmir from 1386 to 1410 CE. The Bhandarkar Oriental Research Institute (BORI) in Pune houses one especially rare manuscript in Śāradā script dated to the late-fourteenth or early-fifteenth century.
19. Pollock, "Sanskrit Literary Culture from the Inside Out," 111–112.
20. See section 1.4 in appendix 1 for Sanskrit text.
21. Lienhard explains the relevant passage as follows: "According to Rājaśekhara, both the poet and connoisseur possess the same poetic imagination (*pratibhā*) though in one it is genuinely creative (*kārayitrī*), in the other imaginatively re-creative (*bhāvayitrī*). Even in the latter's case, it is not a purely receptive or passive faculty . . . but functions in the process of assimilation as an active force which is part of the existence of the poem." See Siegfried Lienhard, *A History of Classical Poetry: Sanskrit, Pali, Prakrit* (Wiesbaden: Otto Harrassowitz, 1984), 41.
22. To borrow Roland Barthes' technical terms, the *Naiṣadhīya* clearly became *the* "writerly" text *par excellence* of the Sanskrit tradition and yet, as a popular text in its initial reception, it also functioned as a highly "readerly" work. In his short essay *S/Z*, the terms "readerly" and "writerly" are formulated by Roland Barthes to describe *kinds* of texts and modes of engagement with them. For Barthes, *writing* a text means that the reader is no longer a "consumer" of texts but rather an active "producer" of them. In this way, *writing* becomes an act of "gaining access to the magic of the signifier." See Roland Barthes, *S/Z: An Essay*, tr. Richard Miller (New York: Hill and Wang, 1974), 4.
23. The verse reads: *ye doṣān pratipādayanti sudhiyaḥ śrīkālidāsoktiṣu śrīmadbhāravi-māghapaṇḍita-mahākāvya-dvaye 'py anvaham / śrīharṣāmṛta-sūkti-naiṣadha-mahākāvye 'pi te kevalaṃ yāvad vṛtti-varṇanena bhagavac-chānteś caritre guṇān //*. Cited in A.N. Jani, *A Critical Study of Śrīharṣa's Naiṣadhacaritam*, 276.
24. The most well known among these are the cases of Tamil and Telugu literary culture. Thus, we know about the "five great *kāvya*" (*aimperunkappiyankal*) formulation in Tamil literary tradition, for example, which is distinguished from the "five lesser *kāvya*" (*ainchirukappiyangal*), and a similar schema in Telugu literary culture begins with the *Manucaritra* and ends with the *Śṛṅgāranaiṣadham* of Śrīnātha.
25. The three, in chronological order, are Pāṇini, Kātyāyana, and Patañjali.
26. In addition to J.A.F. Roodbergen's translation of Mallinātha's *Ghaṇṭāpatha* commentary on *Kirātārjuṇīya* [J.A.F. Roodbergen, *Mallinātha's Ghaṇṭāpatha*], two in-depth studies of Mallinātha in English include Banerji's essay [Sures Chandra Banerji, "Commentaries of Mallinātha," in *S.K. De Memorial Volume*, ed. Hazra and Banerji (Calcutta: Firm K.L. Mukhopadhyay, 1972)] and Lalye's book [P.G. Lalye, *Mallinātha* (New Delhi: Sahitya Akademi, 2002)]. There is also a pioneering book written in Hindi, based on a set of essays on Mallinātha, by Dvivedi [Prabhunāth Dvivedi, *Mallināth kī ṭīkāoṃ kā vimarś* (Varanasi: Kashi Vidyapith, 1982)].

27. See section 1.5 of appendix 1 for Sanskrit text.
28. *durbodhaṃ yadatīva tadvijahati spaṣṭārtham ity uktibhiḥ spaṣṭārtheṣv ativistṛtiṃ vidadhati vyarthaiḥ samāsādikaiḥ / asthāne 'nupayogibhiś ca bahubhir jalpair bhramaṃ tanvate śrotṝṇām iti vastu-viplava-kṛtaḥ prāyeṇa ṭīkākṛtaḥ //* (from the *Rājamārtaṇḍavṛtti* on *Yogasūtra* 1.6).
29. Bourdieu writes of literary critics defending the "interests of their clientele" by holding their position against rival critics. He explains that "the credit attached to any cultural practice tends to decrease with the numbers and especially the social spread of the audience, because the value of the credit of recognition ensured by consumption decreases when the specific competence recognized in the consumer decreases." See Pierre Bourdieu, "The Author's Point of View," in *The Rules of Art: Genesis and Structure of the Literary Field*, tr. Susan Emanuel (Palo Alto: Stanford University Press, 1996), 115ff; 163. We may interpret Mallinātha's aggressive postures as a call for the maintenance of higher professional standards.
30. Although it is doubtful one can trace this idea back to the fifteenth century, U.V. Rao presumably bases this claim on some source. See U.V. Rao, *A Handbook of Classical Sanskrit Literature*, 3rd ed. (Bombay: Orient Longmans, 1967), 94. Rao mentions that commentaries on Udayana's text on logic, *Nyāyakusumāñjali*, and Mammaṭa's work on poetics, *Kāvyaprakāśa*, also had the cachet to earn the title of *mahāmahopadhyāya*.
31. Dvivedi writes (*Mallināth kī ṭīkāoṃ*, 52): "In Mahārāṣṭra, the phrase 'doing a Mallinātha' is very famous. When one sees that a critic becomes overtaken by the poet inside of him and goes on and on about the ideas dancing in his own head before clarifying the poet's expressions, then one says that he's done a Mallinātha. Gratuitously manifesting one's own perspective, therefore, becomes known as a Mallināthi." A similar popular anecdote (*janaśruti* or *lokokti*) exists in Gujarat implicating another famous commentator named Viśveśvara or Gāgābhaṭṭa, who, as we shall see later, also commented on the *Naiṣadhīya* in the seventeenth century. In this case, the expression is to do a "Gāgābhaṭṭi." I am grateful to Jaydev Jani for this interesting detail.
32. Edwin Gerow, "Primary Education in Sanskrit: Methods and Goals," *Journal of the American Oriental Society* 122, no. 4 (Oct.–Dec. 2002): 669; 678.
33. Gerow, "Primary Education in Sanskrit," 679.
34. See, for instance, the UGC textbooks designed to prepare students of Sanskrit to pass their examinations at the university level. For instance, in a preparatory reader (*Sanskrit:* Third *Question Paper*) developed by Chaukhambha Press (Varanasi, 2003), the first four cantos of the *Raghuvaṃśa* are presented with commentary and the first cantos of each of the other four *pañcamahākāvya*.
35. J. Jani provided me with this detail, although I am not aware of any official document supporting it. Manu Bhagavan's research on Gaekwad educational institutions explains their emphasis on modern learning that sought to counter colonial-era directions for intellectual production. This fact about the Gaekwad institutions seems to corroborate the privileging of the *Naiṣadhīya* in the Sanskrit curriculum at MS University during the early- to mid-twentieth century; after all, since the beginning of its critical history, the poem has consistently been praised—and criticized—both for its affirmation and novel challenge to the traditional form of the *mahākāvya*, reflecting both continuity with tradition and a sharp break with it [Manu Bhagavan, "The Rebel Academy: Modernity and the Movement for a University in Princely Baroda, 1908–49," *The Journal of Asian Studies* 61, no. 3 (Aug. 2002): 919–947].

36. A.N. Jani, *A Critical Study of Śrīharṣa's Naiṣadhacaritam*, 275.
37. Chandika Prasad Shukla, *Naiṣadh-pariśīlan* (Allahabad: Hindustani Academy, 1960), 7.
38. *Antyākṣari* is the Sanskrit name for a traditional spoken-word game played throughout India, where one participant recites or composes extempore a verse (or lyric) that the next participant builds upon (along defined rules) with a verse of his or her own until someone fails to come up with something in the allotted time. It is still popular in modern India, known as *antākṣari* in Hindi and *akṣaraśloka* in Malayālam, for example.
39. So far as I can tell, Vārāṇasī receives its first *mahākāvya* paean in the *Naiṣadhīya*. The city, in addition to being the seat of learned paṇḍit culture, was also probably one of Śrīharṣa's homes during his tenure in the Gāhaḍvāla courts. Certainly, his dual role as both poet and philosopher endeared him to the city's scholars who, as Michael Dodson discusses, set the tone for Sanskrit culture's development and dissemination for centuries after Śrīharṣa. Dodson brings notice to the "roles paṇḍits played in facilitating constructive orientalism, and how they utilized and developed their institutionally-consolidated role as India's cultural and intellectual guardians to promote a specific, and often competitive, interpretation of Sanskrit-based knowledge systems" [see Michael Dodson, *Orientalism, Empire and National Culture in India 1770–1880* (Basingstoke, Hampshire; New York: Palgrave Macmillan, 2007), 117]. While Dodson highlights the new roles that pandits played, "through their involvement with colonial education" and their status as "traditional" voices in north India's public sphere contributing to an "emerging national culture" (Dodson, *Orientalism, Empire and National Culture in India*, 173), these "competitive" gestures are, at least in principle, continuations of long-standing practices of older exegetical communities in South Asia that struggled among themselves over interpretive control of canonical Sanskrit texts of Sanskrit culture.
40. See section 1.6 of appendix 1 for Sanskrit text.
41. Handiqui (*Naiṣadhacarita of Śrīharṣa*, xxxii) mentions several cases where a scribe of an earlier commentary (Īśānadeva and Narahari) has placed Cāritravardhana's gloss in the margins, presumably to corroborate or correct the readings they encounter in the work they are copying.
42. Gadādhara's commentary is not listed in the *Catalogus Catalagorum* nor is it listed in other Sanskrit manuscript catalogs. Muni Jinavijayaji mentions the commentary in his lists. Vandana Mehta, in a dissertation filed at the MS University of Baroda (1985), has edited the first eleven cantos of it.
43. See A.N. Jani, *A Critical Study of Śrīharṣa's Naiṣadhacaritam*, 57.
44. The passage from Röer's 1855 edition of the *Naiṣadhīya* (n. 173) is cited in A.N. Jani (*A Critical Study of Śrīharṣa's Naiṣadhacaritam*, 61, fn. 174).
45. Nārāyaṇa's engagement with the *Naiṣadhīya* invites comparison to structuralist and post-structuralist modes of reading literary texts. I especially find that Nārāyaṇa's approach to the reading process resonates with ideas initiated by Barthes and popularized by Derrida, which see reading as actually a special kind of writing (*écriture*), whereby the possibilities of interpretation and what De Man calls "referential aberration" open up to the commentator [Paul De Man, "Semiology and Rhetoric," *Allegories of Reading: Figural Language in Rousseau, Nietzsche, Rilke, and Proust* (New Haven: Yale University Press, 1979), 10]. Also evocative in Nārāyaṇa's approach is Eco's idea of the "open work," where a text is both a "closed form in its

uniqueness as a balanced organic whole" and simultaneously "an open product on account of its susceptibility to countless different interpretations" [Umberto Eco, *The Open Work* (Princeton: Princeton University Press, 1989), 4].

46. The colophon to his commentary, while extensive, lacks the relevant details to fix its provenance securely. For further details, see A.N. Jani (*A Critical Study of Śrīharṣa's Naiṣadhacaritam*, 67).
47. See section 1.7 of appendix 1 for Sanskrit text. I reproduce a portion of his commentary on 1.1 in chapter 5 to demonstrate his point about the *Naiṣadhīya* being able to yield many meanings.
48. See section 1.8 of appendix 1 for Sanskrit text.
49. See section 1.9 of appendix 1 for Sanskrit text.
50. See section 1.10 of appendix 1 for Sanskrit text.
51. See section 2.7 of appendix 2 for Sanskrit text.
52. This point is supported by a fragment of Bhagīrathi's commentary that is preserved in the preface of Pt. Vindhyeśvarīprasād's introduction to the *Tārkikarakṣa*. For details and the full citation, see A.N. Jani (*A Critical Study of Śrīharṣa's Naiṣadhacaritam*, 13).
53. Several *Naiṣadhīya* commentaries come from Jain monastic communities in Gujarat, including those of Cāritravardhana, Municandra, and Ratnacandra. The *Naiṣadhīya* was an important poem for Jain scholars and poets since its inception in the twelfth century, which is indicated by thirteenth-century Jain commentator Mahendrasūri's allusion to the poem in his commentary (1180 CE) on Hemacandra's *Anekārthasaṃgraha*. Jain scholastic interest remained consistent through to the fourteenth, fifteenth, and sixteenth centuries in the creative works of Munibhadrasūri, Nayacandrasūri, Ratnaśekharasūri, Vinayavijaya, and down to the eighteenth century with Meghavaijaya Upādhyāya.
54. See section 1.11 of appendix 1 for Sanskrit text.
55. For further details about his family and many other creative and critical works, see A.N. Jani (*A Critical Study of Śrīharṣa's Naiṣadhacaritam*, 34–35).
56. This conjecture is wholly based on the fact that manuscripts of his commentary are only found in the Madras Government Oriental Manuscripts Library and that another name found for him is Gopinātha Ratha ("Ratha" being a common surname in Orissa).
57. B.N Goswamy, *Pahari Paintings of the Nala-Damayanti Theme* (New Delhi: National Museum, 1995), vii.
58. Goswamy, *Pahari Paintings of the Nala-Damayanti Theme*, 11.
59. Goswamy, *Pahari Paintings of the Nala-Damayanti Theme*, 13. See also Tevet-Dayan for a studied analysis of these paintings in light of Śrīharṣa's language (Maya Tevet-Dayan, *Divine Language Incarnate: The Poetic Metaphysics of Śrīharṣa's Naiṣadhīya-carita*, Ph.D. thesis submitted to Faculty of Humanities, Tel Aviv University, Tel Aviv, Israel, 2010).
60. For further details, see A.N. Jani (*A Critical Study of Śrīharṣa's Naiṣadhacaritam*, 81–83).
61. See A.N. Jani (*A Critical Study of Śrīharṣa's Naiṣadhacaritam*, 76–77) for a description of his other works.
62. T. Bhattacharya portrays Premchandra Tarkabagish (Tarkavāgīśa) as a conservative critic of non-Brahmin entry into the Sanskrit College [Tithi Bhattacharya, *Sentinels of Culture: Class, Education, and the Colonial Intellectual in Bengal (1848–85)* (New Delhi: Oxford University Press, 2005), 197].

63. See section 1.12 of appendix 1 for Sanskrit text.
64. A.N. Jani (*A Critical Study of Śrīharṣa's Naiṣadhacaritam*, 45–48) provides a lengthy comment on Haridāsa's biography.
65. See section 1.13 of appendix 1 for Sanskrit text.
66. The names of these other commentators are as follows: Paramānanda Cakravartin, Govindamiśra, Maheśvara, Mathurānātha Śukla, Narasiṃha, Nārāyaṇa Bhaṭṭa, Ratnacūḍa, Sadānanda, Sarvajña Mādhava Sudhī, Śrīkaṇṭha, Śrīvatsa, Tāṇḍava, Udayakara, and Vātseśvara Sudhī. The scattered details that can be gleaned from the available manuscript fragments of their commentaries are given by A.N. Jani (*A Critical Study of Śrīharṣa's Naiṣadhacaritam*, 32–83).
67. See A.N. Jani (*A Critical Study of Śrīharṣa's Naiṣadhacaritam*, 63–64) for further details about Peḍḍabhaṭṭa's being listed as a *Naiṣadhīya* commentator.
68. A.N. Jani, *A Critical Study of Śrīharṣa's Naiṣadhacaritam*, 50–51.
69. Krishnamachariar believes the commentator and the Telugu poet to be one and the same, but M. Śeśagiri Śāstri cites the evidence of commentator Śrīnātha's patronage to rebut the idea of his being one and the same person. See A.N. Jani (*A Critical Study of Śrīharṣa's Naiṣadhacaritam*, 71–72) for further details.
70. See section 1.14 of appendix 1 for Sanskrit text.
71. Krishnamachariar bases his conclusion on a received tradition that the poet was also a *Naiṣadhīya* commentator, a speculation that A.N. Jani uncritically repeats (*A Critical Study of Śrīharṣa's Naiṣadhacaritam*, 51). For more on *Kṛṣṇānanda*, see chapter 7.
72. T.S. Eliot, "Tradition and the Individual Talent," *The Norton Anthology of Theory and Criticism* (New York: W.W. Norton, 2001), 1093.
73. *upamā kālidāsasya bhāraver-artha-gauravam / naisadhe pada-lālityam māghe santi trayo gunāḥ //*
74. *upamā kālidāsasya bhāraver-artha-gauravam / daṇḍinaḥ padalālityam māghe santi trayogunāḥ //*
75. *upamā bhañja-vīrasya tasyaiva cārtha-gauravam / kallole pada-lālityam santi cintāmaṇau trayah //*. Quoted in Harekrishna Meher, *Upendra Bhañja* (Cuttack, Orissa: Kalinga Bharati, 1990), 54.
76. *tāvad bhā bhāraver bhāti yāvan māghasya nodayaḥ / udite tu punar māghe bhāraver bhā raver iva // kṛtsna-prabodha-kṛd vāṇī bhāraver iva bhāraveḥ / māgheneva ca māghena kampaḥ kasya na jāyate // māghena vighnitotsāhā notsahante pada-krame / smaranto bhāraver eva kavayaḥ kapayo yathā //*
77. *tāvad bhā bhāraver bhāti yāvan māghasya nodayaḥ / udite naiṣadha-kāvye kva māghaḥ kva ca bhāraviḥ //*
78. See Jani (*A Critical Study of Śrīharṣa's Naiṣadhacaritam*, 246) for details.
79. See section 2.8 of appendix 2 for Sanskrit text.
80. See section 2.9 of appendix 2 for Sanskrit text.
81. In tracing the textual lineages of *Naiṣadhīya*'s commentaries, Handiqui contends that Cāṇḍupaṇḍita and Vidyādhara generally, but not always, agree and are followed in their readings by fourteenth-century commentator Īśānadeva and seventeenth-century commentator Jinarāja; he believes that the most popular commentators of *Naiṣadhīya*—Nārāyaṇa (sixteenth century), Mallinātha (fifteenth century), and Narahari (fourteenth century)—often agree on readings, but finds that Mallinātha's "are sometimes very peculiar" and do not seem to agree with either Nārāyaṇa or the earlier commentators. He makes an interesting observation that other readings were almost certainly available even before Vidyādhara and Cāṇḍupaṇḍita's very

early commentaries. Handiqui (*Naiṣadhacarita of Śrīharṣa*, xxxix) cites in support of this observation Cāṇḍupaṇḍita's gloss on *Naiṣadhīya* 6.109, where mention and criticism of other readings are indicated.

82. Eco (*Interpretation and Overinterpretation*, 52) explains "overinterpretation" as follows: "As soon as a text becomes 'sacred' for a certain culture, it becomes subject to the process of suspicious reading and therefore to what is undoubtedly an excess of interpretation."

3. THE *NAIṢADHĪYA* INTERPRETED AND OVERINTERPRETED

1. Oscar Wilde, "The Critic as Artist," *The Norton Anthology of Theory and Criticism* (New York: W.W. Norton, 2001), 901, 911.
2. Umberto Eco, *Interpretation and Overinterpretation* (Cambridge: Cambridge University Press, 1992), 64.
3. Pierre Bourdieu, "The Author's Point of View," *The Rules of Art: Genesis and Structure of the Literary Field*, tr. Susan Emanuel (Palo Alto: Stanford University Press, 1996), 247.
4. See section 1.15 of appendix 1 for Sanskrit text.
5. See section 1.16 of appendix 1 for Sanskrit text.
6. See section 1.17 of appendix 1 for Sanskrit text.
7. See section 1.18 of appendix 1 for Sanskrit text.
8. See section 1.19 of appendix 1 for Sanskrit text.
9. Daud Ali writes of the "widespread tendency in courtly speech and gesture towards self-effacement" as part of a complex strategy for garnering respect and negotiating power. See Daud Ali, *Courtly Culture and Political Life in Early Medieval India* (Cambridge: Cambridge University Press, 2004), 37ff.
10. M.H. Abrams offers this explanation for author-guided readings: "But if we set out not to create meanings, but to understand what the sequences of sentences in a literary work mean, then we have no choice except to read according to the linguistic strategy the author of the work employed, and expected us to employ. We are capable of doing so, because an immense store of cumulative evidence provides assurance that the authors of literary texts belonged to the linguistic community into which we were later born, and so shared our skill, and the consensual regularities on which that skill depends." See M.H. Abrams, "How to Do Things with Texts" in *Critical Theory Since 1965*, ed. H. Adams and L. Searle (Tallahassee: Florida State University Press, 1986), 448.
11. See section 1.20 of appendix 1 for Sanskrit text.
12. I have borrowed these translations from Gary Tubb and Emery Boose, *Scholastic Sanskrit: A Manual for Students* (New York: American Institute of Buddhist Studies, 2007), 150.
13. G. Tubb and E. Boose, *Scholastic Sanskrit*, 150–151.
14. J. Zadoo describes the *anvayamukhī* style as a "long march without posts and stages to gain the object in view [which] necessarily gives rise to a feeling of exhaustion in the mind of the reader; while the [*kathambhūtinī* approach] . . . has clear-cut signposts and easy halting places to lead [the reader] to the destination with a feeling of renewed strength and freshness." See Jaggadhar Zadoo, *A Critical Note on Vallabhadeva's Commentary on the Shishupalavadham* (Srinagar: Normal Press, 1947), 2ff.

15. G. Tubb and E. Boose, *Scholastic Sanskrit*, 111.
16. Devnarayan Jha, *Naiṣadh-samīkṣā* (Delhi: Nag Publishers, 2001), 76.
17. See section 1.21 of appendix 1 for Sanskrit text.
18. The *kathambhūtinī* approach reflects what Tynianov (1924) refers to as the "density" of the verse line, whereby the original text is not minutely bracketed with equivalent paraphrases but allowed to breathe, as it were, and express itself more expansively [Yuri Tynianov, *The Problem of Verse Language*, tr. M. Sosa and H. Brent (Ann Arbor: Ardis, 1981)]. See also the work of other Russian semioticians from the twentieth century, such as Yuri Lotman (1976), who grapples with the problems of representing the significance of verse in simple prose paraphrase [Yuri Lotman, *Analysis of the Poetic Text*, tr. D. Barton Johnson (Ann Arbor: Ardis, 1976)].
19. See section 1.22a of appendix 1 for Sanskrit text.
20. See section 1.22b of appendix 1 for Sanskrit text.
21. See section 1.22c of appendix 1 for Sanskrit text.
22. For a long discussion of the order in which Mallinātha wrote his commentaries, see P.G. Lalye, *Mallinātha* (New Delhi: Sahitya Akademi, 2002), 18–19.
23. G. Tubb and E. Boose (*Scholastic Sanskrit*, 150) write about the relationship of the *anvayamukhī* style's reconfiguration of a verse into a "standard prose word-order" with traditions of Sanskrit education, "the essentials of which are recorded in a verse in the *Samāsacakra*, an elementary handbook used at the beginning stage in the traditional system of Sanskrit education." Mallinātha's approach would perhaps find sympathy among customary New Critical positions, with its commitment to the poem as a fixed object and, as Krieger explains, its "prior commitment to formal closure as the primary characteristic of the successful literary object" [Murray Krieger, "An Apology for Poetics" in *Critical Theory Since 1965*, ed. H. Adams and L. Searle (Tallahassee: Florida State University Press, 1986), 535.
24. The entirety of Nārāyaṇa's text is available in several printed editions, and so, I do not reproduce the whole of his commentary on this verse in the appendix.
25. See G. Tubb and E. Boose (*Scholastic Sanskrit*, 117) for a clear discussion of the different permutations of *anvayamukhī* and *kathambhūtinī* commentaries.
26. As the phonemes "la" and "ra" are often interchanged among speakers of Indic languages (what is commonly described as *ra-layor abhedaḥ* in Sanskrit), it is a long-standing practice among Sanskrit commentators to exploit this feature of the language to create secondary meanings.
27. See section 1.23 of appendix 1 for Sanskrit text.
28. See section 1.24 of appendix 1 for Sanskrit text.
29. Stanley Fish's self-appraisal resonates with Nārāyaṇa's commentarial practice: "Insistence on a right reading and the real text are the fictions of formalism, and as fictions they have the disadvantage of being confining. My fiction is liberating. It relieves me of the obligation to be right (a standard that simply drops out) and demands only that I be interesting (a standard met without any reference at all to an illusory objectivity). Rather than restoring or recovering texts, I am in the business of making texts and of teaching others to make them by adding to their repertoire of strategies" [Stanley Fish, *Is There A Text in This Class* (Cambridge, Mass.: Harvard University Press, 1980), 180].
30. The technical discussion of the various schools of philosophy in Cāṇḍupaṇḍita's commentary is lengthy. I merely summarize the long passage in the paragraphs that follow. See section 1.25 of appendix 1 for the complete Sanskrit text.

31. Cāṇḍupaṇḍita elaborates extensively on the Nyāya position. He explains further, for example, that in saying that there is no pot on the ground, one means that there is an absence of a pot on the ground but not a *complete absence* of pots everywhere. Just so is this false apprehension of silver, the commentator clarifies: the corrective awareness that objects to a shell being silver when one is under a delusion is not universally objecting to the fact that silver exists at all, but only objecting to or blocking the notion that there could not be something other than silver.
32. Cāṇḍupaṇḍita's argument runs as follows: "On account of an awakening of previously experienced sense-impressions, sharing similarity in such qualities as white light, etc., perceived phenomena such as illusions are as real as the bracelets of a young woman or a market street. In that way, the silver superimposed on the shell is remembered. Therefore, both are real. This silver in front of us is real. And because it is remembered from a previous experience, this apprehension of silver is also true."
33. See section 1.25 of appendix 1 for Sanskrit text.
34. Paul Griffiths, *Religious Reading* (Oxford: Oxford University Press, 1999). 64.
35. Robert P. Goldman, "How Fast Do Monkeys Fly? How Long Do Demons Sleep?," *Rivista di Studi Sudasiatici* no. 1: 185–207 (Firenze: Firenze University Press, 2006), 25.

4. STRUGGLES OVER THE TEXT

1. K.K. Handiqui, *Naiṣadhacarita of Śrīharṣa: English Translation with Notes*, 2nd ed. (Poona: Deccan College, 1965), xxxix.
2. In fact, describing the format of one of Īśānadeva's manuscripts available to him, Handiqui writes: "Īśānadeva's manuscript frequently quotes Cāṇḍupaṇḍita's commentary, the citations being usually placed in a supplementary section at the end of the gloss on each verse." See Handiqui (*Naiṣadhacarita of Śrīharṣa*, xxvii) for more details about Īśānadeva's manuscript tradition.
3. See Handiqui (*Naiṣadhacarita of Śrīharṣa*, xxxix–xli) for the specific arguments regarding these statements.
4. Cāṇḍupaṇḍita's gloss on *Naiṣadhīya* 6.109, for example, indicates this fact. Here, the commentator extensively refutes a reading of which no later commentators even show awareness. An earlier, alternative reading reads the narrator of the verse to be the poet himself and not Damayantī; see Cāṇḍupaṇḍita's text on this verse for a more extensive discussion [see Jaydev Jani, *Naiṣadhamahākāvya with Cāṇḍupaṇḍita's Commentary* (Jodhpur: Rajasthan Oriental Research Institute, 1997), 332–333].
5. Sheldon Pollock, *The Language of the Gods in the World of Men* (Berkeley: University of California Press, 2006), 165.
6. For more on Parameśvarānanda's Hindi essay ("*Doṣākaratvaṃ naiṣadhasya ṣaṣṭho guṇaḥ*") and R.N. Bhatt's essay ("*Śrīharṣ ki Niraṅkuśatā*"), see A.N. Jani, *A Critical Study of Śrīharṣa's Naiṣadhacaritam* (Baroda: Oriental Institute, 1957), 271.
7. Krishnamachariar gives a reference for Sivakamesvara Rao's essay, entitled *Naisadhacarita-aucityacarca* [*Mimamsa*, I.5 (Tenali, 1922) and Jl. of Sam. Sah. Bar, vol. XIII]. See M. Krishnamachariar, *History of Classical Sanskrit Literature* (Delhi: Motilal Banarsidass, 1974), 181, fn. 3.
8. A.N. Jani cites this story as being current among Bühler's paṇḍits. See Jani (*A Critical Study of Śrīharṣa's Naiṣadhacaritam*, 128).

9. *salila-krīḍāyā avarṇane 'pi na mahākāvyatva-bhaṅga-prasaṅgaḥ.*
10. *nyūnam apy atra yaiḥ kaiścid aṅgaiḥ kāvyaṃ na duṣyatīty uktatvāt.*
11. For a study and translation of this text, see David Rustin Mellins, *The Cool Rays of Aesthetics and Reasoning: Jayadeva's 'Candrāloka' and Its Role in the Evolution of Alaṃkāraśāstra* (Ann Arbor: UMI, Microform, 2004).
12. See the seventh chapter of the *Sāhityadarpaṇa*, which details the various types of *doṣa* found in poetry.
13. See section 1.26 of appendix 1 for the Sanskrit text of Gāgābhaṭṭa's comment.
14. See section 1.27a of appendix 1 for Sanskrit text.
15. See section 1.27b of appendix 1 for Sanskrit text.
16. Gadādhara's text literally reads that one mouth (the earlier verse) requires the other mouth (verse) and only then can there be a kiss (a single meaning); a kisser becomes a kisser because of a kiss (*mukha-rūpasya pūrva-ślokasyaikārthatvena pratimukha-rūpatayā cumbanāc cumbako'yam ity apare*).
17. See section 1.27c of appendix 1 for Sanskrit text.
18. The relevant verse from the *Mahābhārata* about the Nala story's intrinsic power to purify listeners was cited in the introduction, as was Śrīharṣa's own suggestion of this theme in *Naiṣadhīya* 1.3.
19. Quite a few verses in the *Naiṣadhīya* are soberly considered for suspected interpolation by *Naiṣadhīya* commentators, including 9.119, 11.41–42, 13.5, 15.22, 16.79, 17.161, 18.18, 18.27, 18.65, 18.80a, 19.57a, and 21.85–86. Many of these are not found in the oldest manuscripts or are they available in the oldest commentaries, while 18.27 and 18.65 are in Vidyādhara's reading and 19.57a in Cāṇḍupaṇḍita's. Nārāyaṇa comments on all of them, however, a fact that suggests the spurious character of only 15.22, 16.79, 19.57a.
20. On 14.1, for example, Jinarāja remarks that this particular verse is not available in some manuscripts (*keṣucid ādarśeṣu tv ayam śloko nāsty eva*).
21. For example, as Handiqui notes, a scribe of Īśānadeva's commentary on 17.66 declares that the verse in question is "not in the commentary," contrary to the fact that the verse appears in many manuscripts of Īśānadeva's commentary (Handiqui, *Naiṣadhacarita of Śrīharṣa*, xxviii).
22. See A.N. Jani, *A Critical Study of Śrīharṣa's Naiṣadhacaritam*, 270ff.
23. See section 1.28 of appendix 1 for Sanskrit text.
24. This is the version quoted in the notes by Paṇḍit Śivadatta in the Nirṇayasāgar Nārāyaṇi-ṭīkā edition. Pt. Śivadatta says that having considered it a repetition, Mallinātha and others do not even comment on it (*iti nirdiśya na vyākhyātaḥ*). This notion, however, is contradicted by evidence from other manuscripts used by the Krishnadas Academy edition where Mallinātha does indeed comment on the verse.
25. For details on this example, see Goodall and Isaacson, *The Raghupañcikā of Vallabhadeva, Critical Edition with Introduction and Notes*, vol. 1 (Groningen: Egbert Forsten, 2003), 288.
26. J. Jani (*Naiṣadhamahākāvya with Cāṇḍupaṇḍita's Commentary*, ix–xi) gives further details about this manuscript, which is from the Bhandarkar Oriental Research Institute (BORI) and carries the accession no. 389. He notes that the manuscript's owner is mentioned in a line written in Gujarati, which translates to: "This is the complete commentary of Cāṇḍupaṇḍita on *Naiṣadha* and it belongs to Bhaṭṭa Kṛpārāma."

27. This manuscript can be found in the Bhandarkar Oriental Research Institute (accession no. 415). See J. Jani (*Naiṣadhamahākāvya with Cāṇḍupaṇḍita's Commentary*, viii–ix) for details about it. Samira Sheikh, citing the seventeenth-century Persian historian Firishta, writes as follows about this last of the Tughluq governors of Gujarat before Ẓafar Khan's arrival: "One complaint against Farḥat al-Mulk . . . was that he was friendly with the locals and tolerated idolatry. While this may have been a retrospective smear to discredit him, it shows that he was becoming a threat to central authority on account of the fact that he had set down local roots" [Samira Sheikh, *Forging a Region: Sultans, Traders, and Pilgrims in Gujarat 1200–1500* (New Delhi: Oxford University Press, 2010), 186].
28. See Handiqui (*Naiṣadhacarita of Śrīharṣa*, xxviii) for the Sanskrit text.
29. Lienhard, for example, agrees with a common view among traditional and modern readers that perceives Kālidāsa's ending the *Raghuvaṃśa* on an "unseemly note" (as it currently does) as indicative of the fact that "either Kālidāsa did not finish the poem or that a short concluding section in which the succeeding rulers are mentioned has been lost" [Seigfried Lienhard, *A History of Classical Poetry: Sanskrit, Pali, Prakrit* (Wiesbaden: Otto Harrassowitz), 177ff].
30. See section 1.29 of appendix 1 for Sanskrit text.
31. See section 1.30 of appendix 1 for Sanskrit text.
32. In his Sanskrit introduction to a 1926 edition of the *Naiṣadhīya*, Śrī Vyāsarāya Śāstri seconds Nārāyaṇa's idea by declaring: "At the end of the twenty second canto, the benedictory words 'May that divine moon be for our happiness' indicates the culmination of the poem" (*tatra dvāviṃśasya sargasyānte śrūyamāṇā śrīr astu nas tuṣṭaye ity eva rūpā maṅgalāśaṃsā kāvyasyaitāvan mātratvam eva jñāpayati*) [K.L. Vyasarāya Shastri, *Naiṣadhacaritam with the Commentary of Mallinātha*. Cantos 1–12, 2 pts. (Palghat: Palghat Sanskrit Series, 1926), 12–13].
33. See A.N. Jani (*A Critical Study of Śrīharṣa's Naiṣadhacaritam*, 23ff) for a longer discussion on arguments for the poem's incompleteness.
34. A.N. Jani, *A Critical Study of Śrīharṣa's Naiṣadhacaritam*, 24.
35. Jani, *A Critical Study of Śrīharṣa's Naiṣadhacaritam*, 24.
36. A.N. Jani (*A Critical Study of Śrīharṣa's Naiṣadhacaritam*, 85) explains that Bühler notes that "all the MSS of the *Kāvyaprakāśa* found in Kashmir, to which region Mammaṭa belonged, read 'Bāṇa' instead of 'Dhāvaka,' and he furthermore pointed out that in the Śāradā script it would be quite possible for a copyist to mistake the reading of Bāṇa's name as Dhāvaka."
37. Jani, *A Critical Study of Śrīharṣa's Naiṣadhacaritam*, 25–28.
38. Sheldon Pollock, "Sanskrit Literary Culture from the Inside Out" in *Literary Cultures in History: Reconstructions from South Asia*, ed. Sheldon Pollock (Berkeley: University of California Press, 2003), 111–112.
39. The Sanskrit text reads: *sukavi-vacasi pāṭhānanyathākṛtya mohād rasa-gatim avadhūya prauḍham arthaṃ vihāya / vibudha-vara-samāje vyākriyā-kāmukānāṃ guru-kula-vimukhānāṃ dhṛṣṭāyai namo 'stu //*. For details, see N.V.P Unithiri, "The Sanskrit Commentary Considered," *Journal of Kerala Studies* 10 (1983): 219–232.
40. For other illuminating examples of the ways in which text criticism and the application of text-critical methodologies on the *mahākāvya* aid in the reconstruction of a poem's receptive history and its critical appreciation, see Michael Hahn's appendix to Gauri Shankar's edition of Śivasvāmin's *Kapphiṇābhyudaya* [Michael

Hahn, "Appendix" in *Śivasvāmin's Kapphiṇābhyudaya or Exaltation of King Kapphiṇa*, ed. Gauri Shankar (New Delhi: Aditya Prakashan, 1989), i–xxxvi] and more recently, Isaacson and Goodall's critical edition, introductory discussion, and notes of Vallabhadeva's commentary on Kālidāsa's *Raghuvaṃśa* [Dominic Goodall and Harunaga Isaacson (eds.), *The Raghupañcikā of Vallabhadeva, Critical Edition with Introduction and Notes*, vol. 1 (Groningen: Egbert Forsten, 2003)].

41. At several points in a collection of essays entitled *Beyond Translation: Essays Toward a Modern Philology*, A.L. Becker discusses Ortega y Gasset's "new philology" [A.L. Becker, *Beyond Translation: Essays Toward a Modern Philology* (Ann Arbor: University of Michigan Press, 1995), 106]. See especially the essays entitled "The Linguistics of Particularity" and "On Recapitulation." I thank David Shulman for directing me to this source.

5. SECONDARY WAVES OF READING

1. Yigal Bronner, *Extreme Poetry* (New York: Columbia University Press, 2010), 181.
2. Aditya Behl discusses the nature of spiritual allegory in the context of sixteenth-century Indian Sufi romances (*masnavi*) as aiming for these "point-to-point correspondences" that serve as "a critical strategy [designed] to explain away everything by recourse to this key to all mythologies, motifs, and symbols." For an extensive discussion of allegory in medieval South Asia, see Aditya Behl, *The Magic Doe*, ed. Wendy Doniger (New York: Oxford University Press, 2012), 25ff.
3. Y. Bronner, *Extreme Poetry*, 181.
4. Y. Bronner, *Extreme Poetry*, 85.
5. This fact is noted in Aufrecht's *Catalogus Catalogorum* (1891: 763) and cited in A.N. Jani, *A Critical Study of Śrīharṣa's Naiṣadhacaritam* (Baroda: Oriental Institute, 1957), 119.
6. Nārāyaṇa explains the distinctive quality of this episode, naming the piece as the *pañca-nalīya: idānīm indrādi-pañca-nalī-saṃjñaṃ trayodaśaṃ sargam ārabhate.*
7. *Naiṣadhīya* 14.16: *śliṣyanti vāco yad-amūr amuṣyāḥ kavitva-śakteḥ khalu te vilāsāḥ.*
8. Mallinātha chooses not to read verse 13.5 (in Nārāyaṇa's text). I suspect Mallinātha removes this verse (which begins with the word *kṣoṇita*) because, otherwise, Indra would have five verses devoted to him and the rest of the divinities only four. Mallinātha perhaps seeks to preserve the structural symmetry.
9. See section 1.31 of appendix 1 for Sanskrit text.
10. See section 1.32 of appendix 1 for Sanskrit text.
11. See section 1.33 of appendix 1 for Sanskrit text.
12. A well-known myth describes Indra as clipping the mountains of their wings, thus establishing them in a fixed place so they do not dangerously collide with the earth and its inhabitants.
13. Yama's vehicle is a buffalo.
14. Bronner, *Extreme Poetry*, 84.
15. Y. Bronner, *Extreme Poetry*, 192. For a comprehensive discussion on *śleṣa* as a reading practice, see Y. Bronner, *Extreme Poetry*, 155–194.
16. Y. Bronner, *Extreme Poetry*, 183.
17. A.B. Keith, *A History of Sanskrit Literature* (Oxford: The Clarendon Press, 1928), 141. Incidentally, Keith's extrapolation that Damayantī could not understand Sanskrit is unsubstantiated. Nothing stated or implied in Śrīharṣa's poem gives that impression.

18. S.N. Dasgupta and S.K. De, *History of Sanskrit Literature*, vol. 1 (Calcutta: University of Calcutta, 1947), 328.
19. See Y. Bronner (*Extreme Poetry*, 87ff) for an extensive discussion of this interpretation.
20. Mallinātha's text reads *prāptum* for *sāptum* and *satyapare* for *satyatare*. Vidyādhara, Cāṇḍupaṇḍita, and Jinarāja also cite this reading. See Handiqui's note on 13.36 for details [K.K. Handiqui, *Naiṣadhacarita of Śrīharṣa: English Translation with Notes*, 2nd ed. (Poona: Deccan College, 1965), 344].
21. The discussion of *catuṣkoṭi* in the Advaita context is partially built on the famous verses 4.83 and 4.84 of the *Māṇḍukyakārikās* of Gauḍapāda. See Handiqui (*Naiṣadhacarita of Śrīharṣa*, 529–530) for a full exposition of the primary sources and a thoroughgoing summary of the entire philosophical tradition that stems from these *kārikās*.
22. Phyllis Granoff, *Philosophy and Argument in Late Vedānta: Śrīharṣa's Khaṇḍanakhaṇḍakhādya* (Dordrecht: D. Reidel Publishing Company, 1978), 252ff.
23. K.K. Handiqui (*Naiṣadhacarita of Śrīharṣa*, 529–532) has a lengthy technical discussion of the philosophical significance of *Naiṣadhīya* 13.36 for various commentators.
24. See chapter 3 for a developed treatment of these commentators' analysis.
25. See K.K. Handiqui (*Naiṣadhacarita of Śrīharṣa*, 580) for an extensive discussion of the mantra in early India's various religious cultures.
26. See chapter 1 for a translation of all three verses.
27. Cāṇḍupaṇḍita, according to Jaydev Jani, also gives *klīṃ hrīm* as the mantra, which he alternatively calls the *sārasvata-mantra*. For details, see Jaydev Jani, *Naiṣadhamahākāvya with Cāṇḍupaṇḍita's Commentary* (Jodhpur: Rajasthan Oriental Research Institute, 1997), 663.
28. See section 1.34 of appendix 1 for Sanskrit text.
29. Although enough evidence has not been marshaled to make a solid argument that connects scholars of Sanskrit during this period with intellectuals from various sectarian religious groups, it is plausible to assume that Sanskrit commentators seeking to read allegorical significance in *kāvya* inhabited similar social and intellectual worlds as Sufis, Vaiṣṇavas, Gorakhpanthis, and *nirguṇi* poets. See Allison Busch's discussion of the interaction of Sanskrit and vernacular intellectual and religious traditions during the sixteenth century [Allison Busch, *Poetry of Kings: The Classical Hindi Literature of Mughal India* (New York: Oxford University Press, 2011), 24ff]. To understand better *bhakti* culture's influence on poets working in the sixteenth-century courts of northern India, see also Heidi Pauwels, "The Saint, the Warlord, and the Emperor: Discourses of Braj Bhakti and Bundelā Loyalty," *Journal of the Economic and Social History of the Orient* 52 (2009): 187–228.
30. See Christopher Minkowski ["On the Success of Nīlakaṇṭha's *Mahābhārata* Commentary" in *Boundaries, Dynamics and Construction of Traditions in South Asia* , ed. F. Squarcini (Florence: Firenze University Press, 2005)] for a discussion of Nīlakaṇṭha's commentary. Drawing from the commentarial interpretations of *Rāmāyaṇa* (from the thirteenth to eighteenth centuries), at various points in their translation, Robert and Sally Goldman provide examples of such allegorical readings of Vālmīki's great epic. For example, they explain in a note on *Sundarakāṇḍa* 36.28 that sixteenth-century Śrīvaiṣṇava commentator Govindarāja reads the crow episode "as a parable of the soul's flight to Rāma as the ultimate source of salvation" [Robert P. Goldman and Sally Sutherland-Goldman (trans.), *The Ramayana of Vālmīki: An Epic of Ancient India. Vol. 5, Sundarakāṇḍa* (Princeton:

Princeton University Press, 1996), 457]. The authors cite a number of instances where events and characters in the epic are translated into Śrīvaiṣṇava "parables." See also A.K. Rao's article on theologically motivated *śleṣa* readings of *Rāmāyaṇa* commentators [Ajay K. Rao, "Theologising the Inaugural Verse: Śleṣa Reading in *Rāmāyaṇa* Commentary," *Journal of Hindu Studies* 1, no. 1–2 (2008): 77–92].

31. Baldev Upadhyay, *Kāśī kī pāṇḍitya-paramparā* (Vārāṇasī: Viśvavidyālaya Prakāśana, 1983), 148ff.
32. Jaya Seetaramasastri, *The Elements of Darśanas in Śrīharṣa's Naiṣadha* (Repalle, Andhra Pradesh: Kiran Hindi Press, 1987), xvii.
33. Seetaramasastri, *The Elements of Darśanas*, lxiii–lxvii.
34. Seetaramasastri, *The Elements of Darśanas*, xv.
35. See section 1.35 of appendix 1 for Sanskrit text.
36. Sheshedra Sharma, *Svarṇahaṃsa*, translated into Hindi from Telugu by Jagdish Sharma (Ujjain: Kalidas Akademi, 1990), 68.
37. Meher, in discussing this verse, elaborates their position: "In the present verse, the words 'haṃsa', 'eka' and 'nirupākhya-rūpa' are applicable for both the swan and Brahman. But the nature of the two must not be identical. The sages devoted to yogic austerities, and having renounced terrestrial temptations, reach the close proximity of Brahman. Though realization of Brahman cannot be seen through human eyes, yet it is compared with the act of observing the swan from an empirical point of view. In the Vedānta system, Brahman is known as indescribable Supreme Self" [Harekrishna Meher, *Philosophical Reflections in the Naiṣadhacarita* (Calcutta: Punthi Pustak, 1989), 296].
38. See section 1.36 of appendix 1 for Sanskrit text.
39. See section 1.37 of appendix 1 for Sanskrit text.
40. Seetaramasastri, *The Elements of Darśanas*, ix.
41. Sometimes, the mantra is spoken of as having sixteen syllables, corresponding to the sixteen digits of the moon. Douglass Brooks describes the silent repetition of this mantra as the "centerpiece" of Śrīvidyā practice. For details, see Douglas Brooks, *The Secret of the Three Cities* (Chicago: University of Chicago Press, 1990), 119–120. For more on *hrīṃ* and the mantras associated with Bhuvaneśvarī, see also C.M. Brown, *The Devī Gītā* (Albany: State University of New York, 1998), 57–58, 67–68, 71–73.
42. Seetaramasastri, *The Elements of Darśanas*, xii–xiii.
43. Sharma, *Svarṇahaṃsa*, 5.
44. Seetaramasastri, *The Elements of Darśanas*, xx.

6. LEGENDS OF THE *NAIṢADHĪYA*

1. See section 2.10 of appendix 2 for Sanskrit text.
2. See section 1.38a of appendix 1 for Sanskrit text.
3. See section 1.38b of appendix 1 for Sanskrit text.
4. See section 1.38c of appendix 1 for Sanskrit text.
5. See section 1.39 of appendix 1 for Sanskrit text.
6. Other famous examples include the *Prabhāvakacarita* (thirteenth century) and the *Prabandhacintāmaṇi* (fourteenth century). For a good preliminary discussion of the Jain *prabandha* literature from western India, see Phyllis Granoff, "Jain Biographies

of Nāgārjuna: Notes on the Composing of a Biography in Medieval India" in *Monks and Magicians: Religious Biographies in Asia*, ed. P. Granoff and K. Shinohar (New Delhi: Motilal Banarsidass 1994), 45–66.

7. See section 1.40 of appendix 1 for Sanskrit text.
8. Another story cites the eating of beans as the means undertaken by Śrīharṣa to dull the intellect. See Bronner, Shulman, and Tubb's translation and discussion of this story in *Innovations and Turning Points in the History of Sanskrit Poetry*, ed. Y. Bronner, D. Shulman, G. Tubb (Delhi: Oxford University Press; forthcoming).
9. As discussed in chapter 2, Cāṇḍupaṇḍita mentions at the beginning of his commentary that earlier commentators like Vidyādhara, while learned, did not appreciate the *Naiṣadhīya*'s depth of reference to philosophical issues.
10. *govinda-nandanatayā ca vapuḥ śriyā ca mā 'smin nṛpe kuruta kāmadhiyaṃ taruṇyaḥ / astrī-karoti jagatāṃ vijaye smaraḥ strīr astrī-janaḥ punar anena vidhīyate strī //.*
11. See section 1.41 of appendix 1 for Sanskrit text.
12. See section 1.42a of appendix 1 for Sanskrit text.
13. Here is Śrīharṣa's description: *pavitrita-caturbhuja-vāma-bhāgā vāg*; and here is the passage he cites from the *Purāṇa*: *tvaṃ purāṇeṣvapi viṣṇoḥ patnīti paṭhyase*. One such example is found in *Brahmavaivarta Purāṇa* 2.6.13–95. Here Viṣṇu is the husband of Lakṣmī, Sarasvatī, and Gaṅgā; when the quarrelling becomes excessive, Viṣṇu sends Gaṅgā to Śiva and Sarasvatī to Brahmā.
14. See section 1.42b of appendix 1 for Sanskrit text.
15. A.N. Jani cites this oral story being current among Bühler's pandits [A.N. Jani, *A Critical Study of Śrīharṣa's Naiṣadhacaritam* (Baroda: Oriental Institute, 1957), 456]. See chapter 4 for the narrative.
16. See section 1.43 of appendix 1 for Sanskrit text.
17. See section 1.44a of appendix 1 for Sanskrit text. Śrīharṣa's connection to Bengal has been discussed in detail by A.N. Jani (*A Critical Study of Śrīharṣa's Naiṣadhacaritam*, 95–109). The basic arguments in favor of Śrīharṣa's being a Bengali, or at least his having a deep familiarity with Bengali culture, are based on the poet's supposed use of Bengali diction and his knowledge of certain customs popular in the region. Arguments against locating Śrīharṣa in Bengal with certitude point to the wider geographical distribution implied by his linguistic usages and to his affiliation with other regions such as Benares and Kashmir.
18. See section 1.44b of appendix 1 for Sanskrit text.
19. See section 1.44c of appendix 1 for Sanskrit text.
20. See section 1.44d of appendix 1 for Sanskrit text.
21. Sheldon Pollock, *The Language of the Gods in the World of Men* (Berkeley: University of California Press, 2006), 88.
22. See section 1.45 of appendix 1 for Sanskrit text.
23. U.V. Rao suggests a connection among these three works. See U.V. Rao, *A Handbook of Classical Sanskrit Literature*, 3rd ed. (Bombay: Orient Longmans, 1967), 94.
24. In a famous remembered verse addressed indignantly to the temple priests of the Jagannātha temple in Puri (or to Lord Jagannātha himself) who refused him entry to the temple, Udayana sharply reminds that had it not been for him there would have been no one to defend the existence of God (and the existence of the priests) against the atheist Buddhists (*aiśvarya-mada-matto 'si mām avajñāya vartase / upasthiteṣu bauddheṣu mad-adhīnā tava sthitiḥ //*) [V. Narayana Rao and David Shulman, *A Poem at the Right Moment* (Berkeley: University of California Press, 1998), 37].

25. See especially a relatively recent volume by Arnold and Blackburn (*Telling Lives in India*. Bloomington: Indiana University Press, 2004).
26. Narayana Rao and D. Shulman, *Poem at the Right Moment*, 4.
27. Bhogilal Sandesara, *Literary Circle of Mahāmātya Vastupāla and Its Contribution to Sanskrit Literature* (Bombay: Singhi Jain Shastra Sikshapith, Bharatiya Vidya Bhavan, 1953), 54.
28. Velcheru Narayana Rao, "Multiple Literary Cultures in Telugu" in *Literary Cultures in History: Reconstructions from South Asia*, ed. Sheldon Pollock (Berkeley: University of California Press, 2003), 424.
29. Narayana Rao and D. Shulman, *Poem at the Right Moment*, 136.

7. THE TRADITION EXPANDS TO THE REGIONS

1. Franco Moretti, *Signs Taken for Wonders* (London: Verso, 1983), 7.
2. I borrow these terms from Rita Copeland's study of vernacular translations of Latin works in medieval Europe [Rita Copeland, *Rhetoric, Hermeneutics, and Translation in the Middle Ages* (Cambridge: Cambridge University Press, 1991)].
3. From the point of view of their aesthetic choices and engagement with the rising vernacular languages, the poet Maṅkha (early twelfth century) is perhaps closest to Śrīharṣa in spirit. In addition to his complex verse and frequent tendency for *śleṣa*, Maṅkha's *Śrīkaṇṭhacarita*, for example, like Śriharṣa's *Naiṣadhīyacarita*, uses diction and syntactical structures that resemble usages in the newly developing vernacular languages. For details about Maṅkha's vernacular-inflected language, see Bhagavatprasad Bhatt, *Śrīkaṇṭhacaritam—A Study* (Baroda: MS University of Baroda, 1973), 108ff. Both Maṅkha (11.42–50) and Śrīharṣa (seventh canto) also include set pieces that become ubiquitous in later non-Sanskrit poetry, such as the head-to-toe description of women (*nakha-śikha-varṇana*). While the *nakha-śikha-varṇana* is found earlier in the works of Sanskrit authors such as Subandhu and Bilhaṇa, Maṅkha and Śrīharṣa take the subgenre to new imaginative heights.
4. A.N. Jani provides nearly fifty examples (in his appendix 8) of the ways in which the idiomatic registers of various South Asian languages have been affected by newly created Sanskrit expressions in the *Naiṣadhīya*, concluding that "Śrīharṣa's language gives, on the one hand, a colloquial tinge to his poetry while on the other, it enriches the Sanskrit vocabulary—a contribution which is indeed valuable" [A.N. Jani, *A Critical Study of Śrīharṣa's Naiṣadhacaritam* (Baroda: Oriental Institute, 1957), 242].
5. For example, like Jayadeva (*Gītagovinda*), it appears Śrīharṣa uses *mātrā* meters (of sixteen morae or "short syllables"), except that he treats it, as Hemacandra did for the first time in the early twelfth century, as a Sanskrit syllabic meter. Mitra cites *Naiṣadhīya* 22.46 as an example of the poet's treating an originally non-Sanskrit *mātrā* meter (sixteen morae, sometimes called "short syllables") as a Sanskrit syllabic meter (here, the eleven-syllabled *upendravajrā* meter) [Arati Mitra, *Origin and Development of Sanskrit Metrics* (Calcutta: The Asiatic Society, 1989), 267; 318]. Other than what she interprets as Śrīharṣa's use of a *mātrā* meter, Mitra cites the earliest case of a vernacular meter being used in a classic non-Jain Sanskrit *mahākāvya* to occur in Maṅkha's *Śrīkaṇṭhacarita*, where the poet uses the Apabhraṃśa *dohā* meter

in verses 12.74 to 12.86 (see Arati Mitra, *Origin and Development of Sanskrit Metrics*, 318).

6. Nārāyaṇa on 22.51: *ḍimbaṃ laladimbam iti vā gauḍa-deśa-bhāṣāyāṃ bhramarakasya saṃjñā mahārāṣṭra-bhāṣāyāṃ kānyakubja-bhāṣāyāṃ ca 'bhāvarā' iti saṃjñā.* Cāṇḍupaṇḍita, Vidyādhara, and Jinarāja all read "laladḍimbam" for "lasaḍḍimbam" (Nārāyaṇa and Mallinātha's reading).
7. See A.N. Jani's appendix 1 (*A Critical Study of Śrīharṣa's Naiṣadhacaritam*, 4–5).
8. Krishnamachariar describes Kṛṣṇarāma as a "paṇḍit in the court of Jaipur, of great merit and writer of other poems" [M. Krishnamachariar, *History of Classical Sanskrit Literature* (Delhi: Motilal Banarsidass, 1974), 185]. Kṛṣṇarāma's poetic summary of the *Naiṣadhīya* is available in Pt. Śivadatta's introductory preface to the Nirnaya Sagar Press edition of the poem. For an English translation of the *Naiṣadhacaritasāra*, see Deven Patel, *The Evolution of a Sanskrit Literary Culture: A Study of the Naiṣadha Tradition in Light of Its Commentaries and Receptive Histories* (Ann Arbor: UMI Microform, 2006), 17–25.
9. The *Kāvyakalānidhi* is listed as published by the Hindi Sahitya Sammelan (Allahabad, 1942). I have been unable, however, to gain access to it. Jani writes that it was first published by the Venkatesvara Press in Bombay (ed. Varma Satya Jivana, 1936) as a "free translation of the original into Sanskrit and Hindi metres" (A.N. Jani, appendix 1, *A Critical Study of Śrīharṣa's Naiṣadhacaritam*, 4). George Grierson [*The Modern Vernacular Literature of Hindustan* (Calcutta: Asiatic Society, 1889), 93] writes that Gumān jī Misar, "skilled in composition and in Sanskrit," flourished in the Mughal courts of Muhammad Shāh (1719–1748) "under the protection of Jugul Kishor Bhaṭṭ" and later in Ali Akbar Khān Muhammadī's court. Written in the latter king's court, the *Kalānidhi* is "an excellent line-for-line commentary in various metres of the *Naiṣadha* of Śrī Harṣa." Mishra also, according to Grierson, "wrote a special commentary called *Salil* on the *Pañcanalīya*, which is the name of a difficult portion of the *Naiṣadha*."
10. N.P. Unni, *Nala Episode in Sanskrit Literature* (Trivandrum: College Book House, 1977), 35.
11. Unni, *Nala Episode in Sanskrit Literature*, 55. The four-day dramatic performance follows Śrīharṣa's *Naiṣadhīya* closely during the first day, after which certain changes are made according to taste. A director of *kathakali* performances, Kavalam Pannikar explained to me the graceful verses that contain the dialogue between the *haṃsa* and Damayantī (*Naiṣadhīya* 3.1–3.15) are treated with special innovation and enacted with gusto by the actors. In addition to the annual presentation of the *Nalacaritam*, Pannikar has recently produced a modern *kathakali* play called *Kaliveshanam* (Possession of Kali), which deals with the figure of Kali along the lines that Śrīharṣa has envisioned him in the seventeenth canto of the *Naiṣadhīya*. Apparently, there is also a tradition of folk songs related to the *Naiṣadhīya* that might have been attached to *kathakali* tradition. Dr. T.N. Satheesan, a professor of Malayalam at Aligarh University, informs me that during the early twentieth century, a few musical plays in Malayalam came to be written on the *Naiṣadhīya*'s theme. *Sangeeta Naishadham* of T.C. Achutamenon was the most popular among them, fusing folk themes with the familiar elements from the *kathakali* text of *Nalacaritam*. As of 1931, according to Dr. Satheesan, it had eighteen editions with 33,000 known copies, a distinction that no other Malayalam drama shares.

12. A.N. Jani, *A Critical Study of Śrīharṣa's Naiṣadhacaritam*, 279.
13. A.N. Jani, *A Critical Study of Śrīharṣa's Naiṣadhacaritam*, 281.
14. Sitanshu Yashaschandra, "From Hemacandra to *Hind Svarāj*: Region and Power in Gujarati Literary Culture" in *Literary Cultures in History: Reconstructions from South Asia*, ed. Sheldon Pollock (Berkeley: University of California Press, 2003), 580–581; 588.
15. S.N. Dasgupta and S.K. De, *History of Sanskrit Literature*, vol. 1 (Calcutta: University of Calcutta, 1947), 629.
16. A.N. Jani, *A Critical Study of Śrīharṣa's Naiṣadhacaritam*, 278.
17. Ananta Tripathy Sharma, *Lāvaṇyavatī* (Brahmapura: Śiromaṇi Mudraṇālaye, 1978), 8.
18. Meher writes in his study of Upendra Bhañja: "In the epic *'Koṭi-Brahmāṇḍa-Sundarī'* (Chapter-XX), Upendra has neatly declared: *'ghena naishadha parāye'* (Take this epic as *Naishadha*). He is immensely influenced by the *'Naishadhacharita'* of Śrīharsha, mostly in regard to similarity of ideas, puns, expressions and style. Also in some verses of his other epic poems such as *'Lābanyabatī'* and *'Subhadrā-Pariṇaya,'* the style and ideas of *'Naishadha Mahākāvya'* are fluently reflected" [Harekrishna Meher, *Upendra Bhañja* (Cuttack, Orissa: Kalinga Bharati, 1990), 45].
19. Sharma, *Lāvaṇyavatī*, 15.
20. The *rāmatāraka mantra* (lit., "saving grace of Rāma") is a repetition of Rāma's name in thirteen syllables [*śrīrāma jaya rāma jaya jaya rāma*], and, like the *cintāmaṇi mantra*, is thought to be especially efficacious for the attainment of creative powers. For a discussion of the mantra's influence in the career of the great eighteenth-/nineteenth-century South Indian musician-composer Tyāgarāja, see W.J. Jackson, *Tyāgarāja and the Renewal of Tradition* (Delhi: Motilal Banarsidass, 1994), 125; 234.
21. Sharma writes (*Lāvaṇyavatī*, 6): "We are told that when he confronted the Pandits of Orissa in a conference held at Puri under the chairmanship of the then Raja of Puri, he had to undergo an acid test to establish his poetic individuality openly."
22. For a good introduction to Upendra Bhañja and his reception in Oriya literary culture, see Mayadhar Mansinha, *History of Oriya Literature* (New Delhi: Sahitya Akademi, 1962), 114–117. See also Joanna Williams, *The Two-Headed Deer: Illustrations of the Rāmāyaṇa in Orissa* (Berkeley: University of California Press, 1996), 28ff.
23. K.V. Zvelebil, *Tamil Literature* (Weisbaden: Otto Harrasowitz, 1974), 145.
24. I cite this passage from a draft copy of David Shulman's article, provisionally entitled "Ativīrarāma Pāṇṭiyaṉ's *Naiṭatam* and the Sixteenth-Century Imagination." It was presented during the Summer Academy held at The Institute for Advanced Studies at The Hebrew University of Jerusalem in 2008. I thank David Shulman for allowing me access to this early form of the essay.
25. Shulman and Narayana Rao have recently published the first comprehensive English-language study of Śrīnātha [Velcheru Narayana Rao and David Shulman, *Śrīnātha: The Poet Who Made Gods and Kings* (Oxford: Oxford University Press, 2012)].
26. A.N. Jani, *A Critical Study of Śrīharṣa's Naiṣadhacaritam*, 278.
27. S.G. Tulpule, *Classical Marāṭhī Literature: From the Beginning to A.D. 1818* (Wiesbaden: Harrassowitz, 1979), 339.
28. Tulpule, *Classical Marāṭhī Literature*, 338–339.
29. Important discussions of this subject include Sheldon Pollock ["Sanskrit Literary Culture from the Inside Out" in *Literary Cultures in History: Reconstructions from South*

Asia, ed. Sheldon Pollock (Berkeley: University of California Press, 2003)], which contains essays on the literary histories of Sanskrit and India's regional literatures; Pollock [*The Language of the Gods in the World of Men* (Berkeley: University of California Press, 2006), 39–130], which comprehensively treats the role Sanskrit literature played historically in India's regions; and David Shulman and Yigal Bronner ["A Cloud Turned Goose: Sanskrit in the Vernacular Millennium," *Indian Economic & Social Review* 43, no. 1 (2006): 1–30], an introductory essay on the complex role of Sanskrit literary culture in many of the regions of South Asia and, in particular, southern India. See also Robert Goldman's essay on Sanskrit commentary and translation practices in the late medieval and early modern period ["Translating Texts Translating Texts: Issues in the Translation of Popular Literary Texts with Multiple Commentaries" in *Translation, East and West: A Cross-Cultural Approach (Selected Conference Papers)*, ed. Cornelia N. Moore (Honolulu: University of Hawaii and East West Center, 1992), 93–105].

30. In articulating a Gujarati literary consciousness through his *Nalākhyān*—this is the first time the word *ākhyān* is used and the first time the language (*bhākā*) is called something akin to Gujarati (*gujara-bhākā*)—Bhālaṇ's prefatory remarks position the poet and his work in terms of the Sanskrit literary world's cultural capital through an economic code of power disparity: the mighty, wealthy, and successful Sanskrit *literati* contrasted with the lowly, poor, and downtrodden Gujarati (*Nalākhyān* 1.1–1.5). See Yashaschandra ("From Hemacandra to *Hind Svarāj*," 580–581; 588) for a discussion on Bhālaṇ and his pivotal role in the formation of early Gujarati literary culture.
31. *candra sūraya pākhali kūṇḍālūṃ thaī chi varasāti / tihāṃ kalpanā māhākavi nī mani ehavī āvī vāta // nalanā tej-rūpiyu sūraya yaśarūpi śaśi dekhī /brahmā sācā jūṭhā juī antargati ūvekhī // jim nāmūṃ jūṭhūṃ jāṇi te vaṇik leīni vāli / tima dhyātāe jūṭhā jāṇī raviśaśini kuṇḍāli //* [1.10–12].
32. See section 1.46a of appendix 1 for Sanskrit text.
33. See section 1.46b of appendix 1 for Sanskrit text.
34. V. Narayana Rao and David Shulman, "Notes on *Naiṣadhamu*" (unpublished, 2008), 5.
35. See V. Narayana Rao and David Shulman, *Classical Telugu Poetry: An Anthology* (Berkeley: University of California Press, 2002), 26–27; and Mohan Lal, *Encyclopedia of Indian Literature, Volume 5* (New Delhi: Sahitya Akademi, 1992), 4171.
36. The Pāṇinian *sūtra* in question is 7.1.35 [*tuhyos tātaṅ āśiṣy anyatarasyām*]. The two sounds are "*tu*" and "*hi*," which are also the markers for forms in the imperative mode. The *sūtra* indicates that the imperative markers of "*tu*" and "*hi*" can optionally (*anyatarasyām*) be replaced by the affix "*tāt*" when a benedictory sense (*āśiḥ*) is intended. [And so, instead of "*jīvatu*" ("Let one live"), for example, we get forms like "*jīvatāt*" ("May one live")].
37. Nārāyaṇa, for example, says: *phaṇinaḥ śeṣād bhavam utpannaṃ mahābhāṣya-lakṣaṇa-śāstram*. Mallinātha also clearly explains: *śāstre pāṇinīye mahābhāṣye*.
38. Cāṇḍupaṇḍita thus explicates *paṇibhavaḥ* as *paṇino'patyam*, cross-referencing Pāṇini's *sūtra* 6.4.165 [*gāthi-vidathi-keśi-gaṇi-paṇinaś ca*] to arrive at his conclusion [*tathā ca paṇino 'patyaṃ pāṇiniḥ. 'gāthi-vidathi-keśi-gaṇi-paṇinaś ca' iti. phaṇi-bhava ity aśuddhaḥ pāṭhaḥ. tuhyor iti hi sūtraṃ pāṇineḥ. na tu bhāṣyakārasya*]. In all likelihood, the reference probably refers to the *Mahābhāṣya*, as there is a long discussion in the *Bhāṣya* on *sūtra* 1.1.53 that interrogates the replacement by *tāt* of the entire

endings of "*tu*" and "*hi*" and not just their final sounds. Still, as Patañjali does not deal with the actual *sūtra* 7.1.35 (*tuhyos tātaṅ āśiṣyanyatarasyām*), Cāṇḍupaṇḍita is justified to think that the poet's explicit mention of the *sūtra* in the verse signals that his intention was to reference Pāṇini's work and not Patañjali's.

39. See section 1.47 of appendix 1 for Sanskrit text.
40. See section 1.48 of appendix 1 for Sanskrit text.
41. Bhālaṇ, like many of the Sanskrit commentators on *Naiṣadhīya*, begins the preface of his work with a deferential nod to his sources and to those more learned or fortunate than he. In particular, Bhālaṇ congratulates (tongue-in-cheek) those who can enjoy the great sources of Sanskrit literature in the original. For vernacular audiences, however, who are like "children"/ "uninitiated" (*bāla*) or the "dull-witted" (*mūraka-jana*), Bhālaṇ writes, he has composed his *Nalākhyān*. As the Gujarati poet is obviously proud of his own work, the playful insincerity mimics, in some form, the self-deprecation one often sees in the prefaces of Sanskrit commentators. See especially *Nalākhyān* 1.2 [*naiṣadha caṃpū māhābhāratamāṃ kavi kīriti ati līdhī / kālāṃne prīchavā bhālaṇe bhākāe e kīdhī //* "Poet Vyāsa wrote about the Nala episode in the *Mahābhārata* and became famous. But Bhālaṇ did it in a regional tongue so that even a child could understand] and *Nalākhyān* 1.6 [*tālamaye sakala artha-pada-bandhe bandhūṃ nalākhyān / mūraka-jana moho karavāne bhālana kave abhimāne //* "My Nalākhyān: everywhere word and meaning is joined with rhythmic cadence. Bhālaṇ proudly sings to enchant the dull-witted"].
42. C.N. Shastri ["Commentary—Telugu," in *The Encyclopedia of Indian Literature*, vol. 1, ed. Amaresh Datta (New Delhi: Sahitya Akademi, 1987)] explains that there are also at least two known commentaries of *Naiṣadhamu* in Telugu on this poem, the *Guḍhārtha Prakāśikā* of Ketavarupu Venkata Sastri (late nineteenth century) and the *Sarvaṃkaśa Vyākhyā* of Vedam Venkataraya Sastri (late-nineteenth and twentieth century).
43. V. Narayana Rao and David Shulman, "Notes on *Naiṣadhamu*," 5.
44. In their recent work (*Śrīnātha*, 178), V. Narayana Rao and David Shulman write: "Slightly restated, [Śrīnātha's] diction sounds like Sanskrit, and the syntax speaks Telugu. Śrīnātha has re-Sanskritized Sanskrit so that it becomes a kind of Telugu; long, lexically electrifying compounds follow Telugu metrical and syntactic breaks and rhythms." One is especially directed to chapter 2 of this volume for an intensive and extensive discussion of the *Naiṣadhīya* in light of the *Naiṣadhamu*.
45. In their thesis about regional Sanskrit literature's functional relationship with vernacular literary production, the authors observe: "Sanskrit participated along with the vernaculars in the project of inventing and elaborating distinctive regional cultures and identities. Far from occluding such regional distinctiveness or uniqueness, Sanskrit is now employed precisely to articulate it" (Shulman and Bronner, "A Cloud Turned Goose," 6). It may be useful to explore elsewhere the ways in which Sanskrit poems like *Sahṛdayānanda* function alongside texts composed in the vernaculars not only to articulate a "regionality" but also to reflect a shared compositional practice heavily reliant on exegetical purpose and strategy.
46. Krishnamachariar (*History of Classical Sanskrit Literature*, 184) explains that Kṛṣṇānanda's "indebtedness to *Naiṣadhīya* being apparent, it is easy to fix his time between Śrīharṣa and Viśvanātha [well-known Oriya author of the Sanskrit

poetics text *Sāhityadarpaṇa*], thus placing him at about the thirteenth century." Kṛṣṇānanda, as the manuscript colophons make clear, was a minister from a Kāyastha family in Puri. He was born in the Kapiñjala *kula* and held the title (*upādhi*) of "*Sāndhi-vigrahika mahāpātra*" (shared by Viśvanātha).

47. Vachaspati Dvivedi, *Sahṛdayānanda of Mahākavi Śrīkṛṣṇānanda* (Varanasi: Chowkhambha Vidyabhavan, 1968), 12.
48. Dvivedi, *Sahṛdayānanda*, 21.
49. See Dvivedi (*Sahṛdayānanda*, 22–23) for a discussion of the poem in light of the *Naiṣadhīya*. Krishnamachariar (*History of Classical Sanskrit Literature*, 184) concurs in his comparative assessment: "[Kṛṣṇānanda's] poetry is very charming and in this respect contrasts very favorably with the work of Śrīharṣa, on which tradition says he wrote also a commentary." In forming their judgments comparing Śrīharṣa's and Kṛṣṇānanda's style, both Dvivedi and Krishnamachariar seem to be influenced by the *Sāhityadarpaṇa*'s citing of a *Sahṛdayānanda* verse as a model of clear and natural expression—incidentally, the most important functional feature of the Sanskrit commentary.
50. Mallinātha on *Naiṣadhīya* 1.117: *haṃsam abodhi dadarśetyarthaḥ*.
51. See chapter 5 for a discussion of the allegorical readings of this verse.
52. See section 1.49 of appendix 1 for Sanskrit text.
53. Śrīharṣa imaginatively exploits the imagery of the *trivali* and the *romāvalī* (delicate line of hair above the naval) in no less than nine verses (2.34–35, 7.81–86, 10.27) through an array of metaphors.
54. See section 1.50 of appendix 1 for Sanskrit text.
55. The interactions between formal and content-related features of Sanskrit commentary writing and regional-language translation are present not only in translations of Sanskrit *kāvya* but also of other genres, especially *purāṇa* and *alaṃkāraśāstra*. Narayana Rao proposes, for example, that Pottana's Telugu translation of the *Bhāgavata Purāṇa* can be fruitfully studied alongside the famous commentary of Śrīdhara on the Sanskrit *Bhāgavatam* to tease out the kinds of relationships I have sought here to form between Sanskrit *kāvya*, commentary, and regional-language translation. Similarly, Narayana Rao suggests, one may also look at the ways in which Śrīnātha incorporates into his poem the language and insights of such works as Mammaṭa's *Kāvyaprakāśa*, the well-known Sanskrit encomium *Sūryaśataka*, and Hala's Prakrit *Sattasai*. I thank Prof. Narayana Rao for alerting me to these subjects for future research.

CONCLUSION

1. See section 2.11 of appendix 2 for Sanskrit text.
2. See section 2.12 of appendix 2 for Sanskrit text.
3. *jāyante kati jajñire kati janiṣyante katīha kṣitau sraṣṭāro nitarām idam tu kavibhir nirmatsaraiḥ kathyatām / āpūrvāpara-dakṣiṇottara-harit-sāhitya-siṃhāsana-svair āroha-parākramaṃ bhajatu kaḥ śrīharṣasūreḥ paraḥ //.*
4. James Porter, "Introduction: What Is Classical about Classical Antiquity" in *The Classical Traditions of Greece and Rome*, ed. James Porter (Princeton: Princeton University Press, 2006), 54.

5. Charles Altieri, "Literary Procedures and the Question of Indeterminacy," *Act and Quality: A Theory of Literary Meaning and Humanistic Understanding* (Amherst: University of Massachusetts Press, 1981), 13.
6. S.N. Dasgupta and S.K. De, *History of Sanskrit Literature*, vol. 1 (Calcutta: University of Calcutta, 1947), 325; 330. See the introduction for a full quotation of their remarks.

APPENDIX 2

Many of these verses are collected in A.N. Jani, *A Critical Study of Śrīharṣa's Naiṣadhacaritam* (Baroda: Oriental Institute, 1957), appendices 10 and 11: 45ff.

1. *pratyakṣa-lakṣaṇa-vicakṣaṇa-vādi-vṛnda-durdanti-danta-dalanāni vilāsa-mātram / yeṣāṃ jayanti ta ime jagati pratītāḥ śrīharṣa-siṃha-nara-rūpa-kara-prahārāḥ //.*
2. *jīyān nalaḥ sakala-rājaka-mauli-ratnaṃ yat-kīrtanaṃ sakala-maṅgalam-ātanoti / yat-kīrti-mauktika-gaṇābharaṇāpta-harṣa-śrīharṣa-śuddha-kavitā parito bhramantī //.*
3. *anyaiḥ kavibhir akṣuṇṇāṃ padārabdhāṃ supaddhitam / samādāya kaviḥ śreyaḥ śrīmān harṣaḥ pratiṣṭhate //.*
4. *yad vaktrastha-sarasvatī-śruti-vacaḥ śāstre 'bhavat-khaṇḍanam kāvye naiṣadham uṣṇa-raśmi-śaśinau jāgīyate yad-yugam / sphūrjat-sphīti-vipakṣa-pakṣa-dalana-spardhiṣṇu-vidvad-bhaṭair vidyāsaṃyati harṣa-miśra iḍito gauḍair agauḍair guṇaiḥ //.*
5. *oṃkārādi-vibhūṣaṇā guru-gaṇā vācyā suvākyojjvalā ramyā sādhu-pada-kramāñcita-gatiḥ śrīdevatā-prītidā / eṣā sat-puruṣārtha-sādhana-parā svānte cirānandadā śrīharṣoktir iyaṃ para-śrutir aho dedīpyate sat-priyā //.*
6. *yaḥ sāhitya-rasāmṛtābdhi-laharī-jāleṣu khelācalo yaś cātyartha-gabhīra-tarka-jaladher māthe sa manthācalaḥ / mīmāṃsā-yuga-sindhu-tāraṇa-vidhau yaḥ karṇa-dhāraḥ paraḥ keṣām eṣa mano vinodayati na śrīharṣa nāmā kaviḥ //.*
7. *śrīharṣāt kavi-rājataḥ kṛtir abhūt sā kāpi lokottarā yasyāḥ khelana-bhūr-manīṣi-hṛdaya-prāsāda-śṛṅgasthalī / nepathyasya vidhir navārtha-ghaṭanā sakhyo rasa-vyaktayaḥ śīlaṃ śabda-nayaḥ svayaṃvara-patiś caiṣa svayaṃ naiṣadhaḥ //.*
8. *śabdārthobhaya-mūla-śakti-kalitā sad-vṛtta-bandhojjvalā nānā-tarka-śiphācchala-cchada-vṛtā bhāva-prasūnā vṛtā / śṛṅgāraika-phalā rasaugha-vilasat-pakvā jagaj-jīvikā śrīharṣokti-mayī mahauṣadhi-latā yasyeti kas taṃ jayet //.*
9. *kavi-kula-pateḥ śrīharṣasya prabandha-rasāyaṇaṃ pibata śrotrair antar-vibhāvya sacetasaḥ / acatura-para-granthāvadyaiḥ prakopam upeyuṣaḥ prakṛti-viṣamāṃś ceto-rogān nv etad apohatu //.*
10. *kāvye 'sminn anumānam eva vilasaty ekam khalu prāyikī mukhyālaṅkṛtir ujjvalo 'pi ca rasaḥ sākṣād asākṣād api / ity etat pratipādyam udyatam iva dvandvaṃ sudhā-dugdhayor gāḍha-śleṣam amuṃ ca deva-sudhiyā saṃvāhanīyaṃ bahu //.*
11. *kāvye naiṣadha-nāmni dhāmni subṛhaty arthasya muktā 'vadher bhāvān dūra-nigūhitān katham ahaṃ sarvān pramātuṃ kṣamaḥ / etasmin dyutimanti santi subahūny etāni madhye bhuvaḥ sākalyena labheta ko 'pi khanitā vajrāṇi vajrākāre //.*
12. *etaiḥ khaṇḍana-khaṇḍa-khādya-sahaja-syandair amandaiḥ śuca kulyāvartma-visṛtvaraiḥ sumanasām āplāvitānāṃ muhuḥ / unmīlat pulakāvalī-vikasana-vyājena jānīmahe sarvāṅgīṇatayā sphuranty aviralodbhedhāḥ pramodāṅkurāḥ //.*

BIBLIOGRAPHY

UNPUBLISHED MANUSCRIPT SOURCES

Bhandarkar Institute (Pune, India)

Manuscript No. 376, Jinarāja's *Sukhāvabodhā*
Manuscript No. 385, Rājānaka Ānanda's *Naiṣadhīyatattvavivṛti*
Manuscript No. 377, Vidyādhara's *Sāhityavidhyādharī*
Manuscript No. 369, Narahari's *Dīpikā*

Madras Government Oriental Manuscripts Library (Chennai, India)

Manuscript No. 10553, Gopinātharatha's *Harṣahṛdayā*
Manuscript No. 10555, Viśveśvara's *Padavākyārthacandrikā*
Manuscript No. 10561, Sarvajñamādhavasudhi's *Kāmadhenu*
Manuscript No. 10597, Śrīdhara's *Śrīdharīya*

Scindia Oriental Research Institute (Ujjain, India)

Manuscript No. 10393, Śeśarāmacandra's *Bhāvadyotanikā*

Sarasvati Bhavana at Sampurnanand Sanskrit University (Varanasi, India)

Manuscript No. 104414-16, Cāritravardhana's *Tilaka*

PUBLISHED SOURCES

Abrams, M.H. "How to Do Things with Texts." In *Critical Theory Since 1965*, edited by H. Adams and L. Searle, 436–449. Tallahassee: Florida State University Press, 1986.

Ali, Daud. *Courtly Culture and Political Life in Early Medieval India*. Cambridge: Cambridge University Press, 2004.

——. "Anxieties of Attachment: The Dynamics of Courtship in Medieval India." *Modern Asian Studies* 36, no. 1 (2002): 103–139.

Altieri, Charles. "Literary Procedures and the Question of Indeterminacy." In *Critical Theory Since 1965*, edited by H. Adams and L. Searle, 545–558. Tallahassee: Florida State University, 1986.

Arnold, D. and Blackburn, S. *Telling Lives in India*. Bloomington: Indiana University Press, 2004.

Baghela, Harivir Sinha. *Mahākāvya meṃ Naiṣadhcarit kā mūlyāṅkan*. Agra: Y.K. Publishers, 2000.

Banerji, Sures Chandra. "Commentaries of Mallinātha." In *S.K. De Memorial Volume*, edited by R.C. Hazra and S.C. Banerji, 298–368. Calcutta: Firm K.L. Mukhopadhyay, 1972.

Barthes, Roland. *S/Z: An Essay*, translated by Richard Miller. New York: Hill and Wang, 1974.

——. *The Pleasure of the Text*, translated by Richard Miller. New York: Hill and Wang, 1975.

Becker, A.L. *Beyond Translation: Essays toward a Modern Philology*. Ann Arbor: University of Michigan Press, 1995.

Behl, Aditya. *The Magic Doe*, edited by Wendy Doniger. New York: Oxford University Press, 2012.

Bhagavan, Manu. "The Rebel Academy: Modernity and the Movement for a University in Princely Baroda, 1908-49." *The Journal of Asian Studies* 61, no. 3 (Aug. 2002): 919–947.

Bhatt, Bhagavatprasad N. *Śrīkaṇṭhacaritam—A Study*. Baroda: MS University of Baroda, 1973.

Bhattacharya, Tithi. *Sentinels of Culture: Class, Education, and the Colonial Intellectual in Bengal (1848-85)*. New Delhi: Oxford University Press, 2005.

Bourdieu, Pierre. "The Author's Point of View." In *The Rules of Art: Genesis and Structure of the Literary Field*, translated by Susan Emanuel. Palo Alto: Stanford University Press, 1996.

Brooks, Douglass Renfrew. *The Secret of the Three Cities*. Chicago: University of Chicago Press, 1990.

Brown, C.M. *The Devī Gitā*. Albany: State University of New York, 1998.

Bühler, G. "Age of Śrīharṣa." *JBBRAS* 10, Old Series (1875): 31–37.

Busch, Allison. *Poetry of Kings: The Classical Hindi Literature of Mughal India*. New York: Oxford University Press, 2011.

Bronner, Yigal. *Extreme Poetry*. New York: Columbia University Press, 2010.

Chatterji, K.C. "Some Notes on the *Naiṣadhacarita* of Śrīharṣa." *Calcutta Oriental Journal* 3, no. 6 (1936): 153–157.

Copeland, Rita. *Rhetoric, Hermeneutics, and Translation in the Middle Ages*. Cambridge: Cambridge University Press, 1991.

Dasgupta, S.N. and De, S.K. *History of Sanskrit Literature*, vol. 1. Calcutta: University of Calcutta, 1947.

De Man, Paul. "Semiology and Rhetoric." In *Allegories of Reading: Figural Language in Rousseau, Nietzsche, Rilke, and Proust*, 3–19. New Haven: Yale University Press, 1979.

Derrida, Jacques. *Of Grammatology*, translated by Gayatri C. Spivak. Baltimore: Johns Hopkins University, 1976.

Dodson, Michael. *Orientalism, Empire and National Culture in India 1770-1880*. New York: Palgrave Macmillan, 2007.

Dvivedi, Prabhunath. *Mallināth kī ṭīkāoṃ kā vimarś*. Varanasi: Kashi Vidyapith, 1982.

Dvivedi, Vachaspati. *Sahṛdayānanda of Mahākavi Śrīkṛṣṇānanda*. Varanasi: Chowkhambha Vidyabhavan, 1968.

Eastman, A.C. "The *Naiṣadhacarita* as the Source Text of the Nala-Damayantī Paintings." *Journal of the American Oriental Society* 70 (1950): 238–242.

Eco, Umberto. *The Open Work*. Princeton: Princeton University Press, 1989.

——. *Interpretation and Overinterpretation*. Cambridge: Cambridge University Press, 1992.

Eliot, T.S. "Tradition and the Individual Talent." In *Norton Anthology of Theory and Criticism*. New York: W.W. Norton, 2001.

Emeneau, M.B. "Notes on Śrīharṣa's *Naiṣadhacarita*." *Semitic and Oriental Studies* 4 (1951): 87–102.

Fish, Stanley. *Is There A Text in This Class*. Cambridge, Mass.: Harvard University Press, 1980.

Gerow, Edwin. "Primary Education in Sanskrit: Methods and Goals." *Journal of the American Oriental Society* 122, no. 4 (Oct.–Dec. 2002): 661–690.

Gode, P.K. (ed.). *Descriptive Catalogue of the Government Collections of Manuscripts at Bhandarkar Oriental Research Institute*, vol. XIII, Kāvya, 432–490. Poona: BORI, 1940.

——. "Bühler's Mistaken Identity of Vidyādhara, the Author of the *Sāhityavidyādharī*, a Commentary on *Naiṣadhacaritam* and of Cāritravardhana, the Author of a Commentary on *Raghuvaṃśa, Kumārasambhava*, etc." *Journal of Bhandarkar Oriental Research Institute* 1 (1940): 251–254.

Goldman, Robert P. "How Fast Do Monkeys Fly? How Long Do Demons Sleep?" In *Rivista di Studi Sudasiatici* no. 1: 185–207. Firenze: Firenze University Press, 2006.

——. "Translating Texts Translating Texts: Issues in the Translation of Popular Literary Texts with Multiple Commentaries." In *Translation, East and West: A Cross-Cultural Approach (Selected Conference Papers)*, edited by Cornelia N. Moore, 93–105. Honolulu: University of Hawaii and East West Center, 1992.

——. *The Ramayana of Vālmīki: An Epic of Ancient India. Vol. I, Bālakāṇḍa*, edited and translated by Robert P. Goldman. Princeton: Princeton University Press, 1984.

Goldman, Robert P. and Goldman, Sally Sutherland [eds. and trans.]. *The Ramayana of Vālmīki: An Epic of Ancient India. Vol. 5, Sundarakāṇḍa*. Princeton: Princeton University Press, 1996.

Goodall, Dominic and Isaacson, Harunaga (eds.). *The Raghupañcikā of Vallabhadeva, Critical Edition with Introduction and Notes*, vol. 1. Groningen: Egbert Forsten, 2003.

Griffiths, Paul J. *Religious Reading*. Oxford: Oxford University Press, 1999.

Goswamy, B.N. (ed.). *Pahari Paintings of the Nala-Damayanti Theme*. New Delhi: National Museum, 1995.

Granoff, Phyllis. *Philosophy and Argument in Late Vedānta: Śrīharṣa's Khaṇḍanakhaṇḍakhādya*. Dordrecht: D. Reidel Publishing Company, 1978.

——. "Jain Biographies of Nāgārjuna: Notes on the Composing of a Biography in Medieval India." In *Monks and Magicians: Religious Biographies in Asia*, edited by P. Granoff and K. Shinohara, 45–66. New Delhi: Motilal Banarsidass, 1994.

Grierson, George A. *The Modern Vernacular Literature of Hindustan*. Calcutta: Asiatic Society, 1889.

Guillory, John. *Cultural Capital: The Problem of Literary Canon Formation*. Chicago: University of Chicago Press, 1993.

Hahn, Michael. "Appendix." In *Śivasvāmin's Kapphiṇābhyudaya or Exaltation of King Kapphiṇa*, edited by Gauri Shankar, i–xxxvi. New Delhi: Aditya Prakashan, 1989.

Handiqui, K.K. *Naiṣadhacarita of Śrīharṣa: English Translation with Notes*, 2nd ed. Poona: Deccan College, 1965.

Hueckstedt, Robert A. *The Style of Bāṇa: An Introduction to Sanskrit Prose Poetry*. Lanham: University Press of America, 1985.

Iser, Wolfgang. "Chapter 3: The Repertoire" (from *The Act of Reading*)." In *Critical Theory Since 1965*, edited by H. Adams and L. Searle, 359–380. Tallahassee: Florida State University Press, 1986.

Iyer, V. Subramania. (tr.) *Nalacharitam of Unnayi Warrier*. Trichur: Kerala Sahitya Akademi, 1977.

Jackson, W.J. *Tyāgarāja and the Renewal of Tradition*. Delhi: Motilal Banarsidass, 1994.

Jani, A.N. *A Critical Study of Śrīharṣa's Naiṣadhacaritam*. Baroda: Oriental Institute, 1957.

——. "Did Nandanandana Write a Commentary on *Naiṣadhacaritam*?" *Journal of Madras University (JMSU)* 16.1 (1967): 01–102.

Jani, Jaydev (ed.). *Naiṣadhamahākāvya with Cāṇḍupaṇḍita's Commentary*. Jodhpur: Rajasthan Oriental Research Institute, 1997.

Jauss, Hans Robert. *Toward an Aesthetic of Reception*, translated by Timothy Bahti. Minneapolis: University of Minnesota Press, 1982.

Jha, Amarnath. *The Veiled Moon: Translations of Bihāri's Satsai*, edited by G. Mathur. New Delhi: ICCR, 1973.

Jha, Devnarayan. *Naiṣadh-samīkṣā*. Delhi: Nag Publishers, 2001.

Jhala, G.C. "The *Naiṣadhacarita* of Śrīharṣa—A Linguistic Study." *Journal of Oriental Institute Baroda* 22.2 (1973): 157–214.

Joshi, Mathura D. *Naiṣadh kā kāvya-śāstrīya adhyayana*. Delhi: Vitark Parimal Publications, 1999.

Keith, A.B. *A History of Sanskrit Literature*. Oxford: The Clarendon Press, 1928.

Krieger, Murray. "An Apology for Poetics." In *Critical Theory Since 1965*, edited by H. Adams and L. Searle, 535–542. Tallahassee: Florida State University Press, 1986.

Krishnamachariar, M. *History of Classical Sanskrit Literature*. Delhi: Motilal Banarsidass, 1974.

Lal, Mohan (ed.). *Encyclopedia of Indian Literature, Volume 5*. New Delhi: Sahitya Akademi, 1992.

Lalye, P.G. *Mallināth*a. New Delhi: Sahitya Akademi, 2002.

Lienhard, Siegfried. *A History of Classical Poetry: Sanskrit, Pali, Prakrit*. Wiesbaden: Otto Harrassowitz, 1984.

Lotman, Yuri. *Analysis of the Poetic Text*, translated by D. Barton Johnson. Ann Arbor: Ardis, 1976.

Lutgendorf, Philip. *The Life of a Text: Performing the Rāmcaritmānas of Tulsidas*. Berkeley: University of California Press, 1995.

Mansinha, Mayadhar. *History of Oriya Literature*. New Delhi: Sahitya Akademi, 1962.

Matilal, B.K. "Skepticism and Mysticism." *Journal of the American Oriental Society* 105, no. 3 (July–Sep. 1985): 479–484.

McCrea, Lawrence. "The Conquest of Cool: Theology and Aesthetics in Māgha's *Śiśupālavadha*." In *Innovations and Turning Points: Toward a History of Sanskrit Literature*, edited by Y. Bronner, D. Shulman, and G. Tubb. Delhi: Oxford University Press (forthcoming).

McGregor, Ronald Stuart. *Hindi Literature from Its Beginnings to the Nineteenth Century*. Weisbaden: Otto Harrassowitz, 1984.

Meher, Harekrishna. *Upendra Bhañja*. Cuttack, Orissa: Kalinga Bharati, 1990.
—. *Philosophical Reflections in the Naiṣadhacarita*. Calcutta: Punthi Pustak, 1989.
Mehta, Vandana Dhirajlal. *Gadādharī: A Commentary on Naiṣadhacarita of Śrīharṣa by Gadādhara*. Text with introduction, chapters 1–11. Baroda: The MS University of Baroda, 1985.
Mellins, David Rustin. *The Cool Rays of Aesthetics and Reasoning: Jayadeva's 'Candrāloka' and Its Role in the Evolution of Alaṃkāraśāstra*. Ann Arbor: UMI, Microform, 2004.
Minkowski, Christopher. "The Paṇḍit as Public Intellectual: The Controversy Over Virodha or Inconsistency in the Astronomical Sciences." In *The Paṇḍit: Traditional Sanskrit Scholarship in India*, edited by Axel Michaels, 79–103. Heidelberg: South Asia Institute; New Delhi: Manohar Publications, 2001.
—. "What Makes a Work 'Traditional'? On the Success of Nīlakaṇṭha's *Mahābhārata* Commentary." In *Boundaries, Dynamics and Construction of Traditions in South Asia*, edited by F. Squarcini, 225–244. Florence: Firenze University Press, 2005.
Mishra, Anand Svarup. *Mahākavi Śrīharṣa tathā unkā Naiṣadh kāvya*. Lucknow: Sulabh Prakashan, 1988.
Mitra, Arati. *Origin and Development of Sanskrit Metrics*. Calcutta: The Asiatic Society, 1989.
Moretti, Franco. *Signs Taken for Wonders*. London: Verso, 1983.
Narahari, H.G. "A Rare Commentary on *Naiṣadhacarita*." *Adyar Library Bulletin* 9 (1945): 20–24. Manuscript in Adyar [Shelf number XXXVIII, F. 30].
Narayana Rao, Velcheru. "Multiple Literary Cultures in Telugu." In *Literary Cultures in History: Reconstructions from South Asia*, edited by Sheldon Pollock, 383–436. Berkeley: University of California Press, 2003.
Narayana Rao, Velcheru and Shulman, David. *Śrīnātha: The Poet Who Made Gods and Kings*. Oxford: Oxford University Press, 2012.
—. "Nala: The Life of a Story." In *Damayantī and Nala: The Many Lives of a Story*, edited by Susan Wadley. New Delhi: Chronicle Books, 2011.
—. "Notes on *Naiṣadhamu*." Unpublished, 2008.
—. *Classical Telugu Poetry: An Anthology*. Berkeley: University of California Press, 2002.
—. *A Poem at the Right Moment*. Berkeley: University of California Press, 1998.
Nayaka, Vrajakishor. *Introduction and Commentary (in Sanskrit and Oriya) of Navamasarga of Naiṣadhīyacaritam*. Puri: Sadgranthaniketanam, 1997.
Niyogi, Roma. *The History of the Gāhaḍavāla Dynasty*. Calcutta: Calcutta Oriental Book Agency, 1959.
Ortega y Gasset, José and Parmenter, Clarence E. "The Difficulty of Reading." *Diogenes* (December 1959): 1–17.
Patel, Deven M. "Shared Typologies of Kāmaśāstra, Alaṅkāraśāstra and Literary Criticism." *Journal of Indian Philosophy* 39, no. 1 (Feb. 2011): 101–122.
—. "Source, Exegesis, and Translation: Sanskrit Commentary and Regional Language Translation in South Asia." *Journal of the American Oriental Society* 131, no. 2 (April–June 2011): 245–266.
—. *The Evolution of a Sanskrit Literary Culture: A Study of the Naiṣadha Tradition in Light of Its Commentaries and Receptive Histories*. Ann Arbor: UMI Microform, 2006.
Pauwels, Heidi. "The Saint, the Warlord, and the Emperor: Discourses of Braj Bhakti and Bundelā Loyalty." *Journal of the Economic and Social History of the Orient* 52 (2009): 187–228.

Peterson, Indira Viswanathan. *Design and Rhetoric in a Sanskrit Court Epic: The Kirātārjunīya of Bhāravi.* Albany: State University of New York Press, 2003.

Phillips, Stephen H. *Classical Indian Metaphysics.* Chicago: Open Court, 1995.

Pollock, Sheldon. *The Language of the Gods in the World of Men.* Berkeley: University of California Press, 2006.

—. "Sanskrit Literary Culture from the Inside Out." In *Literary Cultures in History: Reconstructions from South Asia,* edited by Sheldon Pollock, 39–130. Berkeley: University of California Press, 2003.

—. "India in the Vernacular Millennium: Literary Culture and Polity, 1000-1500." *Daedalus: Journal of the American Academy of Arts and Sciences* 127 (1998): 41–74.

Porter, James. "Introduction: What Is Classical about Classical Antiquity." In *The Classical Traditions of Greece and Rome,* edited by James Porter, 1–65. Princeton: Princeton University Press, 2006.

Rājaśekharasūri. *Prabandhakośa,* edited by Jina Vijaya. Śāntiniketan: Adhiṣṭhātā-siṃghī Jainjñānapīṭh, 1935.

Rao, Ajay K. "Theologising the Inaugural Verse: Śleṣa Reading in *Rāmāyaṇa* Commentary." *Journal of Hindu Studies* 1, no. 1–2 (2008): 77–92.

Rao, U. Venkatakrishna. *A Handbook of Classical Sanskrit Literature,* 3rd ed. Bombay: Orient Longmans, 1967.

Ricoeur, Paul. *Time and Narrative,* vol. 1–3. Translated by K. McLaughlin and D. Pellauer. Chicago: University of Chicago Press, 1984.

Röer, E. (ed.). *Naiṣadhīyacarita of Śrīharṣa with Premacandra Tarkavāgīśa's Commentary (Cantos 1-11) and Nārāyaṇa's Commentary (Cantos 12-22). Biblioteca Indica.* Calcutta: Asiatic Society, 1836–1855.

Roodbergen, J.A.F. *Mallinātha's Ghaṇṭāpatha on Kirātārjunīyah, I-VI: Introduction, Translation, and Notes.* Leiden: Brill Publishers, 1984.

Sawhney, Simona. *The Modernity of Sanskrit.* Minneapolis: University of Minnesota Press, 2009.

Sanadhyashastri, Devarsi (ed.). *Naiṣadhacaritam with Jīvātu Commentary of Mallinātha.* Krishnadas Sanskrit Series, 52. Varanasi: Krishnadas Akademi, 1984–1987.

Sandesara, Bhogilal J. *Literary Circle of Mahāmātya Vastupāla and Its Contribution to Sanskrit Literature.* Bombay: Singhi Jain Shastra Sikshapith, Bharatiya Vidya Bhavan, 1953.

Seetaramasastri, M. Jaya. *The Elements of Darśanas in Śrīharṣa's Naiṣadha.* Repalle, Andhra Pradesh: Kiran Hindi Press, 1987.

Sharma, Ananta Tripathy. *Lāvaṇyavatī.* Brahmapura: Śiromaṇi Mudraṇālaye, 1978.

Sharma, Rekha. *Naiṣadhīya nārāyaṇī ṭīkā kā vivecanātmak adhyayan.* Delhi: Eastern Books, 1998.

Sharma, Sheshendra. *Svarṇahaṃsa,* translated into Hindi from Telugu by Jagdish Sharma. Ujjain: Kalidas Akademi, 1990.

Sharma, Shivadatta (ed.). *Naiṣadhacaritam: Śrīmannārāyaṇaṭīkayā.* Lucknow: Uttarpradeśa Saṃskṛta Samsthāna, 1998.

Sharma, Sukhdev. "The Identity, Date, Works, and Erudition of Narahari." *Samskrita Vimarśaḥ* 1.2 (1974): 47–52.

—. "A Critical Estimate of Narahari's Commentary on *Naiṣadhīyacarita.*" *The Mysore Orientalist* 9 (1976): 7–9.

Shastri, C.N. "Commentary—Telugu." In *The Encyclopedia of Indian Literature*, vol. 1, edited by Amaresh Datta. New Delhi: Sahitya Akademi, 1987.

Shastri, K.K. (ed.). *Bhālaṇakṛta Nalākhyāna*. Vadodara: Prācīna Gurjara-Granthamālā; Baroda: MS University of Baroda Press, 1957.

Shastri, Vyasarāya K.L. (ed.). *Naiṣadhacaritam with the Commentary of Mallinātha*. Cantos 1–12. 2 pts. Palghat: Palghat Sanskrit Series, 1924–1926.

Sheikh, Samira. *Forging a Region: Sultans, Traders, and Pilgrims in Gujarat 1200-1500*. New Delhi: Oxford University Press, 2010.

Shukla, Chandika Prasad. *Naiṣadh-pariśīlan*. Allahabad: Hindustani Academy, 1960.

Shulman, David. *Spring, Heat, Rains: A South Indian Diary*. Chicago: University of Chicago Press, 2009.

Shulman, David and Bronner, Yigal. "A Cloud Turned Goose: Sanskrit in the Vernacular Millennium." *Indian Economic & Social Review* 43, no. 1 (2006): 1–30.

Smith, David. *Ratnākara's Haravijaya: An Introduction to the Sanskrit Court Epic*. Delhi: Oxford University Press, 1985.

Stein, Burton. *A History of India*. Malden, Mass.: Wiley-Blackwell Press, 1998.

Sundaram, C.S. *Contributions of Tamil Nadu to Sanskrit Literature*. Chemmanchery, Chennai: Institute of Asian Studies, 1999.

Tevet-Dayan, Maya. *Divine Language Incarnate: The Poetic Metaphysics of Śrīharṣa's Naiṣadhīya-carita*. Ph.D. thesis submitted to Faculty of Humanities, Tel Aviv University, Tel Aviv, Israel, 2010.

Trigg, Stephanie. *Congenial Souls: Reading Chaucer from Medieval to Postmodern*. Minneapolis: University of Minnesota Press, 2002.

Trynkowska, A. "Mallinātha and Classical Indian Theoreticians of Literature on Descriptions in the *Mahākāvya*." In *Kāvya, Theory and Practice*, edited by L. Sudyka, 37–48. Krakow: Ksiegarnia Akademicka, 2000.

Tubb, G. and Boose, E. *Scholastic Sanskrit: A Manual for Students*. New York: American Institute of Buddhist Studies, 2007.

Tulpule, S.G. *Classical Marāṭhī Literature: From the Beginning to A.D. 1818*. Wiesbaden: Harrassowitz, 1979.

Tynianov, Yuri. *The Problem of Verse Language*. Translated by Michael Sosa and Brent Harvey. Ann Arbor: Ardis, 1981.

Unithiri, N.V.P. "The Sanskrit Commentary Considered." *Journal of Kerala Studies* 10 (1983): 219–232.

——. "Commentaries in Sanskrit Literature." In *Dr. K.K. Raja Felicitation Volume. The Adyar Library Bulletin* 44–45 (1980–1981): 572–580.

Unni, N.P. *Nala Episode in Sanskrit Literature*. Trivandrum: College Book House, 1977.

Upadhyay, Baldev. *Kāśī kī pāṇḍitya-paramparā*. Vārāṇasī: Viśvavidyālaya Prakāśana, 1983.

Vidyāpati. *Puruṣaparīkṣā*, edited by Ramanath Jha. Darbhanga: University of Patna, 1960.

White, Hayden. *Tropics of Discourse: Essays in Cultural Criticism*. Baltimore: The Johns Hopkins University Press, 1978.

Wilde, Oscar. "The Critic as Artist." In *Norton Anthology of Theory and Criticism*. New York: W.W. Norton, 2001.

Williams, Joanna. *The Two-Headed Deer: Illustrations of the Rāmāyaṇa in Orissa*. Berkeley: University of California Press, 1996.

Winternitz, Moritz. *History of Indian Literature*. New Delhi: Motilal Banarsidass, 1966.
Yates, W. "Review of the *Naiṣadhacarita*." *Asiatic Researches* XX (1836): 318–337.
Yashaschandra, Sitanshu. "From Hemacandra to *Hind Svarāj*: Region and Power in Gujarati Literary Culture." In *Literary Cultures in History: Reconstructions from South Asia*, edited by Sheldon Pollock, 567–611. Berkeley: University of California Press, 2003.
Zadoo, Jaggadhar. "A Critical Note on Vallabhadeva's Commentary on the *Shishupalavadham*." Srinagar: Normal Press, 1947.
Zvelebil, K.V. *Tamil Literature*. Weisbaden: Otto Harrasowitz, 1974.

INDEX

SOUTH ASIA ACROSS THE DISCIPLINES

Extreme Poetry: The South Asian Movement of Simultaneous Narration by Yigal Bronner (Columbia)

The Social Space of Language: Vernacular Culture in British Colonial Punjab by Farina Mir (California)

Unifying Hinduism: Philosophy and Identity in Indian Intellectual History by Andrew J. Nicholson (Columbia)

The Powerful Ephemeral: Everyday Healing in an Ambiguously Islamic Place by Carla Bellamy (California)

Secularizing Islamists? Jama'at-e-Islami and Jama'at-ud-Da'wa in Urban Pakistan by Humeira Iqtidar (Chicago)

Islam Translated: Literature, Conversion, and the Arabic Cosmopolis of South and Southeast Asia by Ronit Ricci (Chicago)

Conjugations: Marriage and Form in New Bollywood Cinema by Sangita Gopal (Chicago)

Unfinished Gestures: Devadāsīs, Memory, and Modernity in South India by Davesh Soneji (Chicago)

Document Raj: Writing and Scribes in Early Colonial South India by Bhavani Raman (Chicago)

The Millennial Sovereign: Sacred Kingship and Sainthood in Islam by A. Azfar Moin (Columbia)

Making Sense of Tantric Buddhism: History, Semiology, and Transgression in the Indian Traditions by Christian K. Wedemeyer (Columbia)

The Yogin and the Madman: Reading the Biographical Corpus of Tibet's Great Saint Milarepa by Andrew Quintman (Columbia)

Body of Victim, Body of Warrior: Refugee Families and the Making of Kashmiri Jihadists by Cabeiri deBergh Robinson (California)

Receptacle of the Sacred: Illustrated Manuscripts and the Buddhist Book Cult in South Asia by Jinah Kim (California)

Cut-Pieces: Celluloid Obscenity and Popular Cinema in Bangladesh by Lotte Hoek (Columbia)

Text to Tradition: The Naisadhīyacarita and Literary Community in South Asia by Deven M. Patel (Columbia)

Democracy against Development: Lower Caste Politics and Political Modernity in Postcolonial India by Jeffrey Witsoe (Chicago)

GPSR Authorized Representative: Easy Access System Europe, Mustamäe tee 50, 10621 Tallinn, Estonia, gpsr.requests@easproject.com

www.ingramcontent.com/pod-product-compliance
Lightning Source LLC
Chambersburg PA
CBHW020933310726
48980CB00007B/755/J

* 9 7 8 0 2 3 1 1 6 6 8 0 5 *